Reimagining Thoreau is a major reconsideration of Thoreau's career from his graduation from Harvard in 1837 to his death in 1862. Combining biographical and manuscript evidence with a fresh reading of nearly all of Thoreau's texts, Robert Milder focuses on the drama of psychosocial adjustment occurring within and beneath the written work. Rooted in the microcosm of ante-bellum Concord but also in the private urgencies of his nature, Thoreau's writings, in Milder's view, are rhetorical efforts to mediate his troubled relations with his fellow townsmen and to inscribe and thereby realize an ideal self. At the center of *Reimagining Thoreau* is the first detailed interpretation of *Walden* as a temporally layered text that changed as Thoreau himself changed during the years of composition and whose shifts and discontinuities suggest a subtler, more conflicted story than the myth of triumph Thoreau deliberately shaped.

Milder also looks beyond *Walden* to counter the traditional view of Thoreau's "decline." His discussion of the late natural-history essays is not only one of the fullest we have; it completes Milder's reconfiguration of Thoreau's career, which is neither a parabola whose vertex is *Walden* nor a continuous line, but a rising arc with periodic disruptions and recommencements, constant only in its impulse toward ascent.

CAMBRIDGE STUDIES IN AMERICAN LITERATURE AND CULTURE 85

Reimagining Thoreau

Cambridge Studies in American Literature and Culture

Editor: Eric Sundquist, University of California, Los Angeles
Founding editor: Albert Gelpi, Stanford University

Advisory Board

Nina Baym, University of Illinois, Champaign-Urbana
Sacvan Bercovitch, Harvard University
Albert Gelpi, Stanford University
Myra Jehlen, University of Pennsylvania
Carolyn Porter, University of California, Berkeley
Robert Stepto, Yale University
Tony Tanner, King's College, Cambridge University

Books in the series

Continues on pages following the Index.

Reimagining Thoreau

ROBERT MILDER

Washington University in St. Louis

CAMBRIDGE
UNIVERSITY PRESS

Published by the Press Syndicate of the University of Cambridge
The Pitt Building, Trumpington Street, Cambridge CB2 1RP
40 West 20th Street, New York, NY 10011-4211, USA
10 Stamford Road, Oakleigh, Melbourne 3166, Australia

© Cambridge University Press 1995

First published 1995

Printed in the United States of America

Library of Congress Cataloging-in-Publication Data
Milder, Robert.
Reimagining Thoreau / Robert Milder.
p.   cm. – (Cambridge studies in American literature and
culture; 85)
Includes bibliographical references (p.) and index.
ISBN 0-521-46149-9
1. Thoreau, Henry David, 1817–1862. 2. Authors, American – 19th
century – Biography. I. Title. II. Series.
PS3053.M49   1994
818'.309–dc20
[B]   94-12094
                                         CIP

A catalog record for this book is available from the British Library.

ISBN 0-521-46149-9 hardback

Contents

Abbreviations of Frequently Cited Sources

CC   Thoreau, *Cape Cod,* ed. Joseph J. Moldenhauer (Princeton: Princeton Univ. Press, 1988)

Corr   *The Correspondence of Henry David Thoreau,* ed. Walter Harding and Carl Bode (New York: New York Univ. Press, 1958)

CW   *The Collected Works of Ralph Waldo Emerson,* ed. Robert E. Spiller et al. (Cambridge, Mass.: Harvard Univ. Press, 1971–   )

EEM   Thoreau, *Early Essays and Miscellanies,* ed. Joseph J. Moldenhauer et al. (Princeton: Princeton Univ. Press, 1975)

EmJ   *Emerson in His Journals,* ed. Joel Porte (Cambridge, Mass.: Harvard Univ. Press, 1982)

EP   Thoreau, *Excursions and Poems. The Writings of Henry David Thoreau,* Vol. V (Boston: Houghton Mifflin, 1906)

EW   Emerson, *Complete Works* (Boston: Houghton Mifflin, 1911)

FS   *Henry D. Thoreau: Faith in a Seed,* ed. Bradley P. Dean (Washington, D.C.: Island Press, 1993)

J   *The Journal of Henry D. Thoreau,* ed. Bradford Torrey and Francis H. Allen (1906; rpt. Boston: Houghton Mifflin, 1949), 14 vols. (numbered Vols. VII–XX in 1906 edition)

JMN   *The Journals and Miscellaneous Notebooks of Ralph Waldo Emerson,* ed. William H. Gilman et al. (Cambridge, Mass.: Harvard Univ. Press, 1960–   )

Log   *The Thoreau Log,* ed. Raymond R. Borst (New York: G. K. Hall, 1992)

MW   Thoreau, *The Maine Woods,* ed. Joseph J. Moldenhauer (Princeton: Princeton Univ. Press, 1972)

NHE   Thoreau, *The Natural History Essays,* ed. Robert Sattelmeyer (Salt Lake City: Gibbs–Smith, 1980)

PJ   Thoreau, *Journal,* ed. John C. Broderick et al. (Princeton: Princeton Univ. Press, 1981–   ), 4 vols. to date

RP   Thoreau, *Reform Papers,* ed. Wendell Glick (Princeton: Princeton Univ. Press, 1973)

W   Thoreau, *Walden,* ed. J. Lyndon Shanley (Princeton: Princeton Univ. Press, 1971)

Wk   Thoreau, *A Week on the Concord and Merrimack Rivers,* ed. Carl F. Hovde et al. (Princeton: Princeton Univ. Press, 1980)

Preface

Perhaps the best introduction to this book would be a brief account of how it came to be written. It began as part of a more inclusive study of Emerson and the American Renaissance that originated in my sense of a deep structural kinship among three of the major canonical texts of the period – *Moby-Dick, Walden,* and the 1855 and 1856 editions of *Leaves of Grass* – and between these midcentury writings and Emerson's 1837 oration "The American Scholar." By "structural kinship" I had in mind something more than affinities of content or form rooted in the contemporary zeitgeist or traceable in conventional ways to the literary and philosophical influence of Emerson. Despite enormous differences of genre, occasion, sensibility, and idea, the works seemed to share a common rhetorical architecture that could not be explained through the usual vocabularies of criticism and that seemed to point beyond the initiative of particular authors to a source in collective experience.

My subject, as I grew to understand it, centered on the complex relationship among individual and group consciousness, social processes, and literary form. Nothing I had read equipped me to undertake such a project or offered itself as a usable model. While New Historical theory and practice have gone far toward dissolving the traditional distinction between literary foreground and historical background, they have done so in large part by reducing the author to an inconsequential cipher amid the play of discourses and ideologies. More suggestive was the work of theorists on or beyond the edges of literary criticism – Erik H. Erikson, Lucien Goldmann, Raymond Williams, sociologist Alvin W. Gouldner, and Clifford Geertz, all of whom were concerned with the mental structures individuals and groups generated to mediate their relation with the world. In their different idioms, moreover, all these writers seemed to circle around a remark by Kenneth Burke: "Critical and imaginative works are answers to questions posed by the situation in which they arose. They are not merely answers, they are *strategic* answers, *stylized* answers," that "size up the situations, name their structure and outstanding ingredients, and name them in a way that contains an attitude towards them."[1] Approaching the American Renaissance through Burke's notion of literature as symbolic action, I came to see the writings of the 1850s as "stylized answers" to a vocational problem defined by Emerson for an entire literary generation. The process I wanted to illustrate was how the writers of the American Renaissance – pronounced individuals yet members, too, of a literary class that sought to rescue itself from the margins of national life – reshaped their world according to the imperatives of personal and collective need and expressed themselves in literary works as congruent in their underlying narrative and rhetorical form as they were *in*congruent in most outward respects.

The first fruit of this project was an essay on Emerson entitled "'The American Scholar' as Cultural Event."[2] A chapter on Thoreau's early writings and *Walden* was to be the second. The evolution from chapter to book was initially a response to the wealth and character of the available materials – fourteen volumes of journals in the 1906 Torrey-Allen edition (currently being superseded by the Princeton text), which, together with Ronald E. Clapper's genetic edition of *Walden,* enabled readers to trace the development of author and book through most of a decade. Alongside this living record of how and why *Walden* assumed its particular shape, generalizations about history, ideology, vocation, and literary structure seemed bloodless, formulaic, and often beside the point. To modify Emerson's remark that "there is no history; only biography" (*JMN* VII, 202), I increasingly felt there was no literary history of the kind I wanted to write except *through* biography. Comparing Thoreau's first draft of *Walden* (1846–47) with the published text, one interpreter has argued that "history forcibly enters [the book] in the changes and additions" of the intervening years.[3] So it does, yet "history" involves substantially more than Thoreau's declining "confidence in the likelihood of civic reform" and the role of his own work in "instigating" it.[4] The history that altered *Walden* is the organic history of its author as a psychosocial being, and until one understood *that* history with reasonable fullness there seemed little chance of sympathetically understanding any other. The circumstances of the case at hand – what I came to think of as "practical history" – would have to suggest whatever larger claims might be made for the intertextuality of the American Renaissance.

I do not pretend to have come full circle and written the historical book I projected. As I worked with the journals and the genetic text of *Walden,* together with the contemporaneous writings and the juvenilia, Thoreau's career assumed an interest of its own, and having charted its development up to and within the successive drafts of *Walden,* it was impossible not to pursue it farther, beyond *Walden,* to discover how and where the journey ended. Reputedly, the terrain was not inviting. Despite the 1980s work of Robert D. Richardson, John Hildebidle, William Howarth, and others, the myth of Thoreau's "decline" is still nearly as entrenched as the myth of Melville's. Yet both writers went forward to other lives and other achievements – Melville, most impressively in *Clarel,* by endowing his lifelong concerns with a new depth and historical reflectiveness as well as a new literary form, Thoreau in his late natural history essays by extending his range of interests and themes and coming before the public in a new incarnation. Not least among the aims of this book is to help reconfigure the shape of Thoreau's career, which is neither a parabola whose vertex is *Walden* nor a continuous line, but a rising arc with periodic disruptions and recommencements, constant only in its impulse toward ascent.

A note on vocabulary and method. For the most part I have tried to avoid pedagogical sermons and to use literary theory pragmatically for limited ends in response to immediate problems. I do, however, acknowledge a bent toward a reconstituted authorial criticism. "What matter who's speaking?"[5] Foucault asked. Everything, I believe, provided one rejects Foucault's straw man, "the free subject,"[6] and identifies the speaker as a distinctive consciousness receiving and processing sociohistorical experience and working to adapt itself favorably to the community. Erikson and Goldmann were useful counterweights to Foucault in their emphasis on the power of individuals and groups to remold their internalized world and forge new mental structures to meet crises of psychosocial adjustment. On a different side, I was encouraged to find (after the fact) that the approach to textual (dis)unity I had taken with *Walden* and *A Week on the Concord and Merrimack Rivers* has elsewhere received a name. "The empirical critic," as Frederick C. Crews denominates him or her, "is inclined to accept [the work's] contradictions without attempting to sublimate them into a higher unity, and then to investigate their origin in an irresolute or conflicted authorial mind. Such a critic demands order not from the text per se but from the congruence between textual and biographical evidence."[7] Since even the empiricist's kind of order may be more than a book or a literary career can neatly supply, it seems necessary to add that empiricism is a relative matter, a choice not so much to be "objective" as to submit one's inescapable subjectivity to a responsibility to facts and an open inquisitiveness toward literary form.

"Reimagining Thoreau," though applicable to my own project in constructing a version of Thoreau, refers primarily to the enterprise of self-mythologizing in which Thoreau himself was continuously engaged. At the center of this activity was Thoreau's concern with what I call his "problem of relation." "I have almost completed thirty nine years and I have not yet adjusted my relation to my fellows on the planet, or to my own work" (*JMN* VII, 458), Emerson remarked in 1842 in words that might equally have been Thoreau's – indeed, in one form or another *were* Thoreau's in journal confessions spanning nearly twenty-five years and in rare confidences to friends like Harrison Blake.[8] While it includes vocation as a chief element, "relation" takes in the several coordinates involved in defining a satisfactory posture toward experience; it begins in personal identity and ends in a justifiable calling in the world, its adaptational thrusts mediated along the way by the self's connection with other selves, with the local community, with society and humankind at large, and with history, nature, and God.

Thoreau himself liked to believe that "with regard to essentials" he never "had occasion to change [his] mind" (*Corr* 491); in truth, the emphases of his thinking, and still more of his self-conception, were nearly always in flux. What did not change was his transcendentalist conviction that he was embarked on a life pilgrimage whose celestial city was fullness of being, to be reached within or beyond secular time. Interpreting this journey as it appears in, shapes, and is reflexively shaped by his writings – and in terms other than Thoreau himself would have chosen to use – is the main object of this book. A vast commentary has gathered on the substance of Thoreau's beliefs and his artistry in announcing them; my own focus is on the drama of adjustment I see occurring within and beneath his work, generating its rhetorical architecture and charging its expression. Like Stanley Cavell, I would insist that *Walden* (and nearly all Thoreau's writing) "means in every word it says,"⁹ but I would emphasize the preposition "in," which implies for me an actional significance quite different at times from the literal or poetic content of Thoreau's words. In their origin and achieved form – the lines of energy that course through them and mold content into argument – Thoreau's writings are dramatized answers to the social and psychological problem of how to live, answers that assumed new character as Thoreau's efforts to inscribe (and thereby realize) an ideal self met unexpected resistances in nature, society, and his own being. Thoreau rarely overcame such problems; still less did he allow himself to be stymied by them. His special quality was a resilience that enabled him to mythologize himself anew and reformulate the terms of success. Refusing to admit defeat even to himself, Thoreau made good on his refusal through a resourcefulness of mind and spirit inexhaustible in its life-giving efficacy, if sometimes exasperating in its readiness to shed the burden of intellectual memory. Where Emersonian growth is a bursting of boundaries and a recrystallizing of the self around a new mental "helm" (*CW* II, 180), Thoreauvian growth is more typically a redirection of energies, commitments, expectations, and hopes in response to some inner or outer check. Though fond of images of upward metamorphosis (the worm into the butterfly), Thoreau was a Proteus who eluded tragedy, chronic frustration, remorse, and despair through a sidelong change of form which, if not immediately the transmutation he sought, had the salutary effect of reviving his constitutional optimism and giving new creative impetus to his life and work.

I do not expect that my presentation of Thoreau will satisfy all readers. Hagiographers will prefer not to consider the underpinnings of his rhetorical stances, nor will formalists be pleased by my emphasis on disjunctions in his major texts, which changed as he changed and in ways he seems not always to have recognized, much less to have acknowledged. "By ignoring [Thoreau's] weaknesses," however, "we do violence to what is strongest in the man," as Michael West remarked; and by turning an eye from the shifts and discontinuities in his texts, we neglect much of what is most humanly vital in them. Other stories are unfolding in Thoreau's public and private writings than the narrative of self-celebration he would have us attend to. The story I try to tell is in many respects a complement to his; it describes the pressures that generated his identic and literary forms, the experiences that strained or fractured them, and the structures that rose and subsequently fell in their stead. The Thoreau who counts most in my reading is the journalizer and writer of 1851–62: the author of the later drafts of *Walden* and of the life and career after *Walden*. The older Thoreau is a deeper, more sympathetic, more truthful figure – a riper one, too, nowhere more than toward the last in what is still commonly regarded as his intellectual and literary winter.

This book could not have been written without the textual scholarship of J. Lyndon Shanley and, especially, Ronald E. Clapper. Intellectual debts are numerous, considerable, and sometimes elusive, but I would particularly like to acknowledge the work of Charles R. Anderson, John Hildebidle, William Howarth, Linck C. Johnson, Richard Lebeaux, Sherman Paul, Stephen Railton, Robert D. Richardson, and Robert Sattelmeyer. Steven Fink's *Prophet in the Marketplace* appeared after a draft of my manuscript was completed but was a valuable source of information and provocation during the final revision. Teachers routinely credit their students, but the wealth of suggestion offered by my graduate and undergraduate students at Washington University is real and substantial. I am grateful to former Dean Edward N. Wilson and the Graduate School of Arts and Sciences at Washington University for summer grants that helped fund the project, and to the National Endowment for the Humanities for a research grant for an earlier work that contributed formatively to the present one. Above all, I thank my wife, Gail, and my sons, Jeffrey and Brian, for their understanding and support through the difficult work of what Melville called taking a book off the brain.

Part I

1837–1849

1

"A False Position in Society"

Until [a man] can manage to communicate himself to others in his full stature and proportion, he does not yet find his vocation. He must find an outlet for his character, so that he may justify his work to their eyes.

Emerson (*CW* II, 83)

I must confess I have felt mean enough when asked how I was to act on society – what errand I had to mankind – undoubtedly I did not feel mean without a reason – and yet my loitering is not without defence.

Thoreau (*PJ* 1, 339)

I

Like many of his Harvard classmates of 1837, Henry Thoreau left Cambridge for a provincial world in which times were hard, jobs scarce, and prospects uncertain. Ultimately the Panic of 1837 would cause less practical suffering among middle-class New Englanders than was initially feared,[1] but for the literary-minded of Thoreau's generation the apparent collapse of the economic order served to confirm an alienation from commercial America already widely felt and in some cases profound. By any objective measure Emerson vastly overdramatized the case in "The American Scholar" when he described "young men of the fairest promise" who "are hindered from action by the disgust which the principles on which business is managed inspire," and who "turn drudges, or die of disgust, – some of them suicides" (*CW* I, 69). Yet an objective measure was far from the minds of Emerson's young Phi Beta Kappa auditors, would-be scholars diverted to the professions of law, divinity, medicine, and teaching, often unhappily, and now feeling themselves betrayed by their elders even on the primary ground of livelihood they had taken for granted.[2]

For Thoreau, the generational problem of vocation would have been acute even in more prosperous times. As a Harvard undergraduate Thoreau had debated ideas and politics in one of the private literary societies, borrowed *Nature* from the college library in April 1837, and again in June, and shared broadly in the "great excitement of thought on moral and intellectual questions" that Transcendentalism had stimulated among the young,[3] often to the prejudice of their worldly ambitions. Emerson spoke flatteringly but not inaccurately of Thoreau when he commended the "rare decision" it required of the young graduate to "refuse all the accustomed paths" of society and aim instead "at a much more comprehensive calling, the art of living well" (*EW* X, 422, 423). "What may a man do and not be ashamed of it?" Thoreau asked in March 1838, barely six months after his graduation: "He may not do nothing surely, for straightway he is dubbed Dolittle! – aye! christen[s] himself first – and reasonably, for he was first to duck" (*PJ* 1, 34). And yet, he added, "let him do something, is he the less a Dolittle? Is it actually something done – or not rather something undone?" (*PJ* 1, 34). The outward matter of maintaining himself in the world was the least part of the vocational problem for Thoreau, whose requirements were small and who could (and occasionally did) fall back on the family business of pencilmaking when all else failed.[4] But "earning a living" was a phrase always replete with meaning for Thoreau. Beneath the literal necessity of making money lay the social one of securing a right to exist (*earn*ing a living) through labor at some useful and communally recognized calling. A "living" was also a kind of quasi-clerical installment, or material basis for the spiritual "end of life," which Thoreau defined in Emersonian fashion in a college essay of 1837 as "the bringing out, or developement [*sic*], of that which is in man, by contact with the Not Me" (*EEM* 108, 110). More than any of his contemporaries save perhaps Margaret Fuller, Thoreau took seriously the Transcendentalist injunction to self-culture and sought to make his life his vocation: to join the ideals of philosopher and man of action (or hero), and to do so, moreover, as a writer. Finally, because self-culture was a process of limitless unfolding rather than an achieved or achievable state, "earning a living" meant continually winning through to new and higher levels of self; it was the arduous, all-absorbing "business" of life, to which all practical business was subordinate. When Thoreau wrote in *Walden* of a time "when how to get my life honestly, with freedom left for my proper pursuits, was a question which vexed me even more than it does now" (*W* 29), he was referring to the crisis of postgraduation years when even the vocation of teaching, the least uncongenial of the professions respectably open to him, seemed incommensurate with the grand aims of life and peripheral to the concerns of his own life.

Living for one's inward growth was difficult enough in an age of commerce, but it was especially difficult for Thoreau, who felt routed, dissipated, ill at ease in society, and "whole and entire," "God-propt," only in nature (*PJ* 1, 344). "I almost shrink from the arduousness of meeting men erectly day by day," he wrote in 1841, wishing he could "be in society as in the landscape," without "reserve" or "effrontery" (*PJ* 1, 230; v. 201). The obsession with bravery that pervades his early journals and colors so much of his later work is an effort to counter this feeling of masculine insufficiency at once peculiar to Thoreau and endemic to the position of the literary man in America. "Anyone preoccupied with manhood, in whatever time or culture, harbors fears of being humiliated, usually by other men," David Leverenz observes.[5] So it was with the young Thoreau, an aspiring writer in a village world subject to the common doubts of the Jacksonian literary class and deprived even of the residual traditions and mutual support that sustained the Boston and Cambridge literati. "Ignorant, low lived, [and] unambitious, save in the money making line," former townsman Horace Hosmer recalled, "the Concord people did not understand Emerson, or Thoreau, or wish to, even."[6] Thoreau liked to profess an equal indifference, but there is no question that "he cared about, and took to heart, what [his neighbors] thought of him."[7] "How can he appear to be well employed to the mass of men whose profession is to climb resolutely the heights of life?" he would ask in 1846 (*PJ* 2, 357), echoing a plaint Emerson had made years earlier in "The American Scholar" and Hawthorne earlier still in *Fanshawe* (1828) and the semi-autobiographical Oberon stories of the mid-1830s.[8] Hawthorne never fully overcame what he took to be utilitarian America's judgment of him, internalized as a self-judgment and compulsively aired not only in prefaces (where modesty lent charm) but in letters and journals. Thoreau never overcame it either but learned to direct his neighbors' suspicion back against themselves, converting his "feelings of depression and alienation into aggressive satire."[9]

Beyond Thoreau's concern with masculine identity, if not entirely separable from it, was a deeper anxiety about identity itself, a consciousness of being (or appearing) a "fraction" and not an "integer" (*PJ* 1, 236), that impaired his social relations even where manliness was not at stake. "An optimal sense of identity," Erik Erikson writes, "is experienced merely as a sense of psychosocial well-being" and includes "a feeling of being at home in one's body, a sense of 'knowing where one is going,' and an inner assuredness of anticipated recognition from those who count."[10] By contrast, the young Thoreau's experience of life was one of almost chronic estrangement from his physical and emotional nature, from others, and from the community, relieved by moments of harmony and fullness achieved in solitary communion with nature. Reticent, lacking in the conventional graces, and unable to express his feelings even (or especially) when they were deep, Thoreau bore witness to what Emerson called the "porcupine impossibility of contact with men" (*JMN* VII, 301), a solitude grievous in itself yet still more so for the reminders of psychic dis-integration that accompanied efforts to bridge it. "Commonly I am not at home in the world" (*PJ* 3, 124), he summarized his condition in 1850 with an acquiescence impossible in his more turbulent postcollege years. What he meant but was loath to acknowledge, then or earlier, was that he was not at home in himself. Even his journal, begun partly to consolidate his identity, at times mirrored back a mystifying self-dissociation; "I am startled when I consider how little I am *actually* concerned about the things I write in my journal" (*PJ* 1, 131), he noted in 1840 after nearly twenty months of entries. His characteristic trope for his malaise – drawn, appropriately, from nature – was "rootlessness." "I am a parcel of vain strivings tied / By a chance bond together, / Dangling this way and that," he began a poem of 1837:

> . . . A bunch of violets without their roots,
>   And sorrel intermixed,
>   Encircled by a wisp of straw
>   Once coiled about their shoots,
>   The law
>   By which I'm fixed. . . .
>   . . .
> And here I bloom for a short hour unseen,
>   Drinking my juices up,
>   With no root in the land
>   To keep my branches green,
>   But stand
>   In a bare cup.[11]

Against this feeling of rootlessness, Thoreau's settlement at Walden Pond and the imagery of settling, planting, and laying a "foundation" in *Walden* itself take on a special psychic significance. To "settle" himself, whether in a home, a daily regimen, or the sanctuary of an impregnable moral stance, was always the precondition for Thoreau's literal and imaginative sallies into the world. But the most crucial legacy of this sense of nonbelonging was the explanatory metamyth Thoreau gradually evolved to meet it. In Emerson's youthful journals the received pieties of class and tradition are accompanied by a sincere aspiration to truth rarely warped by the deficiencies of character he broodingly lays out for inspection: indolence and apathy, emotional coldness, and "a sore uneasiness in the company of most men & women" that seemed to mock his ambition of public greatness (*JMN* II, 238). Thoreau was also given to inner stock-taking, but his pained self-estimate, rather than being a subject for periodic, almost ritualized lament, was the lens through which he habitually saw and related to the world. As a result, ideas in Thoreau's early journals commonly have the status of mediations, or vehicles for easing frustration and adapting inner necessity to outer fact. At odds not only with his time and place but with the very conditions of secular, corporeal life, Thoreau grew to feel that his proper sphere was another realm of being from which he came (like the child in Wordsworth's Immortality Ode), to which he returned nightly in "divine slumber" (*PJ* 1, 184), and in which he would ultimately find peace and self-justification.[12] Eternity, or "the final migration of souls out of nature to a serener summer" (*PJ* 1, 231), was the antitype of this pacific realm glimpsed fleetingly in dreams, memories of childhood, and strange, rhapsodic moments of self-forgetfulness associated with floating (literally or metaphorically) on water. "Drifting in a sultry day on the sluggish waters of the pond," he wrote in 1839, in one of several such entries, "I almost cease to live – and begin to be. . . . I am never so prone to lose my identity. I am dissolved in the haze" (*PJ* 1, 70). Self-surrender allured Thoreau not only because it suspended the difficulties of living and doing but because it reattached him umbilically to nature as "a restful kernel in the magazine of the universe" (*PJ* 1, 51). Years later, recalling a frequent dream from his childhood, Thoreau specified the connection between floating and psychic peace when he described "all [his youthful] experience, all satisfaction and dissatisfaction" as having been symbolized for him by two conditions he retrospectively named "Rough and Smooth." In the first he envisioned himself "lying and tossing, perchance, on a horrible, a fatal rough surface, . . . the symbol merely of my misery"; in the second he "was lying on a delicious smooth surface, as of a summer sea, as of gossamer or down or softest plush, and life was such a luxury to live. My waking experience," he added pointedly, "*always* has been and is such an alternate Rough and Smooth."[13]

It is more than a shared image that links Thoreau's floating on water to the "oceanic experience" in which Freud saw a reminder that "our present ego-feeling is . . . only a shrunken residue of a much more inclusive – indeed, all-embracing – feeling which corresponded to a more intimate bond between the ego and the world about it."[14] An anticipatory sense of this "bond" had previously led Freud to speculate about an "urge inherent in organic life to restore an earlier state of things," an aboriginal harmony "from which the living entity has at one time or another departed and to which it is striving to return."[15] One path of return led forward through experience, guided by "the efforts of Eros" to enlarge the domain of the self and build networks of relation to the world;[16] an opposite path, that of Thanatos, led backward through the dissolution of identity in self-abandonment or death.

Thoreau knew Eros (as soul union) primarily through his charged friendship with Emerson, but in the fall of 1839 (perhaps with reference to Ellen Sewall, the seventeen-year-old Scituate girl with whom he and his brother, John, both fell in love) he noted, uncharacteristically, "I am only introduced once again to myself. Conversation – contact – familiarity – are the steps to it, and instruments of it, but it is most perfect when these are done, and distance and time oppose no barrier" (*PJ* 1, 99). The relationship with Ellen ended in a spurned proposal of marriage,[17] and never again, save with Emerson, would Thoreau look to intimacy to deliver him from isolation and solidify his sense of self. "Of all phenomena my own race are the most mysterious and undiscoverable," he wrote in 1840: "For how many years have I striven to meet one; even on common manly ground; and have not succeeded!" (*PJ* 1, 145). He would never succeed. His nearest friends – Emerson, Bronson Alcott, Ellery Channing – were a trial to him in proportion to the hopes he had of them, and in time he ceased having hopes at all. Alternatively, the backward path toward unity through self-extinction and trance was inaccessible, he knew, unless the paradise of "Smooth" could be naturalized in the physical world. This is the thought that immediately follows the "restful kernel" entry of 1839. Thoreau delights in floating mentally on "an unknown & infinite sea," but he is equally concerned with "fathom[ing] unceasingly for a bottom that will hold an anchor, that it may not drag" (*PJ* 1, 51). As he would in *Walden,* Thoreau wishes to found his life on the demonstrably true and locate the dreams of consciousness in solid reality. The promise of morning, when his "thoughts and actions" seemed "on a higher level" after his "frequent[ing] a higher society during sleep" (*PJ* 1, 167), recalled to him the cultural morning of the Greeks and Orientals, an epoch recoverable to some degree, he liked to believe, through the purity and simplicity of a natural life. The lesson of such hours was that temporality itself was only an illusion, a function of distance from the fount of life traversable at any moment through a reattachment to essentials. What we call "sin," he wrote in 1841, "is not in overt acts or indeed in acts of any kind, but is in proportion to the time which has come behind us and displaced eternity" (*PJ* 1, 348). The source of our discordant state was the misconceived effort called "progress" or "civilization," the entire outward course of history from the ancients through the present, which was recapitulated on the level of the individual life by the process of socialization that divested each of us of the child's visionary inheritance.[18]

Largely from his private experience of self-division, but with hints also from his reading, Thoreau thus came to replicate the secularized Romantic myth of the Fall widespread in the early nineteenth century and common well into the mid-twentieth – "the claim," in M. H. Abrams's words,

> that man, who was once well, is now ill, and that at the core of the modern malaise lies his fragmentation, dissociation, estrangement, or (in the most highly charged of these parallel terms) "alienation." The individual (so runs the familiar analysis) has become radically split in three main aspects. He is divided within himself, he is divided from other men, and he is divided from his environment; his only hope for recovery (for those writers who hold out hope) is to find the way to a reintegration which will restore his unity with himself, his community with his fellow men, and his companionability with an alien and hostile outer world.[19]

In his own version of the myth, Thoreau subsumed his feeling of inner disharmony to his estrangement from commercial America in such a way as to shift the maladjustment from himself to society and recast a spiritual problem as a sociohistorical one. The Fall arose from no inherent flaw in human nature but from the interposition of artifice and economic temptation that disrupted our proper intimacy with experience and debased character, society, and language alike. Wordsworth and Emerson could also fable in this vein, but their reading of the age was complicated by an awareness that the individual perversely cooperated in his fall (Wordsworth) or was helpless to tap the springs of vision within him (Emerson). By 1852 Thoreau would founder on both these paradoxes, but in earlier years he was more the sociologist of culture joining strains of the radical Emerson with likenesses to the precommunist Marx. By faulting society for his alienation Thoreau avoided inquiring too closely into its private origins. The corollary of his view, however, was that only by swerving the path of history in his direction could he make a home for himself in the communal world. In the face of this quixotic labor, he met his estrangement by cultivating what Erikson calls a "negative identity," in which a tenuous sense of self "is expressed in a scornful and snobbish hostility toward the roles offered as proper and desirable in one's family or immediate community."[20] Painfully sensitive to Concord's judgment of him, Thoreau responded by disparaging his townsmen en masse and defining himself by what he was not. As Emerson was to observe, Thoreau "did not feel himself except in opposition" (*EW* X, 455–56),[21] a remark all the keener if taken literally: Thoreau never *felt* himself, brushed up against the distinguishing contours of his being, unless he had a negative reference point for self-affirmation. "In what I am unlike others," he wrote in January 1841, "in that I am" (*PJ* 1, 224). Confronted with the private uncertainties and public discomfitures he commonly called his "meanness," Thoreau ascribed that meanness to the world and reformulated his discontent as noble disdain. In more tentative moments he adopted a passive-aggressive stance: "How shall I help myself?" he asked in 1840: "By withdrawing into the garret, and associating with spiders and mice – determining to meet myself face to face sooner or later. . . . The most positive life that history notices has been a constant retiring out of life – a wiping ones' [*sic*] hands of it – seeing how mean it is, and having nothing to do with it" (*PJ* 1, 121). But more typically, Thoreau answered the "Roughness" of living with an antinomian roughness of his own, savoring resistance as "a very wholesome and delicious morsel at times" (*PJ* 1, 234) and drawing, so he said, redoubled strength from his failures. "Defeat is heaven's success," he assured himself in 1840: "He cannot be said to succeed to whom the world shows any favor. In fact it is the hero's point d'appui, which by offering resistance to his action enables him to act at all. At each step he spurns the world. He vaults the higher in proportion as he employs the greater resistance of the earth" (*PJ* 1, 179).

"Vaulting higher by resistance" is the hidden subtext of Thoreau's first address to his townsmen, delivered before the Concord Lyceum in April 1838 and inscribed in his journal as "Scraps from a Lecture on 'Society.'" "Society was made for man," Thoreau told his audience, not man for society (*PJ* 1, 35); "the mass never comes up to the standard of its best member, but on the contrary degrades itself to a level with the lowest" (*PJ* 1, 36); "the field of battle possesses many advantages over the drawing room" (*PJ* 1, 37); "the utmost nearness to which men approach each other amounts barely to a mechanical contact" (*PJ* 1, 38); and so on. Though awkwardly assumed, the embattled posture of this first performance is distinctively Thoreauvian, down to what Lawrence Buell calls Thoreau's "natural mode of argument," "triumph by aphorism."[22] If the wit of the lecture is more bludgeon- than rapier-like, it nonetheless has the effect, like *Walden*'s, of routing Thoreau's real or fancied antagonists and leaving the moral terrain entirely his own – as, for example, when Thoreau demolishes the worlds of labor and high culture both and justifies withdrawal to the garret as virtually the only course for a man of integrity to take:

> One goes to a cattleshow expecting to find many men and women assembled, and beholds only working oxen and neat cattle. He goes to a commencement thinking that there at least he may find the men of the country, but such, if there were any, are completely merged in the day, and have become so many walking commencements – so that he is fain to take himself out of sight and hearing of the orator, lest he lose his own identity in the non-entities around him. (*PJ* 1, 36)

Beneath its ostensible purpose of chastising its audience and goading it toward reform, Thoreau's lecture seems meant to record the superiority of the lecturer to his village world; it is "ethical," that is, in the Aristotelian sense of attesting to the moral character of the speaker, who is not so much the actual Thoreau as an ideal self Thoreau is trying to write into being.[23] A like impulse betrays itself in his *Dial* essay "The Service" (1840), a hymn to moral bravery culled from journal entries of the late 1830s and inspired in part by Emerson's lecture "Heroism," presented before the Concord Lyceum in June 1838.[24] "Virtue" in Emerson, Stephen Whicher has said, "is not purity but *virtus,* the manliness proper to man in his integrity."[25] Thoreau made the connection explicitly: "The state of complete manhood is virtue – and virtue and bravery are one – This truth has long been in the languages" and is "hinted at in the derivation and analogies of the Latin words *vir* and *virtus*" (*PJ* 1, 92). With its imagery of war and moral defiance and its celebration of an isolate individualism bordering on spiritual pride ("There is somewhat not philosophical in heroism; there is somewhat not holy in it; it seems not to know that other souls are of one texture with it" [*CW* II, 148]), "Heroism" seems almost to appall Emerson himself, but it would have been balm to Thoreau. "I have a deep sympathy with war[,] it so apes the gait and bearing of the soul" (*PJ* 1, 146), he wrote in June 1840 as he worked on "The Service." Thoreau had no illusions about the character and activity of modern-day soldiers; what he admired and took to himself in "The Service" as a quality of being rather than of doing was the martial attitude of "liv[ing] on the stretch, retiring to our rest like soldiers on the eve of a battle, [and] looking forward with ardor to the strenuous sortie of the morrow" (*RP* 14) – in plain terms, the Transcendental impulse to self-culture heightened by metaphor to what William James called "the moral equivalent of war."[26]

James sheds an especially valuable cross-light on Thoreau because if as a psychologist he was aware of the temperamental origins of the military attitude of soul, as a moralist he honored it, like Thoreau, as an antidote to "the worship of material luxury and wealth" that made for "effeminacy" and "unmanliness" in the age.[27] "Some men and women . . . there are," James observes, "who can live on smiles and the word 'yes' forever. But for others (indeed for most), this is too tepid and relaxed a moral climate. . . . Some austerity and wintry negativity, some roughness, danger, stringency, and effort, some 'no! no!' must be mixed in, to produce the sense of an existence with character and texture and power."[28] Thoreau's soldierly bent was partly constitutional, though it would be hard to distinguish temperament from the armor (and armaments) his position in Concord induced him to wear. As Emerson noted, "there was somewhat military in his nature"; he "found it much easier" to say No "than to say Yes" (EW X, 455, 456). The conditions of austerity, hardship, wintry negativity, even danger (if he could find it), were Thoreau's congenial element; "as our bodies court physical encounters, and languish in the mild and even climate of the tropics," he wrote in 1840, "so our souls thrive best on unrest and discontent" (PJ 1, 107). The notion of a quasi-martial order of spiritual knights lent a heroic cast to the resistance he felt by nature, cultivated as a defense against his townsmen, and justified by appeal to the moral wants of the age. James, too, associated strenuousness and heroism (along with other qualities he detested) with war; his concern was to redirect the spirit of adventure to moral ends, yet when it came to imagining the actional means to these ends, all he could offer as a locus for "'the strenuous life'" was an ascetic renunciation remarkably like Thoreau's: "the liberation from material attachments, the unbribed soul, the manlier indifference, the paying our way by what we are or do and not by what we have . . . — the more athletic trim, in short, the moral fighting shape."[29] James fails to indicate what these moral calisthenics are preparation for, nor does Thoreau in "The Service." The "grandeur" of the clouds, he laments, seems "thrown away on the meanness of my employment. . . . We look in vain over earth for a Roman greatness, to take up the gauntlet which the heavens have thrown down" (RP 12). In the absence of a work commensurate with his ideals and latent powers, Thoreau identifies greatness with a mode of being, the signet of which is loftiness of style. The swelling abstractions of "The Service" become themselves a proof of valor, as if to celebrate a transcendent manliness were tantamount to having attained it.

Long before he went to Walden Pond, then, Thoreau met the demands of his temperament and situation by associating heroism with resistance to society, portraying self-culture as moral warfare, and invoking wit and paradox as double-edged weapons of attack and defense. Thus "healthy and assured rest" became the highest bravery (PJ 1, 91; RP 3), silence the most eloquent conversation, solitude the truest society (PJ 1, 60), and contemplation the most strenuous travel (PJ 1, 171). It was once common to regard Romantic literary form as the Romantics themselves did, as the expression content took when allowed to flower of its own from within. With Thoreau's writing, it would be more accurate to say that form antecedes and structures content – "form" in the sense of patterning impulses that precondition the relationship of speaker to audience and establish the lines of what may (or must) be said and the persuasional ends toward which it is directed. The dispositions that generate and control the early writings, mold *A Week on the Concord and Merrimack Rivers,* and show themselves to one degree or another in nearly everything Thoreau wrote for publication solidified in the years 1837–44 as he struggled toward a personal and vocational identity; even *Walden*'s forays against the world can be seen as the climax of a long campaign whose themes and rhetorical strategies took shape well before Thoreau attained his intellectual majority. In brief, Thoreau knew how he wanted to engage an audience before he was certain what he had to say. "Structure," Robert Weimann theorizes, "is born out of [the] interaction by which the poet and his audience, and also the self and the social within the poet, are all genetically connected."[30] In Thoreau's case, both the external audience and the internalized voice of the community may be represented, literally or figuratively, by "Concord." "He was forever talking of getting away from the world," James Russell Lowell remarked shrewdly of Thoreau, "but he must always be near enough to it, nay, to the Concord corner of it, to feel the impression he makes there."[31] To embed Thoreau's writings in history, therefore, is not merely to describe or ideologically "unmask" their opinions on materialism, the factory system, the railroad, the demise of New England pastoralism, or the character and destiny of America, but to understand how his observations on these and other subjects assumed their peculiar inflection of attitude and tone – and served purposes quite apart from their nominal ones – as they were refracted through the troubled relationship to his townsmen that was always their tacit point of reference. The ultimate "provincial" – a man so "acutely distrustful of convention and artifice" as to "shut himself off from what is legitimately available to him," as Warner Berthoff said with primary reference to Emerson[32] – Thoreau was never more candid (under the guise of irony) than when he acknowledged being "confined" to the theme of himself by "the narrowness of my experience" (*W* 3). His experience *was* narrow, tragically and almost willfully so, since, vulnerable at so many points yet intensely proud, he felt obliged to craft a verbal armor of renunciation and scorn. By inverting the values of Concord, the young Thoreau sought to recenter the world upon his own, yet his efforts rang hollow, he knew, so long as his relation to the community went no further than that of town scold. The literary hero needed to be a man of action, not simply a man of spleen. "I occasionally find myself to be nothing at all, because the gods give me nothing to do. . . . In idleness I am of no thickness," he complained in March 1842 (*PJ* 1, 387). And later that same month: "I must confess I have felt mean enough when asked how I was to act on society – what errand I had to mankind. . . . I would fain communicate the wealth of my life to men – would really give them what is most precious in my gift" (*PJ* 1, 393). But how?

II

If Thoreau was one of the younger generation of idealists described by Emerson as languishing for want of an adequate task to perform, he was also (to cite Emerson again) an eye of genius "too convex or too concave" to "find a focal distance within the actual horizon of human life" (*CW* III, 30). It was Emerson himself who first supplied him with the rudiments of an adjusting lens. "Born, as he said, in the nick of time," Sherman Paul begins *The Shores of America,* Thoreau "did not have to formulate a 'first philosophy' as Emerson had; he found one ready to hand"[33] — all too ready, some of his neighbors felt, exasperated by what they considered Thoreau's imitation of Emerson, down (as one local said) to his imitation of Emerson's nose. "I am very familiar with all his thoughts — they are my own quite originally dressed" (*JMN* VIII, 96), Emerson himself remarked in 1841, not without reason. Yet to observe merely that Thoreau's ideas seem borrowed from Emerson as if both could be mined for their doctrinal content is to neglect extraordinary differences in the manner in which the ideas are held — in their truth-status, epistemological underpinnings, affective coloration, and place within an organic world-view; it is also to forget that Thoreau was not a systematic thinker even by Emersonian measures, and that his absorption of the attitudes of a book like *Nature* without a careful sifting of its metaphysical assumptions made for curious lacunae and contradictions in his own work, *Walden* especially.

For the young Thoreau, of more immediate consequence than Emerson's ideas was the exemplary model he presented of the trials and vindication of the literary man in philistine America. Overcoming his own personal and vocational doubts, Emerson had set out in the early 1830s to use the lecture platform as a medium for individual and cultural reform. "The whole secret of the teacher's force lies in the conviction that men are convertible," he noted to himself in 1834, as if in preparation for the work ahead: "And they are. They want awakening. Get the soul out of bed, out of her deep habitual sleep, out into God's universe, to a perception of its beauty & hearing of its Call and your prosy, selfish sensualist [originally, 'selfish Capitalist'] awakes a God & is conscious of force to shake the world" (*JMN* IV, 278). Emerson's first and most congenial task was to awaken the would-be awakeners themselves, the literary class unsure of its position, beliefs, and duties within the new commercial hegemony. "In that sermon to Literary Men which I propose to make, be sure to admonish them not to be ashamed of their gospel" (*JMN* V, 164), he reminded himself in May 1836, echoing words from Paul ("I am not ashamed of the Gospel of Christ") with reference to what would become "The American Scholar." In the oration itself, delivered to Thoreau's graduating class in August 1837, Emerson appealed intimately to the disaffected young by enclosing within his portrait of the scholar a wish-fulfilling myth of triumph and service to the nation. Beset not only by the sneers of "so-called 'practical men'" but by "the self-accusation, the faint heart, the frequent uncertainties and loss of time which are the nettles and tangling vines in the way of the self-relying and self-directed" (*CW* I, 59, 62), the scholar needed to develop a consummate self-trust and pursue his solitary course till he discovered the truths that were peculiarly his to find. Yet withdrawal and study were only part of his work; truth had to be communicated to the people. Returning to society, the scholar was anxious how his lessons would be received, but he found "to his wonder" that those who had belittled him now hung upon his words because he "fulfil[led] for them their own nature" (*CW* I, 63); he awakened them from the worship of "money or power," the highest good that they "in their sleep-walking" had been able to conceive (*CW* I, 65), and taught them that "the main enterprise of the world for splendor, for extent, [was] the upbuilding of a man" (*CW* I, 65). For the individual mired in sensualism, the scholar served as an agent of conversion, like the minister in Calvinist times; for America itself, lapsed from a worthy vision of human possibility, he was the prophet and creator of a "nation of men" (*CW* I, 70) and a stimulus for the distinctive American literature still wanting more than a half century after independence. To its audience of literary undergraduates poised to enter the Jacksonian commercial world, the meaning of Emerson's fable would have been clear. Addressing a people who persistently undervalued intellect and art, the man of letters needed to do nothing less than refashion the American world, converting his outsider's position into a locus of alternative vision and establishing himself, or the values of the literary class, as the gravitational center of a new order.[34]

Whether or not Thoreau was present to hear Emerson's address, he could hardly have escaped its influence on the literary generation of the 1830s.[35] By tapping a widespread discontent among the young and joining it to a diagnosis of the cultural, spiritual, and economic failure of America, Emerson redrew the lines of sociohistorical reality so as to transform an age of apparent collapse (the Panic of 1837 seemed to many the death knell of capitalism) into one of revolutionary opportunity and to summon the marginalized intellectual to the very forefront of epochal change (*CW* I, 67). "His personal influence upon young persons [is] greater than any man's" (*PJ* 2, 224), Thoreau observed of Emerson in 1845–46 in a rare tribute to a literary contemporary. The nature of Emerson's service to the young in general and Thoreau in particular can be gauged by comparing "The American Scholar" to Thoreau's own commencement address, "The commercial spirit of modern times considered in its influence on the Political, Moral, and Literary character of a Nation," delivered on August 30, 1837, the day before Emerson's oration. In an undergraduate essay on the "Advantages and disadvantages of foreign influence on American literature" Thoreau had echoed the familiar complaint that the literature of New England was at once overly dependent on English tastes and inclined toward a market-oriented mediocrity. His class-day exercise returns to the latter problem, identifying the principal feature of the age as a "freedom of thought and action" which "has generated the *commercial spirit*" and led to "a blind and unmanly love of wealth" that "infuses into all our thoughts and affections a degree of its own selfishness" (*EEM* 115, 116, 117). Against this debasement of character, Thoreau exhorts his audience to "cultivate the moral affections" and shift its definition of manhood from material acquisition to self-culture. Lacking, however, a clear and usable interpretation of history, along with a vision of the role literary men might play in cultural change, Thoreau can only appeal to the ultimate beneficence of social processes and hope that "most devoted and selfish worshipper of Mammon . . . is preparing, gradually and unconsciously it may be, to lead a more intellectual and spiritual life" (*EEM* 117). The address concludes lamely with a forced optimism in which "those very excesses" that trouble "the wise and good" (*EEM* 118) are seen as prophesying their own demise and auguring a more spiritual future.

The effect of "The American Scholar" (which I use synecdochically for the prophetic Emersonianism of the late 1830s) was to crystallize the sullen antimaterialist protest of youths like Thoreau into a prospect of cultural reformation that addressed what Erikson calls youth's chronic "problems of *ideology* and *aristocracy*": the desire to believe "that within a defined world image and a predestined course of history, the best people will come to rule."[36] Like most ideologies of the alienated and insurgent, Emerson's rested on a new "map" of experience whose root coordinates were IS and OUGHT TO BE (a critique of the present from the standpoint of a spiritual/social ideal), WAS and WILL BE (a reading of historical design), WE and THEY (an opposition of progressive and resistant forces), and HOW (a program for change centering on the activity of the intellectual).[37] To speak of ideology at all may be to overconceptualize the sense of possibility Emerson awoke in his most receptive listeners; a more appropriate term might be Raymond Williams's "structure of feeling," a fusion of thought and emotion reflective of "practical consciousness" as it is lived, especially as it is just emerging among a social group and finds expression in works of art rather than in formal systems of belief.[38]

Beyond its broad appeal to a literary generation shunted to the cultural fringes and eager for a task to perform, "The American Scholar" would have helped to solidify Thoreau's quarrel with Concord and to lend a heroic cast to his isolation and self-doubt. His growing friendship with Emerson and membership in the Hedge Club (both dating from the fall of 1837) brought him closer to the center of the Transcendental movement and provided the personal and ideological assurance of belonging to what Emerson called "the party of the Future" (*CW* I, 172). Even so, his practical role within the group was far from clear. Although Emerson could speak glowingly of "my brave Henry here who is content to live now, & feels no shame in not studying any profession" (*JMN* VII, 201–2), in fact he increasingly laid upon Thoreau the burden of public action he himself found uncongenial,[39] vastly mistaking his friend's fitness for mediating "between God or pure mind, and the multitude of uneducated men," as the "man of genius" was charged to do (*CW* I, 113). Emerson's own audience was the decorous and sympathetic literary class; his disciples' audience would be the materialists and scoffers in the cultural provinces whose gaze Thoreau had difficulty meeting and whose harsh words cut him to the bone. The Emersonian requirement that the prophet "come down from the mountaintop to impart his vision among the people"[40] pressed doubly hard, moreover, on a youth who had not even found his mountaintop. Better suited to Thoreau's temperament and circumstances in Concord was the office of the scholar sketched by Frederick Henry Hedge in a *Dial* essay of 1840, "The Art of Life – The Scholar's Calling." The notion of an "art of life" was itself a happy alternative to the arduousness of Emersonian duty, especially since it was an art commanded only by an "honored few," the "heroes and saints of the world" as distinguished from "the rest of mankind."[41] For Hedge, the responsibilities of the scholar began and ended with self-culture, which he was to "pursue with exclusive devotion" (179). Anticipations of "Economy" abound in "The Scholar's Calling" – in Hedge's praise for renunciation and withdrawal, his criticism of a society that loses "the end . . . in the means" (178), his notion that "truth must be lived before it can be adequately known or taught" (181), and his suggestion that the scholar maintain himself by day labor so that he might "live in the present" emancipated from schemes of wealth and with his free hours assigned to "his proper calling" (178, 179). The crux of Hedge's argument, however, was that the scholar's retirement was in the service of (self-)discovery only; his retreat from the world needn't (and shouldn't) be complemented by an Emersonian return.[42] Rather than assist directly in the work of cultural renovation, the scholar was to preserve the aloofness of a moral censor, instructing "a puny and servile age" as the Athenian Cynics and Stoics had (180), by the severity of his example:

> By taste averse, by calling exempt, from the practical movements around him, to him is committed the movement of thought. He must be a radical in speculation, an ascetic in devotion, a cynic in independence, an anchorite in his habits, a perfectionist in discipline. Secluded from without, and nourished from within, self-sustained and self-sufficing, careless of praise or blame, intent always upon the highest, he must rebuke the superficial attainments, the hollow pretensions, the feeble efforts, and trivial productions, of his contemporaries, in the thoroughness of his acquisitions, the reach of his views, the earnestness of his endeavor. (182)

It would be hard to imagine a more idealized rendering of the stance Thoreau had projected for himself in his 1838 lecture on society or tried to assume rhetorically in "The Service." Yet on two critical points Hedge would have failed Thoreau. Although a writer, and ultimately a famous writer, Hedge's scholar labored in obscurity longer than Thoreau, anxious to impress himself on the world, could afford. Second, while Hedge emphasized the need of the age for "deeds," not "words" (181), he gave no more definite idea of the substance of a "high, heroic example" (181) than Thoreau had in "The Service." Useful as moral cheerleading, Hedge's essay left Thoreau in the situation of the "many intelligent and religious persons" described by Emerson in "The Transcenden-

talist" (1841) who "withdraw themselves from the common labors and competi-
tions of the market and the caucus" and develop "a certain solitary and critical
way of living" for lack of an enterprise adequate to their faculties (*CW* I, 207).
Such persons are "miserable with inaction" (*CW* I, 212), Emerson added, and
though they assume a proud posture of indefinite waiting, they are secretly
tormented (as Emerson himself had been at a similar stage in his career) by a sense
of passing time mocking their pretensions to greatness. So Thoreau himself
confessed in a poem of 1840, modeled closely on Milton's Sonnet VII ("How
soon hath time . . . "). The poem begins:

> Two years and twenty now have flown –
> Their meanness time away has flung,
> These limbs to man's estate have grown,
> But cannot claim a manly tongue. (*PJ* 1, 116)[43]

By March 1841 the pressures of vocation had become acute for Thoreau as the
school he conducted with his brother wound to a close and he dallied with
buying the Hollowell farm only to decide at the last that he "must not lose any of
[his] freedom by being a farmer and land holder. Most who enter on any
profession are doomed men" (*PJ* 1, 291). What Thoreau seems to have wanted,
and found when he joined the Emerson household that April, was the "delay of
adult commitments" Erikson calls a "moratorium";[44] yet having lived at home
dependently as a son and younger brother, he was irked by a feeling of prolonged
juvenility and a suspicion that the "grandeur" of life required a more elemental
"back ground" (*PJ* 1, 186) than a new domestic arrangement could provide. His
family's house was insupportable – "the very haunt and lair of our vice," "an
unclean spot" (*PJ* 1, 289, 290) – but even as he prepared to move in with the
Emersons he resisted what struck him as an emasculating compromise and
dreamed of "build[ing] my lodge on the southern slope of some hill, and tak[ing]
there the life the gods send me" (*PJ* 1, 296). "A greater baldness my life seeks, as
the crest of some bare hill, which town and cities do not afford – I want a directer
relation to the sun" (*PJ* l, 300), he reiterated six days later, pitching his spiritual
tent in nature while carrying his belongings to the small crest-of-the-stairs room
of a house on the Cambridge Turnpike. The very comfort and convenience of
his new arrangement – a "very dangerous prosperity," he wryly called it (*Corr*
53) – seem to have sat uneasily on him and provoked a compensatory idyll of
wildness and independence. "The charm of the Indian to me is that he stands free
and unconstrained in nature," he wrote on April 26, 1841, his first day under
Emerson's roof (*PJ* 1, 304), as if obliged to rattle on the bars of his captivity. "Life
in gardens and parlors is unpalatable to me," he added on May 1, still protesting:
"it wants rudeness and necessity to give it relish" (*PJ* 1, 307).

In many respects, of course, the proximity to Emerson (and Emerson's library)
was an ideal opportunity for Thoreau, but it was also the beginning of an
intimacy that would strain both parties, in Thoreau's case recurrently to the

breaking point. In their two years' residence together Emerson was a generous sponsor, Thoreau a ready pupil, but if "it was not within [Thoreau's] conditions of friendship to be grateful,"[45] as Sherman Paul remarks, neither was it within the conditions of Emerson's to be benignly, tactfully forgiving. "Emerson gave Thoreau more than help, advice, and ideas, more even than a model of the writer," Robert D. Richardson comments, "he gave a tender and affectionate concern."[46] If so, it was more than Emerson succeeded in giving anyone else after the deaths of his first wife, Ellen, and his brothers Edward and Charles. Inhibition – read by others as coldness – was Emerson's tragic but unalterable law. Rebuked by Margaret Fuller for "inhospitality of soul," Emerson "confess[ed] to all this charge with humility unfeigned," adding, "nothing would be so grateful to me as to melt once for all these icy barriers" (*JMN* VII, 509). Fuller had ardor enough for both parties and friends to fall back upon when Emerson failed her; Thoreau had neither in abundance yet exacted a sympathy that an infinitely warmer and more sensitive man than Emerson would have been hard-pressed to provide. No two friends were temperamentally more star-crossed, each holding to an impossibly high ideal of friendship yet disabled by nature from even the simplest emotional exchanges. Tensions in the relationship openly appear by 1848–49,[47] with crises occurring every two or three years thereafter. As early as April 1843, however, Emerson was telling Hawthorne of "some inconveniency from his experience of Mr. Thoreau as an inmate," leading Hawthorne to speculate that "such a sturdy and uncompromising person" as Thoreau may be "fitter to meet occasionally in the open air, than to have as a permanent guest at table and fireside."[48] Thoreau himself presciently identified the core of the problem in 1840:

> For the most part I find that in another man [Emerson?] and myself the key note is not the same – so that there are no perfect chords in our gamuts. But if we do not chord by whole tones, nevertheless his sharps are sometimes my flats, and so we play some very difficult pieces together, though the sameness at last fatigues the ear. We never rest on a natural note – but I sacrifice my naturalness and he his. We play no tune though – only chromatic strains – or trill upon the same note till our ears ache. (*PJ* 1, 192)

The same month Thoreau went to reside with Emerson, *The Dial* published an essay of Emerson's that reads like a prospectus for the Walden experiment and an abstract of the chapter "Economy." The essay was "Man the Reformer," delivered in Boston before the Mechanics' Apprentices' Library Association the preceding January. Emerson liked to generalize about the times from the experience of his young disciples, and it is possible that Thoreau influenced "Man the Reformer" as strongly as it seems to have influenced him. Certainly the problem Emerson sketched for his audience could not have been closer to Thoreau's. "Our life, as we lead it, is common and mean," the essay begins; how may we become "brave and upright" and benefit posterity as well as ourselves? (*CW* I,

145). The "general system of our trade" is "a system of selfishness" unfit for "all such ingenuous souls as feel within themselves the irrepressible strivings of a noble aim" (*CW* I, 148). Yet even "by coming out of trade [we] have not cleared" ourselves, for "the evil custom reaches into the whole institution of property" to implicate everyone enmeshed in market relations (*CW* I, 148). To illustrate his point, Emerson supposes the case of a man "so unhappy as to be born a saint, with keen perceptions, but with the conscience and love of an angel." How is such a man to live? "He finds himself excluded from all lucrative works" by the abuses attending them; "he has no farm, and he cannot get one; for, to earn money enough to buy one, requires a sort of concentration toward money, which is the selling himself for a number of years, and to him the present hour is as sacred and inviolable as any future hour" (*CW* I, 148–49). "Has [such a young man] genius and virtue? the less does he find them fit for him to grow in, and if he would thrive in them, he must sacrifice all the brilliant dreams of boyhood and youth as dreams . . . and take on him the harness and routine of obsequiousness" (*CW* I, 147).

If wage labor is alienating and inherited wealth "tainted," Emerson continues, perhaps we should renounce the present order and "put ourselves in primary relations with the soil and nature," "abstaining from whatever is dishonest and unclean" and establishing our culture on the solid foundation of the farm (*CW* I, 149). If a man would be a poet or philosopher, moreover, perhaps he "ought to ransom himself" entirely "from the duties of economy, by a certain rigor and privation in his habits. . . . Let him be a caenobite, a pauper, and if need be, celibate also" (*CW* I, 153).[49] Against the luxury produced by the emerging division of labor, Emerson exhorts his audience to reexamine its modes of living and to simplify: "Let us learn the meaning of economy. . . . Can anything be so elegant as to have few wants and to serve them one's self . . . ?" (*CW* I, 154, 155). Simplifying, however, is only a preliminary act enabling us to "clear ourselves of every usage which has not its roots in our own mind" and thereby to "revise the whole of our social structure" with fittingly human ends in view (*CW* I, 156). "What is man born for," Emerson asks, "but to be a Reformer, a Re-maker of what man has made; a renouncer of lies; a restorer of truth and good . . . ?" (*CW* I, 156). So conceived, reform is not a Jacobin razing of social institutions but the public face of self-culture originating in the reformer's faith in an "infinite worthiness in [man] which will appear at the call of worth" (*CW* I, 156). As examples of such men of faith, Emerson cites three (unnamed but identifiable) whose lives stand as rebukes to the settled order and signposts of the future: "a sincere wise man and my friend" (Bronson Alcott), "a poet" (Ellery Channing), and "a conscientious youth who is still under the dominion of his own wild thoughts, and not yet harnessed in the team of society to drag with us all in the ruts of custom" (Thoreau) (*CW* I, 157). Each of these suggests to Emerson "what one brave man, what one great thought executed might effect" (*CW* I, 157). With a final nod to Thoreau, or to the practical genius he ascribed to him against his own sublime impracticality, Emerson "add[s] one trait more to this portrait of man the reformer": he shall "have a great prospective prudence" to fit him for "the high office of mediator between the spiritual and the actual world" (*CW* I, 159). The role Emerson assigns the reformer is substantially that of the man of letters in "The American Scholar," but here he links the cultural hero to the specifically Thoreauvian ideals of re(and de-)nunciation, asceticism, bravery, celibacy, and secular sainthood.

Thoreau's journals are silent on "Man the Reformer," as on virtually all literary subjects, but its influence may have been partly responsible for his wish of December 1841 to detach himself from society and "go soon and live away by the pond. . . . I dont want to feel as if my life were a sojourn any longer. . . . It is time now that I begin to live" (*PJ* 1, 347). "The pond" here is Flint's (or Sandy) Pond, where Thoreau and a college friend spent six weeks in 1837. Although the current plan fell through when the owner of the land denied Thoreau permission to build a cabin, the impulse behind it seems to have been quickened by, and mediated through, Emerson's sketch of the high-minded youth repelled by the practices of trade who finds "nothing is left him but to begin the world anew, as he does who puts the spade into the ground for food" (*CW* I, 147). Emerson himself, of course, had no thought whatever of returning to the soil beyond a morning's work in his garden; his illustrative "as" signals a figurative use of "the doctrine of the Farm" (*CW* I, 152), a symptom, in his view, of the extremity to which idealists like the Brook Farmers have been driven. In Thoreau's appropriation of "Man the Reformer," a picturesque trope becomes a proposal for living in response to his dream of elevating his life by locating it against the backdrop of nature. A more Bloomian "misprision" may also have been at work here, since to take Emerson at his word by returning to the land, or even by recording a wish to do so, was to triumph over the decorous friend whose generosity and intellectual patronage weighed on Thoreau to the degree he felt beholden to them.

From the vantage point of *Walden,* "Man the Reformer" seems the pivotal text in a curious sequence of art imitating life imitating art imitating life: *Walden* builds upon the Walden experience, whose rationale looks back to "Man the Reformer," which patterns its sketch of disaffected youth heavily after Thoreau. Reading the essay in 1841, Thoreau would have found the idealized portrait he himself had been unable to draw; he might even have glimpsed, embryonically, how the retirement to nature that originated as a flight from meanness and identity diffusion – "It will be success if I shall have left myself behind" (*PJ* 1, 347), he wrote of his plan to live by the pond – might be reshaped within the terms of Emerson's model into a principled renunciation rooted in the historical moment and conceived as an exemplary spiritual quest. Instead of a social misfit, Thoreau could begin to imagine himself a representative of idealistic youth seeking a new order. What he did not yet grasp, and would not until the circumstances of the Walden experiment forced the synthesis upon him, was how the themes of "Man the Reformer" – the return to a simple life and the cultural mission of the scholar – might be combined in a vision of removal to the woods as the appropriate dramatic action for the literary hero to take.

Had Emerson bought his acreage at Walden a few years earlier, Thoreau might nonetheless have been its pioneer settler. As it was, he chafed in vocational idleness, "the perfect transcendental handy man,"[50] as Sherman Paul called him, useful in everything except finding a reason for the "low and grovelling" life that seemed purposeless "even to [him]self" (*PJ* 1, 382). Indeed, use and uselessness are virtual obsessions in the journals of 1841–42, which belie the notion that Thoreau was enjoying a cozy apprenticeship at Emerson's. What he wanted was work. "Are there not [men]," he asked in December 1841, "who would rise to much heigher [*sic*] levels whom the world has never provoked to make the effort – . . . Who pine for an occasion worthy of them, and will pine till they are dead[?]" (*PJ* 1, 345–46). "The world" was not the only party at fault; sometimes Thoreau rhetorically looked skyward at the gods, who not only gave him "nothing to do" (*PJ* 1, 387) but answered his believer's trust ("I must not be for myself, but God's work" [*PJ* 1, 371]) with an exasperating silence. "Why God," he asked, "did you include me in your great scheme? Will ye not make me a partner at last?" (*PJ* 1, 372). The plan to live by the pond, like the removal to Walden three years later, was an effort to force the question, to determine why his life continued to "linger" and whether God was "so indifferent to my career" as he sometimes seemed (*PJ* 1, 371). The "crisis of use," as it might be called, waxed and waned for more than a year, culminating in a grand summation of March 1842, which, if neither resolutional nor cathartic, had the effect, like later summations of different problems, of making additional complaint seem redundant:

> I must confess I have felt mean enough when asked how I was to act on society – what errand I had to mankind – undoubtedly I did not feel mean without a reason – and yet my loitering is not without defence –
> I would fain communicate the wealth of my life to men – would really give them what is most precious in my gift. . . .
> It is hard to be a good citizen of the world in any great sense – but if we do render no interest or increase to mankind out of that talent God gave us – we can at least preserve the principal unimpaired.
> One would like to be making large dividends to society out that deposited capital in us – but he does well for the most part if he proves a secure investment only – without adding to the stock. (*PJ* 1, 393)

Thoreau states the problem in order to argue himself beyond it, yet he could hardly have been unaware that in speaking of "that talent God gave us" he was invoking the parable of the talents in Matthew 25: 14–30, along with Milton's vocational meditation on it in Sonnet XIX ("When I consider how my light is spent"), both of which told against him. The story in Matthew is one of the most troublesome in the New Testament, save from the standpoint of entrepreneurial capitalism. A master gives five talents (a unit of currency) to one servant, two to another, and one to a third. In time the first and second servants double their gift and present the increase to their master, for which they are praised and rewarded, while the third servant, who out of fear has buried his master's talent and returns it to him unmultiplied, is chastised as "wicked and slothful" (Matt. 25:26) and his single talent is given to the servant with ten: "For unto every one that hath shall be given, and he shall have abundance: but from him that hath not shall be taken away even that which he hath" (Matt. 25:29). In Milton's sonnet "that one Talent which is death to hide" is his poetic gift, which he would willingly use but cannot because of his blindness. He fears he may nonetheless be held accountable for his gift, but his deeper concern is that the injustice of God's demanding from him what God himself has made impossible to deliver will drive him to religious protest. "Patience" intervenes to save the day by reminding the poet, "They also serve who only stand and wait." The resolution of the sonnet is poetically and psychologically weaker than the exposition, however, and only a naïve or doctrinally straitened reader will suppose Milton satisfied by Patience's timely didacticism. Like Milton, Thoreau also finds himself prevented from rendering "interest or increase" from the talent God gave him, but instead of laboring under the biblical parable, he recasts the servant's lack of enterprise as a wise and commendable preservation of capital. He acknowledges his course as a lesser good but insists on its merit nonetheless. The echo of scripture throws a dampening irony on the whole logic, however, and in choosing a context that resonates with the praise of worldly enterprise as an instrument for spiritual growth (for what else can the parable creditably mean?) Thoreau tacitly indicts his vocational dereliction. It would be hard to say on precisely what level of intention this tortuous joke is being played, but if Thoreau is anxious enough to mount a "defence" to the charge of "loitering," he is also scrupulous enough to cut the moral ground from beneath him and expose the tenuousness of his reasoning. His argument may suffice to answer the accusing world, but it evidently cannot silence the self-accuser.

III

"All men are in a false position in society until they have realized their possibilities and imposed them on their neighbors," George Bernard Shaw wrote, thinking of his younger self: "They are tormented by a continual shortcoming in themselves; yet they irritate others by a continual overweening. This discord can be resolved by acknowledged success or failures only."[51] No public success was imminent for Thoreau so long as "delay quenched [his] aspirations" (*PJ* 1, 371), yet neither was there a clear path for him to follow. The position of the writer in society pressed upon his imagination during these years, and as he surveyed the course of Western poetry – nominally with the thought of compiling an anthology of English verse but with implicit reference to the avenues for contemporary heroism open to him – he saw the poet moving steadily from the center of communal life to the margins. "The bard has lost the dignity and sacredness of his office" (*EEM* 162), he lamented in the *Dial* essay "Homer. Ossian. Chaucer.," adapted from a lyceum lecture of November 1843, "The Ancient Poets." His praise of James Macpherson's Ossianic forgeries, which he read in Macgregor's *Genuine Remains of Ossian* and regarded as genuine himself, is particularly instructive about the kind of literature he admired and wished to write. "Ossian reminds us," he observed, "of the most refined and rudest eras, of Homer, Pindar, Isaiah, and the American Indian" (*EEM* 158) – not surprisingly since Macpherson's "poetic line and cadence were lifted largely from the King James Bible," and the *Iliad* was among "his most common reference points."[52] The modish eighteenth century commingling of pathos and primitivism that cast doubt on the authenticity of the poems was precisely what commended them to the young Thoreau, for whom the elemental was most sublime when filtered through the mists of the elegiac (*PJ* 1, 484). Ossian's poems were "stern and desolate" (*EEM* 162) *and* they were tender, combining modern sentiment with the grandeur of primitive simplicity. Defenders of Macpherson had explained the anachronism of so refined a warrior society by reference to the civilizing influence of the poet.[53] It is telling, therefore, that in his own praise of Macpherson Thoreau should emphasize the rude energy of the bard against what he saw as the latter-day *excess* of civilization and the descent of the poet from warrior-priest to tame versifier:

> [The poet] has no more the bardic rage, and only conceives the deed, which he formerly stood ready to perform. Hosts of warriors, earnest for battle, could not mistake nor dispense with the ancient bard. His lays were heard in the pauses of the fight. There was no danger of his being overlooked by his contemporaries. But now the hero and the bard are of different professions. . . . Poetry is one man's trade, not all men's religion. (*EEM* 162–63)

A preoccupation with the writer-hero also marks the journal entries on Sir Walter Raleigh that began in the summer of 1840 as Thoreau composed "The Service" and that culminated in a February 1843 lecture on Raleigh, unpublished in Thoreau's lifetime though partly incorporated into *A Week on the Concord and Merrimack Rivers*. "A born cavalier" whose courtly graces Thoreau not only lacked but usually felt obliged to disparage, Raleigh seems at first an odd choice to represent "the heroic character," save as Thoreau's admiration for "his constant soldier-like bearing and promise" (*EEM* 181, 178) reflects the quasi-martial valor he liked to ascribe to the man of letters to parry the common charge of effeteness.[54] Soldier, explorer, statesman, and writer, Raleigh was a man of action turned man of thought, and while his physical and intellectual careers were more successive than intertwined, Thoreau esteemed him for the authority a broad experience lent his prose, which in turn spoke nobly for his character. The testimony of style to authorial ethos was what Thoreau himself had tried to achieve in "The Service" and had failed, chiefly because his prose lacked "the warrant of life & experience" (*EEM* 211) that gave sinew to Raleigh's. The lesson Thoreau drew from Raleigh's career was that "the scholar requires hard labor to give an impetus to his thought; he will learn to grasp the pen firmly so, and wield it gracefully and effectually as an axe or sword" (*EEM* 213).

Sherman Paul calls the Raleigh lecture "autobiography projected on biography";[55] one might also think of it as a one-act play with the title figure, Raleigh, flanked by five satellites: the scholar, the laborer, the ethical hero, the reformer, and the saunterer. The analogy is apt not only because Thoreau structures the address as a moral "plot" but because he aims his effects at a lyceum audience whose plaudits are the condition for success. The underlying theme of the performance is the making and vindicating of the author's character, which Thoreau unveils dramatically by setting one human type against another. In choosing Raleigh for his subject rather than Milton or Sidney, Thoreau is already outreaching his audience, whom he expects to share in the "temporary" but misguided eclipse of Raleigh's reputation (*EEM* 178). Eulogizing Raleigh enables Thoreau to take on the higher qualities of his subject, specifically the aristocratic "grace and loftiness" he admired from afar as giving virtue its "current stamp and value" (*EEM* 178; *PJ* 1, 174). But the signal use of Raleigh for Thoreau is to remind the effeminate man of letters of "the necessity of labor, and conversation with many men and things" (*EEM* 212), and of the salutary effect of chores in the workshop or the field. While Emerson had sounded this theme in "The American Scholar," Thoreau takes the lesson as hard practical advice in a way that silently accuses his bookish mentor. Mindful, nonetheless, of his own circumscribed life under Emerson's roof, Thoreau is careful to subordinate Raleigh's swaggering heroism to one more available by temperament and situation to himself: "Yet after all the truly efficient laborer will be found not to crowd his day with work, but saunter to his task surrounded by a wide halo of ease and leisure, and then do but what he likes best" (*EEM* 213). As in "The Service," Thoreau uses paradox to dispatch his moral rivals left and right and authorize his own ideal self-image. A man of physical and moral action but also of psychic "rest," the "saunterer" is superior on one side to Raleigh, who lacked the strenuous "temperament of Geo. Fox or Oliver Cromwell" (*EEM* 215), and on the other to Fox and Cromwell themselves (ancestors of the modern reformer), whose earnestness needed the leaven of cheerfulness and grace. "To march sturdily through life patiently and resolutely looking defiance at one's foes, that is one way," Thoreau summarized, "but we cannot help being more attracted by that kind of heroism which relaxes its brows in the presence of danger, and does not need to maintain itself strictly, but by a kind of sympathy with the universe, generously adorns the scene and the occasion" (*EEM* 217).

Readers looking for consistency of attitude in "Sir Walter Raleigh" are unlikely to find it. The lecture unfolds through a succession of rhetorical agons, with Thoreau assuming the virtues of his several characters as he works toward a conception of the modern writer-hero that would commend itself to the world while resolving what he later called "the struggle in me . . . between a love of contemplation and a love of action – the life of a philosopher & of a hero" (*PJ* 2 240). At the heart of the problem was his desire to make literary activity a heroic form of social participation. Inclined by temperament and circumstance toward withdrawal, he knew that greatness required involvement in the world, and he was far from perceiving how withdrawal might itself be cast as a mode of participatory action. Thus he concludes the Raleigh lecture by subordinating the ascetic to the hero, whose "religion . . . demands not a narrower cell but a wider world. [The hero] is perhaps the very best man of the world; the poet active, the saint enterprising; not the most godlike, but the most manlike" (*EEM* 218). What Thoreau truly wants, though he cannot see his way clear to it, is a union of the anchorite and the man of action, an ascetic/hero who will realize his godlikeness through a deed performed in solitude on behalf of men. One thinks again of William James, who, living in a world divided between the "carnivorous-minded 'strong man'" and the compassionating but pallid "saint," proselytizes for a new man-of-the-age who will do society's work vigorously but justly – an enterprising saint rather than, like Rockefeller or Hill, a saint of enterprise.[56] The pragmatist James must have understood his lecturing and writing as in some sense *eliciting* the hero he described. So with Thoreau and "Sir Walter Raleigh," though in this case the hero is the lecturer himself, who conceives, fulfills, and publicizes his identity through the medium of his words.

By "publicizes" I literally mean "makes public," for until an ideal image registers itself on the world and is validated by communal assent, it is more a daydream than a working reality, even to oneself.[57] To borrow Joel Porte's phrase for Emerson, Thoreau in "Sir Walter Raleigh" is "essaying to be"; his lecture is "an exposition and enactment of what he is becoming *through* his speech," an attempt to summon "into being that which is envisioned or hoped for" and to build "a solid platform on which to stand."[58] Performances like this are significant as much for what they reflexively *do* for the speaker as for what they explicitly *say*. "Writing may be either the record of a deed or a deed. It is nobler when it is a deed" (*PJ* 1, 495), Thoreau himself remarked in January 1844, nearly a year after the Raleigh address. Frederick Garber takes him to mean that action is the higher form of inscription, with mere words having "an inescapable secondariness."[59] Yet there is a complementary way of understanding Thoreau's words: writing may be the distanced chronicle of an action or it may be a variety of action itself. The Ossianic bard, Thoreau had contended, was as much a participant in the battles of his race as the warriors who fought them. Even the objective historian of a deed might "share in that exploit by his discernment," as Sir Thomas Overbury did in describing the demeanor of Raleigh as he walked to his execution: "We admire equally him who could do the deed, and him who could see it done" (*PJ* 1, 174). Writing may thus become not simply a stand-in for doing but a mode of doing itself, entailed on "the truest writer" – a "captive knight" – "by some urgent necessity, even by some misfortune" (*EEM* 212).[60]

Thoreau feels himself such a "captive knight," shackled by his beneficent host and tutor Emerson, by Concord's opinion of him, and by his own hesitations about what to do or write. In lieu of making himself known to his townsmen by outward action or by literature, Thoreau in "Raleigh" publicizes himself by the example of character he enacts in his speech. "You may think me a Dolittle," he in effect tells his neighbors, "but inwardly . . ." Nor is he above pointing to the lesson explicitly: "A man is not to be measured by the virtue of his described actions or the wisdom of his expressed thoughts merely, but by that free character he is, and is felt to be, under all circumstances" (*EEM* 216). Impressing that character upon his townsmen is the impulse that shapes "Sir Walter Raleigh." The address drew praise, though not, apparently, the praise Thoreau most wanted. "*Mr. Thoreau's Lecture,* delivered last Wednesday evening, before the Lyceum, is spoken of as a production very creditable to its author," *The Concord Freeman* reported on February 8, adding a long summary paragraph on Raleigh's character and not a word on the lecturer's.[61]

IV

Beyond the question of what the modern-day literary hero might do was the equally perplexing one of what and how he might write. By late 1841 Thoreau had apparently abandoned his idea of becoming a poet,[62] but for all his love of nature it seems not to have occurred to him to make nature his literary subject, nor should it have: natural history was not an established literary genre.[63] The early journals abound, rather, with sententiae on topics like "Friendship," "Bravery," "Sound and Silence," "Greek Poetry," and "Hindoo Scripture," reminders that Thoreau's first projected book was not a natural history but a volume of essays patterned after Emerson's, without Emerson's acuteness or pungency of style.[64] Looking to encourage Thoreau's special gifts, Emerson gave him the voluminous state report on flora and fauna to review for the *Dial*. The "Natural History of Massachusetts" that followed in 1842 is usually taken as prophetic of Thoreau's genuine vein, but if the essay looks forward in content to *Walden* and the natural history writings of the 1850s, it also looks backward in rhetorical stance to "The Service" and the 1838 lecture on society. Before turning to birds, fish, and quadrupeds, Thoreau finds it necessary to disparage the communities of bipeds ("Society is always diseased, and the best is the most so" [*EP* 105]). Neither can he recommend the scientific observation of nature without praising it as "an admirable training . . . for the more active warfare of life! Indeed, the unchallenged bravery which these studies imply, is far more impressive than the trumpeted valor of the warrior" (*EP* 106). Such poses seem to have been obligatory for the young Thoreau, who was not psychically free to become a naturalist even if he wished, though nature evoked the best in his style and the most unaffected in his thought. Toward the end of the "Natural History" – an essay "so true, minute, and literal in observation, yet giving the spirit as well as the letter of what [the author] sees," Hawthorne wrote in praise[65] – Thoreau unveils a criticism of the "Baconian" approach to nature, identifying the "true man of science," as Emerson had, with the "finer organization" of the philosopher who "can discern a law or couple two facts" (EP 131) but giving Emerson's thought a distinctively empirical slant: "Let us not underrate the value of a fact; it will flower one day in a truth" (EP 130). In one sense or another, this familiar line would become Thoreau's permanent creed, so it is important to note how far he was from any such flowering in 1842. Details in the "Natural History of Massachusetts" are vividly seen, yet rarely do they make for truths, still less for truths of the lofty sort which most engaged the young Thoreau. Nature was one thing and the materials of literature quite another.

Thoreau comes closest to joining facts and ideas in "A Walk to Wachusett" (January 1843), his first attempt in the popular "excursion" form that would become his characteristic genre.[66] The object of the journey is a mountain of the west to which "distance and indistinctness," aided by the associations of wide reading, have lent sublimity and resonance (EP 133); the question that silently frames the narrative is whether "nature is capable of sustaining the imaginative significance" Thoreau ascribes to it.[67] Triadic in structure (the preliminary adventures, the climactic mountaintop experience, the return home), "Wachusett" in fact chronicles two related quests (one for Arcadia, the other for Olympus) that straddle two literary modes (pastoral and epic) and issue, respectively, from the contemplative and active sides of Thoreau's nature. The pastoral impulse expresses itself in the subjection of "raw and modern" America (EP 138) to a Virgilian eye and sensibility, with New England hop fields standing in for Mediterranean vineyards. Virgil, indeed, is the constant companion of the narrator and his unnamed friend, and the occasional rude intrusions of Yankeedom (the Concord newspaper is handed the travelers by their landlord) are softened by a lyricism that gives the account an air of reporting on a faraway country. Like the painters of the Hudson River school, Thoreau is engaged with the bucolic possibilities of the American landscape.[68] His deeper concern, however, is with finding (or making) an America habitable for the poet, an effort frustrated by the homely decency of 1840s Worcester County, which is neither "civil and ancient" like Virgil's world (EP 138) nor darkly mysterious as it was in Mary Rowlandson's time (EP 149). The epic strain in "Wachusett" is even more a promise than a realized effect. Although Thoreau adds nearly a thousand feet to the elevation of the mountain, the ascent itself is described perfunctorily in a sentence, with greater attention paid to the trees than to the climbers. The summit impresses the narrator as "a place where gods might wander, so solemn and solitary, and removed from all contagion with the plain" (EP 144); if so, the gods are silent, for no illumination is granted the narrator beyond a hawk's-eye view of the panorama below. In setting out for Wachusett the travelers had expressed "misgivings" that its grandeur might wane with proximity and that "thereafter no visible fairyland would exist for us" (*EP* 135). Atop the mountain they continue to enjoy a fairyland, but it has been displaced from Wachusett to Monadnock, far in the northwest: from the mountain, evidently, you see only the next mountain. The homeward journey "along the dusty roads" with "thoughts . . . as dusty as they" (*EP* 150) would be wearily anticlimactic if a climax had indeed occurred or if the rarefied atmosphere of the summit had even temporarily inspired the narrator. Nevertheless, with increased distance Wachusett reassumes its "ethereal hues" (*EP* 149), and by the time he has "returned to the desultory life of the plain" the narrator is ready to pronounce the walk a thorough success and reflect on our need "to import a little of that mountain grandeur into" our life (*EP* 151), though he himself demonstrably has not.

To speak of "A Walk to Wachusett" as "enact[ing] a withdrawal from the community into nature, where Thoreau achieves some greater insight into universal truths,"[69] is to describe an essay Thoreau might have written but did not. The nearest the narrator comes to discoveries of any sort is in grasping the topography of mountain ranges and receiving "a dim notion of the flight of birds" (*EP* 149). Neither contemplative in a genuine sense nor arduously heroic, "A Walk to Wachusett" is the first of several "unconsummated quests" in which Thoreau journeys to mountain, pond, ocean, or forest only to find (but never concede) that nature resists the demand for revelation made of it.[70] Jonathan Bishop has observed that "the *near* [in Thoreau] is associated with the profane; the *remote* with the sacred."[71] The specific doubt raised by "Wachusett" is whether a sacredness perceptible only in the distance can be other than a mirage. At odds with settled, utilitarian America, Thoreau removes himself to an alluring country of the west, but the quest for Arcadia only lands him in a rude pioneer version of Concord, while the quest for Olympus carries him to a mountaintop but to no mountaintop vision. The inner life of thought and poetry finds no locus in the actual world, however the narrator tries to gild experience through style; and while certain of the reality of the spiritual, Thoreau can neither join it to the mundane nor find some mediating errand for himself as an ambassador from one realm to the other.

2

"Under the Eyelids of Time":
A Week on the Concord and
Merrimack Rivers

[In Romantic literature] the yearning for fulfillment is sometimes expressed as *Heimweh,* the homesickness for the father or mother or for the lost sheltered place.

M. H. Abrams[1]

I

Based on Thoreau's 1839 expedition with his brother, John, *A Week on the Concord and Merrimack Rivers* began to assume the mental contours of a book sometime after John's death in 1842,[2] the year Thoreau wrote "A Walk to Wachusett." The chronology seems more than coincidental not only because both works are literary excursions but because both draw their energy from Thoreau's search for an imaginatively habitable alternative to Concord. "Wachusett" pursues its quest on land and across space, *A Week* chiefly on water and through time, yet both have as their physical destination a mountain in the distance and as their spiritual destination a mode of being more distant yet. Drafted in 1845 and revised at least twice before its publication four years later, *A Week* overlaps the early versions of *Walden* but is a more youthful work in its retrospective focus, its incorporation of earlier and sometimes outgrown material, and its dreamy, elegiac stance toward experience. It is also a book singularly resistant to interpretive coherence. If its first draft is imaginatively thin and underwritten, its final one is dense with samplings from Thoreau's published and unpublished works, much to the prejudice of a clear narrative or thematic line. "The element of quest is the least prominent aspect of the book,"[3] Robert D. Richardson observes of its digressive form; yet if *A Week* does not *recount* a quest, it does rhetorically *enact* one. The book is a quest for the "sacred" in experience (Jonathan Bishop),[4] for the "origins of poetry in both humanity and nature" (John Carlos Rowe),[5] for "the possibility for original experience in an autumnal age" (Peter Carafiol).[6] At bottom, that is to say, it is a quest for "home."

Like *Moby-Dick, A Week* opens bravely with its narrator responding to the "lure" of water (*Wk* 12) and embarking on a voyage of discovery that will also be the society-bound reader's voyage, in this case a voyage to "the interior of continents" (*Wk* 12) identified at once with the back country of physical adventure and the inward country of human consciousness. An inherent paradox invests an epic journey taken on a river "remarkable for the gentleness of its current" (*Wk* 9) – Hawthorne claimed to have lived by its banks for three weeks before he could determine which way it flowed[7] – and Thoreau's language of hardy enterprise occasionally threatens to collapse under its own weight. But the deeper strain on *A Week*'s heroic intent comes from its opposing ideals of action and contemplation, associated by Thoreau in a journal entry of 1837 with the twin faces of a river excursion:

> If one would reflect let him embark on some placid stream, and float with the current. He cannot resist the Muse. As we ascend the stream, plying the paddle with might and main, snatched and impetuous thoughts course through the brain. We dream of conflict – power – and grandeur. But turn the prow downstream, and rock, tree, kine, knoll, assuming new and varying positions, as wind and water shift the scene – favor the liquid lapse of thought – far-reaching and sublime, but ever calm and gently undulating. (*PJ* 1, 10)

Early in the "Concord River" preface to *A Week* Thoreau urges the reader to an upstream voyage of the sort he has taken in the past: "you shall see . . . wild and noble sights before night, such as they who sit in parlors never dream of," and "men fuller of talk and rare adventure in the sun and wind and rain, than a chestnut is of meat" (*Wk* 7, 8). This is not the voyage we are presently to make, which is a downstream, contemplative one, though Thoreau would have it appear equally heroic. His problem in *A Week,* as in life, was how to objectify a movement of thought, how, figuratively, to travel upstream and downstream at once. "Meditation and water" may be "wedded for ever,"[8] as Ishmael says, but they rarely combine for literary success without help from the dramatist. *Moby-Dick* unites physical and metaphysical adventure in Ishmael's encounter with the immensity of the sea (an "image of the ungraspable phantom of life") and his pursuit of the "portentous and mysterious monster," the whale.[9] In *A Week,* by contrast, the outward and inward journeys are split asunder, and the passage downstream, itself nearly barren of incident, becomes largely an occasion for sermons its narrator scarcely even pretends to find in stones.

The more significant action of *A Week,* carried on through language and structure rather than through event, is Thoreau's search for a realm of being in which an integral life might be lived. "He was always trying to get back to the beginning of things,"[10] Ethel Seybold noted of his reading in the classics and might fairly have said of his relation to experience generally. In *Walden* the act of physical migration brings Thoreau "nearer to those parts of the universe and to those eras in history which had most attracted" him (*W* 87). *A Week* achieves a

similar end by verbally peeling away the layers of culture and artifice Thoreau
regarded as excrescences on the real. Like *Walden* itself, but more urgently, the
book rests on what Joan Burbick calls an "alternative history": the replacement
of a celebratory account of the growth of American liberty with a history that
made nature the "foreground" and reference point for human activity.[11] By
opening *A Week* with a vision of the "Musketaquid, or Grass-ground River,"
anteceding "civilized history" and maintaining its character across and beyond
epochs of human change – "It will be Grass-ground River as long as grass grows
and water runs here" (*Wk* 5) – Thoreau establishes a framework of natural time
and Adamic naming that warrants his search for a reality buried within the
present moment rather than beneath the sediments of chronology at some remote point of origin. "As yesterday and the historical ages are past, as the work of
to-day is present," he writes in "Concord River," "so some flitting perspectives,
and demi-experiences of the life that is in nature are, in time, veritably future, or
rather outside to time, perennial, young, divine, in the wind and rain which
never die" (*Wk* 8). Living near the beginnings of civilization, Thoreau would
have said, the Greeks and Orientals enjoyed such experiences as their birthright,
as do we all in childhood. Fallen into history (or adulthood), we are obliged to
press onward *through* history in a pilgrimage toward the timelessness beyond it. In
heightened moments, however, we miraculously pierce the veil of time to
glimpse the "perennial," and if we are disciplined, or worthy, or fortunate
enough, we can hope to string such moments together to make a beatific life.
"Though I am old enough to have discovered that the dreams of youth are not to
be realized in this state of existence," Thoreau remarked in 1843, "yet I think it
would be the next greatest happiness always to be allowed to look under the
eyelids of time and contemplate the perfect steadily with the clear understanding
that I do not attain it" (*PJ* 1, 480).

This "next greatest happiness" of exalted and continuous vision is Thoreau's
grail in *A Week*. In launching himself on the stream to "float whither it would
bear me" (*Wk* 13), Thoreau is trusting the order of things to set matters right
with himself, sure that the way to redemption is by self-surrender. But the
current that is "an emblem of all progress, following the same law with the
system, with time, and all that is made" (*Wk* 12), is ambiguously a current of
beneficent tendency ("progress" as self-unfolding) and of historical change
("progress" as the rush toward modernism). As Thoreau leaves Concord behind,
he sees a fisherman who "belongs to an era" (*Wk* 23) he himself has outgrown;
"the pleasures of my earliest youth have become the inheritance of other men"
(*Wk* 23), he observes, floating downstream toward later incarnations of himself.
On one level, the river is a symbol for Thoreau's spiritual maturation; on another,
it is a public waterway whose descent from wild, upstream Sudbury to the
commercial Merrimack Valley recapitulates the past, present, and future of the
region.

Traveling through scenes memorialized in chronicle and legend, *A Week* pays tribute to history in its interpolated stories of Indian warfare, but its concern with the New England past is controlled finally by Thoreau's effort to locate himself in a pre- or a-societal timelessness. Indeed, a consciousness of history only strengthens Thoreau's desire to escape it. Bounded on one side by the rude picturesqueness of colonial life and on the other by the dams, factories, and railroads that were changing the face of the countryside, the voyage meanders through a pastoral "middle landscape" (Leo Marx's term) balanced precariously between the peacefulness of Arcadia and the onrush of industrialism that struck Thoreau when he revisited the area during a walking tour of 1848.[12] The railroad, especially, signaled to Thoreau the end of river travel (*Wk* 213), much as in Concord itself the railroad "was sweeping up the remaining old-time farmers on the outskirts into the triumphant new world of agricultural capitalism."[13] The rough provincial culture that had spawned "greater men than Homer, or Chaucer, or Shakespeare" (*Wk* 8) was already becoming an anachronism, and with it the hope that a life of epic hardihood, or at least of bucolic simplicity, might be preserved into the future. An air of historical fatalism thus pervades the late additions to *A Week* that bear on time and change, suggesting a resistless pressure toward "betterment" that could be countered on the individual's part only by withdrawing into an atemporal world apart from the headlong nineteenth century.

But if Thoreau was troubled by the social and ecological disruptions of emerging capitalism, he was scarcely more content with the drowsy pastoralism it was displacing. "Our Golden Age must after all be a pastoral one," he had noted in a journal entry of 1840, fresh from a reading of Virgil (*PJ* 1, 212). Thoreau would always find a "partially cultivated country" most congenial to "the strains of poets" (*MW* 155), especially when travels in the Maine woods or by the seashore made him nostalgic for the more humanly scaled terrain of Concord. Like weathered barn wood in the afternoon sun, however, pastoralism was most attractive from a distance; up close it showed the dry rot of tradition. In *A Week* Thoreau presents the "actual luxury and serenity of these New England dwellings," so Arcadian in aspect, as "the outward gilding" for lives that ought to be, but are not, Arcadian in substance (*Wk* 242). By being "new" (close to nature and comparatively unburdened by history), America should, by all expectation, be "old" (nearer the bucolic life of the "Georgics"), but in fact it is both recent and desiccated, old only in the negative sense of distant from the source. Concord's neighbor Billerica, though "settled not long ago, . . . to all intents and purposes . . . is as old as Fernay or as Mantua, an old gray town, where men grow old and sleep already under moss-grown monuments, outgrow their usefulness" (*Wk* 49–50). The notion that Thoreau's quarrel with capitalism is essentially nostalgic because "inspired by the agrarian ideals of the past"[14] vastly oversimplifies Thoreau's ambivalence toward American history and toward pastoralism generally. On one level, what Thoreau wanted was not any actual pastoralism he imagined to have existed in New England but the ideal pastoralism he found in the classics: Billerica Atticized.[15] Yet so far as he saw his alienation proceeding not from a particular community or form of community but from communal life itself – humanity in *any* aggregate – he was forced to devalue all modes of social living, pastoralism included, and champion a solitude in nature. Even in its prime, he observes – and "I never heard that it was young" (*Wk* 50) – Billerica with its "soft and cultivated English aspect," its "meek" schoolhouse, and its "quiet and very civil life" (*Wk* 54) – trappings of the "middle landscape" from Jefferson to Cooper – strikes Thoreau as a tame, enervating world antipathetic to "the heroic spirit" that dreams of "remoter retirements and more rugged paths" (*Wk* 55). "There is in my nature," he proclaims, "a singular yearning toward all wildness. I know of no redeeming qualities in myself but a sincere love for some things, and when I am reproved I fall back on to this ground. What have I to do with plows? I cut another furrow than you see" (*Wk* 54). If Thoreau's eulogy of the wild looks ahead to *Walden* and the essay "Walking," the air of proud identity with which he defines himself against the cultivation of the village is qualified by the hint that "justification by wildness" is partly a bulwark against social- and self-accusation. Developed from a journal entry of 1841, the passage is still more confessional as it continues in the source: "This is my argument in reserve for all cases. My love [of nature] is invulnerable   meet me on that ground, and you will find me strong. When I am condemned and condemn myself utterly . . . I rely on my love for some things" (*PJ* 1, 344–45).

The underside of Thoreau's appeal to nature is a bitterness toward his village detractors, the terms of which change as the character of society changes but the animus of which remains constant. When Thoreau writes in *Walden* of the bustling Middlesex County of railroad times (1844 and later), he adopts an anti-market rhetoric that looks wistfully back toward a simpler age; but when, as in *A Week,* he returns in memory to the life of that world, its languor oppresses him nearly as much as the restless commercialism of the present. Because settlements like Billerica too closely resemble the Concord that labels him "Dolittle" (and later "woods-burner" after he and a companion accidentally destroyed more than three hundred acres of local forest in 1844),[16] Thoreau needs to disparage their village culture and find his way back to a more sympathetic age he can privilege as the enduringly real. "I am convinced that my genius dates from an older era than the agricultural" (*Wk* 54), he announces following his sketch of Billerica, dispensing in one long paragraph with nearly all of established society since the invention of the plow. Where the republican tradition had revered the farm as the source of private and civic virtue and the bedrock of manly liberty, Thoreau belittles it as an effeminizing soporific. "There may be an excess of cultivation as well as of anything else, until civilization become pathetic" (*Wk* 55), he writes in direct rebuttal of the agrarian ideal. "In civilization, as in a southern latitude," he summarizes flatly, "man degenerates at length, and yields to the incursion of more northern tribes" (*Wk* 56).

Although "wildness" belonged to Thoreau's genuine delight in nature and the "natural" in himself (he would later have reservations), it was a quality he most insisted on, as Richard Lebeaux says, "when he felt besieged by society,"[17] whether the siege was friendly, as at Emerson's house, or hostile, as in Concord generally. What he had not settled by the time of *A Week* was the relationship between wildness and the more steadfast ideal of contemplation, a conflict that expressed itself in what might be called the "Indian-Indian paradox": a simultaneous admiration for the Spartan, unreflective life of the North American primitive (native or woodsman) and for the passive, unworldly life of the Hindu sage. Conscious of the clash of values, Thoreau tries to obviate it through rhetorical sleight-of-hand: "there is an orientalism in the most restless pioneer, and the farthest west is but the farthest east" (*Wk* 150). The true meeting point of west and east, wildness and contemplation, is the transhistorical ground in which the artifice of society drops away and one can enjoy what Emerson called "an original relation to the universe" (*CW* I, 7). Glimpsed by Thoreau in his "flitting perspectives" (*Wk* 8), such a relation appeared to him the fount of psychic wholeness, of an inward certainty that unfailingly issued in right action, and of an adjustment to the world so complete and harmonious as virtually to dissolve the boundaries between self and other.

The opening chapters of *A Week* gravitate toward this beatific ground, less through Thoreau's controlled artistry, perhaps, than through the psychic pressures upon form that give his eclectic material its distinctive lines of force. After a literal and symbolic casting off from society in "Saturday," "Sunday" begins with the evocation of a morning world reminiscent of the prelapsarian origins of poetry, myth, and religion. "The stillness was intense and almost conscious, as if it were a natural Sabbath," with the air "so elastic and crystalline" as to seem a kind of picture glass over the landscape, lending it "an ideal remoteness and perfection" (*Wk* 46). Thoreau has indeed returned to "the beginning of things," or to its eternal presence within or beneath the meanness of the everyday. "Why," he asks, "should not our whole life and its scenery be actually thus fair and distinct?" (*Wk* 46). Two men floating downstream in a skiff prompt the question again by suggesting "how much fairer and nobler all the actions of man might be" (*Wk* 49). But the moment is too idyllic to last, as Thoreau has hinted from the outset; "the impressions which the morning makes vanish with its dews, and not even the most 'persevering mortal' can preserve the memory of its freshness to mid-day" (*Wk* 43–44). What no mortal can achieve, literary style itself does, but style is not a place for Thoreau permanently to live. He would gladly arrest, even reverse, time, "daily bend[ing] my steps to east / While the late risen world goes west,"[18] as he says in the poem that prefaced the first draft of "Sunday." Yet like Wordsworth, whose lines from the Immortality Ode he recasts,[19] Thoreau knows that he must travel "west," or downstream into futurity. Just as the light of morning with its "heathenish integrity" (*Wk* 43) must dissipate into the ordinary light of noon, so the men in the skiff give way to the sight of "ancient Billerica . . . , now in its dotage" (*Wk* 50). Against the backdrop of an imagined life "as beautiful as the fairest works of art or nature" (*Wk* 49), present-day Christian, agricultural New England seems encrusted, mundane, and narrowly provincial. The outward adventure of a river trip has fallen casualty to Thoreau's quest for "a suitable background" for our lives (*Wk* 46), and that in turn has been thwarted by the flow of a current that bears him into ever more *un*suitable historical worlds. If Billerica is treated harshly by Thoreau, industrial Lowell at the confluence of the Concord and Merrimack rivers is neglected entirely, as if its very existence – by 1848 it had become synonymous with labor troubles, Irish immigration, and predatory capitalism[20] – were an affront to the transhistorical premise of the voyage. With its auroral imagery and aspect of returning to the origins of civilized time, "Sunday" occupies the position in *A Week* that "Where I Lived, and What I Lived For" occupies in *Walden;* the difference is that where *Walden* surveys a paradise rooted in the actual world and readily available for descriptive and symbolic treatment, *A Week* imagines a paradise graspable only in poetic vision and communicable through a gauziness of language and reflection far removed from the locks and canal boats of the physical voyage.

It may have been a wish to corporealize his narrative that led Thoreau to return to the active world in "Monday," whose dawn is a clarion call "to unattempted adventures" (*Wk* 117). As befits the first workday of the week, "Monday" is a vigorous chapter devoted to rehearsing scenes from the Indian wars and to exploring a more contemporary avenue for heroism, that of political reform. In the end, however, even this chapter on secular action works round to the wise passivity of the Orientals, as if doing of any concerted sort were inevitably a falling off from pure being. Behind Thoreau's argument, and allusively cited, is his 1846 arrest and imprisonment for refusing to pay his poll tax. No episode in Thoreau's life did so much to validate his dream of heroism as this unsought and essentially passive one, which gave his quarrel with Concord the moral force of opposition to slavery and the Mexican War, and which left him with a standing indignation at the political state that fueled sections of *A Week* and *Walden* as well as "Resistance to Civil Government." Thoreau had spoken out on political matters previously; in a Boston lecture on "The Conservative and the Reformer" (1844) he had tweaked the noses of progressives by advancing an extreme individualism that scorned the collectivist and institutional focus of contemporary reformers.[21] His arrest was crucial in solidifying his position because it provided a high ground of moral accountability from which he might arraign Concord for complicity in social evil without abridging his freedom to live for private ends. By jailing him overnight, moreover, society had convicted itself of the exorbitant folly he had imputed to it; it had broken an uneasy peace and invited retaliation. If Thoreau needed "a blunder to pillory . . . , a roll of the drum, to call his powers into full exercise," as Emerson said (*EW* X, 456), he now had it; he even had a battle scar to show to moral reformers. In "Monday" his appeal to the incident allows him to sever all obligations to the state, to play the philanthropist of sorts in claiming to "love man – kind" while "hat[ing] the institutions of the dead unkind" (*Wk* 131),[22] and to associate himself with the heroine of *Antigone* in elevating conscience above civil law (*Wk* 134–35). Because the state, rightly seen, could "hardly be said to have any existence whatever" (*Wk* 129), a man needn't attend to the irksome task of reforming it but might "properly" give himself to "other concerns" more suitable to his genius (*RP* 71). Despite the intense but short-lived engagements with politics that produced "Resistance to Civil Government" (1849), "Slavery in Massachusetts" (1854), and the three John Brown addresses (1859), the only heroism permanently satisfying to Thoreau was one that related to his primary business in life, self-culture; and as no outward correlative to self-culture offered itself in *A Week,* he withdrew from his skirmish with political society to the contemplative "'forsaking of works'" of the Hindus (*Wk* 138). "What after all does the practicalness of life amount to?" he asks in "Monday," effectually resigning his effort to join the physical and spiritual worlds in an action partaking of both:

> The things immediate to be done are very trivial. I could postpone them all to hear this locust sing. The most glorious fact in my experience is not any thing that I have done or may hope to do, but a transient thought, or vision, or dream, which I have had. I would give all the wealth of the world, and all the deeds of all the heroes, for one true vision. But how can I communicate with the gods who am a pencilmaker on the earth, and not be insane? (*Wk* 140)

In one way or another, all Thoreau's excursions from "A Walk to Wachusett" to the unfinished "Allegash and East Branch" were efforts to establish such a communication – efforts in the journeying itself and efforts in the retrospective composition. With his "one true vision" as a spiritual goal and the excursion as his literary genre, Thoreau might have ignored the problem of literal action and organized *A Week* as a symbolic pilgrimage leading to enlightenment. His nearest approach to the form of quest romance occurs in "Tuesday" when a morning fog leaves nothing to be seen or done and he interpolates an account of his later (1844) ascent of Saddleback Mountain, near Pittsfield. Traveling alone and preferring his own steep way to the common path, Thoreau reaches the summit just before sunset and awakens the next morning surrounded by mist and looking down upon a "country of clouds" hiding the earth:

> As the light in the east steadily increased, it revealed to me more clearly the new world into which I had risen in the night, the new terra-firma perchance of my future life. There was not a crevice left through which the trivial places we name Massachusetts, or, Vermont, or New York, could be seen, while I inhaled the clear atmosphere of a July morning, – if it were July there. . . . It was such a country as we might see in dreams, with all the delights of paradise. . . . It was a favor for which to be forever silent to be shown this vision. The earth beneath had become such a flitting thing of lights and shadows as the clouds had been before. It was not merely veiled to me, but it had passed away like the phantom of a shadow, . . . and this new platform was gained. (*Wk* 188–89)

Thoreau's pilgrimage has won him a glimpse of glory denied "the inhabitants of earth [who] behold commonly but the dark and shadowy under-side of heaven's pavement" (*Wk* 189). The vision is short-lived, however, "owing [he conjectures] to some unworthiness in myself" (*Wk* 189). Jonathan Bishop cites the episode as an example of "the experience of the sacred" in *A Week;* "quasi-sacred" seems nearer the truth,[23] since no revelation comes to Thoreau, no Emersonian beholding of natural law or Edwardsean sense of ineffable "sweet-ness." Thoreau's gaze is directed *downward* toward the "immense snowy pastures" (*Wk* 188) of the clouds below. What seems an "epiphanic moment"[24] is in fact an aesthetic perception heightened by language into a simulacrum of spiritual discovery. Even the promise of a new foundation for life is only metaphorical, at most a "perchance." Experiences of God characteristically transform the subject and alter behavior, as the Calvinists affirmed by their doctrine of "sanctification." By contrast, the fruit of Thoreau's experience is a widened sense of distance between heaven and earth, eternity and time, and oneself and others. Instead of returning him to the community with the obligations of the convert descended from the mountaintop, Thoreau's consciousness of special "favor" atop Saddleback reinforces his separation from plain-dwellers like ourselves confined to the lower world of overcast and drizzle.[25] The episode is offered as a memory cherished in private and shared with us partly that we might feel our difference from the narrator and marvel at his good fortune.

An oft-cited antecedent of the Saddleback passage is Wordsworth's ascent of Mount Snowdon in Book XIV of *The Prelude*. Climbing at night in a dense fog, "with forehead bent / Earthward, as if in opposition set / Against an enemy" (XIV, 28–30), the poet suddenly finds himself in a moonlit world gazing down upon "a hundred hills" that rise above the "silent sea of hoary mist" (XIV, 42–43).[26] The scene is magical, yet only with distance can Wordsworth begin to glorify it as "the type / Of a majestic intellect, its acts / And its possessions, what it has and craves, / What in itself it is, and would become" (XIV, 66–69). Sure of what nature means to him and of the patterns already inscribed in his poem, Wordsworth can shape his mountain experience to suit its position in a narrative of spiritual growth. Thoreau also came to value the alchemy of retrospect, but as much in perplexity as with creative joy. "How is it," he asked years later, "that what actually is present and transpiring is commonly perceived by the common sense and understanding only, is bald and bare, without halo or the blue enamel of intervening air? But let it be past or to come, and it is at once idealized. . . . It is not simply the understanding now, but the imagination, that takes cognizance of it" (*J* XIII, 17). The etherealizing distance "A Walk to Wachusett" had found in space, Thoreau here ascribes to time, with the wondrous moment either ahead of us or behind, never immediately present. As he composed *A Week* it still seemed ahead, and though he was willing enough to write himself into grace if need be, as a young man he believed that his life was on the rise and that experience would yet bestow its crown if he were patient and deserving. Where

The Prelude is narrated from the standpoint of achieved vision, *A Week* describes an action chronologically complete yet imaginatively still in progress as its author works to orient himself to the basic coordinates of God, nature, and self. His goal in *A Week* is not, like Wordsworth's, to demonstrate, but to *find out,* to press experience for what it can legitimately yield but not to manage it in a way that imposes on the facts he is trying earnestly to appraise.

The Saddleback episode is the ambiguously visionary climax of *A Week,* too inconclusive to serve as the resolution of the quest yet rhapsodic enough to make the balance of the narrative seem mundane. "There is no *further* objective to be reached,"[27] Steven Fink remarks – not because Thoreau's experience on the mountain has been illuminating, as Fink suggests, but because it has *not* been and Thoreau is powerless to see beyond it. The difficulty of imagining a symbolic end to the journey may have kept Thoreau from dramatizing what ought to have been the narrative and thematic climax of *A Week* – the ascent of Agiocochook (Mt. Washington) in "Thursday," described prosaically in a sentence or two after a long digression on the Roman satirist Aulus Persius Flaccus borrowed from a *Dial* essay of 1840. The abrupt disintegration of Thoreau's narrative is otherwise puzzling, for as "a journey book with a mountaintop as its turning point" (H. Daniel Peck's words), *A Week* gives promise of following the "classic structure" of "progress toward the source," moment of "enlightenment," and successful "return."[28] Peck himself sees the "climactic mountaintop experience" on Saddleback as precluding a later one on Agiocochook.[29] The compositional evidence tells a different story. The bulk of the Saddleback episode was a late insertion added to the manuscript no earlier than the fall of 1846 after Thoreau had drafted, then decided to omit, a section on the White Mountains (v. *PJ* 2, 266–69).[30] Intervening to change his plan, it would seem, was his September 1846 ascent of Mount Katahdin, the highest point in Maine, a mountain so rugged and inaccessible "that it had been climbed only by a few surveyors and scientists."[31] Having pitched camp beneath the summit, as he wrote in "Ktaadn," composed in 1847 between drafts of *A Week,* Thoreau awoke early the next morning and climbed upward, alone, toward the clouds hiding the peak. He never did reach the mountaintop, but he saw quite enough:

> [The scenery] was vast, Titanic, and such as man never inhabits. Some part of the beholder, even some vital part, seems to escape through the loose grating of his ribs as he ascends. He is more lone than you can imagine. . . . Vast, Titanic, inhuman Nature has got him at disadvantage, caught him alone, and pilfers him of his divine faculty. She does not smile on him as in the plains. She seems to say sternly, why came ye here before your time? . . . Why seek me where I have not called thee, and then complain because you find me but a stepmother? (*MW* 64)

In the absence of contemporary journals and letters, Thoreau's experience on Mount Washington must remain conjectural. Even today, with its cog railway and well-traveled road to the summit, cloudy, windswept Mount Washington can be hostile to climbers.[32] In Thoreau's time, before the railroad opened the region to mass tourism, it was the symbol and dominating feature of a wild, "sparsely settled" country "perceived as savagely beautiful and dangerous."[33] Cultists of the sublime (writers included) made pilgrimages to the area,[34] but the trip was uncomfortable and accommodations primitive, as Thoreau recollected in an 1843 journal entry later adapted for the first draft of *A Week:* "Why should we take the reader who may be gentle and tender, through this rude tract – where the ways are steep and the views none of the best for such as are tenderly bred – Rude men and rough paths would he have to encounter – and many a cool blast over the mountain side" (*PJ* 1, 476). Drafted immediately before Thoreau left for Katahdin and deleted by the following summer, the section on the White Mountains may have been a casualty of his renewed encounter with the "primeval, untamed, and forever untameable *Nature*" (*MW* 69) he would later meet in the sea.[35] His quest in *A Week* had been directed toward a Greco-Hindu paradise located at the imagined origins of civilized time. The trip to Katahdin carried him still farther into the past, beyond human time itself, to a nature "savage and awful, though beautiful":

> This was that Earth of which we have heard, made out of Chaos and Old Night. Here was no man's garden, but the unhandselled globe. . . . Man was not to be associated with it. It was Matter, vast, terrific, – not his Mother Earth that we have heard of, not for him to tread on, or be buried in, – no, it were being too familiar even to let his bones lie there – the home this of Necessity and Fate. There was there felt the presence of a force not bound to be kind to man. (*MW* 70)

Although Thoreau was surely aware that his "sense of having penetrated to the very source of creation [was] part of the conventional rhetoric of the romantic sublime,"[36] too much was at stake for him to indulge casually in what Burke called "that sort of delightful horror, which is the most genuine effect, and truest test of the sublime."[37] Like Melville's Ishmael "horror-struck at [the] ante-mosaic, unsourced existence of the unspeakable terrors of the whale,"[38] Thoreau identified the agelessly old with the quintessentially real; and like Ishmael again, his experience in boundless nature (forest or ocean) forced on him the sense of a vast indifference that seemed to belie creation's seeming benignity. Thoreau did not require that nature be anthropocentric, only that it show a sympathetic "kinship" with humanity, as nature on Katahdin did not. It was only a partial consolation to reflect that "the vast chemistry of nature would anon work up, or work down, [Katahdin's rocks] into the smiling and verdant plains and valleys of earth" (*MW* 63); the process, after all, was material, geologic. Samuel H. Monk remarks that for Wordsworth "the external world was no series of inorganic scenes, but the ever-present symbol of a spiritual Reality, . . . which flowed from the transcendent Being that he sought and found."[39] In *Walden* Thoreau would similarly sanctify matter by affirming "not a fossil earth, but a living earth" in which "there is nothing inorganic" (*W* 309, 308). On Katahdin, however, everything seemed to Thoreau "inorganic," not least his own body:

> I stand in awe of my body, this matter to which I am bound has become so strange to me. I fear not spirits, ghosts, of which I am one, . . . but I fear bodies, I tremble to meet them. What is this Titan that has possession of me? Talk of mysteries! – Think of our life in nature, – daily to be shown matter, to come in contact with it – rocks, trees, wind on our cheeks! the *solid* earth! the *actual* world! the *common sense! Contact! Contact! Who* are we? *where* are we? (*MW* 71)

The Emersonian "NOT ME" included, of course, one's own body (*CW* I, 8), but the encounter between consciousness and physical reality that unlocked the powers of one and revealed the laws of the other was premised on a correspondence between mind and world that seemed not to obtain on Katahdin – or anywhere, perhaps, if Katahdin were an image of the foundationally real. Thoreau's 1846 excursion was not a definitive "turning point" in his view of nature; it rested in a corner of his mind half-suppressed until some new contact with the elemental reenforced the lesson, just as Katahdin itself may have called forth his memory of Agiocochook. Both mountains seem to have represented for him rude, ponderous, intractable "matter," and matter in *A Week,* so far as it resisted spiritualization, was the continual antagonist to his search for a habitable ground of being. To point the quest toward Agiocochook was to subvert its very aim; it was also to confront the fact that wildness was not, in its extremity, a viable basis for self-definition. Appalled by the annihilating emptiness of nature, the Melvillean quester is driven back, temporarily at least, on the human community he had fled in scorn. The ascent of Katahdin, and perhaps of Agiocochook, might well have had a comparable effect on Thoreau save that for psychic reasons all his bridges to the community had been, and needed to remain, burned. He had staked his justification on the wildness of nature as it evoked an epic hardihood he might oppose to the ways of Concord, and when nature at its wildest showed an inhospitality even to would-be acolytes like himself, he had no recourse other than verbal or structural evasion.[40]

As if exploring a Melvillean volte-face, Thoreau fills "Wednesday" with a thirty-page essay on friendship, an obsessive but foredoomed subject for one who felt an agonizing distance between the ideal and the reality. "All men are dreaming" of friendship, he wrote, "and its drama, which is always a tragedy, is enacted daily" (*Wk* 264).[41] "Wednesday" and "Thursday" are freighted with such interpolations, as though, nearing the close of his journey and reluctant to pursue it to its natural culmination on Agiocochook, Thoreau were increasingly uncertain where it had taken him and what it had meant. Some of his late additions have the aspect of filler.[42] A letter from H. G. O. Blake praising the Persius essay of 1840 prompted Thoreau to include it in "Thursday," though the work was so far from his mind, he told Blake, that he had to reread it "to learn what was the tenor of my thoughts then" (*Corr* 214). Similarly, the 1843 *Dial* essay "Homer. Ossian.

Chaucer." made its way into "Friday." Even new and more lively insertions like the Hannah Dustan captivity narrative in "Thursday" are set pieces whose effect is to eclipse the river journey. Outward events retreat ever farther to the margins of the book, "until in 'Friday,'" as Carl F. Hovde remarks, "we are left with little voyage material, and even the meditations follow one another with a lack of coherence often confusing and even careless."[43]

II

About the time Thoreau began to imagine his river excursion as a book, Hawthorne made a journey on the same river, in the same boat, that produced a brief narrative of an instructively different shape. Newly married in the summer of 1842 and settled in the Concord parsonage built by Emerson's grandfather, Hawthorne welcomed his new life as a deliverance from years of solitude and introspection, at age thirty-eight an Edenic beginning. He grew friendly with Emerson, Thoreau, and Margaret Fuller, rediscovered the outdoors he had known as a boy in Maine ("Oh that I could run wild! – that is, that I could put myself into a true relation with nature"),[44] imbibed the reformist spirit of Transcendentalism even as he preserved a skeptical distance, and purchased Thoreau's boat, the "Musketaquid," which he promptly rechristened the "Pond Lily" and was soon handling with reasonable skill. In "The Old Manse" (1846), a familiar preface written partly to unify a collection of tales and sketches given prominently to allegories of reform, Hawthorne describes "strange and happy times" on the river with Thoreau's friend Ellery Channing when "we cast aside all irksome forms and straight-laced habitudes, and delivered ourselves up to the free air, to live like the Indians or any less conventional race, during one bright semi-circle of the sun."[45] One particular excursion gives "The Old Manse" its narrative climax and serves as a political touchstone for the volume that follows. Venturing far upriver, Hawthorne and Channing spend the night in the woods speculating boldly by the campfire and reenacting the arch Transcendental theme of removing to nature to survey life afresh from the vantage point of absolute freedom. "We were so free today, that it was impossible to be slaves again tomorrow,"[46] Hawthorne writes of the vision the voyagers earn through their journey and apply to the social world upon their return. For the conservative Hawthorne this new perspective turns out to be an eye for interior decorating prophetic of *The House of the Seven Gables,* in which the structures of society are renovated from within by the transformed heart without the disruptions of institutional change. Returned to the Manse, his symbol of tradition, Hawthorne finds its "gray, homely aspect rebuk[ing] the speculative extravagances of the day" and teaching him "that all the artifice and conventionalism of life [is] but an impalpable thinness upon its surface, and that the depth below [is] none the worse for it."[47] Outwardly Hawthorne is situated as before, "within the system of society," but now instead of "a dungeon" society seems to him "a stately edifice, whence we could go forth at will into statelier simplicity!"[48] His circular journey to nature and back has been an upward spiral.

It is unlikely Hawthorne came so dramatically to wisdom during a wilderness overnight with Ellery Channing. With the license of a storyteller he approached the episode as material for art and gave it a shapeliness it would not have had in life. Certain of his theme, and clear about the difference between a persona and a confessional "I," he would not have thought to accuse himself of "managing" the truth; all literary truth (being metaphorical) was managed. The young Thoreau was not a storyteller even to the extent of patterning his adventures into illustrative fables of a quasi-self. He did (and would always) mythologize his life, which may seem like much the same thing, but it was chiefly for the purpose of *becoming* the figure he wrote about or of persuading an audience he *had* become it. His narratives were thus, beneath their moral or aesthetic intent, forms of private action – self-reconstituting experiments in which the drive toward apotheosis was held in check by a feeling for what the facts could support. In *A Week,* especially, Thoreau was too concerned with taking his ontological bearings to give his book an unwarranted symmetry or artificial closure. The form I have called the "unconsummated quest" is a function of the way Thoreau sought to use his narratives to advance him toward a spiritual goal he hoped would clarify itself as he wrote. The writings fail as quests because the experiences they recount were inconclusive beyond the power of art and imagination honestly to resolve them. Midway through *A Week,* as through "A Walk to Wachusett," the upward movement of the narrative peaks (literally) in a moment of radiant but ephemeral vision that leaves no legacy of insight or psychic wholeness and consigns the balance of the work to desultory wandering. Where Hawthorne's river journey has a spiral form, Thoreau's excursions are typically parabolic, which is to say "tragic," in the rise and fall of the narrator's spiritual fortunes, though Thoreau never acknowledges them as such. Not the least of *Walden's* numerous accomplishments is to win through structure and language the aura of a success that eluded Thoreau in experience.

A Week was too early and intimate a book for such artfulness. The work is "curative" in the sense that Thoreau's impulse in writing it, aside from memorializing his brother and advancing his literary career, was to relieve his sense of alienation by shaping a mythology that addressed the essential questions posed by all mythologies: Why are we the driven, fragmented creatures we are rather than what we feel ourselves properly to be in our highest moments? How did we lapse into our present condition? And how shall we deliver ourselves, or be delivered, from it? As Emerson (a co-sufferer) explained: "We say Paradise was; Adam fell; the Golden Age; & the like. We mean man is not as he ought to be; but our way of painting this is on Time, and we say *Was*" (*JMN* V, 371). Starting from a sense of his fallenness measured against those moments in nature when he felt complete, Thoreau painted his condition on time by imagining a past of psychic

integration and harmony with the world, a fall into civilization, and a redemption available to those who could penetrate the layers of history to uncover the
real. Beneath its discursiveness and want of thematic line, *A Week* is the record of
Thoreau's search for that reality, which he finds, if at all, only in an ethereal vision
divorced from vital fact.[49]

"If you have built castles in the air, your work need not be lost," Thoreau
would conclude of his Walden experience; "that is where they should be. Now
put the foundations under them" (*W* 324). In "Friday" Thoreau redeems the
otherworldliness of *A Week* by beginning to dig such foundations. The chapter
opens with a change of season – "We had gone to bed in summer, and we awoke
in autumn" (*Wk* 334) – that can signal either a reinvigoration of life after the hot,
dusty Concord summer or the incursion of time, history, decay, and death into
the travelers' and New England's idyll. Focusing on the poet and drawing heavily
from "Homer. Ossian. Chaucer.," "Friday" looks backward to the dawn of
civilization and forward to its future with an ambivalent, even contradictory,
sense of whether the best lies behind or ahead. The borrowings from "Homer.
Ossian. Chaucer." argue for a declension from the "simple, fibrous life" of the
ancients to "our civilized . . . chronicle of debility, of fashion, and the arts of
luxury" (*Wk* 345). Yet alongside this historical pessimism appears, for the first
time in Thoreau's writing, an Emersonian faith in the perfect correspondence of
natural laws, moral laws, and language perceptible to all who "restore the primitive meaning" of words (*Wk* 362), that is, to the poet. Pressing further, Thoreau
revives the Transcendental empiricism of the "Natural History of Massachusetts," until now dormant in *A Week:* "The poet uses the results of science and
philosophy, and generalizes their widest deductions. The process of discovery is
very simple. An unwearied and systematic application of known laws to nature,
causes the unknown to reveal themselves" (*Wk* 363). Facts, Thoreau now implies, can be *made* to flower into truths. He stops short of joining this vision of
the poet's work to the modern decline in "the dignity and sacredness of his
office" (*Wk* 367), but the very proximity of the ideas points ahead to their
convergence in *Walden* in the working belief that while the poet has lost his
former role as inspirer and celebrant of warriors, he may assume a new and more
exalted one in coming ages by realizing in himself, and causing others to realize,
an ideal life prefigured historically in the ancients and ontogenetically in the
remembered "dreams of our childhood" (*Wk* 380). By projecting a prelapsarian
past upon the future, Thoreau can begin to imagine for himself a home in society
as it is to be remade and a fitting "errand to mankind" as one of its remakers.

While an integrated vision of this kind is more than Thoreau was able to
articulate in *A Week,* he seems clearly to have been advancing in this direction as
his life at Walden wooed him from the postures of the early 1840s even as he
busied himself inscribing them in his first book. The extant manuscript of *A
Week* lends weight to such a theory, for while the initial draft of "Friday" dwelt
elegiacally on the coming of autumn,[50] later insertions suggest the springtime of

Thoreau's recent life at the pond. "Thus we go home to find some autumnal work to do – & help in the revolution of the seasons," an early passage began acquiescently: "Perhaps nature may condescend to make use of us, even without our knowledge, as when we help to scatter her seeds in our walks, or carry burrs and cockles on our clothes from field to field" ("FD" 389; cf. *Wk* 389–90). As befits a narrative with no climactic discoveries to report, the first draft ends on a note of wordlessness. Rowing home in the dark, the travelers (like those in "A Walk to Wachusett") have "little to say but suffered any thoughts to be soothed by the monotonous sound of our oars" ("FD" 390).[51] To put a heroic construction on their silence, Thoreau reaches back ten years or more to some of his earliest journal entries: "As the truest society always approaches nearer to solitude – so the most excellent speech finally falls into Silence . . . . Silence is the universal refuge" ("FD" 390, 391; cf. *Wk* 391, 392; *PJ* 1, 60, 62). The aphorisms remain in the published text, but they are overwhelmed by a call to "a natural life" ("FD" 387) only incipiently present in the first draft. Most suggestive of all is an early passage hinting that Thoreau has already begun to put *A Week* behind him: "A good book is the plectrum with which our silent lyres are struck. We not unfrequently refer the interest which belongs to our own unwritten sequel to the written and comparatively lifeless body of the work" ("FD" 392). In the long term, the "unwritten sequel" is Thoreau's life-development; immediately, it is *Walden,* soon to be drafted and about to make its spirit felt in the additions to "Friday." By the final version of the chapter Thoreau has shed his tentativeness and become active and hortatory:

> Men nowhere, east or west, live yet a *natural* life. . . . [Man] needs not only to be spiritualized, but *naturalized,* on the soil of earth. Who shall conceive what kind of roof the heavens might extend over him, what seasons might minister to him, and what employment dignify his life! . . . Here or nowhere is our heaven.
>   . . . We need pray for no higher heaven than the pure senses can furnish, a *purely* sensuous life. Our present senses are but the rudiments of what they are destined to become. . . . The eyes were not made for such grovelling uses as they are now put to and worn out by, but to behold beauty now invisible. May we not *see* God? . . . Is not Nature, rightly read, that of which she is commonly taken to be the symbol merely? (*Wk* 379–80, 382)

The words seem familiarly Thoreauvian until we recall how minor a place the natural has occupied in *A Week.* Thoreau's exhortation to find spirit in nature, so at odds with the subordination of sense to intellect throughout his book, is a lesson drawn not from the success of the narrated voyage but from its failure. Thoreau seems to acknowledge as much when he appends to his vision of the redeemed life a rare confession of estrangement and personal inadequacy: the 1841 poem "Sic Vita" ("I am a parcel of vain strivings tied / By a chance bond together"), reprinted from *The Dial.* Nothing could be further in spirit from Thoreau's present exuberance,[52] yet confession and humiliation may be requisites in his mind for absolution, for only by speaking his condition aloud can he disemburden himself of it and begin anew. His advice in "Friday" that "every man, if he is wise, will stand on such bottom as will sustain him" (*Wk* 387) is startling and poignant coming from a man who has been standing on no discernible bottom at all. But having wafted in air through seven chapters to no satisfactory end, Thoreau seems genuinely prepared to search for "bottom" – a word from *Walden*'s vocabulary, not from *A Week*'s, and a sign, perhaps, that after looking for heaven on mountaintops and in lofty speculation, Thoreau has begun to find it, to his surprise, in the world around him.[53] The journey that lost direction and object after the Saddleback episode has gropingly come full circle (or spiral). Thoreau has found, if not yet a "home," then a place where a home might be constructed.

Part II

1845–1854

3

Disconstructing Walden

When an art product once attains classic status, it somehow becomes isolated from the human conditions under which it was brought into being and from the human consequences it engenders in actual life-experience.

John Dewey[1]

This is a long letter, but you are not at all bound to answer it. Possibly, if you do answer it, and direct it to Herman Melville, you will missend it – for the very fingers that now guide this pen are not precisely the same that just took it up and put it on this paper. Lord, when shall we be done changing?

Melville to Hawthorne, 1851[2]

I

Like the death of Emerson's wife Ellen in 1831 or of his brother Charles five years later, the death of John Thoreau in 1842 was critical in "terminat[ing] an epoch of infancy or of youth which was waiting to be closed" (*CW* II, 73), as Emerson generalized from his own experience of loss. Among other things, *A Week* is Thoreau's elegy for John, who, "freed from the limitations of human life," as Linck Johnson observes, "had begun to assume to Thoreau the status of a pure idea."[3] *A Week* is also, however, Thoreau's valediction to his own outgrown self. The "wholly new life, which no man has lived" (*Wk* 377), and which Thoreau returns to Concord to attempt, will be a life not only without his brother but without many of the attitudes and postures adopted in his first book. For despite passages of deep reflection and beauty, *A Week* is a transitional work analogous within Thoreau's career to *Mardi* within Melville's; both are ambitious books that developed in the writing and whose popular and critical failure was assuaged by the authors' conviction that they were stepping-stones to wisdom.[4] Melville's major works characteristically changed as their author responded exuberantly to what Warner Berthoff called "that rush of interior development which served him for education."[5] Composed over several years through multiple drafts, *A*

Week and *Walden* also changed; but where Melville tended to write himself forward into new attitudes, overrunning all obstructions, Thoreau often felt his way laterally, searching for an aperture to write himself out of an idea or orientation that had become straitening. "If he is wise," Thoreau later remarked, the scholar will set aside fruitless studies and turn elsewhere, "as a plant in a cellar will strive toward the light" (*J* V, 16). Thoreau rarely solved the intellectual or spiritual problems that beset him; neither did he deny or evade them. He met them head-on, brooded on them in his journals, pressed them to an anguished crux of insolubility, then left them behind, beckoned by some new interest or life possibility that presented itself. The pattern would mark his entire career and is at the heart of what pragmatists would call his admirable resilience, purists his philosophical indifference. Thoreau himself called it dwelling "as near as possible to the channel in which your life flows" (*J* V, 17), or, in the more familiar phrase, following one's genius.

In 1845 Thoreau's genius led him to Walden Pond, where the tenor of his new life slowly burned off the mists of his otherworldliness. Undertaken partly in order "to transact some private business with the fewest obstacles" (*W* 19–20) – on one level, the writing of *A Week* – the Walden experiment made the spirit of his book-in-progress increasingly anachronistic. This did not necessarily impair its composition – Thoreau's growth was uneven, and he could work effectively in a residual mode if its tone had been previously struck – but it did guarantee that his next book would be quite different. Begun even as he labored on *A Week*, *Walden* initially took shape less from a deliberate artistic plan than from Thoreau's situation at the pond as it was refracted through his adversarial relationship to Concord and channeled into a corresponding rhetorical form. Partly a self-awarded sabbatical to secure him time and independence to write, partly his substitute for pistol and ball, Thoreau's move to Walden was also by its nature and literary resonance a Transcendental quest in which the ME and the NOT ME would disclose themselves in confrontation with the other. "I wish to meet the facts of life," Thoreau announced on July 6, 1845, two days after settling at the pond,

> the vital facts, which where [*sic*] the phenomena or actuality the Gods meant to show us, – face to face. And so I came down here. Life! who knows what it is – what it does? If I am not quite right here I am less wrong than before – and now let us see what they will have. (*PJ* 2, 156)

Although a greater private urgency informed Thoreau's experiment than the narrator of *Walden* avows, its quality of flight was subsumed from the first to the pattern of withdrawal and discovery Emerson had been preaching for most of a decade. Walden Pond was scarcely the limit of the civilized world, but it represented to Thoreau both a testing ground for the ideal of simplicity proposed in "Man the Reformer" and a spiritual *terra incognita* from whose frontiers a report was clearly due. Whatever his other motives, Thoreau could thus imagine himself, relative to Concord, as an ontological "scout" fronting nature on behalf of the community and offering his projected book as a record of vital truth.

The nominal occasion for *Walden* was the set of inquiries put to Thoreau when he lectured on Carlyle at the Concord Lyceum in February 1846, inquiries that eventuated in a two-part address of the following winter titled "A History of Myself." Walter Harding argues that "the favorable reactions" of Concordians to these and later addresses induced Thoreau "to write a book-length account of his life at the pond."[6] In fact, Thoreau had his answers ready long before the questions were asked. Passages later incorporated into "Economy," "Reading," "Baker Farm," and other chapters appear in the earliest Walden journals of July and August 1845, and by the end of the year Thoreau was already rehearsing before an imagined audience of his fellow townsmen – explaining his own life, attacking theirs, and holding out the prospect of a timely message directed to their "outward condition or circumstances in this world – in this town. [W]hat it is – whether it is necessarily as bad as it is – whether it can't be improved as well as not" (*PJ* 2, 187).[7]

The certainty of voice, audience, and rhetorical purpose in this Ur-*Walden,* so absent from the draft of *A Week* written almost concurrently, seems the happy convergence of Thoreau's physical circumstances, his drive toward apologetics, and his delight in chiding his neighbors, all of which were assimilated to the Emersonian myth of the scholar's withdrawal from society and triumphant return and expressed in a literary posture of beneficent instruction. Much was also owing to the agency of Carlyle, whose "eminently colloquial" style (*EEM* 226) showed Thoreau the power of vigorous personality in literature.[8] Unsuited to the dreamy, elegiac *Week,* Carlyle's prose, rich with exaggeration and seriocomic truculence, was an accomplished version of Thoreau's own youthful satires and an ideal medium for pursuing his quarrel with Concord. As Thoreau saw it, Carlyle's writing did more than simply communicate; it imposed itself upon the reader with such histrionic force that Carlyle came to appear "himself the hero, as literary man" (*EEM* 243). It was "excellent acting," Thoreau noted ambivalently in his journal, admiring Carlyle with his own authorial instincts while chafing under his bullying style: "He does not retire behind the truth he utters – but stands in the foreground. I wish he would just think and tell me what he thinks" (*PJ* 1, 380). The struggle at work here is between a strong writer and a strong reader – the one demanding rhetorical control, the other interpretive freedom, and each intent on occupying the "foreground." As a consciousness, Carlyle both exhilarated and suffocated Thoreau; as a type of the writer-hero, he came dangerously close to preempting him. Even as he celebrated Carlyle in his 1847 essay, Thoreau made room for himself by arguing that the new literary hero must be more responsive than Carlyle or Emerson to the needs of "the Man of the Age, come to be called working-man" (*EEM* 251) – a figure he himself had begun to address in his draft of "Economy."

Above all, perhaps, Thoreau's assurance in *Walden* must be credited to the pride of domestic independence with its connotation of full manhood. Across Concord at the Old Manse, Hawthorne, settled in his own home "after having lived so long homeless in the world," could belatedly feel himself "a man having a tangible existence and locality in the world."[9] Hawthorne had begun a new life with his marriage to Sophia Peabody, and he was pleased to find his identity as husband/householder confirmed when the first callers pulled up at his door. Thoreau did not simply occupy a house; he had built one with his own hands – a house that metonymically *was* his life, or the platform on which he hoped to establish a new literary and personal relationship to Concord.

II

As J. Lyndon Shanley first demonstrated, *Walden* evolved through seven extant drafts or partial drafts between Thoreau's residence in the woods and the book's publication in 1854.[10] In 1849, after twice reworking the initial manuscript written at Walden, Thoreau offered the book to Ticknor and Company, regarding it as near-complete. The company proposed favorable terms but would not undertake *A Week* except at Thoreau's expense. "Adamant about publishing *A Week* first,"[11] Thoreau allowed the deal to fall through, much to his immediate disadvantage and *Walden*'s ultimate benefit. He did not return to the book until early in 1852, by which time his life and literary career had undergone a major transformation, as to some degree had Concord and America itself. Scholars who have studied the *Walden* manuscript date the versions as follows:

> Draft A: 1846–47 (reprinted in full by Shanley)
> Drafts B and C: 1849
> Draft D: 1852
> Draft E: late 1852–53
> Draft F: 1853–54
> Draft G: early 1854[12]

Although Shanley maintained that "the essential nature of [*Walden*] did not change from first to last" (Sh 6), the evidence of the full genetic text assembled by Ronald E. Clapper indicates that the book changed considerably. Published in 1957 during the heyday of New Criticism, Shanley's *The Making of "Walden"* is a testament to the power of critical paradigms to mold the interpretation of scholarly evidence, even (or especially) when the scholar is unaware of being "theoretical" at all. Shanley's model for the creative process and the text it produces is the neo-Coleridgean organicism advanced by Cleanth Brooks and others as a way of describing and implicitly accounting for the perfect accommodation of part to whole presumed to characterize great works of art, however problematic their origins. "The growth of *Walden*," Shanley remarks, echoing Coleridge (or possibly M. H. Abrams's redaction of Coleridge in *The Mirror and the Lamp*),[13] "might be compared to that of a living organism that grows continuously and imperceptibly by absorbing new material into its tissue and structure, so that there is no distinguishing between new and old, or first and last" (Sh 66). Disposed by theory to look for and value evidence of unity, Shanley was less prepared to see important discontinuities. Nor was his particular understanding of organic form appropriate to a text that evolved over several years. Abrams himself notes that in ascribing the literary work to a principle of growth inherent in the seed, Coleridge discounts "the participation of consciousness in the creative process" he emphasizes elsewhere in his thought.[14] As a result, he overlooks the latent tension between organicism as a theory of composition and organicism as a principle of aesthetic unity, a tension minimal perhaps in a lyric poem written in hours or days from a single impulse but potentially disruptive in a book spanning most of a decade. "Time had to pass before [Thoreau] could achieve the right focus," Shanley argues (Sh 57); yet unless one imagines Thoreau working in a psychological and historical vacuum, the time that gave him distance on his subject significantly altered the consciousness which looked upon that subject and the cultural moment which enclosed it. The "right focus" of 1846–47 was not necessarily the "right focus" of 1852–54, though (growth being gradual) not even the author might have able to judge precisely how he and his book had changed.

Hershel Parker theorizes that "in a literary work words written subsequent to a given passage will be written as they are because of the control already built into previous lines and because of the control already projected toward still later passages."[15] Though true as a general rule, this is a principle whose validity decreases with compositional time. Taking issue with Shanley in a well-titled essay, "The Remaking of *Walden*" (1990), Robert Sattelmeyer observes that Thoreau's "revisions were not directed toward filling out or realizing a design that he kept before him but toward incorporating stages of growth within a design that already existed."[16] Because the "design" was fixed and the "growth" wayward and unforeseen, this was a precarious effort liable to strange fractures and inconsistencies not always perceptible to a writer fond of maintaining that his "oldest convictions" never changed (*Corr* 491). The reigning view since F. O. Matthiessen's time that *Walden* is a prose poem in organic form admirably structured according to the cycle of the seasons and dramatizing the exemplary renewal of its hero-narrator[17] is tenable only by cordoning off the development of its author, neglecting the compositional evidence, and turning a blind eye to prominent gaps and contradictions in the text itself – among them, as Sattelmeyer notes, the fact that its witty and polemical opening chapters "are much more closely tied to Thoreau's original design and purposes than the later ones."[18] Sattelmeyer himself argues for two main phases of composition – a first stage which "includes the initial draft [A] written at Walden in 1846–47, along with the second and third drafts [B and C] that were written nearly together in 1848–49 and that primarily polish the first draft"; and a second stage which "consists of the four successive partial drafts [D through G] written between 1852 and the book's publication in 1854."[19] My own reading, based on an analysis of Clapper's genetic text, resembles Sattelmeyer's with the important difference that I would subdivide phase II in recognition of changing emphases in drafts D–G that reflect crucial microstages in Thoreau's development.[20]

The long delay in *Walden*'s publication had a profound and multi-sided effect on the work Thoreau considered complete. Returning to his manuscript in 1852–54, Thoreau greatly enlarged the fall and winter sections, incorporated new material throughout, divided the manuscript into separate chapters, and sharpened the focus of its existing argument much as a sculptor might refine a clay model to bring out his imperfectly wrought conception. At the same time, in expanding "The Ponds" and "Higher Laws" and developing the winter chapters, he brought what amounted to a new spiritual geography to his book, and even those chapters like "Economy" and "Sounds" which evolved primarily along established lines contain interpolations that strike new and discordant notes. As Shanley points out, Thoreau "did not do one sort of work at one time and another at another, but all sorts – critical, expository, narrative, descriptive – at all times" and, after 1851, on all chapters (Sh 63). But this does not mean, as Shanley supposes, that Thoreau's thematic and tonal emphases remained constant. What can be said with some assurance is that the seven drafts of *Walden* belong to two major phases (1846–49 and 1852–54), and that within the second phase Thoreau engaged in four main types of substantive elaboration, only the first two of which were recognized by Shanley: (1) he lengthened and polished existing chapters within the framework of his original design; (2) he expanded the fall and winter sections from a few pages to nearly one-fourth of the completed book, bringing forward the pattern of the seasons; (3) he overlaid expressed attitudes (toward commerce and the railroad; toward nature and truth; above all, toward his own spiritual development) with later ones, creating unanticipated ironies and subversions of meaning; and (4) he introduced major new emphases (on purity, for example) that bore intimately on his private concerns of the early 1850s but were distant from his announced purposes in "Economy."

Between 1852 and 1854, in brief, *Walden*'s original intention was at once focused, qualified, undercut, and superseded. To the extent that the second half of the book received most attention in later drafts, the experience of reading *Walden* may be said to replicate Thoreau's development while writing it.[21] It would be a mistake to press this rough correspondence too literally, as if the order of the published text neatly mirrored the chronology of composition. Nonetheless (with many caveats), two stories, not always congruent, can be described as unfolding through the course of the book: the *narrated* story of discovery and renewal that Thoreau bids us attend to (and that nearly all of his commentators *have* attended to) and the *enacted* story of the writer's efforts to adapt himself to the world that shows itself in his changing commitments of theme and authorial stance and in shifting centers of textual gravity. To "disconstruct" *Walden* with the help of Clapper's genetic text and within the framework of Thoreau's extensive journal is to read its temporally layered surface for the lines of force that generated, strained against, and repeatedly disrupted the author's successive intentions. It is to ask not merely what *Walden* is but how and why it came to be so. Has *Walden* the imaginative unity ascribed to it, or can it be productively read as what Sherman Paul described as Thoreau's "spiritual history of the years 1845 to 1854"?[22]

Paul himself never undertook a close genetic study of *Walden,* which he saw broadly as a record of fading ecstasy recaptured and memorialized through art. There is no question that 1851–52 marked a crisis of sorts in Thoreau's experience, recorded in the journals as a descent – a word I prefer to "decline" as more reflective of Thoreau's sense of vertical movement toward or away from a more celestial plane of being. Descent was contractile movement, or "regressive metamorphosis," as Daniel B. Shea called it with reference to Emerson.[23] It was a process Thoreau was chagrined to find happening to himself, against all expectation; and no sooner did he recognize it as such than he set out to reconsecrate his life, hopeful that discipline and method might supply the interest that once flowed from youthful *"enthusiasm"* (*PJ* 4, 158). When his first effort at self-reconstruction foundered within the terms he imagined for it, Thoreau fashioned new terms, as he would again, never openly conceding his defeats but edging beyond them to reconceived lives. The traces of these experiments are inscribed in drafts D–G of *Walden.* Rather than focus on the elements of loss and retrospection in *Walden,* as Paul does, I see the book as essentially *prospective* in its attempts to create a self-mythology Thoreau can use to reorient himself to time, place, work, and eternity.

To speak of Thoreau's "intentions" in such problematic circumstances, even his stratified or successive intentions, requires a special understanding of the word. It is arguable, of course, whether a book so freely discursive as *Walden* can be said to have "intentions" at all, the "charm" of many of its passages lying "more in their heterogeneity and unpredictableness," as Lawrence Buell has said, "than in their contribution to an overarching whole."[24] Within the familiar Wimsatt and Beardsley idea of intention as "design or plan in the author's mind,"[25] Thoreau (according to Shanley) had no distinct intention at all when he began *Walden* but gradually developed one as his deepening appreciation of his life at the pond crystallized into a vision that implied its own appropriate literary form (Sh 65–66). Without chapter divisions or a clear demarcation of topics, the first drafts of *Walden* do indeed show few signs of an artist working by deliberate plan. Yet "intention" may also refer to something artistically looser but more encompassing: a will to act upon an audience that seems to have been operative in a text, or part of a text, less as an antecedent design than as a continuing pressure upon form arising from the writer's situation and expressing itself in basic decisions of content, structure, language, and point of view, though by no means accounting for the presence or placement of every detail.[26] It is scarcely a denial of intention in this sense that Thoreau should have responded to his naïve admirer Daniel Ricketson by insisting that he had "no designs on men at all"; if intention meant the prosy didacticism Ricketson urged on him – the "manure" rather than the "fruit" of his experience – Thoreau wanted nothing to do with it (*Corr* 384). No writer who proclaims himself a chanticleer crowing to wake his neighbors up can be called wholly innocent of intention even in its most programmatic sense. Yet of the more private reference and meaning of his enterprise, let alone of its psychosocial roots, Thoreau may well have been (and preferred to remain) only partially aware, shaping his materials as seemed contextually proper without inquiring too closely into the imperatives that guided him. "The motivation out of which [an author] writes," Kenneth Burke remarks, "is synonymous with the structural way in which he puts events and values together when he writes,"[27] however obscure his sense of purpose at the time. To expand on Burke, intention is the conduit between motivation and structure; it is motivation expressing itself *as* structure or, viewed from the side of the literary work, structure disclosing its origins and ends by reference to some immanent problem the work seems organized to address.

The motivation behind *Walden* was adaptational: to fashion a text that would resolve the anxieties of identity and vocation, more generally of being-in-the-world, and establish the terms for a satisfying relationship to experience. If *Walden* "means in every word it says,"[28] as Stanley Cavell claims, it does so through the postures its words enact as much as through their intellectual or poetic content. These postures, moreover, change with time and context. The manuscript Thoreau drafted at the pond and offered for publication in 1849 was written to meet one set of psychological and cultural circumstances, the manuscript of 1852–54 quite another, or successions of others. Within its seasonal narrative of rebirth, *Walden* is an intricate record of aspiration, conflict, defeat, and revised aspiration, played out through several cycles and bearing witness not to the limitless prospects of the self (its announced theme), but to the power of recovery with which its author confronts the self's boundaries, his own and possibly humanity's.

4

Walden *and the Rhetoric of Ascent*

There was a man here, Samian born, but he
Had fled from Samos, for he hated tyrants
And chose, instead, an exile's lot. His thought
Reached far aloft, to the great Gods in Heaven,
And his imagination looked on visions
Beyond his mortal sight. All things he studied
With watchful eager mind, and he brought home
What he had learned and sat among the people
Teaching them what was worthy, and they listened
In silence, wondering at the revelations. . . .

Ovid, *Metamorphoses*[1]

Literature. The author's work, no matter how intelligent, elaborate (Proust) or rich and vigorous in imagination, always turns out to constitute a justification for some particular set of values, . . . a melodrama in which, even if the hero is actually defeated, he is morally triumphant. . . . The effort of the author has thus been concentrated on making his life look as if it justified his own ideals – that is, his own desires – and it is the indestructible impulse to make experience, disappointing in actuality, wear a different and more satisfying aspect, which has provided the motive power to carry him through his book. When his work is done, he may feel reassured, half believing that what he has written, because he has asserted it and it has been printed and read by people who assume that the author had some divine revelation of the truth and adopt an attitude toward him based on that assumption – that what he has written must be true.

Edmund Wilson, *The Twenties*[2]

I

Although *Walden* presents itself as the report of an experiment undertaken in open inquiry and set before the reader with a scrupulous regard for truth, the summer journals of 1845 show that the book originated not in the fruits of actual discovery (Thoreau's quest at the pond having scarcely begun) but in a rhetorical stance whose assumption of authority lacked as yet the earned basis of a life in nature. The narrator of *Walden* is "a deliberately created verbal personality," Joseph J. Moldenhauer reminds us,[3] but he is also a consciously mythologized biographical personality, "more resolute, competent, and pioneering," Lawrence Buell observes, "than [Thoreau] actually was,"[4] and more confident of his ontological bearings. To presume such a self and impress it upon the world was not merely to justify its ways but to call it into veritable existence. "What I think of myself – that determines my fate" (*PJ* 2, 220), Thoreau proclaimed in a journal entry of 1845–46 sandwiched between draft passages for "Economy" and reflections on the literary example of Carlyle. The "actual man" (Carlyle or anyone) was "too complex to deal with," Thoreau added; "the way to compare men" was "to compare their respective ideals," by which he meant their dramatized self-images (*PJ* 2, 222). Carlyle had won his fame by re-creating himself in words as "an earnest honest heroic worker" (*PJ* 2, 222). So Thoreau attempted to do in *Walden,* substituting an idealized persona for the "actual man" in the hope that by inscribing such a self he might genuinely become it.

To solidify this image for his neighbors' contemplation and his own, it was essential that Thoreau suppress the feelings of uncertainty at the root of the effort. How successfully he did so is indicated by the readiness of nearly all his interpreters to accept him at his ideal valuation. "For surely [one commentator writes] *Walden* is not the record of a fugitive life – obsessed and desperate – from one man's contemporaries, from society, from woman, perhaps from one's own self, but a purposeful, emphatic, determined journey into the deeps of self."[5] On the strength of a "surely," vast areas of possibility are thus foreclosed. When the tapestry is as glorious as *Walden,* it may seem ungrateful to insist on viewing its reverse side, however instructive this might prove in explaining oddities in the visible pattern. *Walden* entered the world, nonetheless, trailing clouds of complication that cannot be dispelled by appealing to the supposed autonomy of the literary text. In virtually no prose writer is the relationship between origins and effects more intimate and pervasive than in Thoreau, which is not to say that the relationship is ever simple or transparent. The meaning of *Walden* as *Thoreau's* book rather than as anonymous artifact lies somewhere in the space between my two epigraphs: between the writer's idealized portrait of his removal from the community and his literary relationship to its inhabitants (Ovid) and an analytic sense of how his self-mythology emerges from and enacts an ongoing drama of adjustment (Wilson).

At the core of this self-mythology is the headnote printed in many editions of *Walden* and repeated in "Where I Lived, and What I Lived For": "I do not propose to write an ode to dejection, but to brag as lustily as chanticleer in the morning, standing on his roost, if only to wake my neighbors up" (*W* 84). That a rival tale of frustration and defeat was also contained in *Walden's* materials is evidenced by the hint of private failings Thoreau weighed including during a late stage of composition lest he appear "vainglorious": "I could tell a pitiful story respecting myself . . . and flow as humbly as the gutters. I think worse of myself than [the reader] is likely to think of me, and better too perchance, being better acquainted with the man. . . . I put the best face on the matter" (Cl 854) – a confession deleted, as Richard Lebeaux says, because it "grated too harshly against the ego ideal that was so necessary to self-preservation."[6] To sketch himself at his best, or better than his best, was of the essence of Thoreau's labors in *Walden,* the success of which, literary as well as therapeutic, depended on strategically winnowing the truth of his experience and transforming himself from an invalid into a variety of what Stanley Fish called "the good physician": a literary didact of a special sort who "does not preach the truth, but asks that [his] readers discover the truth for themselves," and whose humiliating deflation of their "opinions and values," indeed of their "self-esteem," is justified by his aim of producing "nothing less than a conversion."[7] Thoreau, of course, had been satirizing his neighbors since his 1838 lecture on society. He had also read, heard, and lived under Emerson's directive that the man of genius assume the duties of moral and cultural reformer. "Men are convertible. They want awakening" (*JMN* IV, 278), Emerson had told a literary generation, just as he reminded himself. Now, at Walden and in *Walden,* and without anything so definite in mind as a deliberate plan, Thoreau was prompted by the urgencies of his relation to Concord to adopt the stance of Emersonian awakener in physician's clothes, undertaking to cure his neighbors' sleepwalking through a strong dose of ridicule. It is doubtful, knowing his townsmen as he did, that he could truly have expected his words to find a responsive local hearing, let alone to "change the world,"[8] yet it was only by engaging to play the good physician that he could construct a rationale for addressing Concord at all.

Before he could begin to practice his medicinal art, Thoreau had to gain admittance to the patient. His opening paragraph establishes his credentials by situating the narrative and portraying its speaker as manly, self-reliant, rigorously exact, and licensed to speak by his more than two years' residence in the woods. His second paragraph justifies the occasion and manner of his speaking: he comes forward in response to "very particular inquiries" made by his townsmen (*W* 3), who have solicited him, not he them, though having been asked to speak he will do so in his own fashion.[9] The third paragraph founds his text on a promise of vital knowledge to those desperately in need of it – New Englanders whose "outward condition or circumstances in this world" (*W* 4) are apparently none of the best. Together, the paragraphs stage a rhetorical drama in which speaker and audience play the parts Thoreau had assigned them in his early journals at the pond. The readers of "Economy" are cast as typical Concordians mortgaged to their properties and modes of living while the writer emerges as a man of deep, if circumscribed, experience ("I have travelled a good deal in Concord" [*W* 4]) whose primary basis for authority is the peremptoriness with which he seizes it. Lest the image of Dolittle persist among "readers who are somewhat acquainted with my actual history" (*W* 16), Thoreau counters it in "Economy" with an alternative history in which he appears an active and valorous figure "anxious to improve the nick of time" – a journeyman of miscellaneous talents employed in an unspecified but patently metaphoric "trade" with "more secrets in [it] than in most men's" (*W* 17). Archly elusive (and *al*lusive) even as it cultivates an air of frankness, Thoreau's language permits him to shed a demoralizing identity and assume the beginnings of a heroic one. His cryptic parable of the lost hound, bay horse, and turtle-dove, unsolved today, was probably never meant to be solved but to pique curiosity and invite readers to attach their own associations to its myth of fallenness and wished-for redemption, so that the quester's search becomes theirs. The social marginality of the narrator thus becomes a source of privilege and representativeness: while his neighbors have been busily attending to their callings, he, the reputed idler, has been faithfully pursuing his, which is what theirs would be if they stopped to consider the matter and review their priorities.

As Thoreau's relation to Concord molded his stance toward the reader, so it gave rise to the contrapuntal form of his argument. Paragraphs four through fifteen of "Economy" rehearse the argument in miniature and sermonically frame Thoreau's removal to the pond. Availing himself of "the whole arsenal of wit"[10] (Charles R. Anderson's phrase), Thoreau begins by overturning the values of the community and unmanning its inhabitants – opposing their "mean and sneaking lives" to "a true integrity" (*W* 6), likening them at once to slave drivers and to slaves, and measuring their dull acquiescence against "the chief end of man" (*W* 8), the development of his latent divinity. The distant, generalized indictment of pastoral New England in *A Week* is brought home to an audience through what the old Puritan sermonizers called "a particular application of the truth to the souls of men" characteristic of a "powerful ministry."[11] Having routed his opponents, Thoreau surveys the abandoned field and looks ahead to his own version of the celestial life, his tone relaxing, his rhetorical mode shifting from satire to prophecy: "But alert and healthy natures remember that the sun rose clear. It is never too late to give up our prejudices. No way of thinking or doing, however ancient, can be trusted without proof. . . . Old deeds for old people, and new deeds for new" (*W* 8). The movement from critique to prospect and back again is a main organizing principle of the 1849 *Walden* and of the first half of the published text, linking paired chapters like "Economy" and "Where I Lived, and What I Lived For," "Reading" and "Sounds," "Solitude" and "Visitors," and "The Bean-Field" and "The Village," as well as providing a constant tension within individual chapters. While the chapter divisions themselves belong to a late stage of composition, the carrot-and-stick argument by which Thoreau alternately chides his readers and tempts them with a vision of possibility informed the early *Walden* so completely that its opening pages required few revisions after 1849. The structure seems to have occurred almost spontaneously to Thoreau, partly because it drew upon the double orientation of his life (toward society, toward nature), partly because it answered so well to the requirements of addressing and capturing a resistant audience.

Thoreau's deep but ambivalent engagement with Emerson also shaped the rhetoric of "Economy." The pivotal turn toward prophecy ("But alert and healthy natures . . .") echoes the opening paragraph of *Nature* ("The sun shines today also. . . . There are new lands, new men, new thoughts" [*CW* I, 7]). Equally in Thoreau's mind was "Man the Reformer," whose model of high-minded renunciation he emulates, contends with, disparages, and works to surpass, not least because Emerson's gift of squatter's rights was an ever present reminder of dependence. Thoreau's announcement that he lived in a house of his own construction and supported himself "by the labor of [his] hands only" (*W* 3) is a response to Emerson's call "to put ourselves into primary relations with the soil and nature" and "bravely" take our part "in the manual labor of the world" (*CW* I, 149). So, too, Thoreau's attack on luxury, while rooted in his native asceticism, extends the critique of "Man the Reformer." "Our expense is almost all for conformity. It is for cake that we run in debt," Emerson had complained, preferring (so he said) "to go without" the "conveniences of life" rather than "have them at too great a cost" (*CW* I, 154). In paring consumption to "the grossest groceries" (*W* 12), Thoreau realizes Emerson's vision of a new "sacrament" of "economy" founded on "the prudence of simple tastes, when it is practised for freedom, or love, or devotion" – a "frugality for gods and heroes," Emerson called it in a phrase that would have particularly struck Thoreau (*CW* I, 154–55). Imitating Emerson, Thoreau also obliquely arraigns him, thinking perhaps of Emerson's fixed income, his large house, his outward decorum and inward restraint: "The success of great thinkers and scholars is commonly a courtier-like success, not kingly, not manly. They make shift to live merely by conformity, practically as their fathers did, and are in no sense the progenitors of a nobler race of men" (*W* 15).[12] Though whetted by the anxieties of discipleship, Thoreau's censure of a life of profession unfounded in practice was itself Emersonian in its belief that things of the spirit had their own special economy, so that thoughtless or hypocritical living inevitably dissipated the soul. Emerson professed to find it "odd," as he told Thoreau in 1841, that the "three persons" he knew who seemed "fully to see this law of reciprocity or compensation, – himself, Alcott, & myself . . . should all be neighbors" (*JMN* VIII, 96). He must have found it odder still to discover his erstwhile pupil turning his law of laws against himself by demanding of the scholar "that economy of living which is synonymous with philosophy" (*W* 52).

The difference between "Man the Reformer" and *Walden* is the difference between a jeremiad and a transcendentalized Franklinian "Art of Virtue"; the latter undertakes to show (in Franklin's words) "the *Means* and *Manner* of obtaining Virtue" as distinct "from the mere Exhortation to be good, that does not instruct and indicate the Means."[13] Confident of his eloquence and position in the world, Emerson could address his audience from the heights, relying on the sublimity of his presence to impress sympathizers and disarm critics, though his failure to specify the *means* of self-reform never fooled his shrewdest critic. "I found when I had finished my new lecture that it was a very good house," he remarked in 1851, "only the architect had unfortunately omitted the stairs" (*JMN* XI, 327). Emerson the architect characteristically omitted the stairs. The problem that vexed him was the disjunction between two levels of being, which he recognized from the outset of his intellectual career but seldom acknowledged publicly before "The Transcendentalist" in 1841. "The worst feature of this double consciousness," he wrote then, "is, that the two lives, of the understanding and of the soul, which we lead, really show very little relation to each other, never meet and measure each other: one prevails now, all buzz and din; and the other prevails then, all infinitude and paradise; and, with the progress of life, the two discover no greater disposition to reconcile themselves" (*CW* I, 213–14). Although Emerson sometimes spoke as if the problem could be solved by a simple readjustment of perception (*Nature*), an increased self-trust ("Self-Reliance"), or a bolder love of truth ("Circles"), privately he knew better. "What a benefit if a rule could be given whereby the mind dreaming amidst the gross fogs of matter, could at any moment east itself and find the Sun" (*JMN* V, 275), he remarked in 1835, more in exasperation than in hope, for as deeply as any Calvinist he felt his utter passivity before the ebbs and flows of the spirit.

With his moments of fullness in nature and seasons of spiritual drought, Thoreau, too, labored under this double consciousness. "The life in us is like the water in the river," he wrote in 1850, adopting Emerson's image from "The Over-Soul" and "Experience": "When on the higher levels we can remember the lower, but when on the lower we cannot remember the higher" (*PJ* 3, 84; v. *CW* II, 159–60; *CW* III, 27). Like Emerson, Thoreau wanted continuously to live at the height of vision, and *un*like Emerson, who soon despaired of a touchstone for grace, he believed early on, and in some form would always believe, that sanctity could be earned. His trope for this activity in *Walden* was house-building, which began, necessarily, at the bottom. "The man of practice is laying the foundations of a poetic life," he remarked in 1846, firmly established at Walden, whereas "the poet of great sensibility is rearing a superstructure without foundation" (*PJ* 2, 240). After the foundation came the staircase. The instrumentalities of self-reform that Emerson neglected were precisely what absorbed Thoreau, burdened with shaping a text that would convert an oppositional audience at the same time it crystallized an ideal self. The structure I call *Walden*'s "rhetoric of ascent" is the architectural staircase designed to conduct the reader gradationally from one plane of being to another *and* to prompt, methodize, and confirm the writer's own self-transcendence.

"Economy" lays the basis for this structure both in the literal sense of resolving the physical preliminaries of Thoreau's experiment and in the figurative sense of shedding received ways and opinions in preparation for the act of discovery. Two images govern the chapter: settling oneself on the bedrock of the solidly real and embarking on a spiritual journey. Walden Pond "is a good port and a good foundation" (*W* 21), Thoreau proclaims, joining both ideas. The images belong to a more encompassing trope of organic growth that controls the chapter-by-chapter organization of *Walden* as well as its vision of metamorphosis, and that Thoreau adumbrates in a kind of thesis statement: "The soil, it appears, is suited to the seed, for it has sent its radicle downward, and it may now send its shoot upward also with confidence. Why has man rooted himself thus firmly in the earth, but that he may rise in the same proportion into the heavens above?" (*W* 15).

Ascent in *Walden* begins in "Where I Lived, and What I Lived For" as Thoreau assumes residence at the pond and baptizes himself in its waters. "Economy" is chiefly concerned with the precondition of simplifying one's life, or clearing away the cultural and material impediments to growth. Enlarged at every stage of composition, the chapter takes its impulse from the 1846–47 manuscript and may be read in all but a few passages as belonging to or elaborating Thoreau's initial intent.[14] While its attacks on getting and spending, on the tyranny of fashion, and on the human costs of the emerging factory system retain much of their force today, they assume particular meaning in light of the semantic constriction of the 1840s in which words like "industry," "wealth," and "profit," as Leonard N. Neufeldt has shown, were drained of moral significance and attached to economic phenomena alone.[15] This narrowing of language was itself symptomatic of the narrowed ideal of human achievement in Jacksonian America remarked by foreign observers like Tocqueville as well as by critics like Emerson. If democracy had come to signify "universal participation in the opportunities the United States held out to all men,"[16] the substance of these opportunities had grown widely identified with the goods and pleasures obtainable by wealth. "The usurpation by the senses of the entire practical energy of individuals," Emerson called this betrayal of national promise, the results of which were "low and unworthy views of the manly character" that it fell to the scholar to reform.[17]

Thoreau's contribution to this project was most notably a style. Reading his friend's journal in 1863, Emerson was impressed by the "oaken strength" of its language: "I find the same thought, the same spirit that is in me, but he takes a step beyond, & illustrates by excellent images what which I should have conveyed in a sleepy generality" (*EmJ* 511). Emerson undervalues his own pungency here, but he is right so far as the authors' criticism of the times is concerned. There is no great substantive difference between (for example) Emerson's "men are subject to things. They are overcrowed by their own creation"[18] and Thoreau's "men have become the tools of their tools" (*W* 37). Within their New England context, both men were responding to the "commodity fetishism" later described by Marx, who "saw the capitalist market as a force created by man but alien to man, having its own quasi-natural laws of development, opposing man and dominating him," so that "man became enslaved by his own products, by things," and even his interpersonal relationships took shape from the logic of material exchange.[19] Observing these tendencies at work in the microcosm of Concord, Thoreau satirized them with a pithiness unmatched by his contemporaries and given special effect by the puns (often etymological) that allowed him to parody or subvert economic values by restoring words to their older, morally resonant meanings.[20] Thus "wealth" in "Economy" is redefined by Thoreau as fullness of being, "business" as the journey toward this fullness, "capital" as the resources of head that fund the journey, "profit" as the spiritual dividends accruing from wise investments of time and commitment, and "economy" itself as the daily management of the "enterprise" (a trade with the "Celestial Empire") according to "strict business habits" (*W* 19, 20). Like Emerson in "The American Scholar," but with livelier wit, Thoreau met the popular notion of the writer's effeminacy by turning the tables on the American materialist, charging *him* with a want of manlinesss, and appropriating the vocabulary of entrepreneurial capitalism for the higher activity of self-culture.[21] Beyond the inventiveness of particular passages, Thoreau's achievement as rhetorician was to apply this semantic imperialism to what Kenneth Burke calls the "priestly" or "transcendental" office of literature – "pontification": "the building of a terministic bridge whereby one realm is transcended by being viewed *in terms* of a realm 'beyond' it."[22] Through a systematic wordplay, objects and processes of the material world commonly regarded as desiderata themselves are displaced in *Walden* by a set of *interior* processes and ends analogous to them on the level of spirit. The laws of economy are sound, Thoreau wryly suggests; they only require a more capacious application, as in his own well-known measure of price ("The cost of a thing is the amount of what I will call life which is required to be exchanged for it, immediately or in the long run" [*W* 31]), which at once draws upon and deconstructs Adam Smith's theory of value by teasing out the ethical implications of its language.[23]

II

A keen observer of the follies of his neighbors, and therefore of Americans generally, Thoreau was not an analyst of the incisiveness and rigor of Tocqueville, Mill, or the early Marx. He was a moralist whose special qualification was the pained intimacy of his relation to Concord; as Stephen Railton has said, "he whetted his prose on his grudge against his place at home and in the village, improved the isolation he had been consigned to into a visionary vantage point, and disciplined his need to justify himself into a potent set of attacks on our self-complacent, slavish 'prejudices.'"[24] He knew how to rile his townsmen while maintaining the most disinterested of poses, but the very facility with which he learned to do this kept him from mounting the broad-scale critique of capitalism his insight and estrangement singularly empowered him to write. Few would trade Thoreau the artist for a provincial Veblen, yet one can scarcely help wishing (for the integrity of the aesthetic project alone) that Thoreau's hit-and-run guerrilla warfare were launched from a more identifiable social base.[25] "The focal point" of his attack in "Economy" is "not wealth *per se* but 'exchange,'"[26] Walter Benn Michaels argues in one of the many briefs for Thoreau as critic of capitalism; yet for the farmer "creeping down the road of life, pushing before [him] a barn seventy-five feet by forty" (*W* 5), it makes little difference whether the barn is owned outright or by mortgage, or whether the crops he labors to raise are consumed at home or sold in the Boston market. Property of any sort is a deadly encumbrance in *Walden,* as are nearly all forms of conventionalism. While censorious toward its own commercial age, *Walden* could not have been "inspired by the agrarian ideals of the past"[27] if only because vestiges of the past were sufficiently present to Thoreau in the 1840s to disabuse him of any illusions about the "narrow, uninformed, and countrified mind" (as he called it in "Ktaadn") more likely to be found "among the rusty inhabitants of an old-settled country, . . . in the towns about Boston, even on the high road to Concord," than "in the backwoods of Maine" (*MW* 22–23). Save for an occasional yeoman like George Minott, the old-line farmers of Concord were no more sympathetic toward Thoreau, or he toward them, than the rising enterpreneurs; both were antagonists that had to be scourged. As a result, Thoreau is at once more and less than a critic of burgeoning capitalism. Propertyless, of no regular calling, and determined to "live free and uncommitted" for as long as possible (*W* 84; v. *PJ* 1, 291), he is a party of one reluctant to concede merit to any social forms lest the adequacy of his own life seem called into question.

Because *Walden*'s attacks on Concord are so intimately bound to Thoreau's circumstances, they tend to border on a high-minded anarchism emphatic enough as critique but puzzling in its advice to a New England citizenry led to expect words addressed to its "outward condition." The appeal of *Walden*'s foundational act of going to the pond lies in its prospective relevance to a hierarchy of readers from local farmers mired in debt to prosperous burghers "cooked . . . *à la mode*" in a surfeit of luxury (*W* 14), "poor students" looking to economize (*W* 3), poor students of life looking spiritually to "economize," and aspiring poets and philosophers eager to found their dreams in fact. Symbols have the power to fuse and reconcile opposites, but when symbols arise from the pressures of competing agendas – Thoreau's need to engage a practical New England audience *and* to defend and reorder his own idiosyncratic life – they are liable either to collapse from their internal divisions or to grow attenuated as they are stretched to fit divergent cases. Although Walden Pond may be a good port from which to embark, strains within "Economy" make it problematic whether the farmer, the burgher, the student, and the poet-philosopher are sailing to a common destination and whether the navigational instructions directed to one group can serve the needs of another.

The fault lines between *Walden*'s private and public ends grow more evident the nearer Thoreau approaches a defense of his life in Concord. "For more than five years I maintained myself thus solely by the labor of my hands," he writes in a late section of "Economy,"

> and I found, that by working about six weeks in a year, I could meet all the expenses of living. . . . As I preferred some things to others, and especially valued my freedom, . . . I did not wish to spend my time in earning rich carpets or other fine furniture, or delicate cookery, or a house in the Grecian or Gothic style just yet. If there are any to whom it is no interruption to acquire these things, and who know how to use them when acquired, I relinquish to them the pursuit. Some are "industrious," and appear to love labor for its own sake, or perhaps because it keeps them out of worse mischief; to such I have at present nothing to say. Those who would not know what to do with more leisure than they now enjoy, I might advise to work twice as hard as they do, – work till they pay for themselves, and get their free papers. For myself I found that the occupation of a day-laborer was the most independent of any, especially as it required only thirty or forty days in a year to support one. The laborer's day ends with the going down of the sun, and then he is free to devote himself to his chosen pursuit, independent of his labor; but his employer, who speculates from month to month, has no respite from one end of the year to the other. (*W* 69–70)

Thoreau is describing his own considerately fashioned life, not legislating for all, but though he makes it an issue of principle to encourage his readers to "find and pursue [their] *own*" way rather than adopt his (*W* 71), he presents his special variety of independence with an absolutism that opposes it not only to market relations but to property, labor, and citizenship within almost any conceivable social order. The wealthy are impugned for their luxurious tastes, but even the "'industrious'" only "*appear* to love labor for its own sake" or else busy themselves with it to keep boredom or the devil at bay. With mock humility the speaker professes a kind of latitudinarian tolerance ("If there are any to whom it is no interruption to acquire these [luxuries], and who know how to use them when acquired, I relinquish to them the pursuit"), but as commonly happens with this "if" construction in *Walden,* the implication is that no such beings exist. Nominally, Thoreau allows his readers an assortment of lives so long as their choice is deliberately made; practically, he denies them full integrity except on the conditions of asceticism, propertylessness, and social marginality.

To reconcile his self-celebration with his stance of reformer, Thoreau had to bring his readers to an appreciation of his own mode of living that would also, in some manner, constitute a partial redemption for *them*. Such redemption would not mean renouncing their farms and shops (Thoreau never expected they would), nor would it involve the narrator's descending from his lofty vagabondage to concede the merit of farms and shops. Any accommodation had to rest on an agreement that while other lives might be acceptable for the mass of men, his own unencumbered life was best; and despite the tactical fiction of appealing to his neighbors' "outward condition," it had to focus on an inward conversion that would align their values with his without indicating how (or whether) such values might be translated into a social modus vivendi. The later drafts of *Walden* show a vastly diminished interest in reform of any sort, yet even the 1849 manuscript can be called "a reforming text meant to produce results in the world"[28] only so long as one reads it innocently and neglects its double-minded rhetoric. The "results" *Walden* sought to produce were first and foremost a change in the writer's character and status in the community, though the condition for that change was the linguistic persuasion of its audience.

Virtually from its opening pages, then, *Walden* turned upon a precarious effort to woo its readers to a set of values Thoreau felt driven to insist on in its impracticable purity. The same imperative that led him to court his townsman-audience thus threatened him with losing it. His answer to this predicament was to write as pointedly yet elusively as possible, asserting the negative moral force of his criticism but obfuscating its positive norms, often through paradox or symbolism. Aesthetically, this contributes to the wondrous plurisignification that is among *Walden*'s chief delights, but it can also leave a reader questioning what, if anything, the author means. When Thoreau writes, for example, "I see young men, my townsmen, whose misfortune it is to have inherited farms, houses, barns, cattle, and farming tools; for these are more easily acquired than got rid of" (*W* 5), it is impossible to tell how we are to read "misfortune." Is Thoreau speaking "extra-vagantly" to unsettle an audience that regards inheritance as a great boon (the ideal lying somewhere between "fortune" and "misfortune" in a measured attitude toward ownership) or does he genuinely believe, as he maintains elsewhere in *Walden*,[29] that owning anything more than a few books and a serviceable suit of clothes is a great curse? His language may be dialectical (to confound the reader) or it may be pontificatory (to elevate propertylessness above property); the text provides no basis for judgment and therefore no ground for inferring a moral position. We know what the author disapproves; we don't know what he values. The ambiguity is characteristic of "Economy" and seems strategic. Even as Thoreau's resistance to Concord calls forth a vigorous attack on materialism, his stance as nominal reformer requires that he disguise the extremity of his own antimaterialism. He refuses to mitigate his criticism; instead, he detaches it from an identifiable norm, writing as a satirist vis-à-vis Concord but as an ironist with respect to any positive ideal.

Thoreau's elusiveness becomes more artfully complex when he feels himself at a potential disadvantage. "But all this is very selfish, I have heard some of my townsmen say," he writes late in "Economy," as if in answer to some muttered demurral:

> I confess that I have hitherto indulged very little in philanthropic enterprises. I have made some sacrifices to a sense of duty, and among others have sacrificed this pleasure also. . . . While my townsmen and women are devoted in so many ways to the good of their fellows, I trust that one at least may be spared to other

and less humane pursuits. You must have a genius for charity as well as for any thing else. As for Doing-good, that is one of the professions which are full. Moreover, I have tried it fairly, and, strange as it may seem, am satisfied that it does not agree with my constitution. Probably I should not consciously and deliberately forsake my particular calling to do the good which society demands of me, to save the universe from annihilation; and I believe that a like but infinitely greater steadfastness elsewhere is all that now preserves it. But I would not stand between any man and his genius; and to him who does his work, which I decline, with his whole heart and soul and life, I would say, Persevere, even if the world call it doing evil, as it is most likely they will. (*W* 72–73)

Like Emerson, who hated "goodies" (*JMN* VII, 31) and whose quills rose up at the thought of "association," Thoreau disliked organized philanthropy but felt besieged and tacitly reproached by it. He had made his objections plain in his 1843 lecture "The Conservative and the Reformer," which "gained a special energy and intensity from his determined effort to defend his own way of life and work in the face of growing pressures to join with the reformers."[30] The basis for his resistance, as he says in *Walden,* was personal: philanthropy didn't suit him. But temperament alone was not an adequate defense. Arraigned for his selfishness, Thoreau turns the charge back upon his real or fancied accusers. He has "*indulged* very little in philanthropic enterprises," he admits, his verb insinuating a complacent, sensual, almost sinful yielding to vanity or inclination at the heart of the philanthropist's effort. "I have made some sacrifices to a sense of duty," he continues, as if prefacing an account of those "enterprises" he *has* engaged in. But the "sense of duty" turns out to be an austere monitor distinct from philanthropic conscience, and among the "sacrifices" he has made to it has been the "pleasure" of the philanthropist's self-congratulation. "My townsmen and women are devoted in so many ways to the good of their fellows," he adds dryly, "that one at least may be spared to other and less humane pursuits." (The allusion to women is as pointed as it is rare, since "virtue" in Thoreau always retains an aspect of the Latin *virtus* [courage or manliness; from *vir*]. The philanthropist's virtue is compassion, or humaneness – admirable in women, Thoreau was ready to admit, but sickly in men.) Conceding at last that philanthropy "does not agree with my *constitution*" (the law of his being), Thoreau avoids acknowledging a fault by brazenly taking the offensive: "Probably I should not consciously and deliberately forsake my particular calling to do the good which society demands of me, to save the universe from annihilation." Before the reader can protest this outrageous display of egoism, however, Thoreau outflanks his sputtering censors and locates himself firmly on the side of the universe after all: "and I believe that a like but infinitely greater steadfastness elsewhere is all that now preserves it." Providence, too, it seems, minds its own business and keeps devoutly to its calling. Having established his repugnance to good works as the righteous and godly position – the highest and most genuine "philanthropy" in any spiritual view of things – Thoreau can encourage natural reformers in their work and even pretend to take their part against society. But his new tolerance proves only a device for adding a final turn of the screw. "Persevere," he exhorts the reformer, "even if the world call it doing evil, as it is most likely they will."

Dazzling in its play of ironies, Thoreau's paragraph has less to do with philanthropy than with self-vindication as the speaker trains his guns in all directions and leaves nothing standing but the law of his private nature. The passage is extraordinary even in *Walden* for the verbal dexterity it brings to the task of apologetics, but it is only an especially vivid example of forces at work throughout the early chapters of the book in latent opposition to its efforts at cultural persuasion. Henry Golemba has suggested that Thoreau's style rests on "a true contra-diction," or a persistent construction and subversion of meaning intended to "provoke the reader's spirit to attempt to fill the text's vacuum, to strive to span its gaps."[31] The philanthropy passage is dense with such subversions, yet rather than invite us to imaginative play, they tend to overmaster us and leave us breathless and in wonder. Whatever direction we expect Thoreau to take in the next sentence, or phrase, or word, he outfeints us, gives a brilliantly unanticipated turn to things, and shames our paltry efforts to join the game. The end of such virtuosity is self-referential: to "privilege the ideology of a single, authoritative 'I,'" as Malini Schueller says of Thoreau's language,[32] save that the special condition of Thoreau's "ideology" is its refusal to declare itself and be known. Thoreau is continuously on the move, an ambusher firing from the cover of his verbal thickets, often (as here) to guard a psychic base considered vulnerable to attack. The danger of such a style is that its triumphant negations can create a forbidding barrenness reflecting back upon the writer more than upon the objects of his attack. This is what Emerson meant when he likened Thoreau to "the woodgod who solicits the wandering poet & draws him into antres vast & desarts idle, & bereaves him of his memory, & leaves him naked, plaiting vines & with twigs in his hand. Very seductive are the first steps from the town to the woods, but the End is want & madness" (*JMN* X, 344). A more sympathetic analogy would be to the loon in "Brute Neighbors," who "manoeuvred so cunningly" as to confound the calculations of the narrator in his boat, surfacing unexpectedly in some remote part of the pond and laughing "in derision of [the narrator's] efforts [to approach him], confident of his own resources" (*W* 234, 236). Whether Thoreau is the woodgod or the loon depends partly on his tone (after "Economy" and in post-1851 drafts he is increasingly the loon) and partly on the reader's tolerance. First-time readers of *Walden,* especially nonliterary ones, are often impatient with what they regard as Thoreau's "righteousness." Critical sophistication brings aesthetic pleasure and psychological distance, but the naïve response should not be discounted, for it reflects an intuition of authorial egotism – "the artist-as-show-off, the stylist nearly as fop" – shared by so astute a critic as Richard Poirier.[33] "Foppishness" in the sense of self-parading personality is what Thoreau had admired in Carlyle as "excellent acting" (*PJ* 1, 380). The philanthropy passage is similarly a one-man show, put on to astonish the reader and display the joyous, upright sensibility its author is, or (his secret) is trying to become.

The extent to which Thoreau rested his self-apology on a feat of style, and therefore on a readership able to appreciate that style, reopens the question of audience ostensibly settled in the third paragraph of *Walden*. For whom was Thoreau writing his book? *Walden* became a more densely allusive text through successive drafts, yet even the initial manuscript presumed a more literary audience than the burdened farmers and tradesmen posited in "Economy" and in Thoreau's subtitle "Addressed to my Townsmen." On purely internal grounds, Joseph J. Moldenhauer distinguishes between two roles the rhetoric of *Walden* invites us to play: "As spectators, or what I will call 'readers,' we are sympathetic toward the witty and engaging narrator" and "applaud [his] rhetorical devastation" of his adversaries; "as projected participants, or what I will term 'audience,'" we are those adversaries ourselves, sharing "the prejudices and short-sightedness which the narrator reproves" and receiving the full brunt of his criticism.[34] Applying Moldenhauer's terms to Thoreau's actual historical readership, *Walden*'s "audience" would consist of those Concordians of the early chapters retained from the journal and lecture origins of the book while its "readers" would constitute the book-buying literati called upon to observe the narrator's contest with his neighbors. "Audience" and "reader" are both literary creations, but their status is quite different. The "audience" is inscribed wholly within the text as a collective fictional character (e.g., the townsmen who push a barn down the road of life). The "reader" is both textual and extra-textual; he is the witness who responds on cue to the book's stage directions and who in applauding the virtuosity of the author's performance confirms his act of self-re-creation.

Literary works have a double existence, Northrop Frye remarked; "besides the internal fiction of the hero and his society, there is an external fiction which is a relation between the writer and the writer's society."[35] The internal fiction in *Walden* is the speaker's announced effort to awaken and convert a commercially minded "audience"; the external fiction is the writer's appeal to literary "readers" to watch, admire, and validate his activity. The internal fiction is *Walden*'s donnée; the external fiction is its raison d'être. While impelled to address his townsmen both as representatives of the world at large and as the local tribunal before which he needed to vindicate his life, Thoreau knew that a village audience could never adequately measure his gifts or supply the full ratification of self he needed. The silencing of Concord skeptics was imperative to him, but the praise he most sought needed to come from the cosmopolitan readership of Boston and New York. I have said that *Walden* is a "pontificatory" text; it is so in a double sense. Within its internal fiction (character "Thoreau" and his townsmen), pontification is a Burkean act of bridge-building designed to lead its audience from a brutish to a semi-divine life; within its external fiction (narrator Thoreau and his reader), pontification is a papal act of speaking across a chasm and recording one's preeminent authority. On one level, Thoreau weaves a rope ladder for his audience's spiritual ascent; on another, like Father Mapple in *Moby-Dick,* he climbs the ladder himself, hauls it into the pulpit, and delivers a two-stranded lesson whose higher significance is reserved for himself as a pilot of the living god.

III

Having sloughed off society in "Economy," literally for himself by removing to the woods, rhetorically for his audience by demolishing village customs and prejudices, Thoreau is free to awaken in "Where I Lived, and What I Lived For" and survey life afresh, ourselves beside him as vicarious participants in his action and auditors of his running commentary. Because "simplicity and antiquity were almost synonymous" for Thoreau in their "reduction to first things,"[36] the quest of *A Week* to return to the fount of experience could be taken as realized in his life at Walden Pond, or at least as auspiciously begun. "It was the very light & atmosphere in which the works of Grecian art were composed, and in which they rest," Thoreau remarked in his journal of the "auroral atmosphere" (*PJ* 2, 155) that struck him his first day in the woods. Where the morning light of "Sunday" had vanished with the dew and been lost even to memory by mid-day, *Walden* perpetuates the spirit of dawn by associating the world of the pond with "those parts of the universe and . . . those eras in history which had most attracted" Thoreau (*W* 87). *Walden*'s hero has not transplanted himself in time so much as he has dispensed with time entirely and situated himself on the eternal substratum of the real. Even more than Emerson's *Nature* with its prospect of "morning knowledge" (*CW* I, 43), "Where I Lived, and What I Lived For" sounds the genuine Adamic note of the American Renaissance in its appeal to discard the past, "throw off sleep" (*W* 90), and build a new world through the "elastic and vigorous thought" of a "perpetual morning" (*W* 89).

The energy of Thoreau's call to awaken is notable in light of the ambiguity that surrounded his notion of morning. If his "most sacred and memorable life," as he said, was "commonly on awaking in the morning," it was not simply because his senses and intellect were then most alive to outward phenomena, but because he "frequently [awoke] with an atmosphere about [him] as if [his] unremembered dreams had been divine – as if [his] spirit had journeyed to its native place, and in the act of reentering its native body had diffused an elysian fragrance round" (*PJ* 3, 233–34). The issue Thoreau needed to settle both privately and as the writer of *Walden* was whether he truly wanted to "awaken" or to "sleep": to go forward toward paradise through the physical world by means of faith, imagination, disciplined striving, and close attention to the actual – the "natural supernaturalism" of "Friday" in *A Week* – or to go backward in dream, reverie, and mystic glimpses of the transcendent. The way of vision was more rapturous and complete, but as a method for permanent self-reconstruction it was an *ignis fatuus.*

Man "needs not only to be spiritualized, but *naturalized,* on the soil of earth" (*Wk* 379), Thoreau came to recognize by the end of *A Week;* more precisely, man needs to be spiritualized *by means of* being naturalized. Jonathan Bishop defined the "natural supernaturalist" (Carlyle's term) as "someone whose experience of the sacred [is] mediated by the most local kind of natural particulars; and whose testimony to the possibility of such experience [is] in turn mediated to us through equally concrete details of language."[37] Historically, the vision belonged to the Romantic secularization of Christian myth, in which, as M. H. Abrams describes it, "the redemptive goal of the history of mankind was shifted from the reconciliation and reunion with a transcendent God to an overcoming of the opposition between ego and non-ego, or a reconciliation of subject with object, or a reunion of the spirit with its own other," a process whose "culmination was represented as occurring in the fully developed consciousness of men living their lives in this world."[38] In Emerson's formulation of 1827, "As religious philosophy advances, men will cease to say 'the future state' & will say instead 'the whole being'" (*JMN* III, 304). Thoreau had always sought heaven in "the whole being," but it was not until "Friday" that he rooted his search in earth and not until *Walden* that he made it a disciplined quest. "I went to the woods because I wished to live deliberately" (*W* 90), he tells the reader in as deliberate a phrase as any in *Walden:* to live from freedom, considering and weighing experience as on a scale, and responding to phenomena leisurely and with purpose rather than haphazardly by reflex or whim.

The achievement of "Where I Lived, and What I Lived For," like that of "Loomings" in *Moby-Dick* and the early sections of "Song of Myself," is to make the narrator's quest an action performed on behalf of the sedentary reader:

> [I wished] to front only the essential facts of life, and see if I could not learn what it had to teach, and not, when I came to die, discover that I had not lived. . . . I wanted to live deep and suck out all the marrow of life, to cut a broad swath and shave close, to drive life into a corner, and reduce it to its lowest terms, and, if it proved to be mean, why then to get the whole and genuine meanness of it, and publish its meanness to the world; or if it were sublime, to know it by experience, and be able to give a true account of it in my next excursion. (*W* 90, 91)

If Thoreau's words are a fair but psychologically reticent account of his motives in going to the woods, they also reveal how aptly the Walden experience conduced toward resolving the split between action and contemplation, outward narrative and inward quest, that had impaired his work from the beginning. To transmute the process of self-refashioning into a grand testing of life conducted in solitude on the frontier by a representative "I" was to elevate one's private "errand into the wilderness" into an "errand to mankind"; further, as Stanley Cavell suggests, it was to reenact the national "moment of origin" (the Puritan flight from an old world) "in order this time to do it right, or to prove that it is impossible; to discover and settle this land, or the question of this land, once for all."[39]

In removing to the woods in the name of all America – taking up residence, as he says, on "Independence Day" (*W* 84) – Thoreau was entering his book in the long debate, intensified during the Transcendental years, about the nature and function of a distinctive American literature. Against complaints by writers and critics about the poverty of native materials, champions of American exceptionalism like William Ellery Channing had made barrenness a virtue by stressing the "peculiar advantages" it afforded "for understanding our own nature" apart from the "political and artificial distinctions" that obscured the claims of the human being in Europe.[40] In the view of Channing and others, it was as if America in the very meagerness of its civilization had managed to drive life into a corner, juxtaposing man against nature and throwing him back upon himself so as to enable him to discover the irreducible truth of his condition. Within this New World context, the American writer might find his subject and vocation as witness to the unfolding prospects of the race, particularly as they testified to the capacities of human beings for democracy; he might even assume the role of explorer himself, making discoveries in his own right, like Emerson's scholar, rather than simply recording them.

By the time of Thoreau's removal to Walden, the thinness of social life in the northeast that Channing could take for granted in 1830 had come to be felt as an oppressive density by literary men caught between a residual philistine agrarianism and a headlong, equally philistine capitalism. After a long inchoateness, American society was suddenly too palpable a reality. Against this sense of squandered New World possibility, writers and intellectuals transferred the American future to an imagined "West." Never mind that Walden Pond lay due south, even a shade southeast, of Concord center; "the West" for Thoreau was the figurative country of "the Wild," crucial as a proving ground for matters of truth and value wherever it happened geographically to lie. The original epigraph to *Walden* – "Where I have been / There was none seen" (Cl 39) – converts a Concord landmark barely a half-hour's walk from the village common into the very boundary of the civilized world, with the speaker assuming the role of a spiritual pioneer returned to the settlements to render a full report. In these terms *Walden* is indeed, as Sacvan Bercovitch has said, "the archetypal Romantic autobiography of the self as 'the only true America.'"[41] If "America" was the idiom of Thoreau's speaking, however, it was never the initiating cause. Where Bercovitch sees the writer's "identification with America as it ought to be impel[ling him] to withdraw" from America as it is,[42] Thoreau's withdrawal, or chronic alienation from the American world, *preceded* his assumption of a prophetically national stance. What Bercovitch calls "the genre of auto-American-biography: the celebration of the representative self as America, and of the American self as the embodiment of a prophetic universal design"[43] was an appropriate vehicle for Thoreau not because he was alive to it as an inherited tradition, or subject to it as a controlling ideology, but because it supplied an eminently useful garb for linking his private values with the *res publica* and giving his quarrel with Concord an epic national importance.

It is as a discoverer returned from his spiritual explorations, in any event, that Thoreau presents himself in "Where I Lived, and What I Lived For." After recounting his settlement at the pond and the "religious exercise" (*W* 88) of his morning bath, Thoreau extends the argument of "Economy" by contrasting two kinds of lives, with his emphasis now upon a prospect of blessedness he has certified by experience:

> Men esteem truth remote, in the outskirts of the system, behind the farthest star, before Adam and after the last man. . . . But all these times and places and occasions are now and here. God himself culminates in the present moment, and will never be more divine in the lapse of all the ages. And we are enabled to apprehend at all what is sublime and noble only by the perpetual instilling and drenching of the reality which surrounds us. The universe constantly and obediently answers to all our conceptions. . . . Let us spend our lives in conceiving then. (*W* 96–97)

The promise of a living world imbued with knowable, anthropomorphic truth (the universe "answers to all our conceptions") is the Transcendental touchstone Thoreau offers for measuring the results of his Walden experiment. Making good on this redemptive vision – convincing his readers that life at the pond was like "the Arabian Nights' Entertainments" (*W* 95) and that their lives in society *might be* so – is the extraordinary task he sets for himself in the balance of his book. Seven years of experience – closer to nine, if one counts the time between *Walden*'s journal beginnings and its publication – would cause Thoreau to modify the terms of success, perhaps unknowingly, certainly covertly. Few readers of *Walden* hold its later sections to the test of "Where I Lived, and What I Lived For," yet this is precisely what Thoreau invites us to do. If the risk was high, so were the stakes, for to create a text that testified in every line to an exalted life was to become – to *have* become – the sensibility capable of living that life.

It may seem odd that a professed experiment should begin with metaphysical propositions at all rather than unfold dramatically as its hero passes through successive trials and illuminations and we as readers are held in suspense as to what his experience will ultimately yield. In *Walden,* however, the dramatic is controlled by the instructional, and the book offers itself as an "experiment" only in the limited sense of a demonstration for our benefit of what the speaker has already tested and proved; in Lawrence Buell's words, "the narrative is encased in a rhetorical appeal to the reader" and exists as "a validation of the speaker's claims to authority rather than a report of how a formerly desperate man found a new life through nature."[44] Instead of comprising a record of inward growth, events in *Walden* are discontinuous, topically organized, and detached from chronology by the "used to" mode of presentation Thoreau cultivates to evoke the tenor of his life in the woods rather than its evolution or day-to-day particulars. Even those incidents tied to the seasons are delinearized by Thoreau's condensation of two years into one. Above all, his recollections of Walden are themselves framed within a distancing authorial commentary, some of it an elaboration of thoughts and impressions *in illo tempore,* much of it an overlay of satire and subsequent reflection. In later drafts Thoreau smoothed the chapter-by-chapter progress of his materials by adding narrative or verbal transitions. The real architecture of *Walden,* however, is rhetorical, as Thoreau undertakes to "prove" the claims of "Where I Lived, and What I Lived For" by conducting the reader stage by stage toward the higher life the narrator is presented as already enjoying. With allowances always for digressions, the logic of the 1849 manuscript is as follows: one simplifies (in "Economy" – I cite chapter titles for convenience; the actual divisions came later) to gain freedom to awaken; one awakens ("Where I Lived, and What I Lived For") in order to renew oneself and perceive; one perceives in order to discover miracle in the world and genius in the self ("Reading" through the early fragments of "The Ponds"); and one follows one's genius in order to ascend ("Baker Farm" and drafts A-C of "Higher Laws"). "Spring" is the peroration of the 1849 text, as "Economy" and "Where I Lived, and What I Lived For" are its exordium.

Within this structural argument, sections arrange themselves, as Charles R. Anderson noted, as successive pairs turning upon a contrast between society and solitude.[45] The sections might also be read as reflections on Emerson's three "influences" on the scholar – books ("Reading"), nature ("Sounds," "Solitude," and "The Bean-Field"), and action, or experience in the world ("Visitors" and "The Village"). But most importantly for Thoreau's "rhetoric of ascent," the earliest of these chapters ("Reading," "Sounds," and "Solitude") all begin with an announced return to the sources of life – Emerson's "original relation to the universe," which Thoreau explores not only for its essential character but for the means of attaining it.

In "Reading" the means are ancient texts. "The oldest Egyptian or Hindoo philosopher raised a corner of the veil from the statue of divinity," Thoreau writes, "and still the trembling robe remains raised, and I gaze upon as fresh a glory as he did. . . . No dust has settled on that robe; no time has elapsed since that divinity was revealed" (*W* 99). While Emerson had commended books as "guid[ing] our steps to the East again, where the dawn is" (*CW* I, 57), his equivalent phrase "the mind of the Past" had implied that all literary transcripts of truth were tinctured by "the conventional, the local, the perishable" (*CW* I, 55), and were therefore in need of constant revision; "each age . . . must write its own books; or rather, each generation for the next succeeding" (*CW* I, 56).[46] With his deep-seated a- or transhistoricism, Thoreau could discount the warp of temporality and view the ancients as undecayed oracles of truth lying before and beneath the artifice of civilization and forever available as conduits to the real. Beyond their immunity to time, the classics in their original tongue had the value of compelling readers "laboriously [to] seek the meaning of each word and line, conjecturing a larger sense than common use permits out of what wisdom and valor and generosity" they have (*W* 100). Thoreau is elaborating here on the notion of participatory interpretation advanced by Emerson (a forefather of reader-response criticism) as "creative reading": "When the mind is braced by labor and invention, the page of whatever book we read becomes luminous with manifold allusion. Every sentence is doubly significant, and the sense of our author is as broad as the world" (*CW* I, 58). In Thoreau's development of this idea, vigorous reading becomes more than a source of intellectual provocation and aesthetic pleasure; it becomes a spiritual calisthenics whose effect is to elevate the soul. Against Emerson's acquiescence before the vicissitudes of creative power, Thoreau sought to discover and align himself with the forces making for ascent, at the least through a kind of "preparationism" (being in the right place, with the proper receptivity) but also, so far as he could, through discipline and method. A paradisical life was something to be earned, and within the "startlingly moral" economy of our experience (*W* 218) in which each act carried its interior consequences, "stand[-ing] on tip-toe" (*W* 104) to read the great books enlarged and ennobled the soul and brought it nearer the purity of a redeemed life, just as the "luxury" of light reading contracted or "dissipated" it by producing a "dulness of sight, a stagnation of the vital circulations, and a general deliquium and sloughing off of all the intellectual faculties" (*W* 105).

Thoreau's main rhetorical challenge in pressing such an argument was to heroicize the claims of self-culture for an audience infatuated with the romance of capitalist enterprise. The act of removing to the woods that established *Walden* as an exemplary quest did not resolve the practical problem of what its hero was to *do*. With no whales to hunt, only beans to raise and an occasional pickerel to catch, Thoreau had to rely almost entirely on language for the spirit of adventure that epic writers distilled from their narrated action. His solution was to invoke the various honorific vocabularies of society and attach them to his life in the woods; thus the language of business and wealth is applied to inward development ("Economy"), that of physical strenuousness to study ("Reading"), of temporal efficiency to contemplation ("Sounds"), of friendship to seclusion ("Solitude"), of Homeric battle to hoeing beans ("The Bean-Field"), and of running the gantlet to strolling down Main Street ("The Village"). The incessant Thoreauvian paradoxes that so exasperated Emerson become in *Walden* a principle of sustained inversion directed toward the Emersonian end of privileging self-exploration over trade. In "Reading" Thoreau signals his theme by elevating "students and observers" (*W* 99) above actors of any sort. The truly valorous and manly, he insists, are those whose efforts and aims are inward. To make his point he likens the study of the untranslated classics to "a training such as the athletes underwent" (*W* 101) and associates readers with military figures like Alexander, who "carried the Iliad with him on his expeditions" (*W* 102), and with epic heroes themselves whose strenuous labors the reader of heroic books must "in some degree emulate" (*W* 100). If readers are a favored class, authors are still more so: "a natural and irresistible aristocracy" who, "more than kings or emperors, exert an influence on mankind," and whose merit is nowhere more tellingly acknowledged than by "the illiterate and perhaps scornful trader" who, gaining leisure and being "admitted to the circles of wealth and fashion, . . . turns inevitably at last to those still higher circles of intellect and genius," where he is made sensible of "the imperfection of his culture and the vanity and insufficiency of all his riches" (*W* 103). In the 1845 source for this passage Thoreau's antagonist had been "the illiterate and scornful rustic" (*PJ* 2, 165). The substitution of "trader" redirects the argument from a waning to a waxing enemy, the merchant princes who disdain the literary class and who are now, in a wish-fulfilling model for social history, disdained in turn. Thoreau not only denies the trader a belated entry into the world of mind; by having him "secure for his children that intellectual culture whose want he so keenly feels" (*W* 103), he makes him concede his inner bankruptcy and bow to the superiority of the literary man in a symbolic transfer of class power.

In "Sounds" Thoreau triumphs again over the entrepreneur, this time by reversing the Franklinian priority of doing to being. "The oriental unlike the western mind," he remarked in a journal entry of 1846, "discerned action in the inactive contemplative mind. And everywhere they affirm that he who is actually & truly inactive is the best employed" (*PJ* 2, 254). Building on this notion of employment, "Sounds" engages to re-"orient" its audience by providing a new measure for efficiency. The activity the narrator performs that is "better" than hoeing beans or even reading books is, to outward appearances, nothing at all – sitting on his doorstep "rapt in a reverie" (*W* 111), absorbing the sounds of the day. "This was sheer idleness to my fellow-townsmen, no doubt" (*W* 112), Thoreau comments, yet never was he better employed, growing "in those seasons like corn in the night" (*W* 111). In good Yankee fashion Thoreau presents time as capital not to be squandered, but where his neighbors view it as a "medium of advancement and prosperity in this world, or [of] preparation for the next" (Hawthorne's words),[47] he makes it the currency for a development and delight "far better than any work of the hands would have been" (*W* 111). The most profitable work turns out to be an Oriental "forsaking of works" (*W* 112); the village "Dolittle," in truth, does most.

Developed gradually over a decade from his earliest writings, the technique of inversion ministered so aptly to Thoreau's need for vindication that he was not always able to keep it within bounds. In "Reading" it carries him beyond a functional dispatching of the "trader" to a censoriousness that clothes him as a nineteenth-century Diogenes searching for an educated man. Along with the commercial classes, "most men" are arraigned for squandering their time and faculties on "easy reading" (*W* 104); Concordians "with a very few exceptions" are berated for their ignorance even of English literature (*W* 106); "college-bred and so called liberally educated men" are likewise accused (*W* 106); and even their professors are faulted for a narrowly philological learning that seldom rises to the needs of "the alert and heroic reader" (*W* 106). The only genuine readers of the great poets, it turns out, are those who are great poets themselves (*W* 104). By the end of "Reading" literary values have accomplished a work of cultural disenfranchisement in which virtually nothing remains but the speaker himself and his book. Although Thoreau patently means *Walden* to be one of those rare texts that marks "a new era" (*W* 107) in the reader's life, his opposition to Concord leads him to a divisiveness at odds with his stated effort to attract and persuade a philistine audience.

A feeling of besetment by family, friends, era, and nation may also have contributed to the note of exclusiveness in "Reading." When Thoreau commends the "father" above the "mother" tongue, writing above speech, for example, it is not from a Derridean bent toward de-authorized language but from a poet's hostility toward the vulgar, ephemeral converse (spoken or printed) of the multitude. The mother tongue represents the democratization of verbal expression in an age of mass culture, one symptom of which is the rhetoric of the popular orator – the Webster or Edward Everett, to some degree even the Emerson – who "yields to the inspiration of a transient occasion, and speaks to the mob before him" (*W* 102), as Thoreau himself, an uncharismatic lyceum performer, generally could not. The mother tongue may also represent the voice of Cynthia Thoreau, a village talker known for her sharp wit and her defense of her younger son, from whose benign sway, and that of a family including two sisters and a mild, unassertive father, he needed to free himself. To speak the "father" tongue one had to "be born again" (*W* 101); to write it, as Thoreau aspired to do, one had to be self-begotten, kin only to a pantheon of literary foster-fathers dating from Homer. In celebrating the father tongue, Thoreau was shedding an emasculated identity as townsman, son, brother, and disciple of Emerson, and serving notice that his genuine self was to be found in his prose, by those initiates who knew how to read it.

Like "Economy," then, "Reading" is rhetorically self-divided due to a basic incongruence between Thoreau's conscious and unconscious purposes: on one level the chapter addresses a local audience in order to awaken and reform it, while on another it dismisses that audience as it plays to a sophisticated readership alone capable of appreciating its moral elevation and linguistic virtuosity. Even its relationship to the aesthetic reader is ambivalent. If in some respects Thoreau's view of the production of literary meaning anticipates, say, Wolfgang Iser's reader-response theories[48] or deconstructionist free-play, the affinities soon break down, chiefly because as a writer laboring to express and ratify a new self, Thoreau had to resist the kind of incorporation-by-the-reader implicit in the theory of books as provocations. His privileging of writing over speech is performed not because writing is unstable and therefore endlessly open to interpretation, as Derrida has it, but (the very opposite reason) because it is "a reserved and select expression" (*W* 101) engraved, as it were, on tablets: an *authori*tative, de-Babelized language, or "*scripture,*" as he puns in the journal source of the passage (*PJ* 2, 164). By deconstructive lights *Walden* is a problematic text, at once unusually congenial to a free-play of signification and unusually oppressive in its weight of authorial presence. The paradox stems largely from Thoreau's double role as a reader and a writer of heroic books, eager on one side to participate in the game of interpretation, even to stretch its rules,[49] and concerned on the other to control the image of himself his text presents. In the same breath he can thus exhort readers "laboriously [to] seek the meaning of each word and line" of a text (reading as an objective *discovery* of meaning) and invite them to "conjectur[e] a larger sense than common use permits" out of their own "wisdom and valor and generosity" (reading as a subjective *creation* of meaning).

With *Walden* itself these seemingly antithetical positions converge in the sense its readers sometimes have of being free but "superintended." More than any text before *Ulysses,* perhaps, *Walden* seems designed to encourage its readers to *produce their own meaning within their finding of authorial meaning.* We read the book according to our ingenuity, that is, but with a constant suspicion that whatever meaning we may generate has been anticipated by the writer, whose air of commanding all conceivable linguistic traces of a word leads us, even in the delight of our invention, to marvel at his orchestration of this wondrous game. Richard Poirier finds Thoreau's "genius with language . . . to an awesome degree self-satisfying" in that he seems to have been "willing to go to his grave without having anyone recognize some of [his] best jokes"[50] — maybe so, but not without making us feel that the jokes are there and that he is cognizant of all of them. "Most men are satisfied if they read or hear read, and perchance have been convicted by the wisdom of one good book, the Bible" (*W* 104), Thoreau begins a relatively unobtrusive sentence in "Reading." But "convicted," oddly used, attracts attention; we think first of the slightly archaic literal sense ("convinced"), then of the pun ("found guilty": the wisdom of the Bible accuses us), but we are unsure even then if we have exhausted Thoreau's meaning. Other possibilities seem to beckon. Are men "convicted" (convinced *or* found guilty) because they have read *only* the Bible ("one good book") rather than the canon of holy books, eastern and western? Further, are they "convicted" (impugned for their narrowness) because the Bible is inferior to the Oriental scriptures, as Thoreau had intimated in *A Week*? And what, if anything, is meant by "perchance"? Is the Bible's power to convince only fortuitous? Is "conviction" (pietistic belief) itself a "perchance," resting on some inscrutable election of temperament, hap, or godly whim? No reading seems too "extra-vagant" with a writer whose diction and rhythms, like Emily Dickinson's dashes, fill his sentences with invisible italics. Thoreau's language has the effect, like Keats's urn, of teasing us out of thought; and just as Keats's ode concedes its inferiority of expression to the silent urn, so we are made to feel that our construction of a simple Thoreauvian sentence falls endlessly short of its intrinsic possibilities. We sense that more is to be seen, that one day we may see it, that sharper readers than ourselves may already see it, but that no reader will approach the omniscience of the author.

Even when nothing unusual may be meant, the positioning of an eyebrow-raising word can hint at mysteries defying solution. Such a rhetoric enlarges readers as a matter of course, and to the degree that they join in the activity of meaning-production they ratify Thoreau's elevation of literary over commercial values and enact the conversion his book was meant to produce. Yet in nearly all of *Walden*'s memorable passages there is a residue of unpenetrated suggestion that directs readers to a sensibility beyond their own, to a master of the game at which they themselves are only novices. An admirer of Thoreau's linguistic effects, the reader of *Walden* is also a competitor – not an antagonist to be defeated (as its inscribed audience is), but a rival for interpretive honors whose function is to run a fine race yet place a distant second to the author.[51] If *Walden* is "in part at least, an auto-biographical saint's life," as John Hildebidle called it,[52] it is Thoreau's literary readers who must perform the canonization.

IV

"Sounds" is the second of those chapters given to exemplifying an original relation to the universe; in its uncertainty about the metaphysics of that relation it is also the most problematic. "But while we are confined to books," Thoreau begins, "we are in danger of forgetting the language which all things and events speak without metaphor, which alone is copious and standard" (*W* 111). Thoreau draws his transition from "The American Scholar" ("Books are for the scholar's idle times" [*CW* I, 57]), but his broader debt is to *Nature*'s flight from tradition to the sources of life in what "Economy" calls "the open air" (*W* 28).[53] As *Walden*'s first extended chapter on nature, "Sounds" marks the practical beginning both of actor Thoreau's quest to "front only the essential facts of life" (*W* 90) and of narrator Thoreau's effort to document his extraordinary claims for experience. "Let us spend one day as deliberately as Nature" (*W* 97), Thoreau had written in "Where I Lived, and What I Lived For"; in "Sounds" he gives us such a day. The initial *Walden* manuscript had prefaced the section with the "Arabian Nights' Entertainments" passage later transposed to "Where I Lived, and What I Lived For" (Sh 154–55), evidence that Thoreau intended "Sounds" to illustrate the life of miracle he had been prophesying. The reference to a "standard" language of "things and events" appears to make a more definite and ambitious claim: "Sounds" will not only demonstrate that "reality is fabulous" (*W* 95); it will show that it is readable.

Thoreau had suggested as much in "Where I Lived, and What I Lived For" when he described the universe as "constantly and obediently answer[ing] to our conceptions" (*W* 97). Presumably he meant what his teacher Emerson had meant in *Nature* when he affirmed a correspondence between the laws of nature and the structure of the human mind: "Undoubtedly we have no questions to ask which are unanswerable. We must trust the perfection of the creation so far, as to believe that whatever curiosity the order of things has awakened in our minds, the order of things can satisfy" (*CW* I, 7). The "order of things" for Emerson was the vast network of interpenetrating laws fashioned by a benign intelligence for human education and accessible to the mind in its proper state, when "the axis of vision" was coincident with "the axis of things" (*CW* I, 43). Thoreau seems hesitant to make quite so specific a claim, though desirous of the *aura* of Emerson's meaning. "If you stand right fronting and face to face to a fact," he writes in a variant on Emerson's image, "you will see the sun glimmer on both its surfaces, as if it were a cimeter, and feel its sweet edge dividing you through the heart and marrow, and so you will happily conclude your mortal career" (*W* 98). It is hard to gauge exactly what Thoreau means, or whether he means anything "exactly." Does "standing right" imply the Emersonian adjustment of perception that causes an "opake" world suddenly to become "transparent" (*CW* I, 43)? Are the two surfaces of the cimeter the material and spiritual worlds as twinned by a symbolic fact in a moment of acute perception – the " 'visible world' " become a " 'dial plate of the invisible,' " as in *Nature* (*CW* I, 20)? Is the "sweet edge" that cuts to our very being a revelation of truth or an experience of noncognitive mystic joy? And is such knowledge or joy a quality of redeemed sublunary life or the fleeting prophecy of an afterstate?

Sharon Cameron notes the difficulty of determining Thoreau's philosophical position in *Walden* owing to his tendency to "theatricaliz[e] attitudes" his journals indicate he did not hold[54] – and in some cases, moreover, seems not to have known he didn't hold. Never a philosopher or student of philosophy as Emerson was, Thoreau drew heavily on Emerson in the 1846–49 *Walden* to clarify his lyrical response to nature and furnish the early chapters of his book with at least the semblance of a metaphysics. The debts were half-unconscious and rarely pondered in the sense of Thoreau weighing how fully he subscribed to (say) the Emersonian idea of Reason (or the Common Mind) that provided the epistemological basis for right perception, or how convincingly his life in nature confirmed Emerson's belief (already qualified by the mid 1840s) that "particular natural facts are symbols of particular spiritual facts" (*CW* I, 17), material laws the duplicate of moral laws (*CW* I, 21), and the world itself a mirror of the soul. If Thoreau "inherited idealism not as a faith but as a problem,"[55] as H. Daniel Peck says, he added to the problem considerably by confusing it with a faith, that is, by submitting his experience of nature to a Transcendental theory he had neither critically examined nor practically put to the test. When Emerson looked at the natural world he saw *structure,* or the spectacle of divine laws makings things what they are: "Behold these infinite relations [he wrote in the Divinity School Address], so like, so unlike; many, yet one. I would study, I would know, I would admire forever" (*CW* I, 76–77). When Thoreau looked at the natural world he saw *texture* – a physical body rather than an X-ray diagram – and *occasionally* he glimpsed something distantly beyond. Universal law was a reality for Thoreau, but it came to him through mediations of matter and mind that allowed only the vaguest apprehension.[56] "Sometimes as through a dim haze we see objects in their eternal relations" (*PJ* 1, 401), he remarked in 1841 (*PJ* 1, 401). The essay "Walking" expands the thought into a metaphysics (or anti-metaphysics) and indicates a life goal:

> My desire for knowledge is intermittent, but my desire to bathe my head in atmospheres unknown to my feet is perennial and constant. The highest that we can attain to is not Knowledge, but Sympathy with Intelligence. I do not know that this higher knowledge amounts to anything more definite than a grand and novel surprise on a sudden revelation of the insufficiency of all that we called Knowledge before, – a discovery that there are more things in heaven and earth than are dreamed of in our philosophy. It is the lighting up of the mist by the sun. Man cannot *know* in any higher sense than this, any more than he can look serenely and with impunity in the face of the sun. (*EP* 240)

By the early 1850s, when "Walking" was first drafted, Thoreau knew his own mind in a way that the writer of "Sounds" did not. The younger Thoreau thought he believed in the correspondences of *Nature,* which he assserted in "Friday" of *A Week* ("all the moral laws are readily translated into natural philosophy" [*Wk* 362]) in reaction to the rootless spirituality of earlier sections of the book. Emersonian metaphysics appealed to Thoreau not as abstract philosophy but so far as it seemed to underwrite a practical method by which close observation might be made to yield moral as well as scientific truth.[57] "Sounds" attempts to apply the theory through a strenuous attention to the normative language of "things and events," a discipline of "being forever on the alert" and "looking always at what is to be seen" (*W* 111).

One difficulty with "reading nature" was that Thoreau in the 1840s lacked the skills to do it, his relationship to nature, as Robert Sattelmeyer points out, being still "largely appreciative and conventional,"[58] or thoroughly *un*disciplined. Still more to the point, nature seemed to resist any effort to be read, even to be fully appreciated. Measured by his Walden journals, Thoreau's experience in the woods can hardly be called a failure, yet neither did it quite fulfill the enormously high expectations for discovery and self-renewal he brought to it. "For the most part I know not how the hours go," he wrote in the entry of April 1846 he would recast as a preface to his day of listening in "Sounds":

> Certainly I am not living that heroic life I had dreamed of – And yet all my veins are full of life – and nature whispers no reproach – *The day advances as if to light some work of mine* – and I defer in my thought as if there were some where busier men – *It was morning & lo! it is now evening – And nothing memorable is accomplished* – Yet my nature is <u>almost</u> content with this – [It hears no reproach in nature.]
>   What are these pines & these birds about? What is this pond a-doing? I must know a little more – & be forever ready. *Instead of singing as the birds I silently smile at my incessant good fortune* but I don't know that I bear any flowers or fruits – Methinks *if they try me by their standards I shall not be found wanting* – but men try one another not so. (*PJ* 2, 242; italics and words between brackets mine)

Except for the bracketed sentence, the whole of the passage appears in the first draft of *Walden* (Sh 152–53), but only the italicized portions survive in the published work, where they receive a more affirmative meaning in context ("nothing memorable," for example, comes to refer to outward events, Thoreau having assured us of the inward value of his days). Deleted entirely are Thoreau's acknowledgments that he is "not living [the] heroic life" he envisioned, that he is only "*almost* content" (his emphasis), that after nine months in the woods he has no more than a puzzled sense of what nature is "about," that his life (while fortunate in many respects) is as yet barren of "flowers and fruits," and that even removed from the eyes of Concord he continues to be sensitive to the judgments of men. *Walden* suppresses these reservations and turns a qualified happiness into an unqualified one, but its claims of discovery are limited by what Thoreau can legitimately report. Life at the pond was indeed an "amusement" that "never ceased to be novel" (*W* 112; *PJ* 2, 243); but while the days brought their respective adventures, they did not seem to build upon one another, to signify heaven on earth or point to a heaven beyond earth. "How to make my life of finer quality – to transplant it into futurity[,] that is a question," Thoreau wrote in May 1846, unsure of his own means of ascent even as he gave himself to preach ascent to his audience.

The inconclusiveness of Thoreau's Walden experience helps account for the central, unremarked paradox of "Sounds": that a chapter which begins by prescribing "the discipline of looking always at what is to be seen" should focus on hearing rather than sight and end by treating nature with the genial anthropomorphism of the familiar essay. At issue are the alternative claims not simply of two senses but of two modes of experiencing, two epistemologies and methods of ascent. In Emerson optical sight is correlative with *in*sight, as befits one who mentally "saw" ideas and felt himself invulnerable to fate so long as he had his eyes (*CW* I, 10). In Thoreau vision (when it is not the aesthetic appreciation of the poet) is a more empirical sense that deals with objects in their singularity and bids us to repossess the world fact by fact through discriminating perception. Hearing, by contrast, is ethereal, receptive, and holistic. The union with God and nature Emerson imaged as a "transparent eye-ball" (*CW* I, 10), Thoreau associated with a finely tuned ear. When at age twenty-three he was already idealizing his ecstatic boyhood and citing Wordsworth's "Heaven lies about us in our infancy," it was with the memory not of a "celestial light" but of a celestial music (*PJ* 1, 242); and when, correspondingly, he lamented his fall into mundaneness, it was as a lapse into the *sound* of "common day."[59] "Why were my ears given to hear those everlasting strains – which haunt my life – and yet to be prophaned much more by these perpetual dull sounds!" (*PJ* 1, 371), he complained in 1842. The divine hum of nature lay just beyond the edge of perception, "always retreat[ing] as I advance" (*PJ* 1, 365), like Emily Dickinson's light in Spring, which "almost speaks to you," then "passes" as "we stay," leaving "A quality of loss / Affecting our Content."[60] But the fall was neither complete nor, Thoreau wanted to believe, irreversible. "Will not this faith and expectation make to itself ears at length" (*PJ* 1, 365), he asked in 1842. And, as if in answer (1846): "I seem to hear a faint music from all the horizon – When our senses are clear and purified we always may hear the notes of music in the air" (*PJ* 2, 242).[61]

This last passage appears in Thoreau's journal just before the entry he adapted for "Sounds" ("For the most part I know not how the hours go"), yet no hint of a celestial music is given in the 1846–49 drafts of the chapter. In a late addition to "Sounds" Thoreau describes the Sunday church bells acquiring "at a sufficient distance . . . a certain vibratory hum, as if the pine needles in the horizon were the strings of a harp which it swept" (*W* 123). The passage has its source in a journal entry of 1851, but many comparable entries dating back to the early 1840s were available to Thoreau had he wished to suggest a remote spiritual music in the air. That he excluded such a favorite conceit points up the crucial questions he felt called upon to settle in "Sounds." What route would he follow toward paradise, close observation or mystical abandonment? And where would he look for paradise, within nature or on its hazy borders?

Thoreau would never unequivocally resolve these matters, except perhaps at the very end of his career. In its main thrust *Walden* is in revolt against the otherworldliness of *A Week;* yet composed during most of a decade, it reflects moments when Thoreau was equally frustrated by the discipline of attentive sight. The "vibratory hum" passage originates in one of these neo-mystical periods (mid to late 1851) and, in its variation on the image of an aeolian harp, reveals some of the conundrums that belonged to the matter-spirit problem for Thoreau and make themselves felt in "Sounds." The aeolian harp, of course, was a Romantic cult object (Emerson had one in his study; Thoreau built one) made famous by Coleridge's poetic speculation, "And what if all of animated nature / Be but organic Harps diversely fram'd, / That tremble into thought, as o'er them sweeps / Plastic and vast, one intellectual breeze, / At once the Soul of each, and God of all?"[62] Cautiously advanced by Coleridge, the trope became a reference point for Romantic pantheism in its suggestion that spirit manifested itself in and through the inflections of living matter. Emerson elaborated on the idea in "The Poet": "Over everything stands its daemon, or soul, and, as the form of the thing is reflected by the eye, so the soul of the thing is reflected by a melody. . . . The condition of true naming, on the poet's part, is his resigning himself to the divine *aura* which breathes through forms, and accompanying that" (*CW* III, 15). Emerson's way of abandonment is in keeping with Coleridge's own pose of passivity,[63] both of which are contrary to Thoreau's method of "being forever on the alert"; yet they all seem varieties of "natural supernaturalism" so far as they see spirit abiding in what Jonathan Bishop called "the most local kind of natural particulars."[64] Thoreau's image, however, turns out to be problematic to the point of subversion. The "vibratory hum" in "Sounds" is occasioned by a mechanical source (church bells), as though nature were a little promiscuous in answering as compliantly to a sexton's bell rope as to God's breath. Physics, not metaphysics, accounts for *this* celestial music, as Thoreau concedes by making the idea only a fanciful conceit ("*as if* the pine needles . . . were the strings of a harp"). In the journal source, the sound of the Lincoln bell prompts Thoreau to think of another artifact of civilization, the telegraph wire (or "telegraph harp," as he liked to call it), an object of endless fascination for the way at odd times it "suddenly & unexpectedly [rose] into melody as if a god had touched it" (*PJ* 4, 302). If a metal wire could vibrate sympathetically to the spirit in the air, then nature had no special status as a register of the divine; it was simply an immensely varied set of material instruments on which heavenly music might be played. The entry continues: "It is not the mere sound of the bell but the humming in the air that enchants me – just [as the] azure tint which much air or distance imparts delights the eye. It is not so much the object as the object clothed with an azure veil" (*PJ* 4, 142–43). Thoreau is less interested here in spirit as it animates matter than as it gathers *about* matter and makes itself known as vapor is known by its condensation on the grass. The "diversely fram'd" particulars of experience become almost incidental; what allures is the azure on the horizon, the distant vibratory hum. Spirit is not "in" objects, to be grasped by a careful study of nature's "language [of] things and events"; it hovers over and around objects, to be sensed sidelong in reverie and only then as an "aural mirage," much as the grandeur of Mount Wachusett years ago had been a visual mirage.

It is easy to see why Thoreau would have suppressed such a thought in the 1849 *Walden*. Reacting against the passivity of *A Week,* he had no wish to stake his growth on an all-or-nothing enjoyment of the music of creation. Neither, however, had he developed the sharp observational skills needed to read nature as an open revelation. The title and content of "Sounds" are his retreat from the problem of spiritual perception he lacked the means to solve. Reluctant to link his ascent to nimbuses on the horizon yet unable to distill meaning from natural fact, Thoreau rejected both paths and fell back upon the Romantic essayist's charming but innocuous display of sensibility. Where his preface to "Sounds" seems to anticipate a decoding of nature's language "without metaphor" (*W* 111), his account of a summer's day rests almost entirely upon metaphor, or a subsuming of natural objects to an anthropomorphic play of fancy in which screech owls become "wise midnight hags" (*W* 124) and bullfrogs "ancient winebibbers and wassailers" (*W* 126).[65] The "humanity of nature," by which Thoreau characteristically meant the deep moral truths suggested by (if not actually contained in) natural objects, is reduced in "Sounds" to a pleasant but trivial effect of literary personification. Thoreau cannot *see* nature as he aspires to do, and he is unwilling to close his eyes and depend on mystically *hearing* it, so in place of the alert intimacy with facts he celebrates at the beginning of "Sounds," he ends the chapter with a consciously literary tour de force satisfying in nearly all terms except those of his opening paragraph.[66]

Unable to mount to heaven by the incremental steps of naturalism, Thoreau vaults himself to it in "Solitude" by invoking a moment of absolute sympathy with nature:

> This is a delicious evening, when the whole body is one sense, and imbibes delight through every pore. . . . As I walk along the stony shore of the pond in my shirt sleeves, though it is cool as well as cloudy and windy, and I see nothing special to attract me, all the elements are unusually congenial to me. (*W* 129)

This is *Walden*'s touchstone experience of grace in nature, theorized about in "Where I Lived, and What I Lived For," sought after in "Reading" and "Sounds," and now intimately realized down to the immediacy of Thoreau's present tense. The description is noteworthy for the unremarkableness of the scene, which suggests that moments like this are not contingent on special revelations or perceptions of the beautiful or sublime but are a matter of harmonious adjustment to the world. Here again, *Nature* stands behind *Walden*, even in the cadences of the prose: "Crossing a bare common, in snow puddles, at twilight, under a cloudy sky, without having in my thoughts any occurrence of special good fortune, I have enjoyed a perfect exhilaration" (*CW* I, 10). The differences are also telling. Where Emerson is passive and wholly spiritual, a bodiless "eye-ball" *receiving* "the currents of the Universal Being" and *seeing* all (*CW* I, 10), Thoreau is active and physical, a permeable skin "*imbib[-ing]* delight through every pore" and *feeling* all.[67] The experience is exceptional in Thoreau for its dissolution of the boundaries between nature, the body, and the self; normally a "strange," unendeared "piece of nature" to Thoreau (*PJ* 1, 365), the body here performs the critical act of mediation. At one with his own body, Thoreau feels at home in the world's body, able to "go and come with a strange liberty in Nature, a part of herself" (*W* 129). No cause is given for this restored physical and ontological innocence beyond the implication that it is the natural outgrowth of the narrator's life at Walden and the spontaneous *next step* in the process of ascent he has been chronicling.

"Solitude" confirms *Walden*'s grounding of heaven in earth, where it will remain through the balance of the 1849 manuscript. In this respect the chapter fills the role later assumed by "The Ponds" (still largely unwritten) in rendering the moral character of nature and the spiritual possibilities of a life in proximity to it. But "Solitude" also, in a different spirit and with a strain upon its portrait of nature, confronts a subject Thoreau could scarcely have avoided. Didn't he "feel lonesome" in the woods (*W* 3)? his neighbors were fond of asking. Solitude itself was rarely an emotional burden to Thoreau, yet he did feel "convicted" when reminded by friends "of the advantages of society[,] of worthy and earnest helpful relations to people" (*PJ* 2, 248–49), an uneasiness all the stronger when he recalled that he was partly in retreat from the failures of an intimacy he deeply craved. "By myself I can live and thrive," he later remarked, "but in the society of incompatible friends I starve. To cultivate their society is to cherish a sore which can only be healed by abandoning them" (*J* V, 86–87). The tragedy of Thoreau's private relations was that all his nearest friends were "incompatible," whether because of inhibitions in himself or them (Emerson, particularly) or because he made "such an enormous demand on men and so [was] constantly disappointed"

(*J* IV, 314). Frustration, anger, sadness, even physical pain (heartache was no metaphor to Thoreau) mark the periodic crises of friendship scattered through twenty-odd years in his journals. Perhaps the most distressing feature of his situation was the sense of losing touch with himself in the presence of others, of growing "dissipated"; "Talked, or tried to talk with R.W. E. Lost my time – nay, almost my identity" (*J* V, 188), he wrote after one such experience. Thoreau learned to adapt to his thwarted hopes (outwardly, at least) through the reversals of paradox. "The truest Society approaches always nearer to Solitude" (*PJ* I, 60), he announced in the earliest of such attempts (1838). "Solitude" converts these bare outcroppings of psychic need into professions of a deep content: "I find it wholesome to be alone the greater part of the time. To be in company, even with the best, is soon wearisome and dissipating. I love to be alone. I have never found the companion that was so companionable as solitude. We are for the most part more lonely when we go abroad among men than when we stay in our chambers" (*W* 135).

In "Solitude" and again in "Visitors," Thoreau also addresses the local charge that he is a recluse or misanthrope, turning the fault back upon his accusers and upon communal life generally. "Society is commonly too cheap," he asserts: "We meet at very short intervals, not having had time to acquire any new value for each other"; further, "we live thick and are in each other's way, and stumble over one another, and . . . thus lose respect for one another" (*W* 136). Lumbering as bodies and repetitious as souls, we must sip, not quaff, society for it to be potable at all. Memories of his mother's boarders may have contributed to Thoreau's sense of a world clogged with human encounters; so, no doubt, did his 1843 residence in New York City, which struck him as "a thousand times meaner than [he] could have imagined" (*Corr* 111). Yet even in semirural Concord or his cabin at Walden, Thoreau rarely felt the physical and psychological ease that allowed for intimacy. Loathing gossip and confession even with his closest friends, Thoreau saw conversation as a meeting of minds and souls (bodies were not asked to attend) that demanded sincerity but also a certain artifice and reserve. "One inconvenience I sometimes experienced in so small a house," he notes in "Visitors," was "the difficulty of getting to a sufficient distance from my guest when we began to utter the big thoughts in big words. . . . Individuals, like nations, must have suitable broad and natural boundaries, even a considerable neutral ground between. . . . If we are merely loquacious and loud talkers, then we can afford to stand very near together, cheek by jowl, and feel each other's breath; but if we speak reservedly and thoughtfully, we want to be further apart, that all animal heat and moisture may have a chance to evaporate" (*W* 140–41). Precious little animal heat, physical or emotional, seems to have warmed twenty-three-year-old William Dean Howells, visiting Thoreau during his Boston pilgrimage of 1860 fresh from Columbus and full of recent events from Harpers Ferry to Lincoln's presidential campaign: "He tried to place me geographically after he had given me a chair not quite so far off as Ohio, though still across the whole room, for he sat against one wall, and I against the other. . . . I do not remember that [he] spoke of his books, or of himself at all, and when he began to speak of John Brown, it was not the warm, palpable, fearful old man of my conception, but a sort of John Brown type, a John Brown ideal, a John Brown principle, which we were to somehow (with long pauses between the vague, orphic phrases) to cherish, and to nourish ourselves upon."[68]

Earnest, deferential, intensely literary-minded but companionable, Howells might have qualified as Thoreau's ideal listener; in fact, Thoreau felt most at ease with plainer men like farmer George Minott who engaged him on the level of fact or, in later years, with admirers like Harrison Blake and Daniel Ricketson who allowed him to stage-manage their relationship. In "Visitors" the single extended portrait Thoreau offers is that of French-Canadian woodchopper Alek Therien, a figure of great "animal spirits" but slight inwardness (Sh 172) who fascinated him for many of the same qualities Melville ascribed to his Polynesians in *Typee* (which Thoreau read at Walden): he was simple, childlike, physical, and utterly unselfconscious, with a certain originality, even perhaps a certain prein-tellectual genius. Like the Indians Thoreau later encountered in Maine, Therien typified the dual nature of the primitive, at once uncorrupted and brutishly corporeal – "a true Homeric boor" (*PJ* 2, 160), Thoreau called him in his journal, joining both traits (*Walden* mutes the phrase: "a true Homeric or Paphlagonian man" [*W* 144]). Within *Walden*'s rhetoric of ascent, Therien is implicitly set against the spiritual man to contradistinguish Thoreau's position (spirituality must be attained) from Romantic sentimentalizations of the rustic, the savage, and the child.[69]

"Solitude" and "Visitors" are perhaps most curious for the sketches of Emer-son, Channing, and Alcott they conspicuously omit. Interest in Emerson, espe-cially, was strong; Horace Greeley, who placed Thoreau's Carlyle essay in *Graham's Magazine,* encouraged him to "write a like article about Emerson" (*Corr* 174), and a portrait of Emerson in "Visitors" would certainly have added to *Walden*'s appeal. Reluctant to cite contemporary men of letters even in his journals, Thoreau had no wish to feed the local prejudice that he trotted after Emerson or, perhaps, to exploit a relationship that was sacred to him, however unsatisfying. *Walden* denies all loneliness except for what Thoreau says briefly assailed him in a mood of "slight insanity" near the beginning of his stay (*W* 131). A yearning for companionship, however, shows itself in the beautifully elegiac journal entries of 1845 later incorporated into "Former Inhabitants; and Winter Visitors" but pointedly omitted from early drafts – the evocations of Irishman Hugh Quoil and freeman Cato Ingraham, among others, "conjured up," as Lawrence Buell says, "to compensate for an excess of the isolation [Thoreau] supposedly wanted when he retreated to the woods,"[70] in much the way a lonely child might surround himself with imaginary playmates. Thoreau's more "usual consolation," Buell adds, was "to reinvent nature as society,"[71] to make "a pine wood" (Thoreau's own words) into "as substantial and as memorable a fact as a friend" (*PJ* 4, 207). The most insistent of the paradoxes that abound in "Solitude" is that of nature's smilingly human face – of its "most sweet and tender, . . . most innocent and encouraging society" (*W* 131), its "infinite and unaccountable friendliness" which renders "the fancied advantages of human neighborhood insignificant" (*W* 132), and its indwelling "sympathy" hinting at "the presence of something kindred to me" (*W* 132).

The effect of making nature fill the place of human intimacy is a confusion about its ethical character that complicates Thoreau's entire relationship to it. Thoreau is nearest the center of Anglo-American Romanticism when he writes, "Sympathy with the fluttering alder and poplar leaves almost takes my breath away" (*W* 129). Sympathy is the power of the imagination as it enters into and apprehends the life principle of an object;[72] it is feeling's analogue to the intellect's grasp of natural law, and though it needn't presume a fixed correspondence between physical and spiritual facts, it does, for transcendental Romantics, imply a *naturgeist* that "breathes through forms" (*CW* I, 15) and molds their defining expression. A wholly different notion of sympathy is at work when Thoreau rhapsodizes, "Every little pine needle expanded and swelled with sympathy and befriended me" (*W* 132). This is Ruskin's "pathetic fallacy," a form of literary personification that ascribes emotion to nonhuman objects but carries no metaphysical weight, indeed is a reflexive sign of the speaker's state of soul, not an illumination of the object. Although Thoreau typically sought a nature infinitely grander than man, even in conflict with man (with the provincialism of the village, anyway), he also required what Richard Lebeaux calls "alternative and compensatory modes of intimacy, family, and community,"[73] which he projected upon nature through his language of companionableness. His affective side sought a "kindred" creation, his philosophical side an immense, transhuman one capable of enclosing the dark and violent in nature and accommodating its visible indifference to human ends. Yet the beneficence of a "sweet and tender" nature and the beneficence of a bracingly vast one could not be harmonized without severely taxing his idea of "goodness." "The gentle rain which waters my beans and keeps me in the house to-day is not drear and melancholy, but good for me too," he begins a key passage in "Solitude": "Though it prevents my hoeing them, it is of far more worth than my hoeing. If it should continue so long as to cause the seeds to rot in the ground and destroy the potatoes in the low lands, it would still be good for the grass on the uplands, and being good for the grass, it would be good for me" (*W* 131).

To affirm nature's benignness Thoreau needs to abandon his ego- and anthropocentric standpoints and identify the good with universal process. The faculty required here is not imagination but what Emerson called "intellect," which "separates the fact considered from *you,* from all local and personal reference, and discerns it as if it existed for its own sake. . . . The intellect goes out of the individual, floats over its own personality, and regards it as a fact, and not as *I* and *mine*" (*CW* II, 193–94). Thoreau appeals to this kind of affectless detachment in a late addition to "Solitude" when he observes, "With thinking we may be beside ourselves in a sane sense. By a conscious effort of the mind we can stand aloof from actions and their consequences; and all things, good and bad, go by us like a torrent" (*W* 134–35). In moments like this the problem of natural evil dissolves, but so does any prospect of nature's "infinite and unaccountable friendliness." Thoreau can stretch himself to fit an epically proportioned universe; in doing so, however, he needs to empty both himself and it of a recognizably human character.

"Solitude" gives reason for qualifying James McIntosh's remark that Thoreau's "relation to nature in the first version [of *Walden*] is comparatively simple, unconscious, and idyllic," while by "the seventh and final version of 1854 he has included much more of the whole conscious man."[74] The first draft only seems simple because Thoreau is innocent about its complexities. The problem of nature's ethical character will return in "The Ponds" and, still more, in the contemporaneous chapters of *Cape Cod*. What Thoreau sought above all, he came to see (if not entirely to find), was a nature larger than and different from the human yet morally related to it by analogy – "kindred" in a profounder sense than the emotionally supportive. In "Sounds" and "Solitude" he pursues his search haltingly, unsure what he wants from nature beyond a refuge from Concord and bound to Romantic categories of thought that were an awkward metaphysical fit. Thoreau is most eloquent and persuasive when he is rendering pure experience, as in the opening lines of "Solitude"; and he is least persuasive (though sometimes no less eloquent) when he is pronouncing upon the *character* of experience, as in the opening of "Sounds." Thoreau's *feeling* for nature never betrayed him in *Walden,* nor did his gift of style. The difficulties began when he borrowed *conceptions* of nature or when his private exigencies caused him to assert more than he knew, or other than he knew. In these instances, style was his philosophical undoing, for it allowed him to beg questions of meaning and dodge contradictions that a less accomplished rhetorician might have been obliged to face.

"The Bean-Field" is Thoreau's final effort in the 1849 text to apply the discipline of "Sounds" and elevate his life through a practical immersion in detail. As it developed over nine years the chapter came to include an "extraordinary mixture of attitudes and tones,"[75] but its root impulse, however elaborated, was always the same. "What shall I learn of beans or beans of me?" (*W* 155), Thoreau asks, setting out "to know beans" (*W* 161) as Ishmael sets out to know the whale in *Moby-Dick:* to subject a piece of creation to exhaustive study as a paradigm for what human beings can know about anything in their world. Working without farm animals, hired labor, and advanced tools, Thoreau becomes "much more intimate with [his] beans than usual" (*W* 157) and is able to offer sound advice to the potential husbandman. Yet his practical knowledge of beans is exactly that; as Leo Marx noted, "the facts do not, cannot, flower into truth."[76] Between the cosmic ("When my hoe tinkled against the stones, that music echoed to the woods and sky . . ." [*W* 159]) and the particular ("For a hoe....... $0 54" [*W* 163]), there is a vast area for mock-heroic literary play but not, as Marx says, for "the kind of meaning the experiment has been designed to establish."[77] Nor, contrary to the theories of the Brook Farmers and others, does labor in the soil necessarily conduce to the elevation of the laborer; to be "attached . . . to the earth" by hands and hoe and receive "strength like Antaeus" (*W* 155) turns out to be a quite different matter from figuratively sending one's "radicle downward" into the ground so that one's shoot may rise toward heaven (*W* 15). Thoreau does harvest a rich literary crop from hacking away at weeds ("Many a lusty crest-waving Hector, that towered a whole foot above his crowding comrades, fell before my weapon and rolled in the dust" [*W* 162]); but unlike the seriocomic exasperation with which Ishmael concludes his quest ("But if I know not even the tail of this whale, how understand his head? much more, how comprehend his face, when face he has none?" [*MD* 379]), Thoreau's mock-heroics seem meant to obscure the results of his inquiry rather than draw an epistemological lesson from them. By lowering the stakes of the chapter, Thoreau avoids the crisis of knowledge Ishmael confronts (and giddily turns to imaginative triumph) but only by burlesquing *Walden*'s central act of meeting "the essential facts of life." Thoreau concedes his limited success in reading nature, and therefore in remaking his life through disciplined attention, when he says he "will not plant beans and corn with so much industry another summer, but such seeds . . . as sincerity, truth, simplicity, faith, innocence, and the like" (*W* 163–64). He will turn inward, that is, privileging *self*-culture above *agri*-culture in a way that separates the spiritual from the practical and reaps the facts of the natural world "only for the sake of tropes and expression" (*W* 162).

In repudiating the labor of farming for the happily vagrant life of the poet, Thoreau goes far toward renouncing the townsman-audience he set out to instruct in "Economy." Late in "The Bean-Field" he seems to argue for a reconsecration of agriculture as a poetical-religious calling and a source of communal ritual. His apparent quarrel is not with farming but with the reification of market capitalism: "By avarice and selfishness, and a grovelling habit, from which none of us is free, of regarding the soil as property, or the means of acquiring property chiefly, the landscape is deformed, husbandry is degraded with us, and the farmer leads the meanest of lives" (*W* 165). Thoreau's touchstone for the "poetical farmer" as distinct from the agrarian capitalist and the dull-witted boor was George Minott, who "makes the most of his labor and takes infinite satisfaction in every part of it. He is not looking forward to the sale of his crops – or any pecuniary profit, but he is paid by the constant satisfaction which his labor yields him. . . . He gets out of each manipulation in the farmers operations a fund of entertainment which the speculating drudge hardly knows" (*PJ* 4, 116–17). A village of yeoman cultivators like Minott seems Thoreau's ideal in "The Bean-Field," but as in "Economy" his disgust with entrepreneurialism spills over into an argument against ownership generally, which drives a wedge between himself and his New England audience. "The true husbandman," he concludes "The Bean-Field," "will cease from anxiety . . . and finish labor with every day, relinquishing all claim to the produce of his fields" (*W* 166). "The landscape is deformed," draft A capped the sermon, "when there is an attempt to appropriate what cannot be appropriated" (Sh 184).

Thoreau's encounter with John Field in "Baker Farm" confirms his indifference to any concordat between himself and his propertied neighbors. Staged as a test case for his efforts to proselytize men of quiet desperation ("I tried to help him with my experience" and "purposely talked to him as if he were a philosopher, or desired to be one" [*W* 205]), "Baker Farm" quickly declares itself a rhetorical rather than a reformist exercise. Thoreau's advice to Field, drowning in debts and children, to live simply and go a-huckleberrying in the summer would be grotesque and downright cruel if it were not meant figuratively, as Charles R. Anderson observed, as part of a "contrast between the elevated and the degraded life, . . . between a poet's desire to soar into the life of the spirit and a clod's resignation to being bogged down in squalid materialism."[78] The point to emphasize against those who see Thoreau writing in 1846–49 as a "reformer-legislator"[79] is that even in the first draft of *Walden* all materialism – which is to say, all ownership – is deprecated as squalid. John Field came to America to rise in the world, yet neither he nor his fellow Concordians will "rise" in any true sense until their notion of ascent becomes preponderantly spiritual. The rejection of property hinted at in "The Bean-Field" becomes an open article of belief in "Baker Farm." "Enjoy the land, but own it not" (*W* 207), Thoreau counsels his neighbors, knowing full well his words disqualify him from any serious hearing. "Through want of enterprise and faith," he continues, "men are where they are, buying and selling, and spending their lives like serfs" (*W* 208). Here, in this ultimate of inversions, the capitalist watchword "enterprise" is pried loose from economics and attached to a life that only the narrator himself, the village "Dolittle," can be said to live. "As a solution to the relationship between culture and nature," Joan Burbick remarks of "Baker Farm," Thoreau "produces only a statement of self-justification, not a realistic blueprint for cultural reform."[80] The tension latent in "Economy" between his avowed purpose of instructing his neighbors and his actuating purpose of defending his life to their eyes and reconstituting it in his own has erupted in what amounts to an abandonment of the fiction that he is addressing his audience's "outward condition." *Walden* remains focused on spiritual ascent, but while it nods formulaically toward a shared activity, it has left its audience behind in the bogs of materialism and ventured on toward a celestial city reachable only, it at all, by the unencumbered pilgrim.

V

Walden's shifts of rhetoric and commitment, even within individual drafts, are a reminder that Thoreau's book, while taking its occasion and argument from his relationship to Concord, is spiritually tentative and inquiring, its author more certain of what he opposes than of what he believes, who he is, where he is going, and how he intends to get there. Conceived almost contemporaneously with his settlement at the pond, *Walden* was meant to be a celebration of his new life, an extended boast saved from egotism by its representativeness. Yet what specific claims it would make for nature and humanity, Thoreau could not anticipate, nor could he foresee what life at the pond would reveal about himself, determined though he was to take whatever encouragement he could and fashion a sustaining self-mythology. The journal sources for his book are scattered almost randomly, certainly plotlessly, through more than two hundred pages in the Princeton edition; fine passages are frequent, epiphanies exceedingly rare. Thoreau's experience at Walden, in short, was largely happy but formless, and it was only in literary composition that it assumed, or was assigned, meaning. Having settled his stance toward the reader ("Economy") and his premises about life ("Where I Lived, and What I Lived For"), Thoreau knew more clearly what he wanted to affirm as well as how he wanted to appear. In reworking his materials, however, he found them unexpectedly problematic, even refractory, in light of his hypotheses about nature, perception, and truth. As a result, the sections of *Walden* ("Sounds" through "The Bean-Field") designed to elaborate and "prove" the propositions of "Where I Lived, and What I Lived For" tend instead to qualify, subvert, or strategically evade them. Nature, it becomes evident, does not speak to us in any language we can decipher; we can only take our blessed moments as they come and learn to position ourselves so as best and most often to receive them. Thoreau never doubts nature's holiness or the value and authority of these elevated states, but he finds himself unable to initiate and sustain, much less to regularize them, and unable to translate their aura into lasting knowledge. Revelation doesn't reveal; it only (temporarily) exalts, with the teasing prospect that exaltation can somehow be made a permanent ground of being. Balked in his own attempts to discover a method for ascent, Thoreau has no method to offer the reader beyond the illusory one created by his staircased literary structure. In the final sections of the 1849 text he will speak *as if* he had attained the life prophesied in "Where I Lived, and What I Lived For"; he will inscribe his highest self in his book to consolidate it against the vagaries of the spirit and persuade Concord that the joyous, saintly figure so inscribed is the essential Henry Thoreau.

"Baker Farm" and the brief 1846–49 "Higher Laws" complete Thoreau's project as amended. "Baker Farm" has its source in an August 1845 visit to John Field (elsewhere in the journal "John Frost"), "an Honest hard-working – but shiftless man plainly" (*PJ* 2, 176) whose life of squalor and profitless toil is set against Thoreau's of purity and independence. Contextually, the entry occupies an important place, following directly upon Thoreau's rejection of farming ("I will not plant beans another summer" [*PJ* 2, 175; *W* 163]) and recording his aspiration toward "a hard and emphatic life . . . full of adventures and work" (*PJ* 2, 177). Within the Walden journals the moment bears no visible fruit, and eight months later Thoreau can voice the reservations about his experience at the pond cited earlier ("Certainly I am not living that heroic life I had dreamed of" [*PJ* 2, 242]). In the 1849 *Walden* the episode is culled out and made the dramatic climax of the narrator's effort toward ascent. Two details absent from the journal but prominent in the text reinforce its symbolic status: the "rainbow over [the narrator's] shoulder" as he leaves Field's hut after a thunderstorm and "some faint tinkling sounds borne to [his] ear through the cleansed air" (*W* 207) – signs of heavenly approval inserted to authorize the voice of his "Good Genius" prompting him toward a new life: "Rise free from care before the dawn, and seek adventures. . . . There are no larger fields than these, no worthier games than may here be played" (*W* 207; v. *PJ* 2, 179). From this point on, following one's genius will replace disciplined sight as the means for ascent, as Thoreau assumes a more articulated version of what in "Sir Walter Raleigh" he had called the "saunterer": a modern-day pilgrim to the Holy Land or knight-errant, as Thoreau was fond of imagining him, but more aptly perhaps a kind of "spiritual picaro" like Whitman's Walt, who "tramp[s] a perpetual journey" ("Shoulder your duds, and I will mine, and let us hasten forth" ["Song of Myself" 1855, ll. 1199, 1212]), or like Melville's Ishmael with his carpet-bag and his abomination of "all honorable respectable toils, trials, and tribulations of every kind whatsoever" (*MD* 5) – drop-outs all, and avatars of a free, uncompromised New World sensibility whose common progenitor is Emerson's self-reliant man.[81] In Thoreau's own words of 1840, "A wise man will always have his duds picked up, and be ready for whatever may happen" (*PJ* 1, 157).

The movement from alert observation to joyous vagabondage (and back again) is one that Thoreau would retrace countless times in his career, seldom for the same immediate reasons but always, at bottom, because neither spontaneity nor method could satisfy his double need for ecstasy *and* teleological assurance. The difference between Thoreau's picaro and Whitman's, especially, is that Thoreau's can never lastingly settle for the pleasures of the journey; he must have a sense of "getting somewhere," or transcending himself and winning through to an increasingly exalted life.

Thoreau uses this image of pilgrimage in the rudimentary "Higher Laws" – the spiritual high-water mark of the 1849 *Walden* – when he speaks of his genius leading him to renunciations of diet bordering on the extreme or insane: "And yet that way as I grow more resolute and faithful my road lies" (Sh 190; v. *W* 216). Thoreau never doubts he is embarked on a life journey, which, with the optimism of the late 1840s, he sees himself prosecuting with single-minded devotion. If the writing of *Walden* has not brought him to the celestial city, as he had hoped, it has at least given him a distant view of it and trained his steps in the right direction. Though added at a later stage of composition, the closing sentences of the published *Walden* – "There is more day to dawn. The sun is but a morning star" (*W* 333) – belong more properly in spirit to this period than to 1854, when Thoreau's heavenly navigation was more clouded. In the earlier *Walden* Thoreau seems confident that his days of adventuring in nature would have an elevating effect and make for a kind of secular beatitude at once spiritual in itself and preparatory to a higher spirituality. Such, at any rate, seems the lesson of the final paragraph of the 1849 "Higher Laws" in which Thoreau sketches his metamorphosis from fisherman to fledgling saint and crowns the argument of his book with a vision of accomplishment to oppose to Concord's: "If the day and the night are such that you greet them with joy – and life emits a fragrance like flowers and scented herb – more elastic – more immortal – more starry – that is your success. All nature is your congratulation and you have cause momentarily to bless yourself" (Sh 191; v. *W* 216). The prospect of a life of wonder extended early in *Walden* is presented here as something authenticated and intimately known, "a segment of the rainbow I have clutched" (Sh 191; v. *W* 217); and while the reader of *Walden* cannot be made a full participant in Thoreau's joy, he has been brought to acknowledge its reality for the speaker and, potentially at least, for himself.

VI

"The noble life is continuous and unintermitting" (*PJ* 2, 177), Thoreau remarked in a source passage for "Baker Farm." The full testimony of his Walden experience indicated otherwise; so, necessarily, did his literary report. After its crescendo in "Higher Laws" the 1849 manuscript trails off into minutiae about birds and field mice (Sh 191–92), as if having risen (or leaped) to a height of spirit, Thoreau were at a loss how to maintain his elevation or gracefully to descend from it. The fragments of what would later become the fall and winter chapters have the randomness of a lost intention. His position resembles that immediately following the Saddleback episode in *A Week,* his structure of ascent having led him to a mountaintop but failed to show him how to live and breathe in its rarefied air. Had his aim in *Walden* been solely to memorialize himself before Concord, he might have ended the 1849 manuscript with "Higher Laws." Yet, having written himself to a peak of vision unsustainable in life, Thoreau was pressed to find not a new *method* of ascent (a dead end, for now), but a reassurance of spiritual direction. He found his reassurance in the cycle of the seasons, elaborated in later drafts but invoked from the beginning as a ready-made confirmation of renewal absent from the spatial narratives of "A Walk to Wachusett" and *A Week*. Like the grass beneath our feet, he wrote in the original of "Spring," "our human life but dies down to the surface of nature – but puts forth its green blade still to eternity" (Sh 205; v. *W* 311). From this modest image of recurrence – quite different from ascent but with an air of hopefulness – the section rises to its well-known celebration of nature: "We need the tonic of wildness. . . . At the same time that we are earnest to learn and explore all things, we require that all things should be mysterious and unexplorable by us[,] that land and sea should be infinitely wild, unsurveyed and unfathomed by us" (Sh 207; v. *W* 317–18). This is resounding language, but it is not the language of *Walden*'s early chapters. Nature is no longer a compliant instructor "constantly and obediently answer[ing] to our conceptions" (*W* 97), nor is it the most "companionable" of companions offering a "sweet and beneficent society" (*W* 135, 132). The nature on which Thoreau now rests his affirmation is no friend to or image of the human; it is the nature of "Ktaadn" shorn of its terror but not of its essential otherness, which Thoreau's thwarted efforts to read creation have forced him to acknowledge, even to extol.

As *Walden* had two beginnings – speaker Thoreau's address to his fellow townsmen, actor Thoreau's removal to the pond – so it might symmetrically have had two endings, a narrative conclusion bringing the experiment to a close and a rhetorical conclusion summarizing its findings for an expectant audience. Thoreau came to recognize this himself and by the late spring or summer of 1849 was incipiently drafting his "report" ("I learned this by my experiments in the woods" [*PJ* 3, 19]). Had Thoreau published *Walden* in 1849, as planned, he almost certainly would have developed its conclusion. As it stands, the 1849 manuscript ends baldly with two statements of fact: "Thus was my first year's life in the woods completed." And interlined in pencil: "I finally left Walden September 6th, 1847" (Sh 208; Cl 845). The words seem brusque given the amplitude of "Economy" and the role of scout Thoreau had assumed in "Where I Lived, and What I Lived For." Yet the absence of a closing summary only formalizes the progressive eclipse of the townsman-reader that marks the later sections of the book. Thoreau has not forgotten his audience; he has simply come to be ruled by other concerns than those he began with. From its journal inceptions *Walden* had contained two "stories," separate but related: a myth of renewal enacted for Thoreau's townsmen in answer to his promise to speak to their condition and a more private quest conducted within this general intention and aimed at reordering the author's relation to the world. The stories were meant to converge in a self-discovery that could stand as the prototype for a new cultural ideal; but as experience stranded him in one philosophical cul-de-sac after another, Thoreau clung more closely to those real but ineffable testimonies of which he felt certain – moments of delight like those in "Solitude" and "Baker Farm" that were exclusively his and that seemed invulnerable to the conundrums of thought if only because they had no propositional content at all. Chosen from the mixed character of his life in nature and invested with authority, such moments sustained Thoreau against his failure to systematize ascent or settle upon a stable body of belief. The fragments of his 1849 conclusion tend to bear out such a reading, for their thrust is to extend these moments into the vision of an available life lying just ahead:

> I learned this by my experiments in the woods, of more value perhaps than all the rest – that if one will advance confidently in the direction of his dreams, and live that life which he has imagined – If he will walk the water, if he will step forth on to the clouds[,] if he will heartily embrace the true, if in his life he will transend [*sic*] the temporal – (He shall walk securely – perfect success shall attend him, there shall be the terra firma or the coelum firmior –). . . . He shall be translated – he shall know no interval[,] he shall be surrounded by new environments, new and more universal and libereal [*sic*] laws shall [*MS torn*] establish themselves around and within [him]. (*PJ* 3, 19; v. *W* 323–24)

Thoreau is writing prophetically of a life that surpasses the one he achieved at Walden. He had not, he knew, been "translated," and however he might have liked his readers to believe he had, he would not impose on them beyond assuming the prerogative of faith and taking his highest moments as an anticipation of the life he would presently come to enjoy. Meanwhile, in place of the blessedness he might have wished to present to Concord, he chose to symbolize his provisional triumph through the figure of a soaring hawk:

> It was the most etherial flight I had ever witnessed. It did not simply flutter like a butterfly, nor soar like the noblest hawks, but it sported with proud reliance in the fields of air; mounting again and again with its strange chuckle it repeated its free and beautiful fall, turning over and over like a kite. It was most high and lofty tumbling, as if it had never set its foot on terra-firma. It seemed to have no companion in the universe, – sporting there alone, – and to need none, but the morning and the ether with which it played. It seemed not lonely, but made all the earth lonely beneath it, though it had no mate in the world. Where was the parent that hatched it, its kindred, and its father in the heavens? The tenant of the air, it seemed related to earth but by an egg hatched in the crevice of a crag, – or was its native nest made in the angle of a cloud, woven of the rainbow's trimmings and the sunset sky, and lined with some sort haze caught up from earth? (Sh 206–7; v. *W* 316–17)

Earth-born (perhaps) but inhabiting the lofty space just beneath heaven, the hawk soars as if toward a ceiling, then tumbles downward just as Thoreau does after each of his thwarted ascents. Far from a defeat, however, its tumbling is depicted as a joyously *willed* and creative act, its alternate soaring and tumbling more exalted than anything else in nature.[83] The hawk is solitary, but its noble self-sufficiency makes the communal world below look "lonely." And though the hawk requires no audience as Thoreau does, it performs for the admiration rather than the instruction of those who do observe it; it has no "errand to mankind," sounds no call to awaken its earthbound neighbors. Nor does it chafe at the upper boundary that seems to constrain its flight. In place of the reformist intent on which he had predicated *Walden* and the drive toward self-transcendence with which he developed it, Thoreau has settled, of necessity, for an idealized rendering of his aspirations and checks as a magnificent oscillating cycle of ascents and falls. "I do not love to entertain doubts & questions" (*PJ* 3, 97), he remarked in 1851; two years earlier, with his life and literary career still, as it seemed, on the rise, there was no compelling reason that he should. The problems he had stumbled against in *Walden,* though disquieting, had nothing as yet of the final or the tragic. And until some new surge of growth should lift him beyond all complications to the life he glimpsed ahead, he seems to have been content, like the hawk, to soar and to tumble – and to wait.

5

Interregnum (1849–1852)

We yearn to see the *Mts* daily – as the Israelites yearned for the Promised land – & we daily live the fate of Moses who only looked into the Promised land from Pisgah before he died.

Thoreau (*PJ* 4, 77)

I

Between Thoreau's completion of the 1849 *Walden* and his return to the manuscript early in 1852, his life underwent a series of outward and inward changes that would seriously affect the emphases of his book. Published at his own expense, *A Week* had sold poorly, leaving Thoreau in debt and forcing him "to confront more directly than before the stark reality that, after nearly a decade of writing for various magazines, lecturing, and publishing a book, he was unlikely to be even moderately remunerated for his work."[1] The family pencil business, prospering now (thanks partly to Thoreau's innovations), provided one source of income, his increasing skill and initiative as a surveyor, another. The debts were a burden that would gradually be lifted; the experience of failure, and concomitantly of humiliation, pressed more heavily, with no end in sight.

Walden's most caustic remarks on trade date largely from this period, as does its parable of the Indian basket-maker, adapted from an anecdote Thoreau heard in 1850 (*PJ* 3, 130–31). The story has such a ring of metaphoric truth ("instead of studying how to make it worth men's while to buy my baskets, I studied rather how to avoid the necessity of selling them" [*W* 19]) that it has generally been taken as literally true. In fact, as Steven Fink has shown, "it was in 1852, just when he was adding the Indian basket anecdote to *Walden,* that Thoreau escalated his assault on the literary marketplace, making a more concerted effort to sell his wares than he had since the publication of *A Week.*"[2] Thoreau's actual relation to his readership was more ambivalent, for while "he could never again [after 1849] be so innocently hopeful in his expectations of the public,"[3] neither was he ready to renounce a popular audience entirely. Money was welcome, of course, if only to pay off publisher Munroe, but its deeper value to Thoreau was as a sign of attention; a lyric poet may soliloquize in private, but a moralist needs the ear of an audience. Thoreau had reason to take pleasure in the success of his January 1850 lectures on Cape Cod, which Emerson reported had his townsmen laughing "till they cried."[4] But he would have rejoiced still further if his personal manifesto "Walking" had been well-received, as he rightly anticipated it would not. He knew what a lyceum audience would applaud and, after 1849, what a popular readership would applaud, and though he was willing to court an audience in his travel writing (while still having his say and rejecting all editorial interference), his attitude toward the public, as Fink observes, "became ever more recalcitrant and uncompromising."[5] An index of his stance of indifference – "stance" because, like his attitude toward friendship, it masks a deep need for approval – is the degree to which he came to regard the artist as one whose work is "all in all" to him, and who rises "above the dread of criticism & the appetite of praise" alike (PJ 4, 107). "Society – Man – has no prize to offer me that can tempt me – not one" (PJ 4, 487), he wrote in 1852, as much perhaps in self-reassurance as in contempt.

Social and economic developments in and around Concord also led Thoreau to relocate the writer's satisfactions inwardly. While his hopes of converting his townsmen had never been very literal or very strong, they were nonetheless the enabling premise that generated and substantially controlled Walden's rhetoric. A faith in reform was near-ubiquitous among New England intellectuals in the early to mid-1840s, "an unquiet period," as Hawthorne wrote, "when mankind [was] seeking to cast off the whole tissue of ancient custom, like a tattered garment."[6] In this respect the seven years between the journal beginnings of Walden in 1845 and Thoreau's resumption of it in 1852 were critical, for they coincided with a watershed in regional socioeconomic history that left the reformist foundation of his book more doubtful than ever.[7] In A Week Thoreau had described the effect of the dams, factories, mills, and, especially, the railroad in transforming New England life between his river journey of 1839 and his walking tour of the area nine years later. The 1849 Walden makes passing reference to these changes, but its bucolic tone is only briefly interrupted by the intrusion of the railroad, in early drafts a kind of sooty miles gloriosus more than a harbinger of uprooted ways. The notion of society regulating itself by railroad time and submitting to "an Atropos" (or fate) it created but could not control enters Walden in 1852, when years of watchful co-existence with the railroad had shown Thoreau its effect in "unsettl[ing] the farmers" and fixing their attention restlessly on the great world (PJ 4, 108). From a provincial market town, Concord increasingly became a "suburb" of Boston, and its "most modern, innovative farmers quickly turned to selling milk, fine fruits, and garden vegetables to the city,"[8] while others, living farther from the depots, found themselves or their children unwilling to remain on the farm at all (PJ 4, 295). "By means of railroads and steamboats and telegraphs," Thoreau observed early in 1854, "the country is denaturized – farmer becomes a market capitalist" (*J* VI, 108). Even Thoreau himself was briefly sucked into the vortex; the late addition to "Economy" that culminates in the phrase "trade curses everything it handles" (*W* 70) recounts his own aborted plan to pick and sell wild huckleberries, for which he did extended penance down through the late manuscript "Huckleberries" (v. *NHE* 247–51). Thoreau's attachment to vanishing ways – to "the quiet retired old-fashioned country-farmer's life," as he called it in 1851 (*PJ* 4, 108) – is more wistful than sincere, given his impatience with gnarly pastoralism wherever it still prevailed. Yet sleepy and narrow as it was, agrarian New England was at least a negotiable, humanly-scaled community in which Thoreau might assume a place, if only as local gadfly. The emerging world was no community at all but a riot of vast impersonal forces (those of the literary market included) in which a dissenting voice was not even met with disapproval because it went unheard.

In these terms industrialism was a personal threat to Thoreau. In early versions of the railroad passage in "Sounds" he could praise the "enterprise and bravery" of commerce (*W* 118) without considering how it contributed to a world of mechanization and bustle that outmoded his own work. By 1853–54 (draft F) his ambivalence toward the railroad has become outright hostility. Watching a cattle train pass, he laments the fate of the drovers displaced by progress, "on a level with their droves now, their vocation gone, but still clinging to their useless sticks as a badge of office" (*W* 122). "So is your pastoral life whirled past and away" (*W* 122), he adds, with a play on "pastoral" ("relating to the care of souls") that extends the image to the literary "drover" anachronistically prodding his sheep-like neighbors with the "useless sticks" (pens and pencils) of *his* office.[9] "But the bell rings, and I must get off the track and let the cars go by," Thoreau continues: ". . . I will not have my eyes put out and my ears spoiled by [the railroad's] smoke and steam and hissing" (*W* 122). "Getting off the track" means retreating to the solitude of the woods and leaving history to its precipitous course. As he enlarged "Economy" after 1851 Thoreau would return to set himself athwart society's tracks (or take a verbal crowbar to them) but more for the literary exhilaration it provided than from a genuine hope of effecting change; social reform is rarely a prominent theme in the newly begun sections of 1852–54. If, as Lawrence Buell observes, ante-bellum New England writing was marked "by a tension between the impulse to seize visionary authority and the awareness of the quixoticism of that desire,"[10] then the 1849 *Walden* may be said to share both tendencies almost equally while the 1852–54 additions are heavily weighted toward the second.

Thoreau's progressive disengagement from society had another, more inward source in the anguish of his personal relations. Large gatherings of any kind continued to discomfit him; "I begin to suspect that it is not necessary that we should see one another" (*PJ* 4, 185), he commented after an evening party of 1851, during which he was expected to converse with eligible young women. But the real crisis was in his friendships, particularly his friendship with Emerson – "a tragedy of more than 5 acts" (*PJ* 3, 29), he called it in 1849, unaware that much of the drama lay ahead. Emerson's postpublication criticisms of *A Week* especially stung Thoreau – less, perhaps, for their substance than for their aspect of betrayal, since Emerson had warmly praised the manuscript beforehand (*PJ* 3, 26).[11] Still more unsettling was the note of formality and condescension Thoreau felt in his successful, worldly friend (recently lionized in England), which balked any hope of intimacy and produced a humiliating "appearance of phlegm and stupidity" in Thoreau himself (*PJ* 4, 209). There was no dramatic estrangement, only a gradual distancing – and self-questioning – that seems to have become particularly acute during the winter and early spring of 1851–52 when Thoreau said or did (or neglected to say or do) something that prompted an accusation of "coldness" – over which Thoreau brooded, ironically, with the same sense of fatalism ("I am under an aweful necessity to be what I am" [*PJ* 4, 213]) that Emerson invoked in answering complaints of *his* coldness. Unable to "confess & explain" (*PJ* 4, 213), even while knowing himself largely in the wrong ("My friends I am aware how I have outraged you[,] how I have seemingly preferred hate to love – . . . sedulously concealed my love – & sooner or later expressed all and more than all my hate" [*PJ* 4, 213]), Thoreau could only remind himself "that inward & essential love may exist even under a superficial cold" (*PJ* 4, 233) while he watched his intimacy with Emerson languish in a succession of missed opportunities and cross-purposes.[12] Rather than abandon his friends (his relationshp with Channing also had difficulties), Thoreau chose to love them from afar, distinguishing his "*actual*" from his "*real* communications with individuals" and building a surrogate emotional world impervious to disappointments. "I *really* communicate with my friends, and congratulate myself & them on our relation – and rejoice in their presence & society – oftenest when they are personally absent," he wrote in 1851, finding a "remarkable gladness" in night thoughts about his friends even as he conceded that "such has never been my actual relation to any" (*PJ* 3, 210). As always, however, Thoreau took primary refuge in his relationship to nature, even to the point of making his social inhibitions a casualty of it. "If I am too cold for human friendship," he reflected in April 1852, "I trust I shall not soon be too cold for natural influences. It appears to be a law that you cannot have a deep sympathy with both man & nature. Those qualities which bring you near to the one estrange you from the other" (*PJ* 4, 435).

The combined effect of Thoreau's frustrations with his audience, his community, and his friends was to distance him from human affairs generally and weaken his consciousness of an "errand." His new orientation shows itself in the character of his expanded journal, which, as Sharon Cameron has said, "writes human beings virtually out of the picture and makes them literally marginal."[13] An entry of August 1851 sounds a waning note of regret for a Whitmanesque road not taken: "I sometimes reproach myself because I do not find anything attractive in certain more trivial employments of men – that I skip men so

commonly & their affairs – the professions and the trades – do not elevate them at
least in my thought and get some material for poetry out of them. . . . It is
narrow to be confined to woods & fields and grand aspects of nature only. – The
greatest & wisest will still be related to men. . . . I will try to enjoy them as
animals at least" (*PJ* 4, 10). He found he could not. Perambulating Concord's
boundaries the following month, he felt "inexpressibly begrimmed" [*sic*] by
"associating even with the *select* men of this and neighboring towns," and he
likened himself as poet-turned-surveyor to "Apollo serving King Admetus" (*PJ*
4, 85), a favorite image for his worldly condition in Concord. "The poet must
keep himself unstained and aloof," he remarked; "A fatal coarseness is the result
of mixing in the trivial affairs of men" (*PJ* 4, 85). "Trivial," indeed, became his
synonym in these years for virtually all the affairs of men, even for politics amid
the turbulent aftermath of the Fugitive Slave Law. In an entry of October 1851
he tells of lodging an escaped slave in the family household and helping him
"into the cars for Canada" (*PJ* 4, 112), but the incident sparks no comment and is
notable in the 1851–52 journals primarily for its anomalousness; it did not
belong to what he considered his essential life. "These processes [of politics,
society, and business] are *infra*-human," he complained in November: "I sometimes awake to a consciousness of these things going on about me . . . as a man
may become conscious of some of the processes of digestion – in a morbid state –
& so have the dyspepsia as it is called" (*PJ* 4, 174). The passion with which
Thoreau could occasionally come forward to battle against slavery (or, more
precisely, to battle his townsmen for their practical acquiescence to slavery) is all
the more remarkable for the impatience with which he regarded such moments
as a distraction from his main business. His "business," as always, was self-culture,
but now he conducted it (so he claimed) on "the heights of philosophy" from
which "mankind & the works of man will have sunk out of sight altogether" (*PJ*
4, 418):

> In order to avoid delusions I would fain let man go by & behold a universe in
> which man is but as a grain of sand. . . . What is the village – city – state –
> nation – aye the civilized world – that it should so concern a man? [the thought
> of them affects me in my wisest hours as when I pass a woodchuck's hole
> (interlined in ms.)] . . . Look at our literature what a poor puny social thing
> seeking sympathy – The author troubles himself about his readers – would fain
> have one before he dies. . . . I do not value any view of the universe into which
> man & the institutions of man enter very largely & absorb much of the
> attention – Man is but the place where I stand & the prospect (thence) hence is
> infinite. (*PJ* 4, 419–20, 780)

The mingling of the cosmically grand and the vocationally pettish is a sign of
how intimately Thoreau's new perspective is related to his frustrations as an
author, which is not to say he didn't believe or come to operate upon the ideas he
expressed. A note of grudgingness toward the reader sours his August 1851

journal introduction to the "Yankee in Canada" lectures he would deliver before the Concord Lyceum early the next year (Thoreau had added reasons for sourness in this case; he didn't enjoy his trip north and felt he had little to say about it). A more instructive measure of his withdrawal is the "genial misanthropy" that colors those portions of *Cape Cod* presented to the Concord Lyceum in January 1850 and submitted (with additions) to *Putnam's Magazine* in November 1852, though it would not see print until 1855, and even then incompletely. If *Cape Cod* is "Thoreau's sunniest, happiest book," full of "jokes, puns, tall tales, and genial good humor,"[14] as Walter Harding says, it is also his rainiest both literally (he and companion Channing are often drenched) and figuratively in its kinship with the "damp, drizzly November" of the soul that drove another jokester-misfit from society to the sea (*MD* 5). Its second chapter, "Stage-Coach Views," strikes an appreciatively Chaucerian tone as it describes "the pleasant equality which reigned among the stage company, and their broad and invulnerable good humor" (*CC* 18). As soon as the travelers reach the elbow of the Cape, however, they begin to avoid the towns, "where [Thoreau says] I am wont to feel unspeakably mean and disgraced" (*CC* 33). Trudging through sand barrens on the plains of Nauset, Thoreau fills the tedium with delightful humor on the sandy barrens of early New England history and theology. But the chronicles Thoreau consulted on his return can sustain him only so long, and between his powerful but intermittent evocations of the sea and his weary accounts of empty, featureless sandscape, only the colorful portrait of his night's host, the Wellfleet oysterman, intervenes to enliven the narrative. Hints of Sarah Orne Jewett's Dunnet's Landing appear in the salty human types on the margins of *Cape Cod,* and Thoreau seems belatedly aware of the social and literary opportunities he has let slip (*CC* 202–3). His portrait of the Cape has been "true so far as it goes," yet he "cannot say how its towns look in front" (*CC* 203), much less how their inhabitants live. It was nature (the ocean), not humanity, he journeyed to the Cape to see, just as it would be nature, not humanity, he would study on his return to Concord. The geniality Harding finds in *Cape Cod* is attributable in great part to the absence of social observation and therefore of the panoply of psychic defenses Thoreau's relation to society called into play. Shunning the towns, Thoreau finds his "spirits [rising] in proportion to the outward dreariness" of the scene (*CC* 32). So he would remark in another work of the period, "Walking" (post. 1862), developed from a lecture first given before the Concord Lyceum in April 1851: "My spirits infallibly rise in proportion to the outward dreariness. Give me the ocean, the desert, or the wilderness! . . . When I would recreate myself, I seek the darkest wood, the thickest and most interminable and, to the citizen, most dismal, swamp" (*EP* 228). In neither work is nature imagined as a "friend" to man; in both, however, solitude in nature frees Thoreau from the tangles of communal life and allows him to refocus, in his own word to re*create,* a diffused self.

The most crucial *human* source of encouragement for Thoreau during these

years – and an indirect influence upon his work – was his correspondence with
Harrison Gray Otis Blake, a former Unitarian minister who had resigned his
pulpit for reasons of conscience, and who in 1848 wrote Thoreau from his home
in Worcester, Massachusetts, praising him for "a depth of resources, a complete-
ness of renunciation, [and] a poise and repose in the universe, which to me is
almost inconceivable" (*Corr* 213). As Thoreau himself keenly understood,
Blake's testimony was the magic touch that gave the literary portrait "Thoreau"
actual life. "I am much indebted to you," he wrote Blake in 1853, "because you
look so steadily at the better side, or rather the true center of me . . . and as I have
elsewhere said 'Give me an opportunity to live.' You speak as if the image or idea
which I see were reflected from me to you, and I see it again reflected from you to
me . . . . Or perhaps what you see directly you refer to me. . . . The meanest
man may glitter with micacious particles to his fellow's eye" (*Corr* 298–99).
Earnest but unimaginative, Blake was no philosopher or poet, and Thoreau,
grateful as he was for his friend's admiration, never let it turn his head. A certain
self-irony marks his letters to Blake, as though, tempting as the prospect was, he
were reluctant to travel under the passport of his literary persona. The image of
mica (extended through ten lines in his letter) resonates subversively in its play
upon Emerson's figure in "Experience": "A man is like a bit of Labrador spar [a
rock with flecks of mica], which has no lustre as you turn it in your hand, until
you come to a particular angle; then it shows deep and beautiful colors. . . .
[T]he mastery of successful men consists in adroitly keeping themselves where
and when that turn shall be oftenest to be practised" (*CW* III, 33). Much of
Thoreau's writing had been an effort of this sort to keep his "better side" to the
light; Blake's letter was proof that the effort could succeed – and might succeed
again. "I rejoice to hear that you have attended so plainly to anything which I
have said heretofore, and have detected any truth in it," he told Blake in July
1852: "It encourages me to say more – not in this letter I fear – but in some book
which I may write one day" (*Corr* 285). By then, of course, Thoreau was once
more deeply engaged in *Walden,* whose imagined audience was no longer his
Concord neighbors (the subtitle "Addressed to My Townsmen" disappears in the
revisions of 1852–54)[15] but a group of ideal readers, modeled partly on Blake,
who were ready to honor him for his example of character irrespective of any
pretensions to social reform.

The outward center of Thoreau's new life was the recently acquired and
renovated family house on Main Street, whose large finished attic he made his
bedroom, study, and burgeoning natural history museum. The inward center was
his journal, expanded now into a regular and detailed account of his daily walks
and a barometer of the moods of his spirit. Settled in the very midst of Concord
and venturing forth afternoons to outlying fields and ponds, Thoreau fashioned a
life of alternating activity and thought – of "undulation" (*CW* I, 61), to borrow
the Emersonian term he had used years earlier when declining to buy the

Hollowell farm on the grounds that his "life must undulate still" (*PJ* 1, 291). Denied the vocation of remunerated author, Thoreau more than ever sought to make his life his vocation and to appear before Concord in the worthy garb of "saunterer," or spiritual pilgrim (*PJ* 3, 176).[16] "They who never go to the Holy Land in their walks, as they pretend, are indeed mere idlers and vagabonds," he explained, "but they who do go there are saunterers in the good sense, such as I mean" (*EP* 205). The lines are from "Walking," his public unveiling of this new persona of "Walker Errant," evolved from the spiritual picaro of "Baker Farm." In a community of mortgagees, the walker was the quintessentially free man, homeless "but equally at home everywhere," who has "paid [his] debts, and made [his] will, and settled all [his] affairs," and is now "ready for a walk" which has "nothing in it akin to taking exercise" but is a search for "the springs of life" (*EP* 206, 209) – a *private* search, for unlike the speaker of *Walden,* a representative man who brags for humanity, the walker belongs to an elect society not to be entered even through a studied apprenticeship: "It requires a direct dispensation from Heaven to become a walker. . . . *Ambulator nascitur, non fit*" (*EP* 207).

While outwardly speaking "a word for Nature, for absolute freedom and wildness" (*EP* 205), "Walking" is essentially about Thoreau's new life, and it mirrors the central uncertainty in that life: where is the walker going? Thoreau admits he doesn't know: "Unto a life which I will call natural I would gladly follow even a will-o'-the-wisp through bogs and sloughs unimaginable, but no moon nor firefly has shown me the causeway to it" (*EP* 242). Although the Holy Land appears to be terrestrial rather than supernal, Thoreau seems hesitant to say with Emily Dickinson, "So, instead of getting to Heaven, at last – / I'm going, all along" (#324). To be "rich enough to be journalized," he remarked early in 1852, "our life should be so active and progressive as to be a journey" (*PJ* 4, 297). Was his own life a "journey" (pilgrimage) or merely a "journal" (succession of days)? And more teasingly, was a "journal," intensely lived and recorded, tantamount to a "journey" even if it wasn't visibly "progressive"? To the first question Thoreau had no final answer; to the second he gave a self-accusatory "no." It was admirable to live in "the present moment; to toe that line" (*W* 17), as he had said in *Walden,* but only if "that line" was part of a spiritual teleology pointing him to heaven on earth. The "going" had to "get" him somewhere, and seemingly it was not. "From time to time I overlook the promised land," he wrote in July 1850, gauging his progress, "but I do not feel that I am travelling toward it" (*PJ* 3, 97). "Walking" ends with a show of optimism – "So we saunter toward the Holy Land, till one day the sun shall shine more brightly than ever he has done, shall perchance shine into our minds and hearts, and light up our whole lives with a great awakening light" (*EP* 247–48). The initiative, however, has quietly passed from the walker to forces outside him (the sun), and the goal of the walk has shifted from a happiness known and authenticated to a future happiness that is only a "perchance."

II

Coincidentally, the final sentence of "Walking" anticipates the final sentence of *The Great Gatsby:* "So we saunter toward the Holy Land . . ."; "So we beat on, boats against the current, borne back ceaselessly into the past."[17] Gatsby's "orgastic future" turns out to be the illusive projection of an irrecoverable past. "Walking" lacks Fitzgerald's poignant sense of human futility in the face of time and loss, but a deep nostalgia virtually governed Thoreau during the spring and summer of 1851. Nearing middle life (he turned thirty-four on July 12), he had reached the bittersweet Romantic peripety at which experience circles back upon the seeker and anticipations of the future give way to laments for the past. "Our most glorious experiences are a kind of regret," he wrote in May 1851: "Our regret is so sublime that we may mistake it for triumph. It is the painful plaintively sad surprise of our Genius remembering our past lives and contemplating what is possible" (*PJ* 3, 233). "Our past lives" has a double, Wordsworthian reference to youth and to the pre-existence of the soul, as it will throughout this season of retrospect when the Immortality Ode became the medium through which Thoreau viewed his life. "Ah, that life that I have known!" he sighed in June 1851, less than two months after celebrating his days in the lecture "The Wild" (the original of "Walking"): "I can sometimes recall to mind the quality[,] the immortality, of my youthful life – but in memory is the only relation to it" (*PJ* 3, 251–52). And in July:

> Methinks my present experience is nothing[,] my past experience is all in all. I think that no experience which I have today comes up to or is comparable with the experiences of my boyhood – And not only is this true – but as far back as I can remember I have unconsciously referred to the experiences of a previous state of existence. "Our life is a forgetting" &c
>
> Formerly methought nature developed as I developed and grew up with me. My life was extacy. In youth before I lost any of my senses – I can remember that I was all alive – and inhabited my body with inexpressible satisfaction. . . . This earth was the most glorious musical instrument, and I was audience to its strains. (*PJ* 3, 305–6)

The nostalgia of mid-1851 is singular in Thoreau, who, as Channing said, "was not of those who linger on the past."[18] Refusing to acquiesce to fate and time, Thoreau struggled to reverse the process of spiritual attrition by assiduously charting and recharting his inner life, by seizing on natural facts that seemed to illuminate the logic of growth, and eventually by working to methodize his days toward the goal of spiritual ascent. The problems of direction and means that had informed sections of the 1849 *Walden* assumed special urgency now as he sought to reorient himself within some enclosing myth of human development. In a curious, spiraled way, the exasperations of his life, together with his new sense of a falling off, reawakened many of his bewilderments from *A Week*. The key questions, once again, were whether paradise was to be enjoyed now or later, on earth or in heaven, and through the body or in suppression of it. "Are our serene moments mere foretastes of heaven[,] joys gratuitously vouchsafed to us as a consolation – or simply a transient realization of what might be the whole tenor of our lives?" (*PJ* 3, 274), he asked in June 1851, uncertain whether to ground his hopes for completion in the temporal world or look beyond it to the eternal.

The life of a plant provided Thoreau with a master analogy both in its successive stages of *"Vegetation"* and *"Fructification,"* or growth and (re)productive activity (*PJ* 3, 224–25), and in the character of its twofold development downward into the soil and upward toward the light, which suggested to a mind so disposed that the route to heaven was through earth (*PJ* 3, 225–27).[19] The cycle of the seasons, invoked in the 1849 *Walden* to confirm the prospect of renewal, was also fraught with meaning, though its application became endlessly problematic as Thoreau pondered it. Because he felt "almost wholly unexpanded," even "unborn" (*PJ* 3, 313), and at the same time superannuated, or in descent from the rapture of his youth, he could not decide whether he was in the early spring of his life awaiting the fruition of summer or in the summer of full manhood – "a season of withering," of "small fruits & trivial experiences" for plants and men alike (*PJ* 4, 62) – with his creative spring far behind him.[20] Still less could he judge whether the course of human development was realizable within the term of physical life. His own experience of thirty-four years seemed to indicate it was not: his "seasons revolve[d] more slowly than those of nature"; he was "differently timed" (*PJ* 3, 313). And "Is it important," he asked defensively,

> that I should mature as soon as an apple tree? Ye[a], as soon as an oak? May not my life in nature, in proportion as it is supernatural, be only the spring & infantile portion of my spirit's life[?] shall I turn my spring to summer? May I not sacrifice a hasty & petty completeness here – to entireness there? If my curve is large – why bend it to a smaller circle? My spirits unfolding observes not the pace of nature. The society which I was made for is not here, shall I then substitute for the anticipation of that this poor reality? I would [rather] have the unmixed expectation of that than this reality. If life is a waiting, so be it. I will not be shipwrecked on a vain reality. (*PJ* 3, 313)

In the end Thoreau waives the question of his proper sphere and falls back upon a cosmic trust: "He that made the demand in me will answer the demand" (*PJ* 3, 314). One possible answer was of the kind given by George Herbert (a favorite poet of Thoreau's) in presenting man's "repining restlessnesse" as the "pulley" that raised him beyond the world to God's breast.[21] Otherworldliness was an ever-available refuge for Thoreau, yet except in moments when all other resources seemed to fail, a life of "waiting" ran counter to his characteristic energy as well as to his need for a home in nature. Pressured to shape a myth that spoke reassuringly to his prospects, he resolved the ambiguities in his seasonal position by teasing out the botanical analogy until it yielded what he sought:

> Plants commonly soon cease to grow for the year unless they may have a fall
> growth – which is a kind of 2nd spring. In the feelings of the man too the year is
> already past & he looks forward to the coming winter. His occasional rejuvenes-
> cence & faith in the current time is like the aftermath of a scanty crop. The
> enterprise which he has not already undertaken – cannot be undertaken this
> year. The period of youth is past. . . . But there is an aftermath in early
> autumn – & some spring flowers bloom again – followed by an Indian summer
> of finer atmosphere & of a pensive beauty. May my life be not destitute of its
> Indian summer– A season of fine & clear mild weather when I may prolong my
> hunting before the winter comes. (*PJ* 4, 62–63)

Having found a confirmatory trope, Thoreau developed it with increasing
assurance, down to employing it as a cleaver to distinguish himself from others:
"most [men] have a spring growth only, and never get over [the] first check to
their youthful hopes; but plants of hardier constitution, or perchance planted in a
more genial soil, speedily recover themselves, and, though they bear the scar or
knot in remembrance of their disappointment, they push forward again and have
a vigorous fall growth which is the equivalent to a new spring" (*J* IV, 227–28).

As the means of encouraging this second growth, Thoreau wavered through
most of 1851 between immersing himself systematically in sense experience and
trying through abandonment to project himself beyond it. On one side, he began
to read widely in natural history, beginning with Stoever's life of Linnaeus, then
graduating to Linnaeus himself and other botanists.[22] His motives were twofold:
to school himself in the methods and vocabulary of the naturalist and to discover,
as Romantic philosophers frequently sought to do, whether knowledge, while
"initially analytic and divisive," might also, "in its higher manifestation, [be]
unifying and integrative."[23] On the other side, he devoted much of the late
spring and summer to taking long walks at night, especially by moonlight, hardly
the ideal medium for the naturalist's study. Emerson, too, had felt the enchant-
ment of moonlight, yet "agitated" as always "with curiosity to know the secret of
nature" (*JMN* V, 423), he had found "the sublime light of night . . . unsatisfying,
provoking[;] it astonishes but explains not" (*JMN* V, 496). For one stymied by the
opacity of natural facts, this was precisely its allure; "I think we fly to Beauty as an
asylum from the terrors of finite nature" (*JMN* VII, 9), he speculated. A suspicion
of such finiteness, terrible chiefly in its banality, contributed to making Thoreau
one of "those who travel in the night" (*PJ* 3, 283). In daylight "I see small objects
better," he acknowledged, "but it does not enlighten me any. The day is more
trivial" (*PJ* 3, 272). Still more disturbingly, he felt himself growing more trivial,
"the character of my knowledge . . . from year to year becoming more distinct &
scientific" (*PJ* 3, 380), he fretted in August 1851, even as he pursued his daytime
botanizing. The night walks of that summer were a compensatory effort to revive
the faculty of wonder in himself and recover at least a semblance of the spiritual
world he believed he had lost. As daylight induction comprised a forward path to
unity, a slow and difficult repossession of the world through accretive knowledge,

so moonlight reverie – greatly more for Thoreau than a Hawthornean site of imagination – signified a backward path, or a regression to preindividuated consciousness, the route of Freud's Thanatos. To walk at night was to wander spellbound through a realm evocative of "a long past season of which I dream" (*PJ* 3, 286). "I go forth to be reminded of a previous state of existence, if perchance any memento of it is to be met with hereabouts" (*PJ* 3, 303), he wrote of a moonlight walk taken on his thirty-fourth birthday. "Reminded," however, was as far as he was willing to carry the likeness: "That kind of life which sleeping we dream that we live awake – in our walks by night, we, waking, dream that we live, while our daily life appears as a dream" (*PJ* 4, 74–75). Night walks were a kind of mild hallucinogen ushering Thoreau, bodiless, into a world of beauty so intense as almost to border on the spiritual yet never so intoxicating as to cause him to mistake the play of light and shadow for the reality of grace.

An actual drug, ether, taken early in May during a dental operation to remove several teeth, brought Thoreau still closer to an intuition of another state:

> By taking the ether the other day I was convinced how far asunder a man could be separated from his senses. You are told that it will make you unconscious – but no one can imagine what it is to be unconscious – how far removed from the state of consciousness & all that we call "this world" until he has experienced it. The value of the experiment is that it does give you experience of an interval as between one life and another– A greater space than you ever travelled. you are a sane mind with out organs – groping for organs – which if it did not soon recover its old sense would get new ones– You expand like a seed in the ground. You exist in your roots – like a tree in the winter. If you have an inclination to travel take the ether – you go beyond the furthest star. (*PJ* 3, 218)

Joining two of his favorite images for growth, a seed in the ground and travel, Thoreau projects a development beyond the limit of physical life as the soul, deprived of sensible feelers, begins to put forth spiritual ones. A rehearsal of death, the unconsciousness wrought by the anesthesia seems to prefigure a passage between ontological states, the future one unimaginable in substance but infinitely alluring. Initiated four days after his taking the ether, Thoreau's moonlight walks of May through September seem efforts to reenter this transition world suggestive of pre- and post-existence, even (who knows?) to call forth strange new senses as darkness suppressed the old ones.

Along with his ambivalence toward natural history, Thoreau's night walks are a symptom of his fractured vision during what Lewis Leary called his "watershed year" of 1851.[24] By the end of the summer he had mostly exorcised his nostalgia and come to see the necessity, and incipiently the means, for reintegrating fact and spirit. His new ideal centered on what, borrowing Wordsworth's phrase, he called "natural piety" (*PJ* 3, 368),[25] an adjustment of his daily life to the progress of the seasons that would not only let him record nature's minute alterations but might serve as a spiritual regimen to focus his energies, check the waywardness of his moods, and confer something of the inexorability of nature's seasonal advance upon his inconstant development.[26] "Ah! if I could so live that there should be no desultory moment in all my life!," he exclaimed in mid-August:

> That in the trivial season, when small fruits are ripe my fruits might be ripe also[,] that I could watch [match?] nature always with my moods! That in each season when some part of nature especially flourishes – then a corresponding part of me may not fail to flourish. Ah, I would walk[,] I would sit and sleep with natural piety! (*PJ* 3, 368)

The very thought of such a state revives Thoreau like an infusion of grace, moving him to an immense gratitude for this "flood of life": "I thank you God. I do not deserve anything. I am unworthy of the least regard & yet I am made to rejoice. I am impure & worthless – & yet the world is gilded for my delight" (*PJ* 3, 368–69). An Edwardsean Calvinist might hardly have expressed himself otherwise. Thoreau, however, is as much the dispenser as the recipient of divine favor, his own resurgent optimism having forged a new channel to the waters of life. "It seems to me that I am more rewarded for my expectations than for anything I do or can do" (*PJ* 3, 369), he adds, giving a special turn to the Protestant "justification by faith." Some new idea (in this case, the seasonal analogy) gives Thoreau cause for hope; on the basis of hope he begins again to aspire; and by aspiring he rekindles dormant spiritual energies that transfigure the outward world and enable, for a time, the life he aspires to. Where the Calvinist and his secular descendant, the visionary Romantic, are dependent on what Emerson called "more or less of vital force supplied from the Eternal" (*CW* III, 40), Thoreau is spiritually a self-starter able to think or write himself into renewal so long as he has the glimmering of an interest or idea to prompt him.

A long journal entry of September 7 suggests the resolution to which four months of brooding on his growth had led him. Indian summer has already begun ("The larches in the front yards – both Scotch & American have turned red. Their fall has come" [*PJ* 4, 50]), and Thoreau feels in himself an almost sexual "fulness of life, which does not find any channels to flow into" (*PJ* 4, 50). (Like Emerson and Whitman, Thoreau associated spiritual vitality with high water: in Emerson, the welling up of an interior stream [*CW* II, 159–60]; in Whitman, the swell of a "flood-tide" ["Crossing Brooklyn Ferry"]; in Thoreau, the overflowing of a river dammed up at its sensual outlets.) Thoreau feels "uncommonly prepared for *some* literary work" but has no particular project in mind so long as it involves "force-ful expression" rather than "contemplation" (*PJ* 4, 50–51). His preference stems partly from his vigorous mood, partly from his sense that his days of vision are over and that his task as writer now and henceforth is to draw on their recollection as "the permanent paint pot" for his "brush" (*PJ* 4, 52). If the result "be not solid gold ['moments of inspiration' themselves] it is at least gold-leaf [art] which gilds the furniture of the mind" (*PJ* 4, 52). His memories are thus "like a pot of ether" (*PJ* 4, 52), an image rich with possibility: the memories share in the rarefied atmosphere of the upper regions (the ether); they are a literary cosmetic to add (quasi-)spirituality to his prose pictures; they are an inhalation to induce a kind of visionary consciousness that life itself presently cannot; and they are a balm to ease the pain of spiritual loss (an *an*aesthetic as well as the ground for an aesthetic).

But "the *Art of life!*" (*PJ* 4, 52), as Thoreau calls it, is more than an art of gilding the life of the past; it involves living joyously in the present, though any new life will obviously require a different basis, and have a different savor to it, than the old. "How to get the most life!" Thoreau exclaims – "How to extract its honey from the flower of the world. That is my every day business" (*PJ* 4, 53). Like Walter Pater later in the century, Thoreau wants "a life of constant and eager observation" lived at the fleeting microseasonal crux where the sweets of nature are most intensely to be found – in Pater's words, to "be present always at the focus where the greatest number of vital forces unite in their purest energy."[27] Where Pater, however, would dissolve the solidity of the world into a flux of aesthetic sensations, Thoreau would "probe" its "rich & fertile mystery" to discover "the divinity in Nature" (*PJ* 4, 54). The "beauty of the flower" (aesthetic perception) is the first allurement, "the honied thought any experience yields" (knowledge or truth) the second; but even the honey is only "a foretaste of the future fruit" (*PJ* 4, 53), which is an intuition of Spirit. "My profession is to be always on the alert to find God in nature," Thoreau announces, "– to know his lurking places. To attend all the oratorios – the operas in nature" (*PJ* 4, 55).

Yet what if this would-be discoverer of God is himself suffering through a dry season, as Thoreau was? What means exist to enliven the faculties when youthful enthusiasm has waned? One means may be sexual sublimation. "The mind," Thoreau speculates, "may perchance be persuaded to act – to energize – by the action and energy of the body. Any kind of liquid will fetch the pump" (*PJ* 4, 55). The body, that is, can prime the imagination so long as its vigor is not dissipated in other activities. "We all have our states of fullness & of emptiness," Thoreau reasons, "– but we overflow at different points," one person through "the sensual outlets," another through the heart or head, and "another perchance only through the higher part of his head or his poetic faculty– It depends on where each is tight & open. We can perchance thus direct our nutriment to those organs we specially use" (*PJ* 4, 55).

The question Thoreau is trying to answer in the September 7 entry is one he had put to himself two days earlier: "How shall a man continue his culture after manhood?" (*PJ* 4, 47). With its string of "perchances," sublimation alone is a marshy ground on which to rear a structure of ascent. The poetic energies that attend a pure life are indispensable, but they must be joined to a method that works upward form natural fact, not (as during his night walks) downward from a counterfeit of spiritual vision. This is the lesson Thoreau draws in November from watching a hawk (a favorite self-image) "soar[ing] so loftily & circl[ing] so steadily and apparently without effort"; it "has earned this power by faithfully crawling on the ground as a reptile in a former state of existence. You must creep before you can run – you must run before you can fly. Better one effective bound upward with elastic limbs from the valley – than a jumping from the mountain tops in the attempt to fly. . . . It is more important to a distinct vision that it be steady than that it be exalted" (*PJ* 4, 179). Thoreau's ideal, of course, was a vision both steady *and* exalted, yet troubled in these months by a sense of spiritual slippage, he was more concerned with stabilizing his experience as a basis for gradual ascent than with miraculously but transiently elevating it. Whatever claims he might make in "Walking" for the joys of the carefree saunterer, he felt beyond the point where he could link his progress to the random adventures of the day; he needed a rationale and the prospect of a direction for his life.

The program he began to sketch for himself by the fall of 1851 was catalyzed by his reading of J. J. Garth Wilkinson's *The Human Body and Its Connection to Man,* a Swedenborgian amalgam of spiritualism and science that addressed the issues occupying him that summer in terms unusually congenial to a writer fascinated with etymologies.[28] "Wilkinson's book to some extent realizes what I have dreamed of[,] a reeturn [*sic*] to the primitive analogical & derivative senses of words" (*PJ* 4, 46), he wrote on September 5 in a rare acknowledgment of a literary or philosophical influence:

> His ability to trace analogies often leads him to a truer word than more remarkable writers have found. . . . The man of science discovers no world for the mind of man with all its faculties to inhabit– Wilkinson finds a *home* for the imagination – & it is no longer out cast and homeless. All perception of truth is the detection of an analogy. – we reason from our hands to our head. (*PJ* 4, 46)

The special importance of Wilkinson's book for Thoreau was to define the relationship between word, fact, and idea (the core of Transcendental epistemology) left unsettled in *Walden* when Thoreau proclaimed a "universe constantly and obediently answer[ing] to our conceptions" (*W* 97). In *Nature* Emerson had posited a preexisting harmony of matter, language, and spirit that imbued experience with built-in correspondences and rendered man "an analogist" (*CW* I, 19) by the very logic of his situation. Thoreau absorbed the idea in the 1840s long after Emerson had strategically abandoned it, but the notion of the world as penetrable symbol that gave the early *Walden* its working metaphysics had faltered before his perception of (and instinctive preference for) a misty translucence that refused to yield up truths in the intellectually formulable way *Nature* promised. Wilkinson's analogism, as grasped by Thoreau, reaffirmed the presence of meaning in nature without binding the knower to a fixed Absolute; unlike Emersonianism, it also provided a method. One of the prime analogies traced by Wilkinson, Thoreau's editors note, was that "between physical and mental 'assimilation' of the external world," or between the body's ingestion and transformation of material nature and the mind's "'translation of nature into thought, and of matter into spirit'" (*PJ* 4, 527). This latter process, while taking its origin from sensible facts, operated more with the suggestiveness of symbol-ism than with the hard certainty of allegory. Truth was still an objective reality, but it was to be discovered chiefly by the disciplined imagination acting upon the results of careful study and extrapolating from physical to moral experience. With Wilkinson in mind, Thoreau could begin to synthesize the empirical and imaginative tendencies that divided him, and in a way that seemed to transcend both. "See not with the eye of science – which is barren – nor of youthful poetry which is impotent," he wrote in November 1851, already deep in his botanical studies: "But taste the world. & digest it" (*PJ* 4, 158).

Wilkinson should prominently be credited for what Stephen Adams and Donald Ross, Jr., misleadingly call "Thoreau's conversion to romanticism in 1851–52,"[29] which was not a conversion so much as a reformulation (George Hochfield's phrase "Transcendentalist empiricism"[30] is apt), and which lost its initial glow by the end of 1852. Although Thoreau never ceased to call himself a "transcendentalist," experience soon forced him to lower his expectations for analogical "truth," and thus to dilute his transcendentalism into an ever more nebulous creed he could profess while practically following other paths. The autumn of 1851, in any event, found him hopeful almost to the point of giddi-ness; "I feel blessed. I love my life" (*PJ* 4, 159), he exclaimed one especially delightful November day. Three or four weeks of surveying set him back for a time, but in mid-December he again expressed a wish "to dive into some deep stream of thoughtful & devoted life" (*PJ* 4, 201), and by January he was exhorting himself to "catch the pace of the seasons" (*PJ* 4, 244). Armed with this new analogism, he approached 1852 as a critical challenge to regain control of his development and counter "the inevitable march of time" he felt had eroded his early "gifts" (*PJ* 4, 281). "A mild spring day," he wrote in mid-March, always the true beginning of his year:

> . . . I go forth to make new demands on life. I wish to begin this summer well– to do something in it worthy of it & me– To transcend my daily routine – & that of my townsmen[,] to have my immortality now – that it be in the *quality* of my daily life. . . . May I attain to a youth never attained[.] I am eager to report the glory of the universe. – may I be worthy to do it– To have got through with human values so as not to be distracted from regarding divine values. It is reasonable that a man be something worthier at the end of the year than he was at the beginning. (*PJ* 4, 390)

Extending through more than 750 pages in the Torrey-Allen edition, the journals for 1852 show Thoreau developing considerable skill as a naturalist and natural history writer. Yet despite his memorandum of September 1851 – "Improve the opportunity to draw analogies" (*PJ* 4, 41) – few bridges from fact to truth appear in his accounts of his daily walks. What H. Daniel Peck describes as "the Journal's endlessly repeated use of the construction 'this reminds me of that'" is not, as Peck argues, an indication of "how deeply analogical Thoreau's imagination was"[31] but a sign of how urgently he was scanning nature to find encouraging tropes for his life. Observing "a young wood springing up" on a tract of burned-over land, he asks, "Shall man then despair? Is he not a sprout-land too after never so many searings & witherings?" (*PJ* 4, 68–69). Similarly, listening to the vibrations of the telegraph harp, he finds himself "reminded . . . with a certain pathetic moderation – of what finer & deeper stirrings [he] was susceptible"; he even fancies the harp moralizing to him, "'Bear in mind, Child – & never forget – that there are higher plains[,] infinitely higher plains of life than this thou art now travelling on. Know that the goal is distant & is upward and is worthy all your life's efforts to attain to" (*PJ* 4, 75, 76). All too frequently the word "reminded" in Thoreau prefaces the forcing of a known or sought-after lesson upon a docile natural fact.[32] Analogism as a method for discovering truth cannot be said to fail in the journal for the simple reason that Thoreau never concertedly tried to apply it. Perhaps he doubted its efficacy, or perhaps he intuited (Wilkinson notwithstanding) that "it [was] impossible for the same person to see things from the poet's point of view and that of the man of science" (*PJ* 4, 356), as he remarked in February 1852. If the latter, he had solid reasons for concern. Compared to the rich thoughtfulness of his 1851 journal, the entries after March 1852 coincident with his new empirical interests are marked by relatively few reflections of any sort, bearing out his July remark to Harrison Blake, "My life is almost altogether outward, all shell and no tender kernel" (*Corr* 284).

Images of loss, waning energies, wintriness, petrifaction, and spiritual descent increasingly dominate the stock-taking exercises that appear in the 1852 journal. "At a very early age," Thoreau wrote in January, "the mind of man – perhaps at the same time with his body, ceases to be elastic. His intellectual power becomes something defined – & limited. He does not think expansively as he would stretch himself in his growing days – What was flexible sap hardens into heart-wood and there is no further change" (*PJ* 4, 265–66). Later that month he bleakly prophesied that his "fertile & expanding seasons . . . shall be fewer & farther between" (*PJ* 4, 281). Even the coming of spring, outpacing his own internal thaw, gave cause for worry. "Perhaps we grow older & older till we no longer sympathize with the revolution of the seasons – & our winters never break up" (*PJ* 4, 403), he speculated in late March, a scant two weeks after setting forth "to make new demands on life." Nothing, after all, guaranteed that human life should renew itself annually with the perpetual youthfulness of nature. Like the wire of the telegraph harp that had "rusted and slackened" with age, "every poet's lyre," he reflected soberly, "loses its tension. It cannot bear the alternate contraction and expansion of the seasons" (*J* IV, 206). His goal for the year was to "be something worthier at [its] end . . . than he was at [its] beginning" (*PJ* 4, 390), but as he measured his progress in late June he found himself "less thought-ful" than he had been "last year at this time" (*J* IV, 144). Less inspired, too. "I came near awaking this morning," he wrote in July, as if this were an exceptional event: "I am older than last year; the mornings are further between; the days are fewer" (*J* IV, 198).

His descent, as he regarded it, was not simply a matter of diminishing spiritual powers but of strong and unanticipated physical drives. "What is peculiar in the life of a man," he wrote in 1850, "consists not in his obedience but his opposition to his instincts" (*PJ* 3, 97). In the early drafts of *Walden* "instincts" had been identified with the promptings of genius toward a higher life; now they come to signify the downward pull of the body as it arrays itself *against* genius. Save for moments in nature when he felt himself a perfectly tuned sensing mechanism, Thoreau looked on his body as, at best, as a kind of alien marionette joined awkwardly by dangling strings to his soul. Some parts of it seemed decidedly better connected than others. "I am struck with the difference between my feet and my hands," he remarked in December 1850: "My feet are much nearer to foreign or inanimate matter or nature than my hands, they are more brute, they are more like the earth they tread on – they are more clod-like & lumpish" (*PJ* 3, 163). As "inanimate matter," his body was "strange" and fearful to Thoreau, as he had written in "Ktaadn" (*MW* 71); his discovery of the early 1850s was that the marionette (all *too* animate) had imperatives of its own at war with the "purely" receptive functions the soul would assign it. Even as he sought to root himself empirically in earth in order to ascend (*PJ* 3, 226), Thoreau worried about an internal earthiness emanating from the grosser parts of his body, the "outlets" that needed to be "tight" if the life energies were to be rechanneled into an overflow of spirit (*PJ* 4, 55). His concern over lapses of diet and other ascetic regimens – the "higher laws" he had glimpsed in *Walden* but was now unaccountably slighting ("As we grow older we live more coarsely – we relax a little in our disciplines" [*PJ* 4, 46]) – dates from this period. So does his preoccupation with sexual purity. Weighing his obscurely hinted sins of thought or deed against the general human turpitude in sexual matters, he is unable to decide "in regard to purity . . . whether [he is] much worse or better than [his] acquaintances"; he is certain, in either case, that he is not as he ought to be (*PJ* 3, 212). At times he can speak ardently of the glories of "becoming pure" (*PJ* 3, 311); elsewhere, however, he is chagrined at his growing indifference to spiritual things and puzzled by the autonomy of the processes ruling him. "I exact less of myself," he complained in October 1851: "I am getting used to my meanness – getting to accept my low estate– O if I could be discontented with myself! If I could feel anguish at each descent!" (*PJ* 4, 141).

A struggle between aspiration and acquiescence, ascent and descent, marks the entire year 1852 during which Thoreau returned to the manuscript of *Walden* and composed a fourth and portions of a fifth draft (stages D and E), expanding "The Ponds" (D and E), recasting "Higher Laws" (primarily E), and beginning to enlarge the fall and winter chapters (E only) (Sh 73). As his dream of success and public vindication gave way before the reception of *A Week* and the pressing uncertainties of his spiritual growth, writing, formerly a medium for adjusting his relationship to the community, became an instrument in his determined effort to win through to a higher life. The drama of his private development absorbed him now to the near-exclusion of society and history, even (with his widening distance from Emerson) of friends. His journals, when not descriptive, were openly experimental in the manner of Puritan diaries: a temperature chart of hopes and anxieties recorded in the faith that a spiritual prognosis might be drawn from the short-term vacillations that kept him in limbo. His public performances ("The Wild" and *Walden,* especially) had a more prophetic aim: to winnow from the divergent strands of the journal – from the several directions his life *might* take, the various contexts in which it *could* be seen – the pattern most encouraging to his spiritual prospects.

When visions fade, orthodox religionists fall back on the framework of a theology to support their faith and preserve at least a semblance of their former intensity; Romantics like Thoreau must fashion their own interpretive structures or do without. "Mythologies," Thoreau called these talismanic fables of spiritual experience as he began to synthesize observation, memory, and desire in a gilded simulacrum of primary vision. "I . . . would fain set down something beside facts," he wrote in November 1851: "Facts should be only as the frame to my pictures – They should be material to the mythology I am writing. . . . Facts to tell who I am – and where I have been – or what I have thought" (*PJ* 4, 170). Most of all, facts to tell (in idealized form) where he was now and where he was heading. To paint mythological pictures was not simply to organize, understand, and vicariously relive his experience at the pond; it was to mold that experience into an active belief he might carry forward into the future, as though to inscribe a fable of growth and metamorphosis were to tip the balance in its favor. While Thoreau saw himself primarily as a maker now rather than as a seer, his crafting of a mythology was in the service of future seeing. As he defined his task in January 1852: "To set down such choice experiences that my own writings may inspire me. – and at last I may make wholes of parts" (*PJ* 4, 277). The "whole" he most urgently wanted to make was a whole self, an integrated life; writing a "whole" book was his means.[33] From a literary structure designed to engage and convert a philistine audience, Thoreau's rhetoric of ascent became in 1852 and 1853 a means for consolidating his drive toward self-transcendence against the downward tug of the body and the spiritual attrition of daily experience.

6

Defying Gravity (1852–1854)

A ball will bounce, but less and less. It's not
A light-hearted thing, resents its own resilience.
Falling is what it loves, and the earth falls
So in our hearts from brilliance,
Settles and is forgot.
It takes a sky-blue juggler with five red balls

To shake our gravity up. . . .

                      Richard Wilbur, "Juggler"[1]

I

With hindsight, it seems inevitable that Thoreau should have returned to *Walden*. It was not quite so inevitable to him, even in September 1851 when he cast about for a project suited to his impulse for "force-ful expression" (*PJ* 4, 51). By mid-January 1852 he did return to his manuscript (Sh 31), visiting the pond several times later that month and recording details he would use in his expansion of "The Ponds" in draft D (1852). And on January 22, in Medford, Massachusetts, he presented a lecture entitled "Life in the Woods at Walden" – "as refreshing a piece as the Lyceum will get from any lecturer going at present in New England," remarked a sympathetic Alcott, who apparently read or heard the lecture beforehand (*Log* 177). That same day Thoreau himself reflected on his Walden experience in a quite different spirit: "But Why I changed–? Why I left the woods. I do not think that I can tell. I have often wished myself back" (*PJ* 4, 275). And two days later: "Why did I not use my eyes when I stood on Pisgah? Now I hear those strains but seldom– My rhythmical mood does not endure. . . . Ah sweet ineffable reminiscences" (*PJ* 4, 281–82).

    "He talked a lot about the past," Nick Carraway says of Gatsby, "and I gathered that he wanted to recover something, some idea of himself," to "return to a certain starting place" and pick up his life again from there.[2] Without a more intimate chronology than the journals supply, there is no knowing whether

Thoreau's resumption of *Walden* early in 1852 was a consequence or a cause of his wistfulness. Did he, too, want to "recover something" and set about using his manuscript to do so, or, having recommenced *Walden* for other reasons, was he overcome (momentarily) by a sweet nostalgia? Both accounts probably have their truth, though not, I think, in equal measure. However he might lament a lost intensity, it was characteristic of Thoreau to look ahead, not behind; and though outwardly about the past, *Walden* was not, as he reworked it, a memorial to a departed life so much as a series of efforts to create a life to come.

Unlike drafts B and C of 1849, which expand the initial manuscript written at the pond without substantively changing it, the revisions of 1852–54 differ both from the 1849 *Walden* and, in subtle but important ways, from each other, though with considerable overlap. In draft D, for example, Thoreau elaborated his critique of getting and spending in "Economy," as he did at every stage of composition, but he also broke new ground in "The Ponds," which drafts E and F would develop with emphases peculiar to each of *those* stages. Sattelmeyer finds *Walden* the work of two Thoreaus, corresponding to its two phases of composition (1846–49 and 1852–54), with "an earlier self subsumed but still present, as it were, within the later."[3] I would divide the second period into identifiable substages and discriminate among three kinds of additions belonging to each: "dominant," "residual," and "emergent."[4] "Dominant" refers to the pattern of the seasons that governed Thoreau's sense of structure and proportion throughout the period; "residual," to the amplification of existing chapters according to their original spirit; and "emergent," to those new and unforeseen elements reflective of Thoreau's development that intruded upon and modified his book within the framework of its seasonal plan.[5] The sourcebook for any such reading is Clapper's genetic text, understood in light of the 1852–54 journals. *Walden* is a book not only marked by perceptible shifts and contradictions, but one for which the compositional and biographical evidence to interpret these dissonances is almost uniquely available.

"We fray into the future, rarely wrought / Save in the tapestries of afterthought,"[6] Richard Wilbur wrote. Even in its final, published version, *Walden* is never quite the harmonious "afterthought" of a fully controlled, fully conscious intention, in large part because Thoreau's development was so singularly "frayed" – not a steady, linear progress but a dynamic interplay of moods and tendencies, some advancing, some retreating, yet nearly all live enough to assert themselves at a given moment against the general tide of months and years. With some chapters ("Economy," for example), the act of revision called into play a side of Thoreau readily provoked even in the quietest psychic times. With other chapters ("Baker Farm," for one), revision could encourage the sympathetic reentry into a dormant or vestigial self. And with still other chapters (notably, "Spring"), revision might involve changes in an idea like self-renewal critical to Thoreau as a core belief yet plastic enough in its specific content as to allow for one or another configuration as present needs and convictions dictated. And because Thoreau was not a conceptual thinker with the thinker's need for clarity and coherence, he was never forced to reconcile the zigs and zags of his interior life or settle precisely what he believed. How he viewed the world and felt about himself at a given moment *was* what he believed, though this is not to say that for all its day-to-day tacking his journey lacks a discernible direction. What most concerns me in the second half of *Walden* are those emergent ideas that best signal this direction – that disrupt established structures of thought, generate new ones, and reflect interests and motifs inscribed in the journal or in contemporaneous writings like *Cape Cod*. To a great extent, the sequence of emergent themes in *Walden* loosely parallels the book's organization from its central triptych – "The Ponds," "Baker Farm," and "Higher Laws" (reworked chiefly in drafts D and E) – through the fall and winter chapters (drafts E and F) to the climactic sandbank passage in "Spring" (revised in F and G) and the "Conclusion" (added primarily in F). To read the second half of *Walden* section by section is thus, in a rough and much qualified way, to retrace the course of Thoreau's spiritual history as he wrote the book.

The main constant through all these revisions is Thoreau's commitment to the cycle of the seasons, adumbrated in the 1849 manuscript but now raised to prominence. More than simply a structural device, the seasonal pattern gives *Walden* its thematic plot, or in Northrop Frye's term its "mythos" – a defining narrative shape that allies it with the upward movement of comedy toward the triumph of the hero and social and psychological integration (Frye's "Mythos of Spring") rather than with the downward movement of tragedy toward defeat, social and psychological *dis*integration, and death (the "Mythos of Autumn").[7] Choosing to end *Walden* with spring is like choosing to end a novel with a happy and symbolically appropriate marriage; the difference is that Thoreau, unlike the novelist, had his ending in mind before he had his middle. As he enlarged his book in 1852–54, he incorporated elements of a spiritual journey still very much in progress, and whose destination seemed to him increasingly problematic. The seasonal pattern guaranteed him an aspect of victory, though what terms this foreordained "victory" might take were by no means certain. In the more than two years he spent expanding and revising *Walden,* Thoreau sought grounds for self- and cosmic affirmation in a variety of experiential stances, none of them entirely successful yet none definitively negative or capable of blighting his constitutional hopefulness. Moments of nostalgia notwithstanding, Thoreau's temporal "country" was the present-bordering-on-the-future, and this was always green. "Regard not your past failures nor successes," he counseled himself in 1850: "all the past is equally a failure & a success[;] it is a success in as much as it offers you the present opportunity" (*PJ* 3, 95). Any "opportunity," of course, had to be actualized in a way of life; it exacted commitments, required a set of practical beliefs, and so was forever subject to betrayal from within or refutation from without. But the closing of one opportunity was typically followed for Thoreau by the opening of another. Within its framework of a seasonally assured renewal, the second half of *Walden* as written or revised in 1852–54 is the record of Thoreau generating provisional structures of belief in response to the opportunities life successively extended – and, with equal regularity, successively foreclosed.

II

The most distinctive element to enter *Walden* in stage D (revised, 1852) is the speaker's stance toward nature, his audience, and himself, signaled quietly by Thoreau's additions to "The Ponds." In place of the metaphysical explorer undertaking "to drive life into a corner" and announce his discoveries to the world, "The Ponds" offers a more chastened figure poised physically and spiritually between the purity of nature and the impurity of the human world, to which he, too, belongs. Building on casual Edenic allusion in his initial draft, Thoreau begins to portray the pond mythologically as the fount of life and the springboard to a new life; the spring-fed pond is "a perennial spring" (*W* 175), a constant "joy and happiness to itself and its Maker, ay, and it *may* be to me" (*W* 193). The italicized *may* indicates the change in the speaker's position: standing outside or beneath pristine nature, he is now a petitioner for its grace rather than the continuous and assured recipient he had been in the 1849 manuscript. He imagines the pond as " 'God's Drop' " (*W* 194) cleansing the railroadmen and passengers who rush by it, but his distance from these symbols of unredeemed humanity has narrowed appreciably. "How much more beautiful than *our* lives, how much more transparent than *our* characters," are White Pond and Walden (*W* 199; my emphasis), he exclaims in the closing paragraph of the chapter, which in draft D immediately followed " 'God's Drop.' " The note of sweeping contempt is atypical of the 1852–54 additions (save those in "Economy"), and it differs from Thoreau's attacks on civilization in the 1849 *Walden* in focusing not on materialism but on filth. In this respect, its target is not so much his townsmen or society at large as it is the entire physical basis of human life, which he brooded on in 1852 journal entries on "uncleanness" and in the squeamishly high-minded meditation "Chastity and Sensuality" he sent Harrison Blake as a nuptial present that September (*Corr* 288; *EEM* 274–78).

In enlarging his account of Walden Pond in draft D, Thoreau sketched a *tableau vivant* in which he was frozen in a posture of moral yearning without the means to activate the redemptive power of nature. In draft E the tableau comes to life, taking on the agency of a mediational process, and "The Ponds" begins to assume the focal position it will occupy in the published text as the ninth chapter of seventeen (omitting the "Conclusion"), the longest chapter next to "Economy," and the mythological fulcrum of a new rhetoric of ascent. In draft A Thoreau had described the strange experience of fishing in the pond at night when a "*faint* jerk" on the line would interrupt his "vast and cosmogonal" thoughts and recall him to nature: "It seemed as if I might next cast my line upward into the air – as well as downward into this element which was scarcely more dense" (Sh 187; *W* 175). Draft E expands the conceit in an announcement of the chapter's literary and philosophical method: "Thus I caught two fishes as it were with one hook" (*W* 175; Cl 491).

Angling downward to fact and upward to meaning is the essence of literary symbolism; the question throughout "The Ponds" is whether Thoreau intends his portrait of Walden to be "only" literary symbolism. Is he fashioning a work of metaphor with an oblique, nonreferential truth to experience or, concerned with writing as a site of discovery and prompted by the analogism of Wilkinson, is he indulging the hope that nature is intrinsically symbolic and literature its faithful decoding? "I thank God that he made this pond deep & pure – for a symbol" (*PJ* 4, 291; v. *W* 287), Thoreau remarked of Walden in a journal entry he later incorporated into his book – without the dash. In presuming that Thoreau is speaking figuratively (God made Walden deep and pure; the perceiver made it a symbol), we may underestimate not only the common Romantic impulse "to find God in nature" (*PJ* 4, 55) but the special Thoreauvian impulse to make deified nature an instrument for spiritual growth. Thoreau's own comments on symbolism are inconsistent. Sometimes he writes as the artist of metaphor his interpreters generally take him to be: "I . . . would fain set down something beside facts. Facts should only be as the frame to my pictures– They should be the material to the mythology which I am writing" (*PJ* 4, 170). Yet elsewhere (eight days earlier, in fact) he could speak as if truth-telling were a high artlessness demanding literal seeing and unadorned reporting: "A fact truly & absolutely stated is taken out of the region of commonsense and acquires a mythologic or universal significance. Say it & have done with it. Express it without expressing yourself" (*PJ* 4, 158). Here the artist is truest to his craft when he most abnegates himself before the inherent significance of things; nature itself is the mythologizer, the writer its devoted scribe.[8] Whenever possible, Thoreau preferred to imagine nature doing the fabling, for it confirmed his faith in a world instinct with meaning and warranted his efforts as its attentive student. When he assumed the stance of fabler himself it was either because nature seemed impenetrable to him *or* because he felt charged with a superabundant energy ("health," he called it) so delightfully fecund as to render questions of meaning inessential. Thoreau openly became a myth*maker,* that is to say, by first resort and by last resort, in creative joy or in epistemological skepticism. More often, he was a seeker who knew first and last resorts only as temporary extremes, and whose enduring aim was to uncover, not construct, the truths that bore upon his condition.[9] Reluctant to scrutinize his beliefs lest they dissolve under analysis, Thoreau never distinguished his roles as bestower and transcriber of nature's meaning. Nor was it unusual for him to oscillate between positions within a single journey entry; thus he could allude to "youth supply[ing] us with colors" to paint our pictures in the same passage that he reminded himself to "let

[his] report be colorless as it respects the hue of the reporter's mind – only let it have the colors of the thing reported" (*PJ* 4, 292). The entry dates from January 1852, when Thoreau had begun to revisit Walden to collect materials for his book and to find that facts could *almost* (but not quite) be allowed to speak for themselves. The qualities he ascribes to Walden Pond are rooted in literal truth, but they are developed in accordance with three redemptive actions he counts on nature to perform: purification, mediation, and instruction.

Purification. The signal characteristic of Walden Pond is its cleanness and inexhaustible power to cleanse. Bathing in Walden during his residence at the Old Manse, Hawthorne found its water so "transparent" as to seem scarcely distinguishable from air: "I threw sticks into it, and saw them float suspended on an almost invisible medium; it seemed as if the pure air was beneath them, as well as above. If I were to be baptized, it should be in this pond."[10] The facts that Hawthorne treats fancifully through simile, Thoreau composes to form a mythological picture that effaces the symbol-making intelligence and offers itself as unretouched truth. Ideas broached in draft D are elaborated, sharpened, and plumbed for meaning but with a seeming inadvertence, as if spiritual applications were an afterthought, a communication of nature's own self-declared meaning. Walden Pond, Thoreau observes in drafts E and F, is the topographical "centre" of its world (*W* 179), the pond of ponds with whose rise and fall the smaller local ponds "sympathize" (*W* 181), and thus the fitting symbol of Concord nature. The pond is "remarkable for its depth and purity" (*W* 175). "It is nowhere muddy" (*W* 178) and has virtually no weeds. Its few plants are "clean and bright like the element they grow in" (*W* 179). Its fish, too, "are much cleaner, handsomer, and firmer fleshed than those in the river and most other ponds" (*W* 184), and it is also home to "a clean race of frogs and tortoises" (*W* 184). The pond is "a mirror which no stone can crack" and whose "surface [is] ever fresh; – a mirror in which all impurity presented to it sinks, swept and dusted by the sun's hazy brush" (*W* 188).

Precisely rendered with a minimum of literary flourish, the details gather until they seem to point to moral realities and to invest nature with a redemptiveness that is not simply metaphoric but actual. The argument turns, as George Hochfield objects, on a sleight-of-hand pun between "'purity' of water and 'purity' of the moral life" that allows Thoreau to evade the question of nature's spiritual agency.[11] One might answer Hochfield with Lionel Trilling's comment on another "redemptive" body of water, the Mississippi in *Huckleberry Finn;* the river "is not ethical and good," Trilling allows, but it "seems to foster the goodness of those who love it and try to fit themselves to its ways."[12] "And to *write* of its ways," Thoreau might have added. "The Ponds" is not merely a paean to nature's purity; for Thoreau composing it in 1852–53, it is an act of self-purification in which the rhetorical celebration of a moral quality helps to call that quality into being.

There are cases, William James argued of "the will to believe," "where a fact cannot come at all unless a preliminary faith exists in its coming, . . . *where faith in a fact can help create the fact.*[13] Whether or not Thoreau's faith generated the settled conviction James had in mind, its expression in prose seems to have had an auto-intoxicating effect with important short-term consequences for feeling and behavior – and immense long-term consequences for literary style. "The possibility of my own improvement, that is to be cherished. As I regard myself so I am," Thoreau wrote in July 1851 on the "glorious condition" of "becoming pure" (*PJ* 3, 312, 311). Chastity (hard to sustain, Thoreau found) was one route to purity; literature was another. Just as to write heroically of the heroic Raleigh was to assume a degree of heroism oneself, so to write "purely" (plainly, unaffectedly) of nature's purity was to reconsecrate oneself to purification and enjoy an enormous upsurge of energy, even (temporarily) a change of being. The practical lesson Thoreau drew was "model your style upon nature's." As a "writer" herself, he observed, nature "never indulges in exclamations" but "uses few gestures – does not add to her verbs – uses few adverbs. uses no expletives. I find that I use many words for the sake of emphasis – which really add nothing to the force of my sentences – and they look relieved the moment I have cancelled these. Words by which I express my mood, my conviction, rather than the simple truth" (*PJ* 4, 291–92). The entry is from January 1852, the month of Thoreau's renewed visits to the pond, his lecture on life in the woods, and his resumption of the *Walden* manuscript. What Thoreau has discovered might be called the intoxication of sobriety, a conceit he later introduced in a draft F addition to "Higher Laws" (Cl 583; *W* 217). To be pure is to be "beautiful" and "transparent" like Walden Pond (*W* 199); to *become* pure is to apprentice oneself to Walden's ways, which, for a writer of prose, means removing "the speaker from his speech" (*PJ* 4, 294) and aiming at a higher simplicity. In its crystalline "purity" (scarcely any other word will do), the language of "The Ponds" is approached in the earlier *Walden* only by portions of "Solitude," which lack, nonetheless, the hard-won authority of fact. Much of the finest writing in the 1852–54 *Walden* (sections of "Brute Neighbors" and "The Pond in Winter," for example) will be in this new impersonal vein, in which "you behold a perfect work, but you do not behold the worker" (*PJ* 4, 294). Thoreau's journals of the period show him conscious of experimenting with a new style, which he regards as considerably more than a style. By suppressing his personality in the service of truth, Thoreau is trying to write himself *beyond* himself. And Walden's purity is at once his subject, his inspiration, his literary model, and his spiritual goal.

Mediation. One of the finest examples of Thoreau's style in "The Ponds" is his "colorless" description of the various colors of Walden's surface:

> All our Concord waters have two colors at least, one when viewed at a distance, and another, more proper, close at hand. The first depends more on the light, and follows the sky. In clear weather, in summer, they appear blue at a little distance, especially if agitated, and at a great distance all appear alike. In stormy weather they are sometimes of a dark slate color. The sea, however, is said to be

> blue one day and green another without any perceptible change in the atmo-
> sphere. I have seen our river, when, the landscape being covered with snow,
> both water and ice were almost as green as grass. Some consider blue "to be the
> color of pure water, whether liquid or solid." But, looking directly down into
> our waters from a boat, they are seen to be of very different colors. Walden is
> blue at one time and green at another, even from the same point of view. Lying
> between the earth and the heavens, it partakes of the color of both. (*W* 176)

Scrupulous in its citation of fact and weighing of opinion, Thoreau's account retains the reader's trust even as it begins to introduce complication, shade off into mystery, and ascend toward symbol. Like all waters viewed at a distance, Walden generally mirrors the color of the sky (fact). But reflection is not entirely responsible for water's hue; the sea, for example, may change from blue to green for no apparent atmospheric reason (puzzling counterfact). Nor can waters be said to borrow their color from the shore, for the Concord River may be green when the surrounding landscape is covered with snow (puzzling counterfact). Some maintain that blue is the genuine color of pure water (scientific or philo-sophical opinion). Yet a glance into the pond from a boat shows its water "to be of very different colors" (opinion tested and refuted by experience). "Walden is blue at one time and green at another, even from the same point of view" (mysterious but warranted conclusion). "Lying between the earth and the heavens, it partakes of the color of both" (conclusion rising to symbol with a verbal assist from the author: "heavens," not "sky").

The description of Walden's color belongs to Thoreau's larger effort to portray the pond qua nature as a point of conjunction between matter and spirit. Though co-planar with the earth, Walden is a "perfect forest mirror" (*W* 188) reflecting the sky (the distant divine), but it is also a tablet on which is inscribed the otherwise invisible writing of worlds beyond sense. In *Moby-Dick* (a foil to "The Ponds" in so many respects) Ahab finds "a most cunning, oh, a most malicious indifference" in the wind, which, like "all the things that most exasperate and outrage mortal man," is "bodiless" and elusive (*MD* 564). In *Walden* the incor-poreal manifests itself through nature, as "a field of water betrays the spirit that is in the air" (*W* 188) both literally as it ripples the surface of the pond and symbolically as its suggests the wind/spirit animating all creation and impressing itself on the alert senses. The image so closely parallels the Romantic aeolian harp that the absence of the analogy is itself notable. But "The Ponds" is and must be a chapter of the eye, not of the ear. To sense the ethereal music on the borders of perception is the privilege of the saint, not of the aspirant, whose journey toward spirit is guided by the more probationary discipline of sight. With his days of gratuitous joy mostly behind him, the Thoreau of 1852–53 is prepared to earn his *in*sights singly and by degree, working upward through observation and analogy according to his Wilkinsonian faith that natural facts can be harvested for their intimations of spirit.

Instruction. Levering oneself upward through nature's intermediacy meant ex-

ploiting the possibilities for growth contained in the metaphor of Walden as
"earth's eye; looking into which the beholder measures the depth of his own
nature" (W 186). "Measures" implies an index, as a child's growth might be
measured by pencilings on the kitchen wall, but the image also suggests an
Emersonian *process* in which a deeper penetration into nature unlocks depths in
the self: "Nature then becomes to [man] the measure of his attainments. So much
of nature as he is ignorant of, so much of his own mind does he not yet possess"
(CW I, 55). By 1852–53 Thoreau had grown skeptical of Emerson's "seal" and
"print" correspondences between nature and the mind (CW I, 55). Wilkinson
had shown him a more empirical and freely imaginative way of approaching
matter-spirit analogies, yet this too was predicated on a basic kindredness between nature and humanity. If the symbolic bottomlessness of Walden Pond
invites the seeker to plumb ever more deeply into nature, the image of "earth's
eye" assures him that the meanings nature yields will have a recognizably human
face. The pond has its "iris" (W 176), its "pulse" (W 178), its "lips . . . on which
no beard grows" (W 181); it "licks its chaps from time to time" (W 181–82).
Thoreau's "pure and deep green well" (W 175) is not the spirit-whelming
Melvillean ocean into which a host of water-gazers peer for hints of life's meaning (only to see their own image reflected back), nor is it Emily Dickinson's more
domestic but equally mysterious and terrifying "well":

> A neighbor from another world
> Residing in a jar
> Whose limit none have ever seen,
> But just his lid of glass –
> Like looking every time you please
> In an abyss's face! (#1400, ll. 3–8)

No human-visaged "eye" (its "lid" is of "glass"), Dickinson's well images
nature's alienness even to its would-be priests, who "know her less / The nearer
her they get" (ll. 23–24). Unfathomableness is also the mark of Robert Frost's
well in "For Once, Then, Something," in which the narcissism of admiring one's
idealized reflection is shattered by a rare and fleeting glimpse of "something"
("Truth? A pebble of quartz?") remotely visible in the water's depths.[14] Dickinson's nature is appalling, Frost's beckoning but elusive, and Melville's all of these
things as well as physically and spiritually perilous to those who chase after it. In a
counter-image to Thoreau peering into earth's eye, Ahab "lean[s] over the side
[of the *Pequod*], and watch[es] how his shadow in the water sank and sank to his
gaze, the more and the more that he strove to pierce the profundity" (MD 543).
Were he to lean farther – to insist on solving nature's mystery and his own – he
would plunge into the water and drown, as in fact he ultimately does.

Thoreau also worried about drowning in nature, though not in "The Ponds,"
which excludes any hint that water darkens and chills with depth and that the
inviting limpidness of nature might shade into annihilating mysteries. In this

respect the chapter seems a studied abridgment of his vision of the ocean in the contemporaneous *Cape Cod:*

> As we looked off, and saw the water growing darker and darker and deeper and deeper the farther we looked, till it was awful to consider, and it appeared to have no relation to the friendly land, either as shore or bottom, – of what use is a bottom if it is out of sight, if it is two or three miles from the surface, and you are to be drowned so long before you get to it, though it were made of the same stuff with your native soil? – over that ocean, where, as the Veda says, "there is nothing to give support, nothing to rest upon, nothing to cling to," I felt that I was a land animal. (*CC* 96)

What Thoreau wants from nature is a "usable bottomlessness" deep enough to be unsoundable by man yet ministrative in its tendency to draw out and elevate the soul. A three-mile bottom is like a mile-high mountaintop (Katahdin's) in its savage mockery of human sympathies, human cognition, and human scale. Thoreau came to know his boundaries and generally to respect them, sampling the sublime on trips to the Maine woods and Cape Cod but flourishing within the picturesque. Even at Walden, however, his requirements that nature purify, mediate, and instruct were challenged by a sense of nature's systemic violence. Observing a fish break the surface of the water to snare an insect, he writes in "The Ponds":

> It is wonderful with what elaborateness this simple fact is advertised, – this piscine murder will out, – and from my distant perch I distinguish the circling undulations when they are half a dozen rods in diameter. . . . It is a soothing employment, on one of those fine days in the fall when all the warmth of the sun is fully appreciated, to sit on a stump on such a height as this, overlooking the pond, and study the dimpling circles which are incessantly inscribed on its otherwise invisible surface amid the reflective skies and trees. . . . Not a fish can leap or an insect fall on the pond but it is reported in circling dimples, in lines of beauty, as it were the constant welling up of its fountain, the gentle pulsing of its life, the heaving of its breast. The thrills of joy and thrills of pain are un-distinguishable. How peaceful the phenomena of the lake! (*W* 187–88; v. *J* IV, 337)

Looking down on the pond from his hillside like a god on Olympus, Thoreau watches the struggle of life and calls it good (ecologically ordered, aesthetically pleasing) with no acknowledgment that he is equally subject to the round of nature, that the "thrills of pain" recorded in "circling dimples" may be human thrills. His "piscine murder" recalls the scene in *Moby-Dick* when Ahab, im-plored by Starbuck to renounce his hunt and half-beguiled by the serenity of the "smiling sky," is confirmed in his purpose by the sight of an albacore breaching the surface to "chase and fang" a flying fish, a reminder for him of the entire cannibalistic scheme of creation against which his quest is a protest (*MD* 545). As in *Walden,* nature in *Moby-Dick* betrays itself most visibly in the interface between air and water – for Melville, not so much in the plane of the surface itself as in the contrast between surface and depth, "seems" and "is," "the tranquil beauty and brilliancy of the ocean's skin" as "gilded" by the sun and "the tiger heart that pants beneath it" (*MD* 491). "The Ponds" also presents nature as a "gilder," but rather than a deceptive tinging of the base metal of creation, the image suggests nature's capacity to absorb disruption and repair its placid, mirror-like surface. Thoreau marks nature's cannibalism as keenly as Ahab does, but from his physical and metaphysical vantage point above the scene of pain, the disturbance quickly dissolves itself into "lines of beauty" testifying to creation's essential innocence.

Here, too, *Cape Cod* suggests a darker view of nature; indeed, written at nearly the same time, *Cape Cod* and "The Ponds" seem designed almost as a diptych. "The ocean is but a larger lake," Thoreau observes in the second of two long meditations on the sea: "At midsummer you may sometimes see a strip of glassy smoothness . . . as if the surface there were covered with a thin pellicle of oil, just as on a country pond" (*CC* 98). The picture is idyllic until Thoreau quotes the explanation of the oily patches given by a local fisherman to Daniel Webster: " 'He said they were caused by the blue-fish chopping up their prey. That is to say, those voracious fellows get into a school of menhaden, which are too large to swallow whole, and they bite them into pieces to suit their tastes. And the oil from this butchery, rising to the surface, makes the "slick" ' " (*CC* 98). Writ large in oily slaughter and viewed from the horizon rather than from above, piscine murder seems harder to accommodate to nature's beneficence. If the ocean "is but a larger lake," moreover, a lake – so peaceful on its surface – is only a miniature of the savage ocean. Thoreau doesn't pursue the thought, but neither is he hesitant to give seaside nature its due. His ocean is fully as treacherous as Melville's – "as civil now as a city's harbor, a place for ships and commerce," he writes, but liable "erelong [to] be lashed into sudden fury, . . . ruthlessly heav[ing] these vessels to and fro, break[ing] them in pieces in its sandy or stony jaws, and deliver[ing] their crews to sea-monsters. It will play with them like sea-weed, distend them like dead frogs, and carry them about, now high, now low, to show to the fishes, giving them a nibble. This gentle Ocean will toss and tear the rag of a man's body like the father of mad bulls, and his relatives may be seen seeking the remnants for weeks along the strand" (*CC* 98). Thoreau's words have the weight of testimony, for he had recently come from two encounters with broken ships and torn bodies – the second in July 1850 when he went to Fire Island to search for the "relics" of Margaret Fuller (*CC* 84), the first, recounted in the opening chapter of *Cape Cod,* in October 1849 when he came on the grisly remains of the emigrant-laden brig *St. John* that had foundered off Cohasset beach two days earlier. "On the whole," he remarks,

> it was not so impressive a scene as I might have expected. If I had found one body cast upon the beach in some lonely place, it would have affected me more. I sympathized rather with the winds and waves, as if to toss and mangle these poor human bodies was the order of the day. If this was the law of Nature, why waste any time in awe or pity? (*CC* 9)

Robert Lowell thought highly enough of "The Shipwreck" to versify lines from it in "The Quaker Graveyard in Nantucket," his elegy for his cousin "Warren Winslow, Dead at Sea." Elegies move from grief to acceptance, even to affirmation, but seldom do they wholly stifle the note of existential protest that arises from their mortal occasion. "The Shipwreck" is nearer to an anti-elegy, extraordinary in how little it feels for the victims, how readily it assumes nature's side in what is not even acknowledged as a human tragedy. In Wordsworth's "Elegiac Stanzas" the memory of his brother's death by shipwreck leads the poet to renounce his youthful faith in nature's benevolence and shift the locus of his moral life to the human community. "The Shipwreck" takes the opposite course. "Why care for these dead bodies?" Thoreau asks, nominally on the grounds that their "owners" were "cast upon some shore yet further west" in "a newer world than Columbus ever dreamed of" (CC 10). But Thoreau has no real interest in the victims' destination; his subject is the self-restorative power of nature, which absorbs the human carnage as easily as Walden had absorbed the piscine murder. Fitting his moral life to nature's, Thoreau takes a grim satisfaction in eschewing the hackneyed impulses toward lamentation, pity, and metaphysical questioning he expects his tender-minded readers to share (the Cape Cod essays were submitted to *Putnam's Magazine,* a good but middlebrow publication). And to prove himself right in his stoicism, he mentions a later visit to the scene, when, with a capsized vessel in sight to remind him of the *St. John,* he finds "the sea-bathing at Cohasset Rocks . . . perfect," the "water purer and more transparent than any I had ever seen" (CC 13). Nature's gilding is shown to operate on the grand scale of the ocean no less than on the diminutive one of a pond, and with time the drowning of a boatload of emigrants is assimilated as completely to nature's calm as the devouring of an insect on Walden. Thoreau compounds the irony by noting in conclusion that the stretch of shore on which he saw the wreck "is called Pleasant Cove" (CC 20). "The ocean did not look, now, as if any were ever shipwrecked in it," he adds: "it was . . . beautiful as a lake. Not a vestige of a wreck was visible, nor could I believe that the bones of many a ship-wrecked man were buried in that pure sand" (CC 14; v. PJ 3, 337).

Roughly contemporaneous with drafts D and E of *Walden,* "The Shipwreck" magnifies the violence of "The Ponds" in a way that reveals the immense human cost of Thoreau's identification with natural process. The premise of his analogism was that a careful study of nature might disclose moral truth, the end of all his investigations. "Nature must be viewed humanly to be viewed at all," he stated flatly in June 1852: "that is, her scenes must be associated with humane affections. . . . A lover of Nature is preëminently a lover of man" (JIV, 163). And yet the character of nature as Thoreau encountered it atop Katahdin, by the sea, and even on the smooth surface of Walden Pond demanded an affirmation that could be made only by a sacrifice of human reference. In "Solitude" Thoreau had been caught between his wish to befriend nature and his awareness of its vast impersonality; "The Shipwreck" and (mutedly) "The Ponds" bring the matter to a head, but now Thoreau's need is not for a "companionable" nature so much as for a pure and purifying one, however alien its purity might to the human, and however distant from the ethical.

III

Directly or indirectly, Thoreau's effort to purify himself and so to reverse the downward tendency of his life lies beneath much of what he wrote in 1852–53 from the descriptive Cape Cod essays to what I would call the "purity triptych" at the center of *Walden:* "The Ponds," the retouched "Baker Farm," and the enlarged and altered "Higher Laws," in all of which humanity in its physical grossness is a contagion Thoreau desperately needs to avoid. Even in the relatively genial *Cape Cod,* skirting the towns is as much a moral choice as a traveler's expedient or a confession of social uneasiness.[15] "The towns need to be ventilated," Thoreau proclaims, leaving behind him "for a season the bar-rooms of Massachusetts, where the full-grown are not weaned from savage and filthy habits, – still sucking a cigar" (*CC* 32). Against this human uncleanness, embodied all too bodily by his corpulent host for a night, the tobacco-spitting Wellfleet oysterman, the "desert" of the Cape was an oasis of sorts, "beautiful" in all aspects and weathers, "so white and pure and level" (*CC* 50–51). A similar opposition between the human and the natural, raised exponentially in pitch, governs the later sections of "The Ponds," which begin in exasperation at the name "Flint's Pond" ("What right had the unclean and stupid farmer, whose farm abutted on this sky-water, whose shores he has ruthlessly laid bare, to give his name to it?" [*W* 195]) and build toward the climactic repudiation of the human, "Talk of heaven! ye disgrace earth" (*W* 200). "A model farm!" Thoreau snorts a few paragraphs earlier,

> where the house stands like a fungus in a muck-heap, chambers for men, horses, oxen, swine, cleansed and uncleansed, all contiguous to one another! Stocked with men! A great grease-spot, redolent of manures and buttermilk! Under a high state of cultivation, being manured with the hearts and brains of men! As if you were to raise your potatoes in the church-yard! Such is a model farm. (*W* 196–97)

Language like this qualifies as what Northrop Frye calls "tantrum prose,"[16] and it is all the more obtrusive for being followed soon after by one of the most lyrical passages in *Walden,* the shrines-and-temples introduction to "Baker Farm" added in stage E. Though occasioned by Thoreau's outrage at "Flint's Pond," the diatribe is aimed, not at man's violation of nature, but at the inherent corruption, the human and animal "muck," of even the best-run farm. Thoreau is beyond any thought of his townsman audience or any judgment of literary appropriateness; he is furious. Among the seven deadly sins, Mary Gordon notes, "only anger is connected in the common tongue to its twinned, entwined virtue:

justice. 'Just anger,' we say."[17] Along with Mark Twain, Thoreau is our nineteenth-century virtuoso of anger, from the novice 1838 lecture on society to the 1859 "A Plea for Captain John Brown." "Economy" makes a high art of controlled, sublimated, keenly penetrating, and largely just anger. The "model farm" passage is *un*just anger – an anger of the curled lip, painful to read not only for its eruptive disgust, but for its hints of art turned to neurotic purposes, of social commentary run amuck. Its excessiveness is precisely the source of its purgative value to Thoreau; for just as in writing purely of purity he works himself into a cleansed frame of mind, so in writing indignantly of human filth he casts out the offending part of his nature. This is the significance of his closing pronoun in the chapter: "Talk of heaven! *ye* disgrace earth" (*W* 200; my emphasis). Within Thoreau's new rhetoric of ascent – a structure designed to foster and record his *own,* not the reader's, self-transcendence – "The Ponds" is a springboard not simply because Walden is a "perennial spring" (or source of renewal) but because its purity inspires a loathing for impurity that Thoreau can brace himself against as he springs upward toward a higher life.

"Baker Farm," as revised, is his self-canonization as a worldly saint, "Higher Laws" his would-be leavetaking of the world. Of all the sections in the 1849 manuscript, "Baker Farm" received fewest enlargements or changes, fitting more aptly into Thoreau's new scheme of personal metamorphosis than it had into his old one of nominal reform. In this respect, "Baker Farm" is a prime illustration of how previously written material comes to have enriching, modifying, and occasionally subverting implications as it is recontextualized by later additions. For example, the contrast between narrator Thoreau's propertyless freedom and bog-trotter John Field's squalor takes on new resonance from the purity–impurity sections of "The Ponds." Thoreau's early focus had been on materialism, the mortgaged life, and sailing by "dead reckoning" as set against celestial navigation; this interest remains, but his concern with moral and physical cleanliness in "The Ponds" serves to bring forward the latent pun in "bog," "bog-trotter," and "bogged down," which plays upon the nineteenth-century slang for excrement.[18] At the other extreme, the rainbow that appears over the narrator's shoulder as he leaves John Field's hut assumes a heightened spirituality from its association with the rainbow of the chapter's preface, added largely during stage E. In the 1849 manuscript, the rainbow connoted heaven's approval of the narrator's life of footloose adventuring; the expanded text raises the stakes by evoking a state of wonder bordering on grace: "Once it chanced that I stood in the very abutment of a rainbow's arch, which filled the lower stratum of the atmosphere, tinging the grass and leaves around, and dazzling me as if I looked through colored crystal. It was a lake of rainbow light, in which, for a short while, I lived like a dolphin" (*W* 202).

Imagery of natural religion dominates the 1852–53 frame to "Baker Farm" and subtly redirects the character and site of blessedness from carefree wandering to spiritual transfiguration. Within Thoreau's now private rhetoric of ascent, the chapter occupies a mid position between the moral cleansing of "The Ponds" and what promises to be the spiritual apotheosis of "Higher Laws." Yet even as Thoreau begins to portray a more exalted condition, he presents it as something behind him, not ahead. Living in a "lake of rainbow light" is the experience of an unspecified, receding "once"; "if it had lasted longer it might have tinged my employments and life" (*W* 202), Thoreau continues, but it did not. Behind him, too, is the "halo of light" that encircled his shadow as he "walked on the railroad causeway" and invited him to "fancy [himself] one of the elect" (*W* 202). Does he still fancy himself so? Will he again? He doesn't say. But within the context of his past glories, the phrase he uses to celebrate his life in nature – "Remember thy Creator in the days of thy youth" (*W* 207) – begins to suggest a contrapuntal Wordsworthian subtext – "Remember thy Creator *from* the days of thy youth."

The submerged countercurrents in the purity triptych surface dramatically in its final chapter, "Higher Laws," a brief but unequivocally triumphant section in the 1849 manuscript, a tortuous and schizophrenic one by 1853. Returning home at night after fishing with John Field, the narrator catches sight of a woodchuck and is "strongly tempted to seize and devour him raw; not that I was hungry then, except for the wildness which he represented" (*W* 210). "I found in myself, and still find," he adds, "an instinct toward a higher, or, as it is named, spiritual life, as do most men, and another toward a primitive rank and savage one, and I reverence them both. I love the wild not less than the good" (*W* 210). The claim has roots in Thoreau's long-standing attraction to both "a mystic spiritual life" and "a primitive savage life" (*PJ* 2, 177), tendencies he managed to persuade himself were not only congruent but coimplicatory. "How near to good is what is wild" (*PJ* 3, 27), he wrote in September 1849, in words he would later include in "Walking" (*EP* 226, 205). In the early "Baker Farm" he could thus exhort himself to "grow wild according to [his] nature," confident that in doing so he was following the hints of his "Good Genius" (*W* 207). "Higher Laws" revives the distinction between the wild and the good, but after praising the impulses as equally worthy, it proceeds to identify the wild with appetites of the body at war with the aspirations of the soul. When Thoreau depicts himself "ranging the woods, like a half-starved hound, with a strange abandonment, seeking some kind of venison [he] might devour" (*W* 210), he is describing a mood of compulsion that resembles nothing so much as unbridled lust. So far as the wild in man signifies psychic drives arising from his kinship with "the lower orders of creation" (*W* 214), growing wild according to one's nature represents a naïve and morally perilous advice. By the end of the chapter Thoreau has worked round to what is probably the most startling sentence in *Walden:* "Nature is hard to be overcome, but she must be overcome" (*W* 221).

By "nature" Thoreau means the carnality of animal life as it is reproduced in humanity, where it becomes a fount of impurity. So long as he believed in nature's essential cleanness, Thoreau could hold to the possibility of his own. By 1852–53, however – the period of major additions to "Higher Laws" – his attention to natural facts had begun to uncover disturbing signs of creation's filth, leaving him to wonder how he might be purified by so morally equivocal an agent.[19] "Shit is a more onerous theological problem than is evil," Milan Kundera observed; "Since God gave man freedom, we can, if need be, accept the idea that He is not responsible for man's crimes. The responsibility for shit, however, rests entirely with Him."[20] So Thoreau seems to have felt as he considered the world's viscera. Noisome odors increasingly offended him, as did slime, fungi, parasites, and some reptiles – natural phenomena repulsive to many but invested by Thoreau with a moral significance that challenged his identification of the wild with the pure. Where in the early *Walden* manuscript he could profess to be "cheered" by the sight of a vulture feeding on carrion and to find "universal innocence" in a nature that sometimes "rained flesh and blood" (*W* 318), in *Cape Cod,* pondering the seashore ("a wild, rank place," with "no flattery in it"), he is appalled by the physical and moral stench of its "vast *morgue,*" whose leveling democracy of decay ("The carcasses of men and beasts together . . . , rotting and bleaching in the sun and waves") reminds him that "we, too, are the product of sea-slime" (*CC* 147). Most disquieting of all was nature's open sexuality, "blazon[ed]" in the visible parts of flowers, in the "Phallus impudicus . . . & other phallus-like fungi" (*PJ* 4, 308), and in certain "orange-colored toadstools . . . cumber[ing] the ground" that led him to ask if "the earth [were] in her monthly courses" (*J* IV, 288).[21] "To correspond to man completely," he speculated, "nature is even perhaps unchaste herself. Or perhaps man's impurity begets a monster somewhere, to proclaim his sin" (*PJ* 4, 309). Anxious "to preserve an immanent divinity from pollution,"[22] as Michael West put it, Thoreau could rationalize nature's foulness only by ascribing it to humanity; he could not concede that nature itself might be impure, still less that the entire issue of nature's purity or impurity was a bugbear. He relied too heavily on nature for his moral life to allow its a- or immorality, yet the other alternative – that nature's obscenity was a reflection of man's – was equally grim. For if nature was an "eye" answering to the moral proclivities of the beholder, what did his shame and outrage at the Phallus impudicus reveal about himself? "If we are shocked," as he later wrote of sexuality in Whitman, "whose experience is it that we are reminded of?" (*Corr* 445). Whitman's poetry was "exhilirating" [*sic*] (*Corr* 445), but it had to be received with caution. So, in "Higher Laws," did nature. In draft A Thoreau had written of his "genius" weaning him away from the grossness of fishing and hunting, "but I see that if I were to live in a wilderness [he added in E] I should again be tempted to become a fisher and hunter in earnest" (*W* 214). Even Concord's more domesticated nature could draw out the brutish in man; the draft E enlargement of "Visitors" retouches the portrait of the woodchopper Therien – an "animal" man, Thoreau now emphasizes, and a "great consumer of meat" (cold woodchucks are a favorite) incapable of taking a "spiritual view of things" (*W* 145, 150). The "tonic of wildness," as Thoreau called it in the first *Walden* (Sh 207; *W* 217), was now something to be prescribed in moderation.

And wildness in the self – a poison more than a restorative – was no longer to be prescribed at all, save in rhetorical opposition to Concord.

In its dramatic self-deconstruction, "Higher Laws" exposes the tensions inherent in Thoreau's project of expanding *Walden* along its existing lines and in its original spirit while at the same time using it to stimulate or record his later development. A notion of metamorphosis as contending with powerful counterforces in the self had been blissfully absent from the 1849 manuscript, in which purity had awakened intimations of a nobler life and pointed infallibly toward ascent. There, too, instincts belonging to physical nature had been elements to master, but the struggle suggested no extraordinary difficulties, nor was it complicated by the association of one drive (hunger) with another (sexuality).[23] In the 1849 *Walden* Thoreau had written confidently of his direction: "If I listen to the faintest but constant suggestions of my genius I see not to what extremes or insanity it would lead me. – And yet that way as I grow more resolute and faithful my road lies" (Sh 190). The revised text of stage E preserves the substance of the thought but replaces the first person with the third ("If *one* listens . . . , *his* road lies" [*W* 190]), and it implicitly disclaims an application to the speaker ("Whatever my own practice may be . . ." [*W* 216]). The logic of ascent seems as valid as ever to Thoreau, but he has drawn back from exemplifying it through his own progress. Having written himself to the brink of metamorphosis, he seems obliged by a consciousness of apostasy to detach himself from the redemptive process even as he traces it to its conclusion.

The result of Thoreau's guilts and anxieties of 1852–53 is a chapter split to the point of incoherence by the conflict between residual and emergent elements. On one side, Thoreau elaborates his account of the ascent from hunter-fisher to poet-naturalist and expands his remarks on the spiritual economy of diet; on the other, he burdens the chapter with a sermon on human bodily and instinctual life charged with revulsion and personalized by confessions of impurity and backsliding. The residual work occurs in the earlier pages and builds toward the vision of ecstasy in nature that had climaxed the original "Higher Laws" ("If the day and night are such that you greet them with joy . . . " [*W* 216–17]). The descent begins almost immediately thereafter: "But to tell the truth, I find myself at present somewhat less particular in these respects. I carry less religion to the table, ask no blessing; not because I am wiser than I was, but, I am obliged to confess, because, however much it is to be regretted, with years I have grown more coarse and indifferent. Perhaps these questions are entertained only in youth, as most believe of poetry. My practice is 'nowhere,' my opinion is here" (*W* 217; v. *PJ* 4, 46–47; *J* IV, 417).

What had been a crescendo in the 1849 manuscript becomes a kind of tragic peripety in the enlarged text, a peaking of the narrator's spiritual fortunes followed by a sudden and precipitous reversal. An unavowedly "tragic" structure is built into nearly all Thoreau's literary excursions, which either rise to a moment of ecstasy in nature that cannot be sustained or turned to lasting account ("A

Walk to Wachusett," *A Week*) or trail off into irresoluteness for lack of a satisfying answer to the curiosities that prompted them (*Cape Cod, A Yankee in Canada,* "The Allegash and East Branch"). "Higher Laws" differs in openly confuting its vision of possibility and turning it to one of human *im*possibility. In the 1849 manuscript Thoreau's objection to animal food had rested on "a faint intimation" only, a feeling that "when I have caught my fish & cooked them, I have gained nothing by it, but perhaps lost" (Sh 190); by draft E the issue of diet has become symptomatic of a deeper opposition between the sensuous and the sensual: between the body as an instrument of cleansed perception (associated with the faculties of sight and hearing) and the body as a source of pleasure (associated with the gratifications of taste and touch). In *Leaves of Grass,* where pleasure is not merely innocent but holy, images of ingestion suggest the nutritive conversion of sense experience into spirit; in "Higher Laws," the soul is nourished to the degree that bodily "appetite" is starved, and even the most casual "devotion to sensual savors" becomes "defil[ing]" (*W* 218). "The wonder is how . . . you and I, can live this slimy beastly life, eating and drinking" (*W* 218), Thoreau writes. The real horror, he implies, is that somehow we do.

Thoreau's revulsion with sensualism of the palate is so extreme that taste seems a surrogate for appetites he is reluctant to name. In a journal entry of September 1851 he links diet with chastity as "disciplines" he finds himself "relax[ing]" with age, though he knows "we should be fastidious to the extreme of Sanity" (*PJ* 4, 46–47). Chastity seems the veiled subject of another entry of the period in which, borrowing Hawthorne's conceit from "Egotism; or, The Bosom-Serpent," he speaks (figuratively) of swallowing a snake when he "drank at stagnant waters once" (*PJ* 3, 370). "I caught him by the throat & drew him out & had a well day after all" (*PJ* 3, 370), he writes, but the image returns in "Higher Laws" in his allusion to "an animal in us," a "reptile and sensual" nature that "perhaps cannot be wholly expelled" and may even "enjoy a certain health of its own," so that "we may be well, yet not pure" (*W* 219). He continues: "The generative energy, which, when we are loose, dissipates and makes us unclean, when we are continent invigorates and inspires us. Chastity is the flowering of man; and what are called Genius, Heroism, Holiness, and the like, are but various fruits which succeed it" (*W* 219–20). In the initial wording from draft D "divine liquors" euphemistically substituted for "generative energy" even as a redundancy of charged language ("profligate," "defile," "bestial") betrayed the force of Thoreau's (self-)disgust (Cl 589). A draft E addition, later excised, is still more openly confessional: "I do not know how it is with other men, but I find it very difficult to be chaste. ⟨Methinks I can be chaste in my relation to persons, and yet I do not find myself clean.⟩ I have ['frequent' interlined in pencil] cause to be ashamed of myself. I am well, but I am not pure" (Cl 588).

In passages like these, muted or generalized in the published text, if not expunged, Thoreau's "idealized versions" of the "'pure' and 'chaste,'" as Richard Bridgman says, run up against the fact of "nocturnal emissions or masturbation."[24] Philip Young describes the protagonist of Hawthorne's "Ego-tism" as a "solitary man in the grip of a solitary vice,"[25] and it seems likely that Thoreau conceived his own snake in a similar way, though *involuntary* sexuality seems to have troubled him fully as much as conscious lust. *Thoughts* about sex he could control, or take responsibility for if he couldn't; emissions were beyond his power but seemed as though they should not be. As early as 1839, before he read the Orientals on the subject, Thoreau was asking whether "by a strong effort" a man might not "command even his brute body in unconscious moments" and thereby realize "the life his imagination paints" (*PJ* 1, 73). For Thoreau this was a life chaste in the strictest sense of continence as well as abstinence. He wished for an innocence (humanity's as well as his own) so complete that men and women might read poems like Whitman's "without harm, that is, without understanding them" (*Corr* 445). Barring that, his characteristic approach to sexual matters was to rarefy them to virtual incorporeality. He condemned Ellery Channing in 1852 for "coarse jesting of facts which should always be treated with delicacy & reverence" (*PJ* 4, 440–41); it is hard to imagine, however, what "reverence" might entail, as newlywed Harrison Blake must have wondered on receiving Thoreau's letter on "Chastity & Sensuality," which leaves it unclear whether married people should copulate at all (v. *EEM* 274–75). Fastidiousness, inhibi-tion, modesty, and a native asceticism contributed to a queasiness about sex quite different from Victorian prudery in being as uncomfortable about conjugal lovemaking as about fornication. "If [copulation] cannot be spoken of for shame," Thoreau told Blake, "how can it be acted upon?" (*EEM* 274).

Beyond an exaggerated heterosexual embarrassment, sex of any sort and in any circumstance was a "dissipating" act for Thoreau within what became by 1852 a vigilant spiritual economy of sublimation. "Man flows at once to God when the channel of purity is open" (*W* 220), he wrote in "Higher Laws," drawing upon a line of thought prominent in the contemporary journals. "What is called genius is the abundance of life or health," he remarked in July 1852, "so that whatever addresses the senses . . . intoxicates with a healthy intoxication. The shrunken stream of life overflows its banks, makes and fertilizes broad intervals, from which generations derive their sustenances. This is the true overflowing of the Nile. . . . If we have not dissipated the vital, the divine fluids, there is, then, a circulation of vitality beyond our bodies" (*J* IV, 218–19). In the continent man, that is, the waters of life flow upward from the loins to irrigate the reaches of perception and creation rather than deplete themselves in voluntary or involun-tary emissions. Ideally, Thoreau wanted to believe with the Orientals that "the spirit can for the time pervade and control every member and function of the body" (*W* 219). His dilemma was that if chastity were a matter of discipline and will, he stood accused by his acknowledged lapses, whereas if, on the other hand, it were not, he was helpless before the necessities of his body. Although shame at first seemed preferable to passivity, the sequence of his phrasing from one draft of *Walden* to another argues a gradual movement toward acquiescence. In draft E, for example, he claims to "have *experienced*" the spirit's control of the body (Cl 589; my emphasis), a testimony he withdrew at a later stage. Similarly, while drafts D and E evoke a Manichaean war between body and spirit that spirit seems capable of winning, the final text retains the idea of struggle but not the prospect of victory. "Perhaps there is none but has cause for shame on account of the inferior and brutish nature to which he is allied, *though his superior divine nature be not subjected to it,*" the earlier drafts had read; the published *Walden* omits the italicized words (Cl 591, my emphasis; *W* 220).

The tragic paradox of "Higher Laws" is that Thoreau maintains his theory of ascent and invokes it against himself to the point of applauding "the laws of the universe" that condemn him (*W* 218–19), much as a faithful Calvinist might consent to be damned for the greater glory of God. From Emerson and the Orientals Thoreau drew an unrelaxing doctrine of behavior as self-retributive – "Our whole life is startlingly moral. There is never an instant's truce between virtue and vice" (*W* 218)[26] – that combined with the slackenings of age to persuade him of a fatal infirmity of will. He was as repelled by his own impurities as he was by others', yet living familiarly with them and despairing of change, he developed a certain defensive immunity that allowed him to function but was as troubling as the disease itself. The curse of indifference, he found, was that at length one grew indifferent to it. A need to vent his self-dissatisfaction, his anguish at not being anguished enough, may explain why (in Robert Sattelmeyer's words) he "confess[es] his apprehensions as openly as he does,"[27] though in late revisions he sought to veil his more lurid breast-barings in a Dimmesdalean obscurity.[28] "Higher Laws" is *Walden*'s confessional; its mood of self-castigation, however, appears elsewhere in the text in hints of moral descent that intrude upon and qualify previously affirmative passages. In "Economy," for instance, Thoreau admits (in a draft D insertion) to having "unfortunately . . . become somewhat callous" about getting his living "honestly" (*W* 29); in "The Bean-Field" he feels "obliged to say" that the seeds of virtue he planted as an experiment "were wormeaten or had lost their vitality, and so did not come up" (*W* 164); and in "The Ponds" (draft G) he adds himself to the list of those who "have profaned Walden" (*W* 197).

What I have called the purity triptych – "The Ponds," the newly framed "Baker Farm," and "Higher Laws" – is a play-within-a-play that enacts Thoreau's struggle of 1852–53 to recover the upward direction of his life by cleansing himself through nature. The effort founders morally and psychologically, but this only means that Thoreau will need to look elsewhere for a vehicle for ascent. His more immediate task is to bring "Higher Laws" to a closing affirmation. Against the downward pull of the body, the final paragraphs of the chapter offer a gospel of labor and self-denial, which, if far from the image of transfiguration that concluded the 1849 "Higher Laws," is at least a rock-bottom that cannot be undermined or swept away. "If you would avoid uncleanness, and all the sins," Thoreau advises, "work earnestly, though it be at cleaning a stable" (*W* 221). A stable is precisely what each of us has to contend with, first and possibly last. The John Farmer epilogue – Thoreau's sermon to himself as much as to the reader – repeats the contrast of "Where I Lived, and What I Lived For" between "this mean moiling life" and the "glorious existence" that seems "possible" for us, but with a deep perplexity about "how to come out of this [former] condition and actually migrate thither" (*W* 222). There is hope for modest improvement in John Farmer's "new austerity" (*W* 222), but missing from Thoreau's conclusion is his earlier belief in a wide-scale sublimation of instinct and with it the prospect of ascent that had crowned the 1849 *Walden* and generated the purity chapters of 1852–53.

IV

Among the consequences of Thoreau's more chastened sense of self are an increased humility toward the reader and the beginnings of what might be termed an unassuming poetry of fact. Although additions to "Economy" will be as caustic as ever, "Higher Laws" marks the abandonment of the narrator's privileged stance so far as the groundbreaking work in *Walden* is concerned. We are all sinners, Thoreau's quieter tone implies, none more so perhaps than those who grasp the laws of ascent and fail to obey them, though Thoreau wastes no time on remorse. "Brute Neighbors" descends sharply from the spiritual peak of "Higher Laws" and begins a movement toward retrenchment that coincides with the turn of the seasons but is neither caused by it nor intrinsically fitted to it. "But practically I was only half-converted by my own arguments, for I still found myself fishing at rare intervals" (Cl 600), Thoreau's draft E transition had begun. The final text makes a cleaner break with "Higher Laws," setting aside its accusations by conspicuously ignoring them and turning to the ordinary ("Sometimes I had a companion in my fishing" [*W* 223]). The title "Brute Neighbors" itself signals a shift from the spiritual to the animal world, and it seems scarcely coincidental that the first "brute neighbor" to appear is a human being who interrupts the narrator's meditation to tempt him to go fishing. Following so closely upon the argument against fishing in "Higher Laws," the dialogue between the Hermit and the Poet, developed from a journal entry of the late 1840s (*PJ* 2, 379–80), becomes a test case for the narrator's perseverance in his "new austerity." Thoreau underscores the point in one of his few additions to the journal source: "Shall I go to heaven or a-fishing?" (*W* 224). By so posing the question Thoreau makes light of it, his irony combining with the artifice of the dialogue to deliver him from the cul-de-sac of "Higher Laws." By the end of the dialogue (which is only minimally related to the content of the chapter; no transition is even attempted), Thoreau has effectually shifted the tone and plane of discourse, put "Higher Laws" behind him, and begun anew.

Walden is a book of such beginnings as the dialectic between aspiration and experience forced Thoreau continually to reframe his expectations for life and reimagine the terms of success. "Brute Neighbors," nonetheless, is a beginning of a different order, the symbolic inauguration of a new phase in Thoreau's career, much as "Friday" had been in *A Week*. Thoreau would have other lives to live after *Walden:* productive literary lives despite the common idea of his aesthetic decline, and vigorous intellectual lives despite his fears about the hardening of the "flexible sap" into "heartwood" (*PJ* 4, 266). But he would also have other lives to live *within Walden,* which, as H. Daniel Peck rightly says, is not a climactic work so much as a "pivotal" one.[29] Adjusting his sights did not come painlessly to Thoreau, especially when "adjusting" seemed to involve "lowering." He worried about the "Medusa" effect of naturalism, which "turn[ed] the man of science to stone" and threatened even the poet with a plethora of dissipating facts (*J* V, 45). "Ah, those youthful days!" he exclaimed in March 1853: "are they never to return? when the walker does not too curiously observe particulars, but sees, hears, scents, tastes, and feels only himself, . . . his expanding body, his intellect and heart" (*J* V, 75). With decreasing frequency he would sound this note for several years. More practically, he took stock of his interests and energies and determined to follow his genius even if it kept to a less exalted road. Having reached thirty-five (in July 1852), he was midway through the biblical three-score and ten, a fact not lost on him. "The youth gets together his materials to build a bridge to the moon, or perchance a palace or temple on the earth," he observed just after his birthday, "and at length the middle-aged man concludes to build a wood-shed with them" (*J* IV, 227).

So far as it anticipates his natural history writings of the late 1850s, "Brute Neighbors" is a trial effort at such a woodshed. "Why do precisely these objects which we behold make a world?" (*W* 225), Thoreau asks in preface to the sketches of domestic nature that fill "Brute Neighbors." The question has its source in a journal entry of April 1852 that hints at his new orientation: "Why should just these sights & sounds accompany our life? . . . I would fain explore the mysterious relation between myself & these things. I would at least know what these things unavoidably are − . . . know why just this circle of creatures completes the world" (*PJ* 4, 468). Several interests are suggested here − indeed, several *levels* of interest. Thoreau would know "at least" what objects are in themselves (empirical); he would "explore" what they are to himself and humanity (moral and spiritual); and he would understand how and why they aggregate to form an environment (teleological; later, ecological).

In time, Thoreau's woodsheds would become small palaces themselves, but not (save stylistically) those in *Walden.* "Brute Neighbors" trains its eye on the natural world but without a clear sense of the questions it is asking of it. The same holds true for the fall and winter chapters as a group, "The Pond in Winter" partly excepted. The materials of the chapters, mined from the journals, are elaborated and reworked, sometimes with great art but rarely for thematic ends. Anthology favorites like the ant war in "Brute Neighbors," for example, are exercises of high rhetorical skill but with limited symbolic ambition or contextual point. The 1852 source for the passage contains most of the substance (and much of the mock-heroic treatment) of the published account. Neither source nor text, however, comes close to fulfilling the literary ideal expressed just after the ant war entry in the journal: "To record truths which shall have the same relation & value to the next world. i.e. the world of thought & of the soul – that political news has to this" (*PJ* 4, 273). Not until the late 1850s would Thoreau develop a method of seeing and writing that would happily unite this world and the next, fact and thought, science and poetry. Meanwhile, despite his wish to "look through and beyond" nature and be "a magnet" to all its "dust and filings" (*J* V, 45), he was uncertain how to arrange and interpret the objects of his world other than through episodic feats of style. The styles themselves (there are many) are supple, inventive, and tonally varied, by turns objectively precise, comic, lyrical, poignant, and ironic – triumphant by nearly all literary measures save structural unity and depth of vision: the spiritual "news" is not reported. In brief, the fall and winter chapters show Thoreau facing a more acute version of the problem of "reading nature" that had beset him in "Sounds." Sometimes he will describe phenomena plainly with an immense verbal authority ("A style in which the matter is all in all & the manner nothing at all" [*PJ* 4, 158]). Sometimes he will rely heavily on "manner" and color objects anthropomorphically (the ant war). And sometimes he will try to penetrate nature, only to find it hard and resistant, or fluid and elusive, in either case frustrating, and he will withdraw in respectful admiration, no closer to the analogical truths he sought.

A symbol of fluid and elusive nature is the loon in "Brute Neighbors," who mocks the narrator's calculations and surfaces precisely where he is least expected. The loon is a happy, whimsical version of the spirit-spout in *Moby-Dick*, beckoning Thoreau onward not to whelm him in some remote corner of the pond but, like the whale's unapproachable silvery jet, to assert nature's tantalizing mystery. Unable to outrace the loon, Thoreau tries to outthink him, but the loon proves the more subtle player and rises unexpectedly on the other side of Thoreau's boat, gloating with "demoniac laughter" (*W* 236) to affirm his superiority to human wit. Far from "anticipating" nature, as he dreamed of doing, Thoreau finds himself trailing helplessly (but delightedly) after it.

In counterpoint to the loon is Thoreau's image of hard and resistant nature, the somnolent barred owl of "Former Inhabitants; and Winter Visitors" (both the loon and owl passages are draft E additions), which lets itself be studied but not understood. Watching the owl for half an hour, Thoreau finds himself yielding as if by empathy to "a slumberous influence" (*W* 266), half becoming the owl himself, as he fancies. The owl nods off toward sleep, with "only a narrow slit left betweeen [his] lids, by which he preserved a peninsular relation to me; thus, with half-shut eyes, looking out from the land of dreams, and endeavoring to realize me, vague object or mote that interrupted his visions" (*W* 266). Perceiver and perceived exchange positions here, with Thoreau adopting the perspective of the owl looking dimly out at a strange, two-legged trespasser upon his domain. The passage tests the limits of Romantic sympathy with nature – and of nature's interest in man. The owl as ME has only a "peninsular relation" to Thoreau as NOT ME, while for Thoreau the observer and would-be owl, the connection is further attenuated because he must cross this neck of land twice – first in entering the owl's consciousness, then in passing back through it to himself. It is a game whose chances of victory (knowledge of nature, reflexive knowledge of the self) are exceedingly small. The owl's "half-shut eyes" are not, like Walden's eye, the sign of a nature that invites itself to be fathomed. Natural objects as seen here are remote and conjectural, whether the object is the owl as studied by Thoreau or Thoreau as registered by the owl. A "peninsular relation" summons Thoreau's fancy into play, but in the end all it yields is a subjective construction of owldom, while the owl itself tires of the game and flies off to do its sleeping elsewhere.[30]

Commentators who find the fall and winter chapters a site of intellectual dormancy sometimes argue that they are very properly so, since to pattern one's book (and life) after the course of the seasons is ipso facto to wane with the waning of the year. Thoreau himself preferred to imagine winter as a time of introspection, not of sleep – of a feeding on memories harvested from summer days like Wordsworthian time spots and furnishing an "armor that can laugh at any blow of fortunes" (PJ 1, 349). "The alert and energetic man leads a more intellectual life in winter than in summer," he wrote in October 1851: "In summer the animal and vegetable in him are perfected as in a torrid zone – he lives in his senses mainly– In winter cold reason & not warm passion has her sway – he lives in thought & reflection– He lives a more spiritual & a less sensual life. . . . He migrates into his mind – to perpetual summer. And to the healthy man the winter of his discontent never comes" (PJ 4, 144–45; v. PJ 4, 180–81).

Readings of Walden so routinely take the seasonal pattern as implying a period of descent that it is startling to find Thoreau imagining the cycle as a continuously ascending spiral in which winter works upon and transcends the experiences of summer, to be transcended in turn by the quickening of life in spring. There is no reason inherent in the logic of the seasons why Walden should not have taken flight after "Higher Laws" and grown more reflective even as it faced a snow-bound world. Stylistically, the fall and winter chapters are not only accomplished but winning in a way that the more combative sections of Walden often are not; it is as if Thoreau the artist heeded the lesson of the melting sandbank – that "Thaw with his gentle persuasion is more powerful than Thor. with his hammer. The one melts the other but breaks in pieces" (PJ 4, 294). Even so, the chapters give voice to a period in which Thoreau felt his interior life contracting, or growing wintry without the "deep inward fires" he liked to associate with winter (PJ 4, 181). Other sections in Walden, including portions of "The Ponds," were also written during stages E and F, when Thoreau enlarged the winter chapters; Thoreau's day-to-day life was mood-dominated and peculiarly compartmentalized, his development "frayed." The mood of "The Ponds" was always potentially available to him, if only as retrospect; so was the mood of

"Economy." It is the fall and winter chapters, however, that represent the emergent work of late 1852–53 and that most closely parallel directions in his private writing. William Howarth sees (as I believe most readers would) "a slow and almost imperceptible change" in Thoreau's journal beginning about September 1852, as his "entries on birds and plants became more precise and detailed, less fanciful in his reading of their metaphysical significance"; the journal, he adds, "increasingly became a repository for data in which he did not see clear patterns."[31] This is not to argue for a "decline" in Thoreau's life and work as he composed *Walden;* it is rather to suggest that he was experiencing a transition between lives that was profoundly disorienting and that, for want of an adequate context, he tended for a time to *regard* as a decline. Belonging neither to *Walden's* original vision of 1846–49 nor to the later obsession with purity that climaxes in "Higher Laws," the fall and winter chapters are a structure of detail without a thematic rationale, an achievement of style operating upon stored-up materials but incapable of freshly endowing them with meaning.

V

"The Pond in Winter" is the symbolic reference point for the later *Walden* as "Where I Lived, and What I Lived For" is for the book's opening sections and "The Ponds" for its middle. Largely the work of drafts E and F, the chapter is a stock-taking exercise analogous within Thoreau's career to the essay "Experience" within Emerson's. The concern of both texts – " 'Interim Report[s] on an Experiment in Self-Reliance,' "[32] as Stephen Whicher called "Experience" – is how to live in a world of sense impressions shut off from the divine and impenetrable to the flagging energies of the self. Both begin with a groggy awakening from sleep, a birth into selfhood and physical experience presented not as an Adamic beginning but an estrangement from the All. "Where do we find ourselves?" Emerson asks, referring at once to the shared human condition and to his own fifteen-year intellectual and spiritual pilgrimage:

> In a series, of which we do not know the extremes, and believe that it has none. We wake and find ourselves on a stair: there are stairs below us, which we seem to have ascended; there are stairs above us, many a one, which go upward and out of sight. But the Genius which, according to the old belief, stands at the door by which we enter, and gives us the Lethe to drink, that we may tell no tales, mixed the cup too strongly, and we cannot shake off the lethargy now at noonday. (*CW* III, 27)

Emerson's metaphor of awakening with a sense of faraway truths was a fact of experience for Thoreau enacted daily on "first returning to consciousness in the night or morning," as he wrote in March 1852:

> I am conscious of having, in my sleep, transcended the limits of the individual – and made observations & carried on conversations which in my waking hours I

can neither recall nor appreciate. As if in sleep our individual fell into the infinite mind – & at the moment of awakening we found ourselves on the confines of the latter – On awakening we resume our enterprise[,] take up our bodies and become limited mind again. . . . There is a moment in the dawn . . . when we see things more truly than at any other time. . . . By afternoon all objects are seen in mirage. (*PJ* 4, 392–93)

"The Pond in Winter" opens with such a moment; befuddlement, not clarity, however, initially reigns, and when Thoreau turns from his receding dreams to the prospect around him, he sees a snow-covered surface brilliant to the eye but opaque to the inquiring mind:

> After a still winter night I awoke with the impression that some question had been put to me, which I had been endeavoring in vain to answer in my sleep, as what – how – when – where? But there was dawning Nature, in whom all creatures live, looking in at my broad windows with serene and satisfied face, and no question on *her* lips. I awoke to an answered question, to Nature and daylight. The snow lying deep on the earth dotted with young pines, and the very slope of the hill of which my house is placed, seemed to say, Forward! Nature puts no questions and answers none which we mortals ask. (*W* 282)

The scene is physically as glittering as in Wallace Stevens's "The Snow Man" – and metaphysically as empty. Earlier in *Walden* Thoreau had posited a universe that "constantly and obediently answers to our conceptions" (*W* 97); now he fronts one that "puts no questions and answers none which we mortals ask." Where Emerson awakens drugged and blear-eyed without the energies for transcendental perception, Thoreau rises exhilarated and ready to heed nature's cry of "Forward!" The spiritual result is much the same, however, since "forward" is into a world that has closed "its eye-lids" (a play upon "earth's eye") and become "dormant" (*W* 282). With Emerson's text allusively behind it, the implicit question in "The Pond in Winter" is how far this frozen world should be construed figuratively as normative. Cutting down through layers of snow and ice, Thoreau uncovers "a perennial waveless serenity" in Walden's depths; "Heaven is under our feet," he writes, "as well as over our heads" (*W* 283). But can he also penetrate the "ice," the low-hanging epistemological ceiling, that presses down on the world from above? Can he still, as in "The Ponds," cast his line upward to hook a celestial fish as well as downward to catch a physical one?

As "Higher Laws" tested and drastically qualified Thoreau's belief in purity, so "The Pond in Winter" tests his analogist's faith that one might pass, by study, from natural fact to moral fact. In the central episode of the chapter, expanded significantly from draft A,[33] Thoreau drops a weighted cod-line to sound Walden's bottom, hoping at the same time to strike moral bottom. But the naturalist in search of empirical truth and the poet seeking analogies soon part ways. Walden, it turns out, has a "remarkable depth for so small an area" (*W* 287) and thus serves as a fitting symbol for nature's inexhaustibility. Nonetheless, like even the deepest ponds, Walden is not so very deep in proportion to its acreage, nor, if drained, would it leave more than "a shallow plate" in the landscape (*W* 287), as would the ocean itself relative to its breadth. "What if all ponds were shallow?" the poet Thoreau asks: "Would it not react on the minds of men" and depress their sense of the infinite (*W* 287)? But all ponds *are* comparatively shallow, the naturalist Thoreau feels compelled to add, countering the poet's enthusiasm with the sober corrective of truth. I say "compelled," but in fact Thoreau is as curious about the empirical particulars of bottoms as he is about the tropes he can draw from them. The problem is that his interests lead him in opposite directions and that the figurative truth he would have nature exemplify must be asserted *against* the plain facts. To the would-be poet, the world doesn't adequately or properly signify. "The amount of it is," Thoreau concludes, "the imagination, give it the least license, dives deeper and soars higher than Nature goes" (*W* 288).

Rather than the agent and index of human growth it had been in "The Ponds," nature in "The Pond in Winter" is a tether on the spirit, whose effort to rise through the poetic resonance of facts is thwarted by their bald, insistent literalness. Empiricism, of course, has its own compensatory satisfactions and circuitous route to heaven. Extrapolating from his measurements of Walden, Thoreau can devise a formula for locating all watery bottoms and find it confirmed by his soundings at White Pond; he can even imagine the world restored to conceptual unity through science's mastery of "seemingly conflicting, but really concurring, [natural] laws" (*W* 290). Wonder may thus be the end-product of a laborious accumulation of knowledge – the empiricist's collective, centuries-hence version of paradise regained in place of the poet's private and immediate one.[34] Even aside from disinheriting the timebound individual, however, science was positivistic and could not provide Thoreau with the moral "alphabet of man"[35] he sought in nature. In *A Week,* before he had begun to train himself as a naturalist, Thoreau had speculated about the poet using "the results of science and philosophy" to pass from "known laws" of nature to "unknown" ones (*Wk* 363). Wilkinson's analogism seemed to ground this effort in a firsthand observation that spoke to Thoreau's emerging scientism of the early 1850s and promised to marry it with poetry in a single unified response to the world. "The Pond in Winter" puts analogism to a paradigmatic trial. "What I have observed of the pond is no less true in ethics" (*W* 291), Thoreau begins, applying his law of bottoms to human character:

> Perhaps we need only to know how [a man's] shores trend and his adjacent country or circumstances, to infer his depth and concealed bottom. If he is surrounded by mountainous circumstances, an Achillean shore, whose peaks overshadow and are reflected in his bosom, they suggest a corresponding depth in him. But a low and smooth shore proves him shallow on that side. In our bodies, a bold projecting brow falls off to and indicates a corresponding depth of thought. (*W* 291)

Reminiscent of old physiognomy books, the passage is deliberately extravagant, as if only through a language that calls attention to its figurativeness can

Thoreau venture to suggest a connection between natural and moral fact. The evolution of the passage sheds light on its problematic truth-status. The 1846 journal source culminates in the assertion, "There is no exclusively moral law – there is no exclusively physical law" (*PJ* 2, 241; cf. *CW* I, 21). In stage E of *Walden,* Thoreau used the sentence to introduce the moral shores paragraph, consistent with his Wilkinsonian faith in the intrinsic meaningfulness of phenomena. Draft F replaces the line with a wording nearly identical to the final text's: "But what I have observed of the pond *is no less true* in morals" (Cl 768, my emphasis; v. *W* 291). Thoreau has gravitated from an apparent belief in built-in correspondences to a much diluted appeal to similitudes. He would like to offer analogism as an empirico-poetic method of discovery, but his instinct warns him it may only be a manner of intellectual punning or a feat of literary style.

At issue is the distinction between types and tropes, or correspondences woven into the fabric of reality by the Creator and metaphoric likenesses grasped or made by the perceiving imagination. Because there is "consentaneity in [God's] manner of working in one thing and another throughout all nature," Jonathan Edwards reasoned, "why should we not suppose that He makes the inferiour in imitation of the superiour, the material of the spiritual, on purpose to have a resemblance and shadow of them?"[36] Armed with this notion of types of one side and with a full explanation of moral and spiritual reality (Scripture and church doctrine) on the other, Edwards could read nature for its countless illustrations of orthodox truth – for example, "The silk-worm is a remarkeable type of Christ, which when it dies yields us that of which we make such glorious clothing. Christ became a worm for our sakes, and by his death kindled that righteousness with which believers are clothed, and thereby procured that we should be clothed with glory."[37] What separates Edwards's type from a metaphysical conceit is the typologist's conviction of its divine origin and objective validity. "In the type," Perry Miller wrote, "there is a rigorous correspondence, which is not a chance resemblance, between the representation and the anti-type; in the trope there is correspondence only between the thing and the associations it happens to excite in the impressionable but treacherous senses of men."[38] While lacking a fixed, antecedent body of doctrine, Romantics like the Emerson of *Nature* could also credit their analogies thanks to their belief in the consonance of divine and human intelligence and the disciplinary function of natural facts. What man in his proper perceptual state saw in the world was what God had instructively placed there to be seen. Thus, when Emerson asks (anticipating Thoreau), "is there no intent of analogy between man's life and the seasons?" (*CW* I, 19), his implied ascription of "intent" to a pedagogical Intender elevates the "grandeur and pathos" (*CW* I, 19) of the likeness from a poetic fiction to an ontological fact. Analogical perception is open-ended in *Nature,* but it is not whimsical.

Without Edwards's Biblicism and Emerson's Transcendental Reason, Thoreau had neither an external text to govern his search for types nor an internal monitor to confer authority on them once they were found. In his journals, some natural fact or process characteristically sets the mind to meditating and fabling, and the result is usually the confirmation of an idea or faith he already holds or is disposed to hold. The activity is exhilarating, both for the substance of the discoveries made and for the joy of imaginative play. At times in the journals Thoreau genuinely seems the ecstatic artist-maker untroubled about the objective referentiality of his truths. "He is richest," he wrote in May 1853, "who has most use for nature as raw material of tropes and symbols with which to describe his life" (J V, 135). This is one recurring strain in Thoreau, but it is not the only strain or even, in the early to mid 1850s, the dominant one. For while Thoreau had no uneasiness about the narcissicism of symbol-hunting (the self was always his point of reference), he could not always quell the thought of its triviality, worse yet of its dissipating effect so far as it distracted him from questions of his spiritual progress and destination.

It is tempting to read "The Pond in Winter" as a hard-won synthesis of naturalism and poetic vision in which science (as John Hildebidle argued of Thoreau generally) "prepares the mind for blessedness" by "finding those mystical facts which may provoke blessedness."[39] Despite his eagerness for a gradational ladder of ascent, however, Thoreau was more a "pietist" than a "preparationist" in his attitude toward nature. Experience, that is, obliged him to admit a chasm between the physical and spiritual worlds bridgeable not by knowledge or method but only by the dim intuition of supersensory realities that occasionally seized the mind. Nature only rarely "provoked" Thoreau to blessedness; rather, buoyed by a preexistent sense of blessedness, he found nature infinitely responsive to the creative energies he brought to it.[40] "If I am overflowing with life," the tropes-and-symbols passage continues, "am rich in experience for which I lack expression, then nature will be my language full of poetry, – all nature will *fable,* and every natural phenomenon will be a myth" (J V, 135). Thoreau could thrive under the ambiguity of tropes so long as he felt confident of his power to generate them continuously and live what amounted to a spiritual life in and through the activity of poetic creation. Yet implied in his conditional "if" was a reminder of the inconstancy of spirit Coleridge lamented in "Dejection: An Ode" – "I may not hope from outward forms to win/ The passion and the life, whose fountains are within."[41] In the absence of psychic vitality, naturalism was a barren, even a dangerous enterprise. As early as August 1851 Thoreau had begun to caution himself against the "distinct & scientific" character of his knowledge (PJ 3, 380), and as the naturalist in him came progressively to the fore in succeeding months, he lectured himself periodically, more in absolution than in hope, on the need to unify fact and poetry. "Man cannot afford to be a naturalist, to look at Nature directly" (J V, 45), he wrote in March 1853. His fears seem partly to have been justified. The journals of mid 1852 and later, as Frederick Garber notes, "are replete with untransmuted material, as though Thoreau were bathing himself in the concrete, hoping that the pressure of all these facts would somehow, by their sheer quantity if nothing else, make them light up into truths. They rarely did so."[42] "We soon get through with Nature. She excites an expectation which she cannot satisfy" (*J* VI, 293), Thoreau complained in May 1854, as if in summation of nearly two years' experience and thirteen hundred pages of journal text. The fault, he knew, was not in nature, but in the naturalist himself, whose fountains of life welled up with decreasing frequency. "We begin to die, not in our senses or extremities," he remarked late in 1853, "but in our divine faculties. Our members may be sound, our sight and hearing perfect, but our genius and imagination betray signs of decay" (*J* VI, 80).

Emerson also liked to envision genius as an "influx," "an ebb of the individual rivulet before the flowing surges of the sea of life" (*CW* II, 166), and in "Experience" he invoked the figure to suggest a Coleridgean depletion in which, "though we have health and reason, . . . we have no superfluity of spirit for new creation. . . . We are like millers on the lower levels of a stream, when the factories above them have exhausted the water" (*CW* III, 27). Whitman drew on a related image in "As I Ebb'd with the Ocean of Life," his autumnal counterpoint to the "flood-tide" poetry of 1855–56 as "Experience" is a counterpoint to "The Over-Soul" and "Circles." The vision in each case is of a world reduced to lifeless fragments, foremost among them the ego itself stranded helplessly on dry banks and mocked for its presumption. "I too am but a trail of drift and debris," Whitman confessed, likening himself to the sediment underfoot: "Chaff, straw, splinters of wood, weeds, and the sea-gluten, / Scum, scales from shining rocks, leaves of salt-lettuce, left by the tide."[43] In a similar fashion Thoreau described himself to Harrison Blake in July 1852, midway through the year that began with a determined reconsecration to his growth and ended in frustration and half-acknowledged failure: "I am glad to know that I am as much to any mortal as a persistent and *con*sistent scarecrow is to a farmer – such a bundle of straw in a man's clothing as I am – with a few bits of tin to sparkle in the sun dangling about me" (*Corr* 285). The midsummer date of the letter is worth remarking to counter the view that *Walden*'s winter retrenchment is aptly seasonal. What Stevens called the "mind of winter" – the void of imagination that sees "Nothing that is not there and the nothing that is"[44] – was not confined for Thoreau to the long months of New England snows; it was the extremity of a stage in the human life cycle – a final earthly stage, he sometimes feared – that he inscribed in the winter chapters partly because he happened to be writing them at the time and partly because, following directly upon the peripety in "Higher Laws," they seemed an appropriate place to give literary expression to the restrained mood of the contemporary journals.

"The Pond in Winter" suggests this theme of spiritual ebbing in an oddly nonsequential coda to the "concealed bottom" passage. In comparing the mind to a pond fathomable by geometric rule, the 1846 journal source had made allowance for private idiosyncrasies and the fits and starts of moral growth by positing "a bar . . . across the entrance of [a man's] every cove," each of which is his "harbor for a season" in which "successively is he detained – land locked" (*PJ* 2, 241). Drafts F and G develop the conceit into an archetypal history of the self:

> Also there is a bar across the entrance of our every cove, or particular inclination; each is our harbor for a season, in which we are detained and partially land-locked. These inclinations are not whimsical usually, but their form, size, and direction are determined by the promontories of the shore, the ancient axes of elevation. When this bar is gradually increased by storms, tides, or currents, or there is a subsidence of the waters, so that it reaches to the surface, that which was at first but an inclination in the shore in which a thought was harbored becomes an individual lake, cut off from the ocean, wherein the thought secures its own conditions, changes, perhaps, from salt to sweet, becomes a sweet sea, dead sea, or a marsh. At the advent of each individual into this life, may we not suppose that such a bar has risen to the surface somewhere? It is true, we are such poor navigators that our thoughts, for the most part, stand off and on upon a harborless coast, are conversant only with the bights of the bays of poesy, or steer for the public ports of entry, and go into the dry docks of science, where they merely refit for this world, and no natural currents concur to individualize them. (*W* 291–92)

As for Emerson and Whitman, the ocean for Thoreau is the transpersonal consciousness from which we are separated at birth. Replicated in the soul, it continues to flow over or around the dividing sandbar in Emersonian "surges of the sea of life" until such time as the waters retreat or the deposits of experience – socialization; the hardening of intellectual and temperamental biases into permanent ridges; the inevitable sedimentation that comes with age – render the bar impassable and we are left in a provincial backwater of being, occasionally "sweet," more often stagnant, but in either case "cut off" from the spiritual fount of life. Experience itself led Thoreau to revise the journal source as he did, but his conception and idiom share in the broader Romantic naturalization of Protestant thought formalized years later in the psychology of Jung. "In Jung's thought," Martin Bickman explains,

> the individual psyche begins in a state of complete undifferentiated unconsciousness, a primordial wholeness that exists prior to and encompasses all opposites. . . . Out of this realm, what Jung calls the 'ego' emerges, a psychic complex that serves as the center of consciousness, a core around which a personal identity is constructed. As the ego grows and develops, it tends to separate itself from the rest of the psyche, setting up barriers between consciousness and what remains and what becomes unconscious. . . . Although this development is necessary in what we call everyday reality, for establishing a life and a living, it creates an imbalance in the 'self,' the entire psychic unit, and leaves a person divided, with only a fragment of his or her potential realized.[45]

Jung was optimistic about the later reintegration of the self. Thoreau seems more conflicted, partially because his image of spiritual oceanlessness operates in competing didactic and ontogenetic contexts. If we are simply "poor navigators" like John Field, perhaps we can be redirected to the sea by a text like *Walden*. Yet the sandbar that surfaces with our birth and mounts steadily with experience seems to suggest inexorable life-processes which preclude a Jungian "rejoining of the ego with the rest of the self."[46] Given the self-regulating moral economy of "Higher Laws," there is also the possibility that we ourselves raise or lower the sandbar according to how vigilantly we dam the waters of life through our chastity. If we feel dry and barren and imagine ourselves beached by the retreating tides of life, it may be because we have dissipated our energies elsewhere and helped create the sandbar we attribute to the logic of human development.

If the special beatitude of the Romantic is his power to animate nature from his own superabundant vitality, the special curse is his utter desolation and helplessness when, in Coleridge's words, his "genial spirits fail."[47] "I am a God in nature; I am a weed by the wall," Emerson complained of "this vast ebb of a vast flow!" (*CW* II, 182) that left him a bewildered spectator of the subterranean currents of his being. "Experience" reenacts this cycle of prostration and revived faith in each of its structural divisions, as no sooner does Emerson acquiesce in his spiritual poverty and consent to live prudentially on the level of the Understanding than "presently comes a day – or is it only a half-hour, with its angel whispering – which discomfits the conclusions of nations and of years!" (*CW* III, 39). The promise of recovery is implicit in the very image of a spiritual tide, as Whitman also comes to find – "Ebb, ocean of life, (the flow will return)" – although the ebb (which will also return) is both too devastating in itself and too prophetic of the general subsidence of waters in middle age for recovery to be complete. Neither Emerson nor Whitman denies the superior authority of flood-tide vision, yet faced with his powerlessness to control or even comprehend the rhythms of the spirit, each is made to recognize his radical dependence on a source as distant and unreachable as the old Calvinist God. As Whitman writes: "We, capricious, brought hither, we know not whence, spread out before You, up there, walking or sitting, / Whoever you are – we too lie in drifts at your feet."[48] And Emerson: "All writing comes by the grace of God, and all doing and having. . . . I can see nothing at last, in success or failure, than more or less of vital force supplied from the Eternal" (*CW* III, 40).

If Thoreau never suffered quite so dramatic a crisis, it was partly because his naturalism called into play alternative powers and gave him a kaleidoscope world of objects to explore while awaiting the spiritual "light" that dawned in him "ever and anon, though with longer intervals" (*Corr* 297). Denied access to Walden's ice-covered depths, Thoreau could take pleasure in the brilliance of its surfaces. The "mind of winter" for him was never a condition of being "nothing himself," as it was for Stevens's snow man; it simply meant living on the horizontal, burden enough for one who would navigate by the sun and stars. "We live amid surfaces," the skeptic in Emerson announced, "and the true art of life is to skate well on them" (*CW* III, 35). An accomplished skater – Sophia Hawthorne described him "figuring dithyrambic dances and Bacchic leaps on the ice" while husband Nathaniel moved sedately along "like a self-impelled Greek statue" and

Emerson breathlessly pitched forward "headforemost"[49] – Thoreau never managed literary surfaces more gracefully than in the fall and winter chapters of *Walden*. Stylistically the sections are excellent of their kind and more anticipatory of the best of Thoreau's post-*Walden* writing than "The Ponds." Their aura of anticlimax comes partially from Thoreau's shift to the understated genre of natural history, which has only recently begun to receive its due appreciation, and which Thoreau himself may have undervalued in 1852–54 for want of a sense of its possibilities. A new phase of his career (as natural historian) was opening up before him while an older one (as Transcendentalist) was closing itself off, but it was impossible for Thoreau to have seen this at the time, or, seeing it, to have accepted the loss of spiritualism it seemed to entail. Working heavily with journal materials, Thoreau could neither assimilate the fall and winter chapters to his departing vision nor generate from them a viable new vision. As he himself might have been the first to say, the chapters are a work of talent rather than of genius, of brilliant pieces held together by the logic of the calendar, not synthesized by a glowing idea.

Considering the vast concessions of "The Pond in Winter" – vast according to the claims of "Where I Lived, and What I Lived For" and "The Ponds" – the wonder is that the fall and winter chapters are as equable as they are, that Thoreau did not suffer his retrenchments more painfully. His chief asset in warding off despair was the extraordinary power of self-recovery that enabled him to adjust to chastened expectations and seek his victories elsewhere. To the dejectionist's plaint warbled by Robert Frost's oven bird – "what to make of a diminished thing"[50] – Thoreau's answer was to alter the terms of plenitude. Where Emerson only plays at metaphysical humility when he claims to expect nothing of the universe and to be "thankful for small mercies" (*CW* III, 36) – no one ever demanded more of life than Emerson through the mid 1840s or had greater difficulty settling for less – Thoreau was almost limitlessly capable of revising his hopes downward, or at least laterally, in response to frustration. If his journals are relatively thin in reflection after mid-1852, they are also thin, after a transitional period, in laments for his unreflectiveness. Even the sexual anxieties of late 1852–53 run their course in a matter of months and vanish from the journals. The most striking thing about an 1854 expression of loss – "There was a time when the beauty and the music were all within, and I sat and listened to my thoughts, and there was a song in them" (*J* VI, 294) – is its anomalousness; it is a rare throwback to the Wordsworthian nostalgia of mid 1851 despite the fact that, objectively speaking, Thoreau may have had ample cause for such feelings.

If Thoreau seldom belabored his spiritual crises and disappointments, it was not because he resolved them but because he refused to dwell upon the negative. "Repression" and "denial" seem blundering terms for a temperamental proclivity that conduced, against all odds, to a robust, if circumscribed psychic health. Like a prudent general, Thoreau met his rebuffs by repositioning himself more favorably and pulling back from untenable ground. It is no judgment of the merit of his natural history writing to observe that it is not the kind of work he proposed to do when he settled at Walden Pond or began the 1846–49 manuscript that set the terms for the published text through "Baker Farm." By his own criteria, announced in the opening chapters of his book, his stance of 1853–54 represented a severe curtailment of the prospects he had envisioned years earlier. One may regard the change as a sober intellectual maturation or as a poignant spiritual defeat; the practical question for Thoreau was how he would choose to present it in *Walden*. Reviewing his experience of nine years, he could make his book a *bildungsroman* detailing how and why a middle-aged man came to settle for his philosophical "woodshed," or he could suppress his long series of adjustments to life and use the formidable resources of his prose to deck the woodshed with all the glories he had prophesied in "Where I Lived, and What I Lived For." At stake was how he wanted to mythologize himself before the world and as a starting point for the life he would assume after *Walden*.

VI

"Only as he refused to conceive life as tragedy could he find the courage to live," Stephen Whicher remarked of Emerson.[51] Thoreau's need for affirmation was proportionately stronger as his interests and relations were narrower than Emerson's, his position in the world more marginal, and his sense of identity more precarious. Even as it reflects the earthbound vision of the 1852–53 journals, "The Pond in Winter" masks its compromises by an exuberant rhetoric that converts loss ("Nature puts no question and answers none which we mortals ask") into putative gain (the phenomenal world is wondrously sufficient). At the very least, the fall and winter chapters are a spiritual holding action meant to assure author and reader that the deprivations of winter have their own attendant joys and are not, in any event, final. The 1849 section on spring had begun with Thoreau noting the signs of seasonal change and had mounted to the climactic statement of redemption through nature ("We need the tonic of wildness" [*W* 317]) that was a central lesson of his experiment at the pond. The long descent of 1852–54 from the expanded "Higher Laws" to "The Pond in Winter" at once disrupted the logic of Thoreau's affirmation and made that affirmation more urgent. The association of spring with renewal gave him the framework for a happy ending, but his success in filling it now depended on his somehow overleaping the downward tendency of experience, on (in all senses) "defying gravity." But what by 1853–54 could he still legitimately affirm?

The enlarged "Spring" of later drafts preserves the structural bookends of the 1849 manuscript, opening with the advent of the season and building as before to a celebration of nature's wildness. The locus of change is the intervening sections, which explore the various grounds for affirmation that seem available to Thoreau. Perhaps because his quest is now so private and its stakes so high, Thoreau seldom confronts his subject openly, choosing instead to test the vehicles for adjustment through metaphor and language. Reading *Walden* as symbolic action, therefore, means attending to the issues that are being dramatized in and through the overt substance of the said. Martin Bickman describes *Walden* as "an attempt to create structures that will make possible a reintegration of ourselves with the world, and of the mind with itself."[52] "Spring" is dense with such structures, though they are more provisional than confidently enabling, and though they are devised only incidentally for us.

The most obvious and longstanding ground for belief is the tendered correspondence between human and seasonal cycles, which has the inherent advantage of ensuring a recovery from winter and the inherent disadvantage of implying renewal but not growth or ascent. "Live in each season as it passes," Thoreau wrote in August 1853: ". . . Grow green with the spring, yellow and ripe with autumn. Drink of each season's influence as a vial, a true panacea of all remedies mixed for your especial use. . . . Why, 'nature' is but another name for health, and the seasons are but different states of health" (*J* V, 394–95). A joyous naturalist in both the avocational and the philosophical senses, Thoreau immerses himself here in the microchanges of the year and unobtrusively shifts his gaze from the earthly heaven he has found he cannot have (spiritual fulfillment here and now) to the heavenly earth he believes he can (delight in nature, spiritualized by a leaven of poetry). So far as "Spring" voices this new allegiance, it seems to join the lessons of the winter chapters to the vision of a renewed life extended in "Where I Lived, and What I Lived For" and "The Ponds." "Renewal," however, has come to mean something markedly different. Formerly an agent of purification anointing man for a higher life, nature now becomes a source of periodic absolution delivering him (temporarily) from a lower one. The thought enters *Walden* late in "Spring" as Thoreau introduces the sacramental idea of "pardon." We pardon ourselves by cutting loose from old commitments and refusing to "spend our time in atoning for the neglect of past opportunities" (*W* 314) – tendencies crucial to Thoreau's own successive repositionings. But what allows us this self-amnesty is nature's own gift of amnesty:

> In a pleasant spring morning all men's sins are forgiven. Such a day is a truce to vice. While such a sun holds out to burn, the vilest sinner may return. Through our own recovered innocence we discern the innocence of our neighbors. . . . Why the jailer does not leave open his prison doors, – why the judge does not dismiss his case, – why the preacher does not dismiss his congregation! It is because they do not obey the hint which God gives them, nor accept the pardon which he freely offers to all. (*W* 314–15)

In place of man's "unquestionable ability . . . to elevate his life by a conscious endeavor" (*W* 90), we have come to depend for whatever self-reform we can achieve on nature's annual pardon. The only real sin, Thoreau implies, is loitering in vain retrospection, which is tantamount to despair.[53] Shedding his disappointments and failures, his exploded intellectual positions and lapses of chastity and diet, Thoreau faces forward, absolved by nature and eager as ever to make new trial of life. To guard his optimism against past and future betrayals, however, Thoreau needs to empty it of specific content and reduce it in his own case, as well as in his neighbors', to "a savor of holiness groping for expression, blindly and ineffectually perhaps, like a new-born instinct," and destined to flourish even then, it seems, only "for a short hour" (*W* 315). Where "Economy" had urged us to send our "radicle downward" so that our "shoot" might ascend toward heaven (*W* 15), "Spring" presents a perennially hopeful but foredoomed reconstitution of things from scratch as "our human life dies down to its root, and still puts forth its green blade to eternity" (*W* 311). Thoreau is sensible, moreover, of how fragile this "green blade" ultimately is. Quoting from the Chinese philosopher Meng-tse, he suggests a prospect of reformation held out to us again and again but not indefinitely: "'After the germs of virtue have . . . been prevented many times from developing themselves [by the evil we do], then the beneficent breath of evening does not suffice to preserve them" and "the nature of man does not differ much from that of the brute" (*W* 315). The words recall the late insertion in "The Bean-Field" in which Thoreau admits that "the seeds of virtue" he planted at Walden "were wormeaten or had lost their vitality, and so did not come up" (*W* 164). More broadly, they reflect his concern of 1852–53 about the gradual attrition of human recuperative powers, so that "perchance as we grow old we cease to spring with the Spring – and we are indifferent to the succession of years" (*PJ* 4, 406). Although he himself was far from that dismal condition, his delight at the quickening March annually brought him was increasingly tempered by an awareness that he was no further along (toward *what* he could hardly say) than he had been a year earlier. To cast one's spiritual lot with the cycle of the seasons was at best to settle for a pageant of revolving surfaces, at worst to resign oneself to a rhythm of hope and blight winding down to permanent blight.

However well it served him as a principle of literary structure and a guide for adjusting the rhythms of his life, the round of the seasons – a cycle rather than an ascending spiral – was too problematic in its spiritual implications for Thoreau to draw assurance from it. An alternative center of belief in "Spring" is the sandbank passage added to *Walden* in stages F and G from journal materials dating back as far as 1848. The sandbank formed by the railroad cut near Walden was one of the shrines Thoreau most liked to visit, and its melting in the spring was as much a vernal rite as the breaking up of Walden Pond. In the journals, and still more in *Walden* itself, the thawing of the sandbank came to represent the eons-long thawing of the earth as directed by a world-spirit whose teleological end was the transformation of matter (man included) into spirit. The context for the idea is what Robert Sattelmeyer calls "the great scientific issue of the age" addressed by theorists of creation: "What was the agency or mechanism by which change and development in nature occurred?"[54] For "progressionists," notably Harvard's Louis Agassiz (whom Thoreau knew both personally and through his work), the mechanism was divine and expressed itself in a series of "special creations" that brought forth a more highly articulated organic world culminating in the appearance of man.[55] The counterposition, a biological uniformitarianism, derived from Sir Charles Lyell's *Principles of Geology* (1830 ff.; Thoreau read it in 1840) as it applied by analogy to the life sciences and emphasized the regular, uninterrupted operation of natural laws. Although there was no reason why a uniformitarian might not also be an evolutionist – Darwin descended intellectually from Lyell – scientists of the 1850s (Lyell among them) were generally wary of evolution, first, because it was tainted by the miraculism and teleology they had spent years opposing, and second, because it offered no naturalistic mechanism of causality for evolutionary change.[56] The absence of such a principle was at the heart of their objection to Robert Chambers's *Vestiges of the Natural History of Creation* (1844), an inventive but amateurish synthesis of progressionism and natural law that ascribed the evolution of species to an impulse that led one type to "[give] birth to the type next above it," so on up to man.[57] Thoreau knew the *Vestiges* and scorned its immanent evolutionism for quite another reason: it seemed rife with "infidelity" (*PJ* 4, 107). His own position, according to Sattelmeyer and Richard A. Hocks, was closer to that of the German *Naturphilosophie* known to him through Goethe and, especially, through Coleridge's *Hints Toward a More Comprehensive Philosophy of Life;* Thoreau believed, that is, in a vital and continuous evolution of nature according to laws that were fundamentally spiritual in character and marked by a transmutation of lower into higher forms.[58] Even before he read Coleridge, his response to the brute materiality of nature had been to posit a sort of evolutionary meliorism at work. The mass of boulders atop Katahdin seemed to him "the raw materials of a planet dropped from an unseen quarry, which the vast chemistry of nature would anon work up, or work down, into the smiling and verdant plains and valleys of earth" (*MW* 63). Similarly, in *Cape Cod* the shore "between high and low water mark" evoked for him the "chaos" that reigned "before the land rose out of the ocean and became *dry* land" (*CC* 54); "in short," he continued, citing the testimony of naturalists but turning it to his own philosophical ends, "the dry land itself came through and out of the water on its way to the heavens" (*CC* 100).

In "Spring" the process of drying becomes one of evolutionary melting as the inert matter of the sandbank liquefies, takes the form of vegetation and animal and human organs, and promises to translate itself still further with time. "True," Thoreau admits, the phenomenon "is somewhat excrementitious in its character, and there is no end to the heaps of liver lights and bowels, as if the globe were turned wrong side outward; but this suggests at least that Nature has some bowels, and there again is mother of humanity" (*W* 308). The concession is astonishing for its scatological about-face. In "The Ponds" it was nature's *lack* of bowels that enabled Thoreau to depend on it for his purification, while in "Higher Laws" the suspicion that nature shared, even promoted man's uncleanness – was bowel-ridden itself – made him look beyond it for deliverance.

Whatever its derivation "from his readings in agronomy and food faddism, from powerful anal drives, from his characteristic morbidity, and from the influence of those Hindu works he loved so well," Thoreau's "homespun fecal cosmology," as Michael West calls the vision of "Spring,"[59] is a tactical answer to Kundera's "onerous theological problem" of "the incompatibility of God and shit." "Either/or," Kundera writes; "either man was created in God's image – and God has intestines! – or God lacks intestines and man is not like Him."[60] Thoreau's God has no viscera, but man and nature are both unavoidably boweled, occupying the vast continuum between inanimate matter and disembodied spirit. An 1848 journal source for "Spring" had only casually likened the forms of the melting sandbank to "human brains or lungs or bowels" (*PJ* 2, 383); the insistence on their "excrementitious" quality is the work of drafts F and G, which postdate all but a few passages of "Higher Laws." What allows Thoreau to acknowledge, even to celebrate nature's bowels in the late additions to "Spring" – to reconcile God with shit and man *to* shit – is his new emphasis on the upward direction of natural processes. Though man and nature are not like God, they are gradually becoming *more* like Him. Shit was and is, Thoreau implies, but in time shit will cease to be.

The problem with such an evolutionary perspective was that it left human beings helplessly "bogged down" in the present. To adopt a meliorist view was to abandon the sense of timelessness that had sacralized reality in *A Week* and "Where I Lived, and What I Lived For" and privileged the simplicity of early races and cultures. It was to submit to the teleology of history, since "not only [the earth], but the institutions upon it" (governments and stock companies included) were "plastic like clay in the hands of the potter" (*W* 309). Above all, it was to accept the inherent spiritual frustrations of life in nature and time. "What is man," Thoreau asks, "but a mass of thawing [not 'thawed'] clay?" (*W* 307). Ourselves half-unmelted, we inhabit a mid-March outer world only partly responsive to our higher impulses. "Who knows what the human body would expand and flow out to under a more genial heaven?" (*W* 307), Thoreau continues in a voice of metaphysical complaint muted but not silenced from the open protest of draft F: "How short and feeble are our roots; how uncongenial is our sky! We extend our arms and legs in vain. Who knows what the human body would expand and flow out to under a more genial heaven – stretched on a bank in paradise? Have we not unsatisfied instincts?" (Cl 814, 815). Just as our "uncongenial" sky recalls the ice-bound world of "The Pond in Winter" more than the spirit-swept one of "The Ponds," so our "short and feeble" roots suggest the futility of efforts to plant ourselves firmly in nature and send our "radicle downward." "The globe is a worthier place to live on for this slumbering life that may awake, that already partially awakens" (Cl 816), Thoreau proclaimed in draft F, but it is worthy for its tendencies more than for its present state, which retains too much of wintry inertness and springtime mire for those who yearn for the genial world of summer. Thoreau's draft G revisions not only excise this note of discontent but replace it with a celebration of those evolutionary processes that doom the self to incompletion: "The earth is not a mere fragment of dead history, . . . but living poetry like the leaves of a tree, which precede flowers and fruit, – not a fossil earth, but a living earth; compared with whose great central life all animal and vegetable life is merely parasitic" (*W* 309).

To silence his spiritual murmurings and preserve a belief in the beneficence of creation, Thoreau suppresses his feeling of the tragic and consents to our living prematurely in a fecal world still in "her swaddling clothes" (*W* 308); we are thawed enough, he implies, to grasp and commend nature's progressive design even as it apprises us of our own transitional place in it. If "The Pond in Winter" corresponds philosophically and psychologically to Emerson's "Experience," "Spring" has its counterpart in the 1851 lecture "Fate" in which Emerson accommodates himself to the defeat of the individual by transferring his allegiance to "the Blessed Unity which . . . compels every atom to serve a universal end" (*EW* VI, 48). In place of the benign anthropocentrism of *Nature,* "Fate" depicts a proto-Darwinian spectacle of "tooth against tooth, devouring war, war for food, a yelp of pain and a grunt of triumph," made to testify in the end to a spiritual selection that "pleases at a sufficient distance" (*EW* VI, 36). In its new evolutionary context, Thoreau's eulogy of wildness in "Spring" takes on a strikingly similar meaning:

> I love to see that Nature is so rife with life that myriads can be afforded to be sacrificed and suffered to prey on one another; that tender organizations can be so serenely squashed out of existence like pulp, – tadpoles which herons gobble up, and tortoises and toads run over in the road; and that it has sometimes rained flesh and blood! With the liability to accident, we must see how little account is to be made of it. The impression made on a wise man is that of universal innocence. (*W* 318)

Along with the "myriads" sacrificed according to nature's benign laws, human beings now take their place as amphibious products and casualties of earth's evolutionary ascent. A rhetorical flourish in the 1849 manuscript, the reframed passage becomes an effort to transcend limitation and tragedy by, in Emerson's words, "rally[ing] on [one's] relation to the Universe, which his ruin benefits" (*EW* VI, 47). "The way of Providence is a little rude" (*EW* VI, 7), as Emerson grimly noted, but by the narrative and compositional end of *Walden* Thoreau seems willing to abide by it if that is the price of belief.

What depreciated even this dearly bought affirmation was Thoreau's feeling that it might be groundless. Type or trope? metaphysics or metaphor? Everything depended on the status of analogies. While the thawing sandbank pointed Thoreau to nature's unfolding design, his thrust toward assertion is repeatedly checked by the qualifiers "like," "as if," "resembling," "you are reminded," and "seems." In the flowing sand one sees "*perchance* how blood vessels are formed"; "in the silicious matter which the water deposits is *perhaps* the bony system" of vertebrates (*W* 307; my emphasis). Respectful of the integrity of facts, Thoreau was suspicious of their inherent meaningfulness, and forced to the point of having to declare or withhold his commitment to an idea, he often resorted to the question-begging device of simile, which retained the savor of belief but not the substance. "When I see on one side the inert bank, . . . and on the other this luxuriant foliage, the creation of an hour," he writes, "I am affected *as if in a peculiar sense* I stood in the laboratory of the Artist who made me and the world [the journal source had been unequivocal: "I am in the studio of an artist" (*PJ* 2, 384)]. . . . I feel *as if* I were nearer to the vitals of the globe, for this sandy overflow is *something such* a foliaceous mass as the vitals of the animal body" (*W* 306; my emphasis). The reminders of a perceiving consciousnsess identify the artist of the sandbank as the author himself, not as God, and endow his likenesses with the limited authority of trope. "The description of the melting railroad bank," as Leo Marx observed, "is an intricately orchestrated paean to the power of the imagination" in which "meaning and value . . . do not reside in the natural facts or in social institutions or in anything 'out there,' but in . . . the analogy-perceiving, metaphor-making, mythopoeic power of the human mind."[61] The "making" is such a giddily delightful activity as sometimes to seem an adequate satisfaction itself, with creator Thoreau "sporting" on his own rhetorical sandbank and "strewing his fresh designs about" (*W* 306). Nowhere is Thoreau more prodigally an image of the divine Artist than in the elaborate wordplay through which he describes, interprets, and linguistically replicates the world's progressive articulation:

> You find thus in the very sands an anticipation of the vegetable leaf. No wonder that the earth expresses itself outwardly in leaves, it so labors with the idea inwardly. The atoms have already learned this law, and are pregnant with it. The overhanging leaf sees here its prototype. *Internally,* whether in the globe or animal body, it is a moist thick *lobe,* a word especially applicable to the liver and lungs and to the *leaves* of fat (λειβω, *labor, lapsus,* to flow or slip downward, a lapsing; λοβος, *globus,* lobe, globe; also lap, flap, and many other words,) *externally* a dry thin *leaf,* even as the *f* and *v* are a pressed and dried *b.* The radicals of lobe are *lb,* the soft mass of the *b* (single lobe, or B, double lobed,) with a liquid *l* behind it pressing it forward. In globe, *glb,* the gutteral *g* adds to the meaning the capacity of the throat. The feathers and wings of birds are still drier and thinner leaves. Thus, also, you pass from the lumpish grub in the earth to the airy and fluttering butterfly. The very globe continually transcends and translates itself, and becomes winged in its orbit. (*W* 306–7)

Behind Thoreau's wordplay, as Michael West and Philip F. Gura have shown, are the linguistic theories of Charles Kraitsir, whose "bizarre doctrine of intrinsic phonological meaning"[62] gave an aural turn to the Romantic Adamicism that would restore the primal harmony between fact, idea, and linguistic sign. In *Nature* Emerson had argued for the "radical correspondence between visible things and human thoughts" (*CW* I, 19) as mediated by etymologies and pungent figures of speech; so had analogists like Wilkinson and the English linguistic philosopher Richard Trench, whose *On the Study of Words* Thoreau read in 1852.[63] Kraitsir's special contribution was a theory of the cross-cultural significance of language that linked "'three fundamental articulations [gutterals, labials and linguals, and dentals], symbolizing the three organs of speech by which they are severally made [throat, lips and tongue, and teeth],'" to "'three obvious categories of nature: – cause, living and moving effect, [and] dead or dormant effect.'"[64] Gutterals expressed the *ca*usal or quasi-*ca*usal, *la*bials and *li*nguals the *fl*owing and *vi*tal, *den*tals the *sta*tic or *dead*. As West points out, many of Kraitsir's etymologies also "equate flowing material with vegetation and the parts of the body."[65]

In the sandbank passage Thoreau reads nature "with every philological lens Kraitsir bequeathed him"[66] as he traces the upward evolution of the earth from inert matter to winged spirit. The absence of serious phonological speculation elsewhere in Thoreau's writing suggests that he found Kraitsir's theories more an intriguing oddity than a matter for sober belief. At a slightly earlier time Thoreau might have drawn on Kraitsir's work for an analogical "hinge" joining fact and idea through the vehicle of poetic language. By drafts F and G of "Spring," however, he had come largely to accept the subjectivity of analogies and the accompanying confinement of the artist to the figurative truths of his imagination. His use of Kraitsir in describing the sandbank is evidence not of a genuine epiphany but of an elaborate literary game that is nonetheless quite significant within a second Kraitsirian context. As West observes, language for Kraitsir was "'the aim and end of the whole complex of human energies, the only adequate memento of . . . a people and [of] each man, while they and he yet live; and still more so after they have made their exeunt from the theatre of their activity'"; in brief, language was "the *telos* of the *weltgeist,* the dynamic of human progress, and the mode of man's immortality."[67]

Kraitsir is present in Thoreau's notion of a world slowly *articulating* itself over vast reaches of time, but even more provocative to Thoreau in 1853–54 may have been Kraitsir's view of language study as "the highest form of mental cultivation" and therefore as "the best worship."[68] As a "memento," the literary work was an enduring testament to the individual self, as language was to a people. But it was as "worship," or as *process* rather than as *product,* that Thoreau may have come to look upon writing as a medium for the private transfiguration that eluded him in his evolutionary optimism. In Hawthorne's Romantic parable of transcendence, "The Artist of the Beautiful," Owen Warland brings two gifts to blacksmith Robert Danforth and his wife, symbolic of his two related achievements – a mechanical butterfly, whose beauty exceeds nature's originals, and a carved jewel box that encases it. The box depicts "a boy in pursuit of a butterfly, which, elsewhere, had become a winged spirit, and was flying heavenward; while the boy, or youth, had found such efficacy in his strong desire, that he ascended from earth to cloud, and from cloud to celestial atmosphere, to win the Beautiful."[69] The butterfly is the work of art, the carving on the box a representation of the

spiritual metamorphosis of the artist. The sandbank passage in "Spring" is at
once Thoreau's butterfly *and* his carved box: a dazzling verbal performance so
demonstrative of its virtuosity that the spectacle of the soaring artist becomes its
reflexive subject. "Thoreau is his style," which "is itself the hero of his book,"
Richard Poirier remarked.[70] More privately, Thoreau seems laboring to *become*
his style, or transform himself through its agency. He was well aware of the
euphoria-inducing effects of language. "True words are those, as [language theo-
rist Richard] Trench says, – transport, rapture, ravishment, ecstasy," he noted in
January 1853: "These are the words I want. . . . These are truly poetical words. I
am inspired, elevated, expanded. I am on the mount" (*J* IV, 466–67). To write
such words was temporarily to realize the states of being they signified, if by
writing one means not casually penning the words but working oneself up to
them through the metamorphic pressures of literary composition. "A man cannot lift himself by his own waist-bands, because he cannot get out of himself,"
Thoreau told Harrison Blake in December 1853, "but he can expand himself . . . , and so split his waist-bands" (*Corr* 311). He did so through creative
work: "Will [work] not . . . be elevating as a ladder, the means by which we are
translated? *How admirably the artist is made to accomplish his self-culture by devotion to
his art!*" (*Corr* 311; my emphasis).

Coming after the aerial act of the sandbank passage, the "ethereal flight" (*W*
316) of the hawk late in "Spring," formerly an image for Thoreau's solitary life in
nature, takes on an additional reference to "the flight of linguistic play."[71] Like
the Divine and literary artists "sporting" on their respective banks (*W* 202), the
hawk "sport[s] with proud reliance" (*W* 316) high above the earth, rising as far as
its wings can carry it, then tumbling downward in joyous free fall. One is
reminded of Richard Wilbur's juggler-artist with his five red balls, "swinging a
small heaven about his ears,"[72] then grandly reeling it in, or of Robert Frost's
boy-artist in "Birches" climbing carefully "*toward* heaven" before launching out
and swinging back to earth.[73] In each case literary composition serves as both the
scene (product) and the vehicle (process) for whatever redemption the artist
might achieve in time. The act of writing is one of transcendental jugglery in
which the downward-tending self reverses the pull of gravity (mundaneness,
sobriety, physical coarseness, and spiritual sloth) and, like Wilbur's juggler, wins
"for once over the world's weight."[74]

"The brave and redemptive act of the will was to root one's self in one's human
individuality and, facing life and death, to gamble on the adventure of the mind
in a world of sense."[75] The words are Albert Gelpi's on Emily Dickinson,
another midcentury writer delighted with nature and literary creation but caught
between a pointillism of wrought impressions and a culturally-imbibed need for
transcendent meaning – between, as Gelpi says, "Edwards' perception of types
and Stevens' elaboration of tropes."[76] To "dwell in possibility," as Dickinson put
the modernist side of the case, was not only to live without a visible roof (so as
better "to gather Paradise" [#657]), but to live without a floor, or platform of

stable belief, a grave deficiency for one like Thoreau who valued foundations. For better or worse, Thoreau never forgot that art was not life; facts might only be the frames for his mythological pictures, but they delimited what the pictures might express and how thickly the coloring could be laid on. Watching a hawk circle aloft, Thoreau is pulled back from his rhetorical fancies by a recollection that "the majesty is in the imagination of the beholder[,] for the bird is intent on its prey" (*PJ* 4, 210). No mind so responsible to fact can long persuade itself that the dizzying Kraitsirian flights of the sandbank passage have much to do with solid reality. However gratifying it was in the making, a world of words was ultimately a world of words; and while at times Thoreau could imagine himself spiritualized by the activity of linguistic play, at other times, and *increasingly,* his interest was drawn to the absorbing spectacle of a real hawk circling for real prey. To fashion a sustained art from *that* world – to join actual (rather than idealized) nature and poetry – was not yet within his literary power (despite local successes in the fall and winter chapters) because it was not yet within his imaginative vision, still attached to Transcendental modes even as the life recorded in his journals was leading him in other directions. Two remarks from Wallace Stevens help frame his situation by the narrative and compositional end of *Walden*. First: "The final belief is to believe in a fiction, which you know to be a fiction, there being nothing else. The exquisite truth is to know that it is a fiction and that you believe in it willingly."[77] No contemporary of Thoreau's could have functioned under such a creed, least of all Thoreau himself. Thoreau was not a modern who could thrive on ironist contingency and literary invention; he was a mid-nineteenth century idealist who held in the end that the spiritual was more than a pressurization of the aesthetic, and who could live without possessing absolute truth so long as he could still be sure of its reality. And second: "The final poem will be the poem of fact in the language of fact. But it will be the poem of fact not realized before."[78] This is the poem Thoreau would aspire to write, would begin to write by the late 1850s, and sometimes seems on the point of writing in the 1852–54 additions to *Walden*. The structure he created years earlier had its own aesthetic imperatives, however, and Thoreau, in any case, was still far from extricating himself from the high Romantic categories through which he approached life and measured his inner progress.

VII

Within the terms of the self-transcendence that mattered most to Thoreau, "Spring" rests on the ground like a precariously balanced three-legged stool. The legs are (1) the cycle of the seasons, which attuned Thoreau to nature, disciplined his observations, and ensured a yearly absolution and renewal; (2) the evolutionary thawing of creation that gave teleological point to nature's cycle and nourished humanity's instinct toward a higher life; and (3) the triumphs of the literary artist, gratifying as aesthetic achievements and ushering the creator into a temporary simulacrum of the spiritual life. The authority readers commonly ascribe to "Spring" is a testament to Thoreau's rhetorical skill in shifting his weight from leg to leg so masterfully that the stool seems barely to wobble at all. The act is necessary because the claims of the chapter, taken singly or together, fail to provide requisite assurance that the spirit can make a fitting home for itself in the sublunary world. In this respect "Spring" pointedly evades the question Thoreau asked in mid-1851 and in one form or another never ceased to ask: "Are our serene moments mere foretastes of heaven[,] joys gratuitously vouchsafed to us as consolation – or simply a transient realization of what might be the whole tenor of our lives?" (*PJ* 3, 274). Is paradise available here and now or only in another world?

The shape of *Walden*'s symbolic action depended on its answer to this question, for the book set out to make trial of life and promised to render its findings in a faithful report whether life "proved to be mean" or "sublime" (*W* 91). Charles R. Anderson voices the common estimate of *Walden*'s experiment when he describes "the skeleton plot" of the book as "the archetypal monomyth of the hero's retreat from society, his initiation, and [his] final return" with the "vision of a better life."[79] Even a psychobiographer like Richard Lebeaux, who approaches *Walden* through Thoreau's development of 1845–54 as interrupted by a crisis of direction in the early 1850s, concludes by essentially translating Anderson's myth into a different idiom: "*Walden* . . . provides a blueprint, archetype, and affirmation of the moratorium and seedtime that will eventually lead to a new, expanded life."[80] This is how Thoreau wished his book to be read and took pains in composing his "Conclusion" to ensure it would be read. "You think that I am impoverishing myself by withdrawing from men," he later wrote, "but in my solitude I have woven for myself a silken web or *crysalis,* and, nymph-like, shall ere long burst forth a more perfect creature, fitted for a higher society" (*J* IX, 246). The journal entry (from 1857) suggests the vulnerability Thoreau felt throughout his career when he considered how his life must look to his fellow townsmen – indeed how, in moments of doubt, it recurrently looked to himself. If life at Walden, and in *Walden,* proved anything less than the "Arabian Nights' Entertainments" (*W* 95) he had forecast in "Where I Lived, and What I Lived For," Thoreau was in no position to acknowledge it, yet neither could he reiterate claims of 1846–49 that the experience of later years had failed to support, in some cases had even refuted. His "Conclusion" to *Walden* is a rhetorical triumph, as it had to be, but its affirmations are as vague as they are urgent. Optimistic by temperament as well as by psychic need, Thoreau was uncertain by 1854 what remained for him to be optimistic about.

One problem his "Conclusion" could not have avoided was why he left Walden at all. In truth he had no distinct answer, any more than he had for why he had gone to the pond; he could only say, in retrospect, "I went there because I had got ready to go – I left it for the same reason" (*PJ* 4, 276). *Walden* echoes the thought but puts a more positive construction on it. Where the journal allows "there was a little stagnation it may be" (*PJ* 4, 275), the text points to a trodden path – fresher, nonetheless, than the "worn and dusty . . . highways of the world," the "ruts of tradition and conformity" (*W* 323) – and cites "several more lives to live" that keep him from "spar[ing] any more time for that one" (*W* 323). The passage is even more revealing for the draft F addition Thoreau ultimately decided to omit: "If ⟨any⟩ think that I am vainglorious, and set myself ⟨up⟩ above others, I assure ⟨them⟩ that I could tell a pitiful story respecting myself as well as ⟨them⟩, if my spirits held out. I could encourage ⟨them⟩ with a sufficient list of failures, and flow as humbly as the ⟨very⟩ gutters. I think worse of myself than ⟨they can possibly⟩ think of me, and better too perchance, being better acquainted with the man. ⟨And⟩ finally I will tell ⟨them⟩ this secret, if ⟨they⟩ will not abuse my confidence – I put the best face on the matter" (Cl 854). Merely to record such feelings – an act analogous to inserting the poem "Sic Vita" near the end of *A Week* – may have been enough to satisfy Thoreau's need for confession and self-absolution; the passage needn't have been printed. The fact that it was written at all, however, indicates how close Thoreau may have come to shaping a "tragic" *Walden*. Though life at the pond and afterward had not by any measure proved "mean," it *had* proved silent, cryptic, unresponsive to man's intellect, and indifferent to his spirit. Still more troubling, Thoreau himself had proved impure and irresolute ("Higher Laws"), too willing to accommodate his aims to his weaknesses. To meet the truth of his experience, however sobering, was nothing less than Thoreau had urged on Harrison Blake, who had evidently been complaining of his life. "Make your failure tragical by the earnestness and steadfastness of your endeavor," he told Blake, "and then it will not differ from success. Prove it to be the inevitable fate of mortals, – of one mortal, – if you can" (*Corr* 313). The advice dates from December 1853, when *Walden* was nearing its final stages. One can imagine a "Conclusion" to *Walden* that heeds Thoreau's words – that confronts the themes of "Higher Laws" and "The Pond in Winter" and either subsumes them to a larger affirmation or squarely admits that no affirmation can be found. But this was not the path Thoreau chose to follow. To show failure "to be the inevitable fate of mortals," even "of one mortal" (himself), was as foreign to his nature as it was obligatory to (say) Melville's. Defeat – even if it made for a greater victory – was simply not a temperamental possibility for Thoreau. Present always in his mind, too, was the need to clothe himself valorously before Concord. His lesson to his fellow townsmen accordingly ran thus:

> I learned this, at least, by my experiment; that if one advances confidently in the direction of his dreams, and endeavors to live the life which he has imagined, he will meet with a success unexpected in common hours. He will put some things behind, will pass an invisible boundary; new, universal, and more liberal laws will begin to establish themselves around and within him; or the old laws be expanded, and interpreted in his favor in a more liberal sense, and he will live with the license of a higher order of beings. . . . If you have built castles in the air, your work need not be lost; that is where they should be. Now put foundations under them. (*W* 323–24)

Distilling more than two years' experience at the pond and another seven of reflection, Thoreau's words are conspicuous for their modesty and studied evasion (*what* things? *what* boundaries? *what* laws?), as though he feared some disgruntled reader of "Economy" might hold his claims to a strict accounting. In spirit the passage seems to belong more closely to the 1849 *Walden* than to the published text – as in fact it does, enlarging on a journal entry of mid 1849 but tempering its enthusiasm to reflect a chastened awareness of limits (for example, "He shall be translated – he shall know no interval" becomes "He will put some things behind him, will pass an invisible boundary" [*PJ* 3, 19; *W* 323]). Even with all its hedging, Thoreau's note of confidence seems philosophically out of place after the long moral and epistemological descent from "Higher Laws." The castles in the air he built in "Where I Lived, and What I Lived For" remain largely in the air, while the ground beneath them has been so eroded by the experience of 1849–54 that the distance between earth and heaven seems greater than ever. Instead of openly reevaluating human prospects according to his revised measure in the journals, Thoreau expurgates his life history (more unconsciously than not, perhaps) to bring it into line with the celebratory character he has foreordained his "Conclusion" to have. That he succeeded in this effort is shown by the willingess of all but a handful of *Walden*'s readers to take its ending at face value without asking very seriously what, after all, the "Conclusion" affirms, how its affirmation comports with the substance of the fall and winter chapters, and to what degree "Love your life, poor as it is" (*W* 328) satisfactorily validates the promises of "Economy" and "Where I Lived, and What I Lived For."

It may have been a feeling for the insufficiency of his communicated results that led Thoreau to excoriate the medium of communication itself: "It is a ridiculous demand which England and America make, that you shall speak so that they can understand you. . . . I fear chiefly lest my expression may not be *extra-vagant* enough, may not wander far enough beyond the narrow limits of my daily experience, so as to be adequate to the truth of which I have been convinced" (*W* 324). By describing how he ideally ought to have spoken, Thoreau imputes whatever shortcomings his experience might be found to have to the constraints of audience and occasion that kept him more closely "yarded" than he would have liked. He is truest to his apprehension of things, he implies, when he most transgresses commonsensical bounds and exaggerates. Style, that is, is a more faithful carrier of intuited truths than any objective correlative of facts or circumstances. Yet if style depends on exceeding "the narrow limits of [his] daily experience," can it be said to have a basis in reality at all, or is it simply another instance of the "world elsewhere" Richard Poirier identifies as the true country of much American literature?[81] Style as Thoreau imagines it here is neither a mirror of the real nor quite a substitute for it; it is a last-ditch attempt to hold together the realms of matter and spirit that were progressively diverging as physical nature claimed more of Thoreau's daily attention and spirit as always claimed his ultimate allegiance. Style was the exponent Thoreau attached to natural facts to raise them to the plane of spirit. It was not because reality was "fabulous" that he cultivated an "extra-vagant" prose but because it needed the gilding of hyperbole to appear so.

For the long-forgotten townsman reader of "Economy" – the man of quiet desperation pushing a barn down the road of life – *Walden*'s "Conclusion," however bracing and hortatory, has no very definite advice. While sure of the disease afflicting his contemporaries, Thoreau is less sure of the remedy. "To the sick the doctors wisely recommend a change of air and scenery" (*W* 320), he begins the chapter, but just what air and scenery (literal or symbolic, earthly or heavenly) this good physician prescribes is left unclear. "Does the writer of *Walden* really believe," Stanley Cavell asks, "that the manner in which one conducts one's affairs can redeem their external meanness – that, for example, one could find one's Walden behind a bank counter, or driving a taxi, or guiding a trip hammer, or selling insurance, or teaching school? . . . Is it the way we live that he despises, or human life as such? Is it merely governments that he scorns, or the human need and capacity for human society altogether? Is it the way we treat our bodies that makes them ugly to him, or is he repelled by existence itself?"[82] If "not one of [his] readers . . . has lived a whole human life" (*W* 331), as Thoreau claims, is it because none has marshaled the insight and will to live "deliberately" or because humanity itself is only in the "spring months" of its development (*W* 331)? In its original wording in draft F, the published line "I do not say that John or Jonathan will realize all this" had read "I do not say that this generation or the next will realize all this" (Cl 877); a moral question of the individual's nature and resolve had initially been conceived as a temporal question of the race's evolutionary status. The sense that we presently live in a crude world, beneath an "uncongenial" sky – inscribed in, then deleted from, the late drafts of "Spring" – returns in displaced form in Thoreau's closing anecdote of the "strong and beautiful bug" (*W* 333) that emerged from the dry wood of an apple-tree table, a parable of death and resurrection rather than of ascent within secular time. Together with his journals of 1853–54, Thoreau's story of the bug suggests not "immortality now,"[83] as Sherman Paul argued of the "Conclusion" generally, but *nature* now and immortality later, whatever and whenever "later" turns out to be. By the end of *Walden* matter and spirit have grown so disjunctive that Thoreau can nourish an impulse toward ascent only by detaching it from the conditions of worldly life and consenting to function, as it were, on parallel planes. In one sense Thoreau has abandoned a good deal (most of his Transcendentalism, in effect, though he will never admit it); in another sense he has healthily secured what remains. In relieving nature of the burden of testifying to spirit and abetting his transformation, he has begun to free himself from mental categories that impeded the lines of development evidenced in the journals. By the time he finished *Walden* Thoreau was already beyond *Walden,* though it would take years for him to articulate his new faith.

Part III

1854–1862

7

"A Point of Interest Somewhere Between" (1854–1857)

I once thought that there were no second acts in American lives.

F. Scott Fitzgerald[1]

I

If the *Walden* I have described is something less – and more – than the unified prose poem in organic form familiar to readers since Matthiessen's time, it is also a text whose shifting emphases and structures of belief Thoreau could never have openly acknowledged. "It is a great satisfaction to find that your oldest convictions are permanent," he told Harrison Blake in 1857, adding: "With regard to essentials, I have never had occasion to change my mind. The aspect of the world varies from year to year, as the landscape is differently clothed, but I find that the *truth* is still *true*" (*Corr* 491). Implicit in Thoreau's words is the odd notion that change is discreditable, an admission of having once been wrong or in only partial possession of "the *truth*." "Occasions" *force* a change of mind; one never grows toward it endogenously. Where a writer like Melville could thrive on change because the "essentials" for him were ideas about experience that developed as the mind unfolded and deepened, Thoreau staked himself on permanence because *his* essentials were wordless intuitions exempt from the shocks that topple formal beliefs and from the gradual psychic attrition that debilitates them. To concede change was equivalent to allowing that his intuitions were groundless. In his assignments of energy, his mental vocabularies, his formulations of identity and of worldly relation – the entire semiconscious area of working belief that mediates between the polestar of fixed ideals and day-to-day thinking and doing – Thoreau changed significantly, and it was critical to his health and productivity that he did. Bitterness, disillusion, and prolonged dejection were foreign to him not only by temperament but also because his genius (as he liked to say) seldom failed to show him a new prospect.[2] "I am enjoying existence as much as ever, and regret nothing" (*Corr* 641), he wrote some six weeks before his death. He meant it. By continually readjusting his stance toward experience even as he maintained what he regarded as a fundamental constancy, Thoreau freed himself from the hold of outworn myths and failed aspirations and recentered his days upon new, more forward-looking impulses and activities. But the transition was not always rapid or painless. If Thoreau "molted" periodically, it was not like a bird but like certain crustaceans who before their new shell hardens are half immobile, tender, and dangerously exposed.

As an imaginative resolution to real problems, *Walden* left Thoreau particularly vulnerable before the return of the actual. While the book was surely "all he could ever have hoped for," as Richard Lebeaux says, Thoreau must have been aware of "the unbridgeable 'interval' between 'the prospect of the heavens' it offered and the hard, imaginatively unmalleable realities of the gross, mundane world."[3] Foremost among these realities was the fact of his own unreconstructed self. Although *Walden* was the apex of his literary career (thus far), it was only a way station in his life progress, directionless as that now seemed. His first thought after completing the book was apparently to have no thoughts at all. Each afternoon's walk brought its outward adventure, which he accepted in a spirit of what Robert D. Richardson calls "culpable aimlessness."[4] The critical and (modest) financial success of *Walden,* rekindling old ambitions, gave his efforts their initial thrust in the late summer of 1854 as he sought to capitalize on his new publicity by offering himself widely as a lecturer. I use "capitalize" in a full Thoreauvian sense to suggest the ironies and dilemmas he himself foresaw in assuming the role of strolling Indian and peddling his intellectual wares. "Ah, how I have thriven on solitude and poverty!" he wrote in September, tempted by the prospect of fame and influence but uneasy about their likely exactions: "If I go abroad lecturing, how shall I ever recover the lost winter?" (*J* VII, 46). The choice Thoreau sketches is between a literary career and a life. He chose the career, lecturing on "Night and Moonlight" (developed from his summer walks of 1851) in Plymouth on October 8, on "Moose-hunting" (a section of "Chesuncook," later included in *The Maine Woods*) in Philadelphia on November 21, and on "Getting a Living" (the ancestor of "Life without Principle") in Providence on December 6.[5] His fears were borne out: "Winter has come unnoticed by me, I have been so busy writing. This is the life most lead in respect to Nature. How different from my habitual one! It is hasty, coarse, and trivial, as if you were a spindle in a factory. The other is leisurely, fine, and glorious, like a flower. In the first case you are merely getting your living; in the second you live as you go along" (*J* VII, 80). "Merely getting your living" echoes Thoreau's lecture title and reflects his ironic sense of the whole enterprise: he had lost a season of his life in trying to get a living by reading a lecture called "Getting a Living" to audiences that had lost their lives. He had done so, moreover, with little practical hope of success, perhaps even little desire to succeed. Thoreau lacked and openly scorned the entertainer's touch needed to engage a popular audience, and while his first two offerings may have been reasonable attempts to please, his third seems intentionally to have courted and exulted in failure. "After lecturing twice this winter," he wrote after the Providence talk (the October one not qualifying as "winter"), "I feel that I am in danger of cheapening myself by trying to become a successful lecturer, *i.e.,* to interest my audience. I am disappointed to find that most that I am and value myself for is lost, or worse than lost, on my audience. I fail to get even the attention of the mass. . . . I feel that the public demand an average man, – average thoughts and manners, – not originality, nor even absolute excellence. You cannot interest them except as you are like them and sympathize with them" (*J* VII, 79). It might be thought that Thoreau is bristling at the cool reception of "Getting a Living," but the theme is prominent in the lecture-essay itself: "The ways by which you may get money almost without exception lead downward. . . . If you would get money as a writer or lecturer, you must be popular, which is to go down perpendicularly" (*RP* 158).[6] Faced with a middlebrow audience, Thoreau "came increasingly to see his public failures as a sign of private success,"[7] even to the point of openly taunting his audience to ensure failure.[8] "Getting a Living" (as revised in "Life Without Principle") is his most abrasive literary performance, resuming the critique of materialism in "Economy" but converting its reformist stance into a moralism calculated to affront his readers and drive a wedge between his own principled but (financially) "profitless" life and their truly profitless lives.[9]

"One of the most cogent essays [Thoreau] ever wrote,"[10] as Walter Harding enthusiastically calls it, "Life Without Principle" is surprising for its date. It belongs thematically to the mid 1840s when Thoreau was most embattled with his Mammonish neighbors, not to 1854 when the satisfaction of having written *Walden* and the lure of natural history might reasonably have produced a more forgiving mood. Reentering the marketplace may have stoked Thoreau's former quarrel with it; so, too, lecturing on the "incessant business" (busyness) of society (*RP* 156) may have rekindled the truculence of the 1840s "idler" forearming himself against the anticipated slights of his townsmen. "If a man walk in the woods for love of them half of each day," he wrote in one of several auto-biographical passages of the essay, "he is in danger of being regarded as a loafer; but if he spends his whole day as a speculator, shearing off those woods and making earth bald before her time, he is esteemed an industrious and enterprising citizen" (*RP* 157). Although such things needed, and still need, to be said, in saying them with such animus Thoreau was betraying old vulnerabilities and reverting to the role of town censor almost as though *Walden* had never been written. In part his severity may have stemmed from the loss of self that attended his venturing into the public world – and from the loss of self-esteem that followed his *choosing* to venture. Lecturing "dissipated" Thoreau in the sense of diffusing his identity both by removing him from the carefully wrought structures of his life and by forcing him to acknowledge his ambivalence toward success and reputation. Virtually the only way in which he could address the public with good conscience was by periodically abusing it and disclaiming any taste for popularity or hope of achieving it. In "Economy" the good physician justifies his caustic medicine by its curative intent; by the time of "Life Without Principle" the treatment has assumed a teleology of its own and the plain speaker has become a Diogenes looking for an honest man and finding only one.

If lecturing for Thoreau was so futile, "cheapening," and anxiety-ridden, why bother with it at all, as he continued to do as long as health permitted?[11] Emily Dickinson spoke disparagingly of publication as "the Auction / Of the Mind of Man" (#709) and founded a life on renunciations of many sorts, content, it seems, with being "Nobody" (#288), and accommodating herself so habitually to hunger that "the Plenty hurt me" when it became available (#579). Thoreau, too, was concerned with making much out of visibly little, but unlike Dickinson he required public witness. It seems strange that the writer of *Walden* – still more, the walker who found so much to interest him in nature – should have sought his witness by returning to the materialist follies of his townsmen. His July 4th address "Slavery in Massachusetts" may have whetted his polemical instinct, but the truth seems rather that Thoreau fell back on defining himself by resistance to Concord because of his feeling of spiritual rudderlessness and his exasperation with nature's opacity. Even as he readied for press his grand paean to the "tonic of wildness" (*W* 317), he was privately lamenting nature's (and his own) finitude:

> We soon get through with Nature. She excites an expectation which she cannot satisfy. . . . Will not Nature select her types from a new fount? The vignette of the year. This earth which is spread out like a map around me is but the lining of my inmost soul exposed. . . . No wholly extraneous object can compel me to recognize it. . . . There was a time when the beauty and the music were all within, and I sat and listened to my thoughts, and there was a song in them. . . . I sat for hours on rocks and wrestled with the melody which possessed me. I sat and listened by the hour to a positive though faint and distant music, not sung by any bird, nor vibrating any earthly harp. When you walked with a joy which knew not its own origin. When you were an organ of which the world was but one poor broken pipe. . . . You sat on the earth as on a raft, listening to music that was not of the earth, but which ruled and arranged it. Man *should be* the harp articulate. When your cords were tense. (*J* VI, 293–94)

The note of lyrical self-pity is atypical of Thoreau, but the mood of deep and chronic alienation is not so different from what he baldly expressed to Blake that December: "I have not yet learned to live in [the world], that I can see, and I fear that I shall not very soon" (*Corr* 354).

II

If there is a discernible turning point to Thoreau's interior life after *Walden,* it would probably be the mysterious weakness in his legs that invalided him through most of the spring and early summer of 1855. Whatever its cause, the illness seems to have acted as a rite of passage, for he returned to nature that autumn with an enthusiasm reminiscent of the opening months of 1852. At times he could even sound like the visionary of the early *Walden*. "To perceive freshly, with fresh senses, is to be inspired," he wrote in December: "My body is all sentient. As I go here or there, I am tickled by this or that I come in contact with, as if I touched the wires of a battery. . . . The age of miracles is each moment thus returned" (*J* VIII, 44). Thoreau's percipience recalls the opening of "Solitude" ("This is a delicious evening, when the whole body is one sense, and imbibes delight through every pore") save that the older man would have been unlikely to add, "Sympathy with the fluttering alder and poplar leaves almost takes my breath away" (*W* 129). Inspiration has come to assume a different meaning than it formerly had; it connotes exhilaration, aesthetic pleasure, or scientific insight but only seldom a Romantic identification with nature, much less one of those mystical "communications from the gods to us [which] are still deep and sweet, indeed, but scanty and transient, – enough only to keep alive the memory of the past" (*J* VIII, 269). "More empirical than transcendental," as William Howarth observes, Thoreau's "Journal became [in 1855] a record of vigorous outdoor activity."[12] It had been tending in that direction for more than two years, but now Thoreau seems to take a positive joy in those surfaces which in "The Pond in Winter" had interposed themselves between the mind and spiritual truth. Walking in a "still, dark, mizzling" November afternoon, Thoreau finds nature "more suggestive and profitable than in bright weather." Although "the view is more contracted," it is also more "favorable to reflection." He feels his thoughts "concentrated," his self made "compact," by the very confinement of the scene, which, far from estranging him from nature, shelters him from its distracting immensity like a cozy dome: "This mist is like a roof and walls over and around, and I walk with a domestic feeling. . . . I am *compelled* to look at near objects. All things have a soothing effect; the very clouds and mist brood over me. My power of observation and contemplation is much increased. My attention does not wander. The world and my life are simplified" (*J* VIII, 14).

A low-ceilinged world need not be an uncongenial one if a person lived keenly within its terms. Learning to thrive on "nothing definite – only a sense of existance" (*Corr* 444) was Thoreau's chief occupation in the mid 1850s, which he pursued by rigorously circumscribing his outward life and encouraging a practical interest in the common (*J* VIII, 204). In its physical advantages, Concord now seemed to him "the most estimable place in the world" (*J* IX, 160), deficient only in that wilder nature he sought out in carefully measured doses on trips to Cape Cod (1855, 1857), the Maine woods (1857), the White Mountains (1858), and Mt. Monadnock (1858, 1860). For Concordians themselves, or those among them who "let [him] alone," he managed to develop "a certain tenderness" (*J* VIII 151), even mildly idealizing them at a distance. References to his neighbors, if only as sources of anecdotes or natural history information, appear more frequently in the journals of 1856, while the town on its side – more in recognition of his competence as a surveyor than his distinction as an author[13] – seemed ready to convert his stigmatic "A" from "Anomalous" to "Able." Even so, Thoreau remained apart, finding his society less in Concord (Emerson, Alcott, and Channing excepted) than in visits to and from New Bedfordite Daniel Ricketson, whose adulation flattered him and, like Blake's in Worcester, introduced him to a small circle of admirers eager to accept him on his own terms.

Intellectually, Thoreau read intensively but narrowly, responding to books and ideas chiefly as they bore upon his special areas of study, which included natural history, regional New England history, and the American Indian,[14] and which excluded nearly all of contemporary literature (save Whitman) as well as philosophy, social theory, and criticism in the fine arts. Ruskin, for example, appealed to him for his themes of "Infinity, Beauty, Imagination, Love of Nature, etc." and for his thoughts on perception – always live issues for Thoreau – but *The Seven Lamps of Architecture* had "too much about art in it for me and the Hottentots" (*Corr* 497), he told Blake with the dismissiveness he often used for aesthetic subjects. Of classical music, he "had almost nothing to say," though music was available to hear "not only in Boston but in Concord itself";[15] when Horace Greeley took him to the opera in New York, he claimed to find it less remarkable than the song of a certain thrush in Beck Stow's swamp.[16] Altogether, Thoreau read less for pleasure or mental provocation than for the equipment that would allow him to make or clarify his own discoveries or that lent support to the life he was cultivating. Among the classical authors, Homer and Virgil gave way in 1854 to what Ethel Seybold calls "the husbandry writers" of the brazen age (Cato, Varro, Columella, and Palladius), in whom he found a kindred interest in "man's existence as closely bound to the turning of the year."[17]

Thoreau's practical aim during this period was to become, through experience and study, an aficionado of the ordinary – "so to live as ever to derive my satisfactions and inspirations from the commonest events, every-day phenomena, so that what my senses hourly perceive, my daily work, the conversation of my neighbors, may inspire me, and I may dream of no heaven but what lies about me" (*J* VIII 204). James Russell Lowell's criticism that Thoreau wasted his time rediscovering what people already knew was the same thought that occurred to Thoreau's father, who saw no "*use*" in Henry's making maple sugar when he "knew it could be done and might have bought sugar cheaper" at the village store (*J* VIII, 217). Both objections were definitive from their respective standpoints – Lowell's from that of civilization as a collective enterprise, John Thoreau's from that of Yankee efficiency and economy – and both were utterly irrelevant from Thoreau's. Living for him had come to mean knowing and savoring reality by "carrying out deliberately and faithfully the hundred little purposes which every man's genius must have suggested to him" (*J* IX, 37). A succession of such purposes – tapping trees for syrup in the spring of 1856, studying the fruits and berries of Concord the following fall – filled Thoreau's days and contributed to the perpetual "thanksgiving" (*Corr* 444) that marked his life. The challenge he faced was how to bring these activities into intellectual focus and define a subject and role for himself as a writer, which to his own mind he still preeminently was. His concern about the literary fitness of his materials shows itself in the energy with which he fended off an imagined criticism of his work:

> Men commonly exaggerate the theme. Some themes they think are significant and others insignificant. I feel that my life is very homely, my pleasures very cheap. . . . I see that my neighbors look with compassion on me, that they think it is a mean and unfortunate destiny which makes me to walk in these fields and woods and sail on this river alone. But so long as I find the only real elysium here, I cannot hesitate in my choice. My work is writing, and I do not hesitate, though I know that no subject is too trivial for me, tried by ordinary standards; for, ye fools, the theme is nothing, the life is everything. . . . That is, man is all in all, Nature nothing, but as she draws him out and reflects him. Give me simple, cheap, and homely themes. (*J* IX, 121; v. *J* IX, 160)

Beneath Thoreau's defense of the common is his recognition that he has no real choice about the scene of his life and work; that in society (as he wrote at the time) he is "almost invariably cheap and dissipated," his life "unspeakably mean"; and that only when "alone in the distant woods or fields" does he "come to [him]self" and find "the problem of existence . . . simplified": "there at last my nerves are steadied, my senses and my mind do their office" (*J* IX, 208–9; v. IX, 200, 205, 245–46). Nonetheless, two issues troubled him. The first was that his days appeared bare and poor before Concord (v. *J* IX, 160), a judgment he himself shared "in the society of many men, or in the midst of what is called success," when he found his life "of no account, and [his] spirits rapidly [fell]" (*J* IX, 246). The second was that his experience lacked connection to men for want of an adequate literary expression. On both counts he found himself beset once more by the problem of "relation" that had occupied him early in his career. "I would fain communicate the wealth of my life to men – would really give them what is most precious in my gift" (*PJ* 1, 393), he had written in 1842 and, in effect, reiterated now when his life was truly rich and his gift impressively developed, though not for the special work at hand. No longer a hieroglyph of God, nature was most significant for Thoreau as it "drew out" and "reflected" man. For literary purposes, however, "man" had to embrace the commonly human, not merely the private. And despite the craftsmanship that had produced *Walden,* Thoreau had yet to master, even clearly to envision, the markedly different art of weaving baskets from his daily walks and persuading his neighbors they were worth buying.

One of his first attempts at such an art is an extended journal entry on cranberrying written in August 1856 (*J* IX, 35–46), probably as the draft of a proposed lecture or essay. An accomplished literary performance, the entry has a visibly transitional quality as Thoreau joins new materials (natural history) to longstanding ones (apologia and sermon). In celebrating a humble New England fruit, Thoreau means to give his audience a glimpse of how he lives (and they ought to live) by offering an example of following one's genius to uncover the wealth near at hand. "Cranberrying" (to title the entry) has five carefully ordered parts: a prospectus of the enterprise; an argument for the wisdom of "obeying the suggestions of a higher light within you" (*J* IX, 38); an account of the excursion itself; a reflection on the "unexpected harvest" of wildness to be gathered from the recesses of domesticated nature (*J* IX, 43); and a final essayette on regeneration through wonder. The newest element in "Cranberrying" is the delight Thoreau takes in looking down and around at the objects before him, not through them to spirit, or above them at a radiant illumination of the mist by the sun, or beside them to the effects to be wrought through style. Sections of the fall and winter chapters in *Walden* had demonstrated a similar interest, but never had Thoreau centered a literary work on such a detailed appreciation of the homely. Without metaphysical fanfare, he has not only accepted the fact of nature's impenetrability, he has learned to thrive on it, so far relaxing the analogist's search for immanent meaning that he "can even worship . . . terrene, titanic matter" because it is "so different" from himself (*J* IX, 45), so stonily *opaque;* it is "meteoric, aerolitic" (*J* IX, 45), he writes happily – a glittering rocklike surface (no "earth's eye") endlessly productive of "reverence." Through the habits of observation he sharp-ened and systematized as his youthful vision dimmed, Thoreau has begun to realize "the discipline of looking always at what is to be seen" (*W* 111) he had commended years earlier in "Sounds." Blessedness no longer depends for him on a discovery of material and spiritual correspondences or a mystic intuition of the All; it can gather incrementally through a mounting apprehension of the remark-ableness of the ordinary. *Man,* not *nature,* is the locus of spirituality, and he becomes more spiritual by marveling at a world of bright superficies, "divine" chiefly in their ministerial power to make *him* divine. "It would imply the regeneration of mankind," Thoreau concludes paradoxically, "if they were to become elevated enough to truly worship stocks and stones" (*J* IX, 45):

> If I could, I would worship the parings of my nails. If he who makes two blades of grass grow where one grew before is a benefactor, he who discovers two gods where there was only known the one (and such a one!) before is a still greater benefactor. I would fain improve every opportunity to wonder and worship, as a sunflower welcomes the light. The more thrilling, wonderful, divine objects I behold in a day, the more expanded and immortal I become. If a stone appeals to me and elevates me, tells me how many miles I have come, how many remain to travel, – and the more, the better, – reveals the future to me in some measure, it is a matter of private rejoicing. If it did the same service to all, it might be a matter of public service. (*J* IX, 45–46)

To teach human beings how to live in or beside nature – how to see it, adjust their ways to it, find unsuspected gods in it, create poetry from it, and use and conserve it – was the new "errand to mankind" Thoreau's life and studies of the mid-1850s were gradually preparing him to undertake. He was still far from the synthesis of poetic, scientific, and ethical perception he would approach in his late natural history essays. Aside, however, from the literary and philosophical question of how best to share nature was the psychological question of whether he could afford to share it at all. Because nature was not simply the site but the very ground of his being and the basis of his defense before Concord, he needed to regard it as a private possession, to feel that only he knew its secrets, savored its beauties, and participated intimately in its life. Instead of a boon he might confer on his neighbors, nature was the standard of value he raised against them. In the late essay "Huckleberries" he would renew his critique of a commercialism that plunders and desecrates nature, but instead of withdrawing from the social community, he would confirm his relationship to it by assuming the role of conservationist and public trustee (*NHE* 256). In "Cranberrying" he prefers to imagine himself a righteous "I" in lone opposition to the multitude:

> I am the only person in the township who regards [the cranberries] or knows of them, and I do not regard them in the light of their pecuniary value. I have no doubt I felt richer wading there with my two pockets full, treading on wonders at every step, than any farmer going to market with a hundred bushels which he has raked, or hired to be raked. . . . I would gladly share my gains, take one, or twenty, into partnership and get this swamp with them, but I do not know an individual whom this berry cheers and nourishes as it does me. When I exhibit it to them I perceive that they take but a momentary interest in it and commonly dismiss it from their thoughts with the consideration that it cannot be profitably cultivated. . . . But I love it the better partly for that reason even. . . . If anybody else – any farmer, at least – should spend an hour thus wading about here in this secluded swamp, barelegged, intent on the sphagnum, filling his pocket only, with no rake in his hand and no bag or bushel on the bank, he would be pronounced insane and have a guardian put over him; but if he'll spend his time skimming and watering his milk and selling his small potatoes for large ones, or generally in skinning flints, he will probably be made guardian of somebody else. (*J* IX, 40–41)

This is accomplished writing reminiscent of the philanthropy section of "Economy" in its backhanded irony. Prose of this sort came easily to Thoreau ("Life Without Principle" is filled with it); yet rather than use his art for communal ends (to instruct and redeem a materialistic audience), Thoreau makes it serve exclusionary ones, as if to validate his own life he needed uniformly to castigate his neighbors'. By mid 1856 he has begun to see how the form of the literary excursion might be applied to the interests of the naturalist. Bound as he is to apologetics, however, he has yet to imagine a social context for his work and an accompanying writerly vocation. "Instead of engineering for all America," Emerson would later complain, Thoreau, wanting ambition, "was the captain of a huckleberry-party" (*EW* X, 480). "Cranberrying" shows him – still more narrowly, if for a different reason – trying to be its only full-fledged member.

III

On two occasions in the 1850s Thoreau did come forward to engineer, as it seemed, for all America. The first was in response to the Anthony Burns case of 1854 in which an escaped slave was returned from Massachusetts to Virginia in accordance with the Fugitive Slave Law; the second was sparked by John Brown's raid on Harpers Ferry in 1859. Antislavery feeling was passionate but intermittent in Thoreau the *writer,* roused whenever government made him a tacit accomplice to social injustice but otherwise dormant; even his assistance to fugitive slave Henry Williams in 1851 claims only a single laconic page in his journal (*PJ* 4, 113). Although deeply enraged by slavery, Thoreau rarely addressed it as literary material or allowed it to disrupt what he considered his "just and proper business" (*J* VI, 356; *RP* 107). It may have been the very strength of his indignation that made him reluctant to think steadily about it at all, since it would have disabled, even invalidated, his carefully wrought life in nature, as the Burns and Brown episodes temporarily did. In any case, disavowal, not protest, was his characteristic stance. "Give me a country where it is the most natural thing in the world for a government that does not understand you to let you alone," he wrote in *A Yankee in Canada,* championing an atomistic individualism – in his view, "the primitive and ultimate condition of man" – against Euro-Canadian notions of corporate citizenship (*EP* 83). Only when the state "interrupted" a man "on his onward and upward path" (*RP* 107), as he said in "Slavery in Massachusetts" (the Burns address), did speech become an obligation. The state's surrender of Burns angered and sickened him, almost to incapacity: "my old and worthiest pursuits have lost I cannot say how much of their attraction, and I feel that my investment in life here is worth many per cent. less" (*J* VI, 356). "The remembrance of my country spoils my walk" (*RP* 108), he rephrased the feeling in the July 4th address, delivered in part before an antislavery convention in nearby Framingham. He meant, of course, that no honest man could function innocently amid the general guilt, but he also meant quite literally that his life had been unsettled: "what signifies the beauty of nature when men are base?" (*RP* 108).

The tension between Thoreau's outwardly directed moral rage and his self-protective resentment at political invasion accounts for the divided focus of "Slavery in Massachusetts," which is not the call to abolition one might expect. Even the title of the address is ambiguous, referring less, it turns out, to the national question of Negro slavery as it impinges upon the New England conscience than to the local question of whether Massachusetts citizens should acquiesce in the derivative evil of slavecatching. The slaves Thoreau is most concerned with freeing are not the civil slaves in the South but the "million" uncivil (pusillanimous) ones in the North (*RP* 91). "Let the State dissolve her union with the slaveholder," he proclaims, echoing William Lloyd Garrison's "No Union with Slaveholders" but taking the words to mean private withdrawal rather than public action: "Let each inhabitant of the State dissolve his union with her, as long as she delays to do her duty" (*RP* 104). Having begun in what seemed a spirit of political activism, "Slavery in Massachusetts," like "Resistance to Civil Government," works round to a stance of dissociation whose aim is not so much to destroy slavery or end the state's complicity with it as to avoid personal defilement.[18] For the writer himself this is achieved through a purely verbal repudiation. More than an argument for abolition or even an ethical protest, "Slavery in Massachusetts" is ultimately a gesture of individual purgation, with Thoreau's anger of mid June rising to a climax in the Independence Day speech, then vanishing from his public and private writings till reawakened more than five years later by John Brown.

Thoreau met Brown twice in Concord, in 1857 and again in May 1859 when Brown spoke at the town hall and sought funds for purposes he mysteriously refused to specify.[19] Brown impressed him on second acquaintance, but it was not till news of Harpers Ferry reached Concord on October 19 that Brown became his archetypal hero, "a man of ideas and principles" (*RP* 115) who was also, like Sir Walter Raleigh, a man of action. Entries on Brown fill forty pages of published journal from October 19 to 22, the source for Thoreau's Concord address of October 30, "A Plea for Captain John Brown." Although Brown was scheduled to be hanged in less than five weeks, Thoreau's "plea" was not "for his life, but for his character" (*RP* 137), which in Thoreau's biographical and spiritual account became an idealized version of his own character. Brown, too, was a surveyor, a native of New England and moral descendant of Cromwellian Puritans, "a man of Spartan habits" who ate "sparingly and fare[d] hard" (*RP* 115), "a transcendentalist" in his allegiance to ideals (*RP* 115), and "a superior man" who "did not recognize unjust human laws, but resisted them as he was bid" (*RP* 125). To praise Brown in the terms Thoreau did was to praise his own lifelong moral stance; it was to identify with Brown to the point of vicariously *becoming* him, imitating Brown's struggle in his own struggle against temporizing editors and politicians from Garrison himself down to Concord's selectmen, who refused to ring the town bell to announce Thoreau's address, obliging the speaker to do it himself.[20]

Yet if Brown inspired Thoreau, he also silently reproached him for his habitual quietism, Brown himself being "a man who did not wait till he was personally interfered with, or thwarted in some harmless business, before he gave his life to the cause of the oppressed" (*RP* 124–25). The words apply so aptly to Thoreau's own reformist occasions that one wonders if some self-lacerating irony isn't at work. Brown is further described as a man who "did not overstate any thing, but spoke within bounds" (*RP* 115) – curious praise coming from a man who loved to overstate things and sought to speak "*without* bounds" (*W* 324). In the moral presence of Brown, Thoreau seems to have felt an intensified version of the shamed admiration he felt before Raleigh – the wordsmith's perception of ineffectuality and unmanliness in the face of the forthright soldier. By taking the soldier's part *against* the man of letters, as he had in the Raleigh essay, Thoreau rhetorically assumes the soldier's virtues: though the deed may be better than the word, the word that aligns itself with the deed acquires something of an associated glory. In the end Thoreau disemburdens himself of Brown by praising his extremism as perhaps the "quickest" route to abolition but arguing that "a man may have other affairs to attend to" (*RP* 133) – not better affairs, perhaps, but ones lying more naturally within his genius. As he had written a decade earlier in "Resistance to Civil Government," "It is not a man's duty, as a matter of course, to devote himself to the eradication of any, even the most enormous wrong; he may still properly have other concerns to engage him." All duty requires is that he "wash his hands" of the wrong (*RP* 71).

So far as his own civic life was concerned, Thoreau's two most important antislavery addresses of the 1850s were both a washing of hands. Little more than a month after "Slavery in Massachusetts" Thoreau told Blake he had been "too much with the world" of late, adding that "the completest performance of the highest duties it imposes would yield [him] but little satisfaction" (*Corr* 330). The excitement of causes and assemblies, though heady for a time, was ultimately distracting for one whose life prospered only in solitude. Protest, moreover, seemed to Thoreau a kind of negation resting on what Henry Adams would call the Puritan New Englander's law of "resistance to something," his "pleasure of hating,"[21] inner realities that Thoreau – "a born protestant" (*EW* X, 452) if ever there was one – knew intimately enough to find lacking. "The attitude of resistance is one of weakness," he wrote in "Cranberrying," "inasmuch as it only faces an enemy; it has its back to all that is truly attractive" (*J* IX, 36); the value of a walk, he added defensively, is that it "drives Kansas [or Burns or Brown] out of your head" and opens you to "the only desirable and free Kansas," that of the self (*J* IX, 36). Although incidents like the Burns affair incensed Thoreau, in the end he came to regret, almost to resent, their power to call him forth. In "Slavery in Massachusetts" he professes to wonder that men can go "about their businesses" amid the events of the times; they must be "unfortunates" who "have not heard the news," he comments ironically (*RP* 107). By the time of the Civil War he can express a wish to be such an unfortunate himself. "As for my prospective reader," he wrote antislavery orator Parker Pillsbury, who had requested a copy of *Walden*,

> I hope that he *ignores* Fort Sumpter, & Old Abe, & all that, for that is just the most fatal and indeed the only fatal, weapon you can direct against evil ever; for as long as you *know* of it, you are *particeps criminis*. . . . I do not so much regret the present condition of things in this country (provided I regret it at all) as I do that I ever heard of it. . . .
>
> Blessed are they who never read a newspaper, for they shall see Nature, and through her, God. (*Corr* 611)

Thoreau was speaking hyperbolically and would certainly never have sounded such a note if there was the remotest chance Pillsbury might have taken him at his word. If anything, Thoreau probably cared too much about the war, more than was advisable for one already in failing health. "The country's misfortune . . . acted on his feelings with great force," Ellery Channing recalled, and "he used to say that he 'could never recover while the war lasted.'"[22] He was doubtless sincere in this, though it would be hard to disentangle the threads of patriotism, moral anguish over slavery and war, guilt concerning his complicity, and petulant individualism that entered into his feelings. References to political events, at any rate, are extremely rare in his journals and letters, confirming his remark of a decade earlier that public affairs are a kind of "dyspepsia" of the body politic, which in its normal state functions quietly enough to leave a man oblivious to it (*PJ* 4, 174). However eloquent and embattled his public utterances, Thoreau was an activist only perforce, turning from the podium as quickly as he took to it and reverting, so far as he could, to solitude. No enduring relationship to an audience was possible for him that was not based on his own rootedness in nature and his readers' in society. The problem of authorial role he faced in the mid 1850s centered on what he could *do* for an audience – on what license and occasion he had to address it, what instructional end he might invoke while at the same time pursuing the kinds of activities that mattered most to him. The stances of the naturalist, the moralist, and the poet were all available to him in these years. Each answered to a strain within his character; none, however, seemed spiritually and aesthetically sufficient by itself, and Thoreau was at a loss how to join them.

IV

Thoreau's primary challenge in the mid 1850s was to locate what he called a "point of interest . . . somewhere *between*" himself and natural objects (*J* X, 165). His words refer directly to his relationship to science, but in a figurative sense they also describe his efforts to position himself mediately between solitude and society, the wild and the civilized, the ideal and the possible. So far as science itself was concerned, he felt the barrenness of a habit of mind that reduced the wonder of the rainbow to a phenomenon of light, but he was scientist enough also to distrust the adequacy of poetry, which saw only the display of color and illusionary form. Instead of fusing fact and impression, however, Thoreau tended to oscillate between them according to his involvement with or revulsion against the empirical methods of the naturalist. At times, science seemed the key to a more discriminating perception and a finer expression: "With the knowledge of the name [of an object] comes a distincter recognition and knowledge of the thing. That shore is more describable, and poetic even. My knowledge was cramped and confined before, and grew rusty because not used, – for it could not be used. My knowledge now becomes communicable, and grows by communication. I can now learn what others know about the same thing" (*J* XI, 137). But the knowledge that sharpened perception and brought it within the public domain also threatened to drain it of immediacy and private meaning.

Rather than "stand fronting to" an object as a scientist would, Thoreau in this latter mood "sometimes" preferred to "get a transient glimpse or side view" of it, for what "really concerns me," he wrote, "is not there [in the object], but in my relation" to it (*J* X, 164), moral or aesthetic. From this standpoint science seemed positively fatal to perception: "It is only when we forget all our learning that we begin to know. I do not get nearer by a hair's breadth to any natural object so long as I presume that I have an introduction to it from some learned man. . . . If you would make acquaintance with the ferns you must forget your botany. You must rid yourself of what is commonly called *knowledge* of them. Not a single scientific term or distinction is the least to the purpose, for you would fain perceive something, and you must approach the object totally unprejudiced. You must be aware that *no thing* is what you have taken it to be. In what book is this world and its beauty described?" (*J* XII, 371).

Divided between impulses toward knowledge and beauty and uncertain how to direct them harmoniously toward what most concerned him – the interior life of human beings, his own above all – Thoreau lacked the imaginative center that might act as a "magnet in the midst of all [his] dust and filings" (*J* V, 45). His related problems of philosophical perspective (toward his material) and authorial stance (toward his audience) are exemplified by the essay "Chesuncook," developed from journal entries on his Maine woods excursion of 1853 and published in the *Atlantic Monthly* five years later. Wanting a mythic pattern analogous to *Walden*'s cycle of the seasons, Thoreau relied on simple chronology to organize the materials of his adventure.[23] The canoe trip is described, more-over, in a prose as extreme in its laconic objectivity as *A Week*'s had been in its prolix subjectivity. Supplementing the matter-of-fact voice of the traveloguer is the still more colorless voice of the naturalist remarking the region's flora and fauna without symbolic comment and compiling the lists of trees, flowers, shrubs, plants, and birds (identified by their Latin names) that would be appended to the essay in the posthumous *Maine Woods*.

The true center of "Chesuncook," obscured by Thoreau's structure, is its ambivalence toward the primitive, represented by the Indian and by the timber explorers who scout for logging companies. A fascination with the ways of the Indian had been a secondary motive behind the trip and the prime motive for enlisting an Indian guide (*MW* 95), young Joe Aitteon, competent enough as a woodsman, it proved, but morally competent neither as an Adamic primitive nor as a civilized New Englander. An enthusiastic moosehunter, Aitteon kills and butchers a cow moose in what constitutes the emotional turning point of the essay. "As it affected the innocence," Thoreau writes, the episode "destroyed the pleasure of my adventure" (*MW* 119). "What had begun with a longing for 'wildness' and a desire to learn more about the woods and Indians," Richard Lebeaux comments, "had become another descent into the heart of darkness."[24] This is luridly overstated, but there is no question that the "tragical business" (*MW* 115) of the moose relieves Thoreau of his romantic primitivism and starts a reaction against the wild in human nature, ultimately against "the wild" itself. The timber explorers, whose "solitary and adventurous life" formerly struck Thoreau as "nearest to that of the trapper of the west" (*MW* 101), now seem "hirelings" with "no more love for wild nature, than wood-sawyers have for forests" (*MW* 119). The Indians of the woods, mostly moosehunters themselves, are seen with an equally jaundiced eye: "What a coarse and imperfect use Indians and hunters make of nature! No wonder that their race is so soon exterminated" (*MW* 120). Indian language continues to interest Thoreau, carrying him "as near to the primitive man of America . . . as any of its discovers" (*MW* 137). Yet the string of etymologies Thoreau manages to coax from a group of Indians has a disappointing literalness ("*Mattawamkeag* was a place where two rivers meet" [*MW* 141])[25] that falls far short of the natural poetry envisioned by Emerson and Charles Kraitsir. Immersed in nature, primitive man turns out to be prereflective, antipoetic, and (except for an uncanny practical acuteness like that of guide Joe Polis in "The Allegash and East Branch") unseeing.[26]

By the end of "Chesuncook," the relationships to nature held by the traveler, the scientist, the woodsman, the hunter, the Indian, and the romantic primitivist have all proved limited or worse; none singly provides a broadly humane "point of interest," and no imaginative triangulation of their perspectives seems feasible. The real "friend and lover of the pine" (Thoreau's symbol of the forest) turns out to be "the poet" (*MW* 121), conspicuously absent from the narrative before the moose-killing incident but introduced now as a counterweight to scientific myopia, commercial rapacity, and savage rudeness. William Howarth finds the "poet" of "Chesuncook" an anachronistic figure who "collects wild flowers" while his companions "slaughter moose," and who "dream[s] of a 'solitary and adventurous' year he might spend in the woods, 'living like a philosopher.'"[27] Howarth is right; although Thoreau has by no means finished with poets, this particular version of one seems to have been dusted off and commissioned to fill a moral void. As the product and representative of an evolved but happily bucolic state of society, the poet is useful for Thoreau in suggesting an ideal to juxtapose against the raw wilderness. And this ideal, in turn, seems to open the prospect of a *new* cultural role to be played by a very *different* sort of poet. Returning from the woods, Thoreau writes,

> it was a relief to get back to our smooth, but still varied landscape. For a permanent residence, it seemed to me that there could be no comparison between this and the wilderness, necessary as the latter is for a resource and a background, the raw material of all our civilization. The wilderness is simple, almost to barrenness. The partially cultivated country it is which chiefly has inspired, and will continue to inspire, the strains of poets . . . . Perhaps our own woods and fields, – with the primitive swamps scattered here and there in their midst, but not prevailing over them, are the perfection of parks and groves, gardens, arbors, paths, vistas, and landscape. They are the natural consequence of what art and refinement we as a people have, – the common which each

village possesses, its true paradise, in comparison with which all elaborately and wilfully wealth-constructed parks and gardens are paltry imitations. Or, I would rather say, such *were* our groves twenty years ago. (*MW* 155–56)

Noteworthy here is not only Thoreau's visible love for the Concord landscape but his willingness to write in the first person plural and take his place as a Concordian. Unlike "Walking," an "extreme statement" for "absolute freedom and wildness, as contrasted with a freedom and culture merely civil" (*EP* 205), "Chesuncook" in its final pages is a mediatory statement as Thoreau locates himself midway between the wild and the civil, nature and culture, absolute freedom and human commonalty. "Walking" is concerned with bringing man to nature, "Chesuncook" with bringing nature to man; and while Thoreau may still be leading a "sort of border life" (*EP* 242), venturing into the wild "not only for strength, but for beauty" (*MW* 156), his allegiance is now firmly attached to the environs of the village (the proper home for poets), whose paradisical blend of the primitive and the cultivated is steadily receding into the past. The "sense of the lateness of the hour"[28] that John Hildebidle finds in the natural history essays of 1859–62 is already present in the 1853 journal source for "Chesuncook," indeed, in an entry of the preceding March on the felling of a Concord woodlot: "The woods I walked in in my youth are cut off – Is it not time that I ceased to sing? My groves are invaded" (*PJ* 4, 385). The "complacent lyric poet" of "Chesuncook,"[29] as Howarth calls him, has in fact long ago ceased to sing, but in the invasion of his groves Thoreau has begun to find the voice of the "conservator" that will resound in his later work. "Why should not we, who have renounced the king's authority," he asks, "have our national preserves, where no villages need be destroyed, in which the bear and panther, and some even of the hunter race, may still exist, and not be 'civilized off the face of the earth' . . . ?" (*MW* 156). Instead of appropriating nature for himself and using it as a ground for superiority to Concord, Thoreau is proposing to mediate between what remains of nature and what seems redeemable in society. This is the stance he will adopt in the late manuscript "Huckleberries" ("Let us try to keep the new world new, and while we make a wary use of the city, preserve as far as we can the advantages of living in the country" [*NHE* 254]), and, with vastly more scientific ambition, in "The Succession of Forest Trees" (1860) and the encyclopedic, uncompleted, and probably uncompletable "Dispersion of Seeds."

8

"Annexing New Territories"
(1857–1862)

Where are the songs of Spring? Ay, where are they?
Think not of them, thou hast thy music too, –
Keats, "To Autumn"[1]

I

If careers, like novels and plays, assume mythic shape according to their endings,
the measure of Thoreau's career as romance, tragedy, divine comedy, or wintry
farce depends heavily on one's reading of the achievement and tendencies of his
late writings.[2] In addition to "Walking," revised for publication in 1862 but
essentially a work of the early 1850s, Thoreau completed three manuscripts in
the last years of his life: "Autumnal Tints," delivered in Worcester in February
1859 and published five months after his death in the *Atlantic Monthly* (October
1862); "Wild Apples," Thoreau's final lecture before the Concord Lyceum,
given in February 1860 and also published posthumously in the *Atlantic* (November
1862); and "The Succession of Forest Trees," an address to the Middlesex
Agricultural Society in September 1860, printed the following month in Horace
Greeley's *Tribune*. A fourth essay, "Huckleberries," was assembled by Leo Stoller
from manuscript leaves. At his death Thoreau also left behind partial drafts of two
immense natural history projects, "The Dispersion of Seeds" (a portion of
which, edited by Bradley H. Dean, appeared in 1993 as *Faith in a Seed*) and "Wild
Fruits," along with more than three thousand pages of notes (mostly extracts or
paraphrases) on "aboriginal North America: its people, geography, and history,"
the literary intention behind which is unclear.[3]

"The Universe has three children," Emerson wrote in "The Poet," "born at
one time, which reappear, under different names, in every system of thought,
. . . but which we will call here, the Knower, the Doer, and the Sayer. They stand
respectively for the love of truth, for the love of good, and for the love of beauty"
(*CW* III, 5). In the late Thoreau these figures incarnate themselves, respectively,
in the Naturalist, the Moralist, and the Poet. The moralist in Thoreau resides not

so much in the structure of the eye as in the modulation of the voice. Even in the journals it implies a hearer, or audience, usually an imagined townsman Thoreau is chiding for his ways. In mental solitude, when Concord was absent from his mind, Thoreau rarely dwelt upon "the good," indeed openly criticized Judeo-Christian ethicism, but he could seldom come before the public without an inflection of "ought" conditioning his rhetoric and authorial stance. The poet was a Sayer (or Maker), also a Seer (in both senses: a mystic *and* an appreciator of sensible beauty); above all, however, the poet was a "Be-er," since "poetry" was Thoreau's word for much of what pertained to his spiritual life. The naturalist was the empiric endlessly curious about the physical world and scrupulously faithful in reporting on it. "How differently the poet and the naturalist look at objects!" Thoreau exclaimed in "Autumnal Tints" (*EP* 286) – "and how differently the moralist relates them to behavior!" he might have added. The thrust of Thoreau's late work is toward a synthesis of these three personae, or rather a synthesis of the poet and the naturalist in some activity of the moralist – some service to himself and the community that might further his intellectual and spiritual growth, accommodate him to his neighbors, provide a literary subject and form, and establish his claim to permanent reputation as a writer.

"Wild Apples," a favorite of many readers, is probably the least ambitious of the natural history essays as well the least representative, drawing on journal entries dating back to the early 1850s, though in its finest passages reflecting the undemonstrative complexity and beauty of Thoreau's late prose. "A fact barely stated is dry," Thoreau noted in 1860: "It must be the vehicle of some humanity in order to interest us" (*J* XIII, 160). The "humanity" that most interested Thoreau was always his own; the success of the natural history essays lies in his new power and willingness to write about himself obliquely, taking a quiet satisfaction in his tropes without the insistent egotism that marked, and to a large degree marred, stylistic triumphs like "Life Without Principle." The wild apple attracted Thoreau, Robert Sattelmeyer notes, "because it was a forgotten and neglected fruit, . . . and because its situation and its qualities were so transparently suggestive of his own: a cultivated plant tending back to the wild, bearing its fruit late and unnoticed by most, crabbed and gnarled perhaps, but bracing if taken in the right spirit."[4] (Sherwood Anderson would use "gnarled, twisted apples" in a similar way in *Winesburg, Ohio* as an image for the hidden "sweetness" of his village grotesques.)[5] Following Sattelmeyer's lead, Steven Fink has superbly explicated the central section of "Wild Apples" in which Thoreau describes the struggle of the growing shoots in contending with "more difficulties" than any other trees and "sturdily resist[ing] their foes" (*EP* 303), especially cattle:

> The cows continue to browse them thus for twenty years or more, keeping them down and compelling them to spread, until at last they are so broad that they become their own fence, when some interior shoot, which their foes

cannot reach, darts upward with joy: for it has not forgotten its high calling, and bears its own peculiar fruit in triumph.

Such are the tactics by which it finally defeats its bovine foes. (*EP* 305)

"Cattle," as Fink reminds us, had been Thoreau's epithet for his Concord antagonists since his 1838 lyceum lecture on society.[6] "The reading public," Fink continues, "have shaped his own 'wild' American self and the expression of that self in writing. In typical Thoreauvian fashion, he has converted hardship and failure into the source of his ultimate triumph."[7] So far as the literal truth serves him, naturalist Thoreau is faithful to it, but the self-mythologist does not hesitate "to manipulate and, to some extent, misrepresent the natural facts in order to make the material conform to his symbolic construct" – suppressing, for example, his journal observation of 1853 that the cows "first planted" and manured the apple seeds and "thus . . . create[d] their own shade and food" (*J* V, 180).[8] In the essay itself the cows are unequivocally the enemy, which the "generous tree" in the fullness of its growth "permits . . . to come in and stand in its shade, and rub against and redden its trunk, which has grown in spite of them, and even to taste a part of its fruit, and so disperse the seed" (*EP* 305–6). The lines are a parable of Thoreau and his townsman-audience, whom the author blesses with the shade and fruit of his work, and who will ultimately bless him in turn by perpetuating his literary reputation.

What distinguishes this elaborate piece of wit from so many in *Walden* is the submersion rather than the blazoning of its personal reference, as if Thoreau has come to see his vindication as lying in a magnanimous forgiveness of Concord (still "cattle," nonetheless) and an absence of self-display. Even the more obtrusive puns in "Wild Apples" are relishable for their nonaggression. Browsed down by the cattle year after year, Thoreau writes, "No wonder [the apple trees] are prompted to grow thorns at last, to defend themselves against such foes. In their thorniness, however, there is no malice [from the Latin *malus* (evil)], only some malic acid [from *malus* (apple tree) and *malum* (apple)]." If Thoreau can't resist a barb or two of his own, he makes light of his "thorniness" by disclaiming a hurtful intent; the apples of his essay, he later puns, are "apples not of Discord, but of Concord!" (*EP* 314), and so for the most part they are.

A second difference between "Wild Apples" and *Walden* is Thoreau's new willingness to put forward his tropes *as* tropes, harvesting them for their metaphoric yield without ascribing an inherent significance to objects. In this he realizes the relationship to nature he had commended during the late *Walden* period – "He is the richest who has most use for nature as raw material of tropes and symbols with which to describe his life" (*J* V, 135) – but was too overswayed by Transcendental impulses to steadily adopt. By the late 1850s the reference of "symbol" has subtly changed for Thoreau; nature is no longer the symbolist, *man* is, and the tropes he engenders are valuable for their figurative truth whatever their ontological status. Thoreau can now explore nature more receptively, both as naturalist and as poet, because the burden of making it *signify* something or *perform* something has been lifted in favor of the more modest and dependably satisfying service of provoking the imagination. Troping had always been part of Thoreau's literary relationship to nature, but too many urgencies had intervened for it to be the dominant part. "In the last essays," as James McIntosh remarks, "Thoreau consistently presents nature as a familiar ally, no longer as a problem."[9] He and nature have become friendly co-workers in the collegial effort of educing the self, an activity uncomplicated now by questions of nature's intrinsic meaning or of its purity and disquieting filth. Without abandoning the search for moral analogies, Thoreau seems ready to grant them a wholly conjectural status and to share his constructions with those readers who are are willing and able to follow him.[10]

II

Of the natural history essays, "Autumnal Tints" works most subtly on the levels of description, moral reflection, social critique, and personal allegory, that is to say, operates with the density and symbolic richness of poetry, which it comes nearest to approaching. Literally, the essay is a painterly scrapbook of the advancing season drawn from the annual "calendar" of Concord Thoreau sometimes imagined writing. The open concern of the essay is beauty, not scientific knowledge – "the rosy cheek" of nature rather than the "particular diet the maiden fed on" (*EP* 250) – and though its rendering of a New England fall is visibly sharpened by learning, it pillories the botanist for an insensitivity to nature's grandeur as dessicated as the practical farmer's. Robert D. Richardson argues convincingly for Ruskin's presence in "Autumnal Tints."[11] Thoreau read *Modern Painters* in 1857 with an enthusiasm qualified chiefly by his regret that it was, after all, only a book about art ("He does not describe Nature as Nature, but as Turner painted her" [*J* X, 69]). It was Ruskin's *Elements of Drawing,* according to Richardson, that still more palpably influenced Thoreau in its emphasis on the artist's "representing 'visual appearances only, never memory knowledge'" – on his "'recovery of what may be called *the innocence of the eye:* that is to say, of a sort of childish perception of these flat stains of colour, merely as such, without consciousness of what they signify.'"[12] Whether Ruskin helped teach Thoreau to see or simply furnished an aesthetic vocabulary for the way he had already begun to see, the journals of October 1857 and, especially, October 1858 show a heightened responsiveness to color, virtually the *only* subject of the lengthy 1858 entries, the prime source for "Autumnal Tints."[13]

In its stance toward the reader, "Autumnal Tints," fittingly, is a pleasantly mellow and meditative performance. Utilitarians of various sorts (market-oriented farmers, town selectmen, field scientists) come in for periodic gibes, but the reader is not presumed to be among them. Neither dull-witted nor morally obtuse, the implied reader is nonetheless conveniently unappreciative, and Thoreau's first object as writer is to show him the "seasons and haunts [of beauty], and the color of its wing" (*EP* 287). His teaching is mostly of the gentlest sort, an overlay of sensibility and light moralizing on what offers itself as a guided tour through rural New England for the uninstructed city dweller (*EP* 249).[14] "If Thoreau is . . . somewhat in advance of [his audience]," as John Hildebidle comments, "the reason has nothing to do with secret initiations he may have undergone; it is simply that, as he tells us, 'I have learned to look.' Thoreau is our model of the man who has trained himself" and whom we may practically hope to emulate.[15]

The essay's second level of "seeing" rests on the proposition that "each humblest plant, or weed, as we call it, stands there to express some thought or mood of ours" (*EP* 257). The correspondence is metaphoric, not transcendental; objects "stand there," that is, for the poet as he articulates himself through the vocabulary of nature rather than for the visionary who would grasp nature itself. At its worst, the poet's search for tropes can end in the moralizing on nature that led Hawthorne to contrast the lovely and fragrant pond lily with the foul-smelling yellow lily, both of which had their roots in the black mud of the Concord River; "Thus we see, too, in the world, that some persons assimilate only what is ugly and evil from the same moral circumstances which supply good and beautiful results – the fragrance of celestial flowers – to the daily life of others."[16] "Autumnal Tints" escapes such platitudes not only because Thoreau's habit of mind is less convention-bound to begin with, but because his perception of nature is acute enough to show him nuances of fact – translatable into nuances of human meaning – that escape the casual eye of a Hawthorne. The naturalist serves the poet and the moralist by discovering a world of finely wrought detail that elicits a corresponding fineness of insight in the perceiver and an accompanying freshness and precision of imagery. Unlike Samuel Johnson's ideal poet in *Rasselas,* the writer of "Autumnal Tints" finds his vocation in "numbering the streaks of the tulip," yet like Johnson's poet he manages to direct his observations toward a just and striking picture of common human nature.[17]

If "Autumnal Tints" is about the species, it is also about Thoreau himself as he meditates on his life and literary career. The progress of the season gave him his subject and principle of structure; the schooling of the reader's eye supplied a didactic rationale; but what lends "Autumnal Tints" its special depth and poignancy – its "point of interest" between outward phenomena and the self – is an evocation of ripeness and impending death intimately confessional in reference. "Perhaps after middle age man ceases to be interested in the morning and in the spring" (*J* V, 393), Thoreau remarked in August 1853. The entry continues with an exclamation on the deep purple bloom of the pokeweed "all afire with ripeness": "What maturity it arrives [at], ripening from leaf to root! May I mature as perfectly, root and branch, as the poke! . . . It is the emblem of a successful life, a not premature death – whose death is an ornament to nature" (*J* V, 393).

"Autumnal Tints" incorporates the passage and through its evocation of the brilliant flaring and dying of fall color extends its conceit of a climactic flourish presaging death, by now a timely subject for Thoreau. As October lapsed into November 1858, the shortening days recalled him to "the shortness of life" and the need "to make haste and finish our work before the night comes" (*J* XI, 273).

The theme of death enters "Autumnal Tints" in a late section on fallen leaves in which Thoreau's use of the pathetic fallacy (falling leaves as falling lives) seems more a sign of philosophical acquiescence than a groping for sentimental effect. One thinks, by contrast, of Richard Wilbur's "Year's End," in which leaves and ferns relinquish life gracefully as a final act of the organic cycle while human beings die "incomplete" with "the random hands, the loose unready eyes / Of men expecting yet another sun / To do the shapely thing they had not done."[18] Thoreau sees none of Wilbur's grotesque truncation; in "Autumnal Tints" humans die serenely at their proper time, like leaves that flutter down in due course "before they rest quietly in their graves! They that soared so loftily, how contentedly they return to dust again, and are laid low, resigned to lie and decay at the foot of the tree, and afford nourishment to new generations of their kind, as well as to flutter on high! They teach us how to die" (*EP* 270). Literally, "they" (our instructors in mortality) are the leaves, but the insistent personification in the passage, the image of soaring, and the particular kind of immortality Thoreau imagines for leaves and men – not an afterlife of the soul but an organic nourishment of future generations – combine to suggest the exemplary life and death of the writer, who has also soared loftily in his time, and whose "leaves" (of prose) will fertilize the world long after his death. The flurry of deathbed activity with which Thoreau revised his manuscripts and arranged for their posthumous publication indicates he had greater ambitions than to become, like most of us, organic mold. "He wanted to assure that his own leaves would survive him," William Howarth observes[19] – more than that, perhaps, that *he* would survive *in* them. It was not simply the deathlessness of the artifact that spurred him on at the last, but the immortality – the persistence of self – to be achieved *through* the artifact.

However this may be, the focus of "Autumnal Tints" is not so much on death as on the celebration of a productive life. Though fall color presages death and owes its aching loveliness to reminders of death, Thoreau chooses to see it as the sign of "a late and perfect maturity, answering to the maturity of fruits" yet nobler than nature's edible harvest because it "address[es] our taste for beauty alone" (*EP* 250–51). In likening a leaf to a fruit, Thoreau takes liberties with scientific fact, converting a symbol of waning vitality into one of rich consummation meant to endow human maturity with the concentrated sweetness of an apple or grape ripened slowly in the sun. Here the poet is not discovering analogies so much as enlisting them in the service of a mythology he is determined to write. In the complex allegory that follows, "every fruit, on ripening," represents both an organic perfection of the earthly and a spiritual attenuation of the earthly. "Just before it falls," Thoreau writes, the fruit/leaf "commences a more independent and individual existence, requiring less nourishment from any source, and that not so much from the earth through its stem as from the sun and air" (*EP* 250). Like the butterfly in *Walden* metamorphosed from "the voracious caterpillar" and feeding only on "a drop or two of honey or some other sweet liquid" (*W* 215), the leaves are essentially finished with earthly sustenance and ready to surrender their corporeal life as they await translation into spirit. With their deeply scalloped lobes, so sparing of "leafy *terra firma*," the scarlet oaks, particularly, the latest and "ripest fruit of the year" (*EP* 284), are the most "ethereal" of their species: "Lifted higher and higher, and sublimated more and more, putting off some earthiness and cultivating more intimacy with the light each year, they have at length the least possible amount of earthy matter, and the greatest spread and grasp of skyey influences" (*EP* 278).

Just as Thoreau would image himself in the long-suffering but triumphant trees of "Wild Apples," so he is each of the trees and plants in "Autumnal Tints," whether in his character, his achievement, or his circumstances in the world. Thoreau is the pokeweed "glowing in the midst of [his] decay" (*EP* 255). He is the "small red maple" flourishing in solitude, "unobserved," attending to its business without "gadding abroad," "neglect[ing] none of its economies," and ripening "at the eleventh hour of the year" in spectacular vindication of its ways, like an artist coming forth from long seclusion with his book: "the tree which no scrutiny could have detected here when it was most industrious is thus, by the tint of its maturity, revealed at last to the careless and distant traveler, and leads his thoughts away from the dusty road into those brave solitudes which it inhabits" (*EP* 260–61). As writer of the late-harvested "Autumnal Tints" Thoreau is likewise the scarlet oak with its "late and unexpected glory" (*EP* 281), rarely appreciated since most people have shut themselves indoors yet "surpass[ing] all that spring or summer could do" (*EP* 284). At each turn Thoreau selects and arranges natural facts with such quiet artistry that the interpretive context for his life seems almost to arise spontaneously from nature itself. He does not present his spiritual life as a long descent from youthful raptures, nor does he regard his artistic life as a lapse from the achievement of *Walden*. The best is now, in the present as it opens toward the future.

Beneath all its particulars, the subject of "Autumnal Tints" is its own meditative and stylistic ripeness as it crowns its author's life and literary career and signals both a worldly fulfillment and a readiness for the spiritual translation to be wrought by death. Thoreau has ceased trying to defy gravity. Acknowledging the organic propriety of change, decay, and death (leaves *fall*), he has come to rejoice in the fruition of earthly life as it prepares to shed its bodily envelope and become spirit. He has learned, moreover, to make an art of exquisite beauty from the poignancy of life in time. To write in such a fashion was nearly to dissolve into spirit oneself, like the sculpted leaves of the scarlet oak "so intimately mingled" as they dance with the light that "you can hardly tell at last what in the dance is leaf and what is light" (*EP* 278–79). The proof of Thoreau's claim of autumnal fulfillment is the serene mastery palpable in his prose.

Through all of this Thoreau has not forgone his quarrel with Concord; he has, however, considerably relaxed it, coming himself to lead a "more independent" existence and "requiring less nourishment" from his townsmen. A section on elms – social trees that line the streets of the village and resemble yellow sheaves of grain – gives him occasion to wonder whether the ripeness of the trees finds "any answering ripeness in the lives of the men who live beneath them" (*EP* 263). As he sees "the market-man driving into the village, and disappearing under its canopy of elm-tops, with *his* crop," he is "tempted" to follow him "as to a husking of thoughts, now dry and ripe," but he fears "it will be chiefly husks and little thought, blasted pig-corn, fit only for cob-meal, – for, as you sow, so shall you reap" (*EP* 264). Where the farmer dully submits to nature's rhythm, the poet imaginatively aligns himself with it, sows with his spirit, reaps accordingly, and ripens by an inner timetable to a harvest of astonishing fruitfulness. An opposition between material and spiritual profit, utility and beauty, runs throughout "Autumnal Tints," but if Thoreau continues to play the good physician well into his mellow autumn, he has at least learned to sugar-coat his pills. Even his most unpalatable medicine, his argument against organized religion – "What meant the [town] fathers by establishing this *perfectly living* institution" (the sugar maples on the common) beside the perfectly dead institution of "the church?" (*EP* 277) – is administered in a genial prose inoffensive to the casual reader. Like Melville in his magazine pieces of 1853–56, Thoreau has learned to write for two audiences, with two purposes; he continues to have his say for those who wish to hear him, but he has mastered the art of the engaging surface unruffled by the contempt of the moral censor or the defensive urgency of the self-apologist.

III

In its effort to join naturalistic detail with moral and aesthetic idealization, "Autumnal Tints" is a literary counterpart to the work of Hudson River painters from Thomas Cole to Frederic Church. "I do feel that I am not a mere leaf-painter. I have higher conceptions than a mere combination of inanimate, uninformed nature,"[20] Cole said of his landscapes, which included several brilliantly colored canvases of New York and New England autumns. With his ambition to "unite discovery, science, and art" and his near-religious awe at nature's grandeur,[21] Church, whose major work emerged in the decade of "Autumnal Tints," seems even closer to Thoreau, though Church liked to paint grandiosely on the scale of the sublime, while Thoreau worked in a miniaturist vein of the picturesque. Beyond appealing to the midcentury love of idealized realism,[22] "Autumnal Tints" was a wonderfully contrived lyceum performance, fresh, vividly pictorial, lending itself to sentiment (if so one took it) but inviting a deeper response from the thoughtful and discerning. Yet Thoreau never sought to repeat the triumph. In its cultivation of the poet-moralist at the expense of the empiricist, "Autumnal Tints" is not only anomalous among his late manuscripts but represents a kind of willed counterthrust to the positivistic direction he saw his interests and character taking.

In the months following the lecture Thoreau's quarrel with the objectivity of science intensified, a sign not of his rejection of empirical methods but, paradoxically, of his increased involvement with them. For want of a theory of nature's inward dynamics, "the science of Thoreau's lifetime was primarily taxonomy," or classification, Walter Harding reminds us,[23] and it was chiefly as a recorder and measurer of phenomena that Thoreau the empiric approached nature with mingled curiosity and impatience. Against the positivist's search for a knowledge of fact distinct from its reference to the perceiver, Thoreau protested in the name of what he called the "humanity" of science, by which he tended to mean a moral subjectivism that satisfied one side of his nature but affronted another. "Autumnal Tints" escaped the vetoes of the Thoreauvian empiricist through a "literariness" that proclaimed with every sentence, "This is a work of metaphor." Poets never lie, as Philip Sidney had answered poetry's sixteenth-century critics, because they never claim to be telling the factual truth. To Thoreau, however, Sidney's victory, like his own in "Autumnal Tints," would have semed a costly one bordering on the Pyrrhic. The factual had come to absorb an increasing part of his attention during his afternoon walks, in his reading, and with regard to the developmental possibilities he saw ahead of him. Yet neither would Thoreau sacrifice the poet in himself – always, he felt, his highest, most spiritual self, if not his very soul.

To find a more imaginative science that might span his diverging interests, Thoreau turned in 1859–60 to the classical naturalists, Aristotle and Pliny especially, and to natural historians of the Renaissance and seventeenth century, whose colorful style was an antidote to the self-impoverishment of modern science.[24] Even when their testimonies were wholly incredible, the old naturalists erred in the healthier direction of "imagin[ing] more than existed, while the moderns cannot imagine so much as exists" (*J* XIII, 155; v. *J* XIII, 150–53). What Thoreau really sought was not the fabulous but the organic: a science of *processes* that confirmed the intuition of the sandbank passage that ours was "not a fossil earth, but a living earth" (*W* 309; v. *J* XIII, 154). "The development theory implies a greater vital force in Nature, because it is more flexible and accommodating, and equivalent to a sort of constant new creation" (*FS* 102), he wrote in the "Dispersion of Seeds" manuscript. Prior to 1859, however, no development theory seemed viable: the spiritualism of Wilkinson and Coleridge had long been discredited by Thoreau's immersion in fact; the progressionism of creation theorists like Louis Agassiz was tainted by its ascription of change to periodic divine interventions; and the naturalistic evolutionism represented by Robert

Chambers's *Vestiges of Creation* had neither the rigor of genuine science nor the idealism of the old *Naturphilosophie.* Thoreau's return to the beginnings of natural history was a search not so much for an alternative to science as for a suggestive model of how to think about science – for what Emerson called "a theory of nature" (*CW* I, 8) or what moderns call a "paradigm."

It was the absence of such a paradigm that seems to have delayed Thoreau in formalizing the hypothesis about forest succession that occupied him in the last half-dozen years of his life and that constitutes, as Harding says, his "major contribution to scientific knowledge."[25] In April 1856 a neighbor called his attention to the fact that when a pine wood was felled, oaks or other hardwoods would generally grow up in its place. He had read this himself years before in G. B. Emerson's *Report on the Trees and Shrubs Growing Naturally in the Forests of Massachusetts* (1846); the alternation of forest trees – hardwoods replacing pines; pines yielding to hardwoods – was even "a matter of common observation in the country around Concord,"[26] though the mechanism of succession (spontaneous generation? seeds lying dormant in the soil for years? the agency of fire?) was poorly understood. By mid-May Thoreau had framed his own explanation: the hardwoods grew from small saplings barely noticeable on the pine needle floor, whose seeds had "probably" been "carried into the thicket by squirrels": "This planting under the shelter of the pines may be carried on annually, and the plants annually die, but when the pines are cleared off, the oaks, etc., having got just the start they want, and now secured favorable conditions, immediately spring up into trees. Scarcely any allowance has been made for the agency of squirrels and birds in dispersing seeds" (*J* VIII, 335).

Leo Stoller sees the April incident as precipitating "a synthesis" of "the hitherto unrelated pieces of information lying dormant in Thoreau's mind."[27] If so, it seems odd that the synthesis should have gone undeveloped for more than four years, particularly after Thoreau found anecdotal confirmation of his theory in September 1857 when he chanced upon a squirrel burying hickory nuts beneath a hemlock: "This, then, is how forests are planted. This nut must have been brought twenty rods at least and was buried at just the right depth. If the squirrel is killed, or neglects its deposit, a hickory springs up" (*J* X, 40). The long interval between discovery and announcement is evidence for William Howarth's conjecture that the catalyst for "The Succession of Forest Trees" (September 1860) was Thoreau's January reading of *The Origin of Species,* which redirected him "from tedious research to interpreting his data more broadly."[28] Studying the *Origin,* Thoreau would have been impressed by Darwin's wide-ranging allusiveness and keen powers of perception and generalization, by the force of his scientific reasoning and the clarity of his style, and by illustrations that drew with an astonishing offhandedness on facts to which he himself had given the most painstaking attention – for Darwin, too, cited the growth of trees from nearly undetectable seedlings, the role of birds and other animals in the dispersion of seeds, and the succession of species in North American forests.[29] Thoreau could scarcely have avoided a feeling of provinciality beside Darwin; but while the invalid Darwin may have known the world – in youth from his travels on the *Beagle,* later from his vast reading and scientific correspondence – the peripatetic Thoreau knew Concord, and under the stimulus of Darwin he may now have begun to regard his microcosm with new eyes. If Aristotle's work was valuable to him as "a very storehouse of scientific nomenclature" (*J* XIII, 55), Darwin's supplied the principle (competition) that caused the accumulated data to spring into life. Darwin himself sometimes spoke as if observation itself generated hypotheses, claiming to have worked toward the *Origin* "on true Baconian principles, and without any theory" to guide his collection of facts; at other times, however, he was more candid about the controlling agency of ideas: "How odd it is that any one should not see that all observation must be for or against some view if it is to be of any service!"[30] Thoreau came to agree; "How is any scientific discovery made?" he asked late in 1860: "Why, the discoverer takes it into his head first. He must all but see it" (*J* XIV, 267).

The specific question Darwinian competition would have helped Thoreau to "see" was the one he left unanswered, even unasked, during his observations of 1856–57: why, when a *hardwood* stand was cut, did pines spring up in its place since pine and hardwood seeds were both presumably buried in the soil? Although the dispersion of seeds exploded the old myth of spontaneous generation, it failed to explain why one species of available seed came to predominate over another. Thoreau's answer to this problem in "The Succession of Forest Trees" and the hundreds of journal pages that follow it shows his increasing dedication and thoroughness as a scientist. His explanation in the lecture itself is tentative, based more on conjecture than on solid observation and showing only a partial assimilation of Darwin:

> [W]hen you cut a lot of hard wood, very often the little pines mixed with it have a similar start, for the squirrels have carried off the nuts to the pines, and not to the more open wood, and they commonly make pretty clean work of it; and moreover, if the wood was old, the sprouts will be feeble, or entirely fail; to say nothing about the soil being, in a measure, exhausted for this kind of crop. (*EP* 190)

Thoreau's reasoning is speculative, plausible, factually undersupported, and sometimes erroneous. He is right about the feebleness of stump sprouts grown from older hardwoods. However, white pines, which "will not tolerate any serious degree of shading, and can grow vigorously only in the open," would probably not have gotten much "start" in an oak forest except where disease, windfalls, fire, or Alek Therien's ax had created a small clearing.[31] Thoreau gives no reason why squirrels should carry acorns from one wooded covert to another, nor does he consider the windborne or bird-distributed birch, poplar, and cherry seeds that commonly take root in a cut forest and (fast growers all) "offer strenuous competition to the new generation of pine."[32] Lacking a single conclusive explanation – it would be decades till foresters discovered that "the specific critical factor [in pine growth] is light" – [33] Thoreau offers several weak and partial ones, appealing at last to the popular but mistaken analogy of crop rotation (*EP* 190).[34] Thoreau's "succession" of forest trees amounts finally to a pine-oak alternation, though the title of his essay is truer to fact than its argument: white pines do not normally "alternate" with hardwoods in mid-New England forests but are succeeded by them, the white pine being a "transient" in any given location in the north woods.[35]

Thoreau could not have known most of this. To grasp fully the pattern of forest succession, he would have needed a broad geographical perspective and a reasonably complete and accurate set of historical records. In the absence of these advantages, he assumed the painstaking task of reconstructing the history of local woodlots from the physical evidence directly at hand. As a scientist, Thoreau had hitherto been an alert but self-trained observer who enjoyed discovering things for himself whether or not they had already been discovered, and who in coming upon a magical phenomenon like phosphorescent wood could be tempted to "let science slide" and revel in pure wonder (*MW* 181). In the succession of forest trees, he found an untouched subject ideally suited to draw out his more rigorous empirical gifts. Thoreau's lectures and published writings typically mark a consummation of some interest or commitment; they work up existing journal materials, that is, rather than stimulate new ones. His address of September 1860, by contrast, represents an engaged beginning. Almost immediately, his accounts of his daily walks take on a purposiveness quite different from the casual, seasonally-oriented sauntering of earlier days. After listing "the trees which *with us* grow in masses," he wondered in mid October "what determines which species of these shall grow on a given tract" (*J* XIV, 134). To this question he devoted an intense and unusually systematic two weeks, the prelude to a still more ambitious investigation that would occupy him through December 3, when he caught the cold that precipitated his final illness. The uncompleted "Dispersion of Seeds," together with the journal entries that underlie it, is Thoreau's *Voyage of the Beagle* – a work of massive observation, classification, and incipient speculation that shows an impulse toward theory but not as yet a discernible theory itself. Its virtues are patience, thoroughness, and a certain ad hoc version of what one historian of science calls "the hypothetico-deductive method," in which the empiricist "invent[s] a plausible hypothesis based on facts available to him and then use[s] this as a guide to further research."[36]

The paradigm that governed Thoreau's research was the Darwinian one of an incessant competition ruling (in Darwin's words) "the whole economy of nature" and showing itself in "every fact on distribution, rarity, abundance, extinction, and variation."[37] Though never squeamish in acknowledging nature's strife, Thoreau could hardly have been comfortable with Darwin's insistence on struggle as the basic mechanism of organic life. Prompted by Thomas Malthus's

Essay on Population, Darwin's "struggle for existence" not only mirrored the ethic (or non-ethic) of laissez-faire capitalism, but it represented the extreme of soul-less materialism: "a natural, mechanical principle operating without the conscious intervention of either human or divine agents, a principle that was self-explanatory, self-sufficient, and self-regulating."[38] The hypothesis of botanical opportunism was too persuasive and convenient to resist, however, and Thoreau let it guide his thinking ("There are always the oaks ready to take advantage of the least feebleness and yielding of the pines" [*J* XIV, 141]) even as he continued to personify Nature as a wise and beneficent goddess. Returning to the field like any responsible scientist conscious of flaws in his theory, he searched for evidences of selection in the predominance of certain trees. He discovered that the pine is indeed a transient (a "pioneer" giving way to the "the more permanent settler," the oak, he wrote in a rare flight of metaphor [*J* XIV, 130; *FS* 167]); that pitch pines require the light of an open field to thrive and white pines at least a substantial clearing in the woods (*J* XIV, 162, 267–68; *FS* 152–53); that oak seedlings fare better under the shade of pines than under mature oaks (*J* XIV, 180); that squirrels who carry acorns to the pine woods may do so because "the ground does not freeze so hard under the dense pines" (*J* XIV, 143), inadvertently benefiting the frost-sensitive acorns even as they serve themselves; and that mixed oak and pine forests were more the rule in and around Concord than his initial theory had allowed. Having gathered his evidence, Thoreau moved to extrapolate laws and conclusions from it (*J* XIV, 181–82). His interest was not philosophical but practical. "May we not *see* God?" (*Wk* 382), he had asked in *A Week*. "Why not control our own woods and destiny more?" (*FS* 166), he now asks. He has discovered the basic principles of forest succession, and instead of simply exhorting his townsmen to conserve nature, he can teach them to use it more profitably (in every sense) by acquainting them with the results of various human interventions – burning and temporary agricultural planting (the most wasteful course), clear-cutting, selective foresting, and benign neglect.

As a preface to these investigations, "The Succession of Forest Trees" gives a very imperfect idea of the scope, penetration, and utility of Thoreau's scientific work or of the excitement of discovery that marks his late journals. The weeks of exploring woodlots brought Thoreau to a new appreciation of nature's harmony that reestablished the poet's sense of miracle and beauty on the solid ground of unillusioned empirical understanding. Although nature seethed with struggle, its processes conduced toward a temporary equilibrium in which, "when sufficient time is given, trees will be found occupying the places most suitable to each" (*J* XIV, 218; v. XIV, 243) – the "climax stage" of forest development described by modern silvicultural theory. Starting from the Darwinian premise of competition, Thoreau has ended with a vision of what can only be called "the good." There seems little in his conclusions inimical to Darwinism save, characteristically, his confidence in a beneficent teleology at work; but that itself is crucial. Long-term cosmic ends – the spiritual evolution of the earth, the "thawing" of man – concern him less than they once did, for, having separated time from eternity, his worldly perspective is now primarily spatial, or ecological: the interrelationship of organisms within a functioning system.

Because Thoreau never lived to develop a full-fledged ecology, it is tempting to conceive one for him and to make him more of a late-twentieth-century thinker than he was or might have become. Forced to decide between Darwinian natural selection and some version of the traditional argument from design, Thoreau would probably have hesitated for a time, looked wishfully at a teleologized natural selection (as Darwin's colleague Alfred Russel Wallace did), then, if pressed to choose definitively, come down on the side of teleology. The scientist was strong in Thoreau, but the poet and residual transcendentalist were even stronger. Occasionally Thoreau put a question that seemed inescapably to invite a Darwinian answer. For example: "What kind of understanding was there between the mind that determined that these [willow] leaves should hang on during the winter, and that of the worm that fastened a few of these leaves to its cocoon in order to disguise it?" (J IX, 221). Posed early in 1857, more than two years before the publication of the *Origin,* Thoreau's question is purely rhetorical, as it had to be. Even after reading Darwin, however, Thoreau, observing that the vast proportion of maple seeds on Mt. Monadnock were eaten by squirrels, could reason that sustaining squirrels "apparently is one of the principal ends which these seeds *were intended* to serve" (J XIV, 6–7; my emphasis). Even when he hypothesizes as a scientist, Thoreau often likes to personify nature and accord it a "design," especially when marveling at the beauty that Darwin saw only as a puzzling, gratuitous by-product of the survival of the fittest.[39] An example of Thoreauvian nature writing at its best and most problematic is his empirical-fanciful description of a maple seed:

> In all our maples a thin membrane, in appearance much like an insect's wing, grows over and around the seed while the latter is being developed within its base. Indeed, this is often perfectly developed, though the seed is abortive – Nature being, you would say, more sure to provide the means of transporting the seed than to provide the seed to be transported. In other words, a beautiful thin sack is woven around the seed, with a handle to it such as the wind can take hold of, and it is then committed to the wind, expressly that it may transport the seed and extend the range of the species; and this it does as effectually as when seeds are sent by mail in a different kind of sack from the Patent Office. There is a Patent Office at the seat of government of the universe, whose managers are as much interested in the dispersion of seeds as any body at Washington can be, and their operations are infinitely more extensive and regular. (*FS* 50)

Robert Sattelmeyer believes that judgments of Thoreau as an unscientific scientist may reflect "our own implicit and unexamined assumption about the unbridgeable gap between scientific and imaginative truth [that] makes it almost impossible [for us] to grasp the nature of his work from the inside."[40] In the case of the maple seed he may well be right, for it is hard to imagine an acceptably positivist description that would combine the factual precision and pictorial suggestiveness Thoreau achieves through simile ("like an insect's wing") and metaphor ("with a handle to it such as the wind can take hold of"). Intentionally or not, however, the passage unavoidably implies a metaphysics, which strains against the limits of empirical-poetic accommodation. "Expressly that it may . . ." suggests not only evolutionary functionalism but teleological intent, while Thoreau's Patent Office conclusion – the *literary* climax of the passage – is a metaphor virtually without referent, dangling free of propositional meaning.

Thoreau himself may have felt how evasive such writerly passages were, for they are exceedingly rare in the late journals and "The Dispersion of Seeds"; on the other hand, they may be rare because Thoreau could rarely achieve them. Although the poet in him could sometimes embroider the discoveries of the naturalist, the two visions and voices seldom worked spontaneously in unison. Reconciling them may have been his ultimate goal in 1860–61, though, as Robert D. Richardson observes, "the publication of *The Dispersion of Seeds* does not clarify the overall intention of [his] late works" (*FS* 6). If Thoreau was indeed trying to unify a divided sensibility, he was battling centrifugal impulses in his culture as well as his temper, for he worked at a time "when the differentiation between amateur and professional, between man of letters and man of science, [was becoming] distinct and irrevocable."[41] But the chief opposition between Thoreau and the Darwinian scientist was not vocational but philosophical. Thoreau's nature, though competitive, is purposive and benign, while Darwin's is a turbid conjunction of chance and necessity whose "astonishing waste" of life, even among successful species, struck the author of the *Origin* as "abhorrent to our ideas of fitness."[42] Thoreau, too, had perceptions of enormous and horrific "waste," which looked, he admitted, "like a glaring imperfection in nature" (*J* XIV, 149); but such moments of doubt were infrequent and quickly suppressed. Even in the scientism of his last years, Thoreau never lost the Romantic's faith in a beneficently spiritual nature, though it would have been difficult for him to specify what his belief consisted in beyond a vague constitutional hopefulness. In this respect, Bradley H. Dean's edition of the "Dispersion" manuscript, *Faith in a Seed,* is aptly titled.

Conscious of the difficulties of teleology, or perhaps simply uninterested in nature's God toward the last, Thoreau found justification for science in its moral reference to humanity – in the case of succession theory, its implications for the behavior of communities in establishing an optimal relation to nature. The rationale for studying the history of Concord woodlots was that by knowing how they developed "we should manage them more wisely" (*J* XIV, 126). In the project that evolved from this impulse, the naturalist, the moralist, and the poet converged in a new Thoreauvian figure, the ecologist, whose errand to mankind was to correct the long "history of cross-purposes" in which human "blundering," "improvidence," and greed frustrated the regenerative efforts of nature (*J*

XIV, 132, 130). The abuse of forests rankled Thoreau like the abuse of animals and reawakened his anger at a system of ownership that allowed shortsighted proprietors to cut a thriving woods and burn the saplings ready to succeed it in order to plant a crop or two of winter rye. Indignation wells up in the journals whenever Thoreau considers the ravages of his thoughtless townsmen. In "The Succession of Forest Trees," his address to the Middlesex Agricultural Society, he restrains his anger and applies it to instructional ends. Once again he presents himself as a man who has traveled a good deal in Concord, but this time he speaks with the practical authority of a surveyor-naturalist who has walked his neighbors' properties more often and more thoroughly perhaps than they have, and who now proposes to "lead [them] back into [their] wood-lots again" (*EP* 186) to explain phenomena they may have noticed but scarcely understood. He addresses them not as a moralist preaching simplicity but as the delegate from a more enlightened Agricultural Society assigned to teach them their own long-term interests by elucidating the ways of "the most extensive and experienced planter of us all" (*EP* 198), nature itself. In *Walden* Thoreau had professed to find farmers "respectable and interesting . . . in proportion as they are poor, – poor farmers" (*W* 196); in "the Succession of Forest Trees" he undertakes to make them good farmers and seems perfectly willing to let them thrive in the process.[43]

This does not mean that by 1860 Thoreau had reconciled himself to market values. One of the last sustained entries in his journal (partly incorporated into "Huckleberries") is an attack on commercialism sharply reminiscent of "Economy":

> How few ever get beyond feeding, clothing, sheltering, and warming themselves in this world, and begin to treat themselves as human beings, – as intellectual and moral beings! Most seem not to see any further, – not to see over the ridge-pole of their barns, – or to be exhausted and accomplish nothing more than a full barn, though it be accompanied by an empty head. . . . He who has the reputation of being the thriftiest farmer and making the best bargains is really the most thriftless and makes the worst. . . .
>
> But most men, it seems to me, do not care for Nature and would sell their share in all her beauty, as long as they may live, for a stated sum – many for a glass of rum. Thank God, men cannot as yet fly, and lay waste the sky as well as the earth! We are safe on that side for the present. It is for the very reason that some do not care for those things that we need to continue to protect all from the vandalism of a few. (*J* XIV, 306–7; v. *NHE* 256)

"All" refers to the community not as an aggregate of individuals but as the organism "society" as it extends across time and region and merges with the destiny of the race. Privately, Thoreau is as hostile as ever to the reifying capitalism in which nothing is deemed "valuable . . . until it is convertible into so much money, that is, can cease to be what it is and become something else which you prefer" (*J* XIV, 283). Yet rather than chide his townsmen for values he knows are unreformable, he is willing to let materialism be its own punishment and work to restrain the outward depredations of nature by showing their inutility. He has resigned himself to the short-term triumph of capitalism and staked his efforts on the belief that humanity as a group may outlive its folly and eventually turn to nature. His errand is to help ensure that enough of nature will remain intact for man when he realizes he needs it. It is not simply to preserve the forests themselves that Thoreau assumes the role of ecological reformer but to stabilize the natural conditions in which humanity may one day grow to fullness. His premises are that, for better or worse, society is where human beings (himself included) must find their home, and that society flourishes best in the precariously balanced "middle landscape" he had disparaged earlier in his career (*A Week*) but has come to view as the most beautiful and potentially fulfilling of human worlds. To perpetuate this world, "Chesuncook" proposed a system of "national preserves" (*MW* 156) resembling our present one of national parks, forests, and seashores. "Huckleberries" returns to the idea on the level of the community. "Let us try to keep the new world new," Thoreau urges his neighbors, "and while we make a wary use of the city, preserve as far as posssible the advantages of living in the country" (*NHE* 254). As a noun and verb both, "preserve" is the key to the late Thoreau's errand to mankind. Unable to redeem his townsmen by morally awakening them, Thoreau could at least work to save a portion of redemptive nature till their descendants should have grown wise enough to profit from it.

"The Succession of Forest Trees" is his practical effort to do this while at the same time reaffirming his private identity as poet. The core of the lecture is his exposition of forest laws as they bear upon the management of local woodlots, but the lecture is also a conscious literary performance that weaves together concerns from his later years in what proved to be his valediction to Concord. It is fitting that this last address should have been delivered before the Middlesex Agricultural Society. Twenty-two years earlier, in his first appearance before his townsmen, Thoreau had spoken caustically of going "to a cattleshow expecting to find many men and women assembled, and behold[-ing] only working oxen and neat cattle" (*PJ* 1, 36). Because a cattle show symbolized for him both the narrow utilitarianism of his neighbors and their bovine spiritual state, there is a poetic symmetry to his closing his public career by petitioning to join the community at its annual fete. "Every man is entitled to come to Cattle-Show, even a transcendentalist" (*EP* 184), he begins his lecture in a tone ambiguously conciliatory, self-deprecating, and truculent, as if he half-expected some curmudgeonly neighbor to bar his way. Conscious of himself as a "crooked stick" in the eyes of his audience (*EP* 184), he exploits the idea with a genial but labored irony, uncertain whether to ingratiate himself with his listeners (by telling them they "come as near being indigenous to the soil as a white man can" [*EP* 184]) or to mystify them (by spinning verbal webs of metaphor, circumlocution, and pun). Altogether, Thoreau seems ready to declare a truce with Concord but is wary and self-withholding lest his offer be rejected or lest he abridge his nature to win acceptance. Oddly, his awkwardness proves quite effective once he introduces his subject and, having paraded around as a misty transcendentalist, proceeds to show how acute and practical-minded a transcendentalist can be. It is a cumbersome but ingeniously appropriate method contrived partly to let Thoreau seem the fool he is reputed to be before winning his neighbors' grudging approval, partly to let him proclaim his full identity even as he addresses this most skeptical audience on this most prosaic occasion. Although willing enough to instruct and even delight his listeners, he will do so only on condition that in some covert manner he may also have his poet's say.

The poet is in abeyance through most of "The Succession of Forest Trees," but he surfaces in its final paragraphs as Thoreau's remarks on germination lead him to the miracle of the seed. "Though I do not believe that a plant will spring up where no seed has been," he writes, "I have great faith in a seed, – a, to me, equally mysterious origin for it. Convince me that you have a seed there, and I am prepared to expect wonders" (EP 203). To illustrate his point, Thoreau describes the prodigious squashes he raised from seeds obtained from the patent office, the largest of the squashes a prize-winner weighing $123\frac{1}{2}$ pounds and containing seeds for countless progeny. The fecundity of nature is astonishing, even to an audience of close calculators. As in "Autumnal Tints," however, Thoreau's natural facts have a second and third order of meaning for the writer and the handful of listeners able to follow him. Among New England Unitarians the seed was a common metaphor for self-culture, transcendentalized by Emerson and others into the notion that all human development was an unfolding of the self from within. "Explore thyself," Thoreau seems again to say as he celebrates the wonder of the seed. Like the story of the beautiful bug in Walden, the seed–into–squash is an image of metamorphosis in which fruition is depicted as a change of state so wondrous and disjunctive, and yet so demonstrably true, as to turn the unlikelihood of a human metamorphosis into a kind of fideistic certainty. The tall-tale quality of the account is a reminder of its figurativeness even as Thoreau's precision about numbers and weights (down to the half pound) ties it to fact. "Perfect alchemists I keep who can transmute substances without end," Thoreau writes of the "inexhaustible treasure-chest" of seeds in his garden (EP 204), closing the address with a paragraph of almost dizzying metaphor that must have left his Yankee auditors winking knowingly at each other even as they carried home his practical advice. The enlightened use of nature is Thoreau's parting lesson to mankind, but the "conservation" that most deeply concerned him, as ever, was the conservation of his spirit, whose impulses toward a higher life – as a poet in this world, as a disembodied soul in the next – he was not about to suppress for the good opinion of his neighbors.

William Howarth speculates that beneath its welter of observations and botanical reasonings "The Dispersion of Seeds" was intended to "offer a rational proof of [Thoreau's] ideas about life and death."[44] This seems very likely if "rational proof" is softened to "metaphor." Thoreau never regained his fleetingly held belief of 1851–52 that disciplined observation of nature could yield anything so definite as moral or spiritual "truth." The study of nature had its own intellectual, aesthetic, and practical rewards, and to the naturalist-poet it might also be a source of provocative analogies. "But is analogy argument?" as Melville's show-me Missourian, Pitch, asks in The Confidence-Man.[45] Thoreau had immense "confidence" to the very end, but it was the confidence of a faith that regarded spiritual things through the poet's imagination and was content to use science as a source of factual knowledge and a stimulus for fabling without confusing the truth claims of these very different activities. "The Succession of Forest Trees" botanizes and it fables; it never pretends to find proof of its fables in facts.

In thinking about death, moreover, Thoreau seems to have made a working distinction between his body, his soul, and his temporal identity as inscribed in his writings. His body, he felt sure, would be resolved back into the "inextinguishable vitality" of nature (J XIV, 268) like the fallen leaves of "Autumnal Tints." Of his soul – though constitutionally hopeful – he declined to speculate; "One world at a time," he is reported to have said on his deathbed when asked if he had had a glimpse ahead.[46] His practical efforts toward the last were aimed at securing his survival in literature, by which he imagined something more intimate and inclusive than posthumous reputation, gratifying as that itself was. He worked feverishly during his final illness preparing lectures for publication in the Atlantic Monthly, revising errors in the text of A Week, arranging for a new edition of Walden, and organizing, if never satisfactorily completing, The Maine Woods.[47] No doubt he would have taken the consolation Melville did from a fragment in Schopenhauer that the long-forgotten author of Moby-Dick noted in the last year of his life: "the more a man belongs to posterity, in other words, to humanity in general, the more of an alien he is to his contemporaries; since his work is not meant for them as such, but only for them in so far as they form part of mankind at large."[48] For Melville, who long ago told Hawthorne he had "pretty much made up his mind to be annihilated,"[49] literary fame was the most probable immortality he could expect. Melville's own writings were not simply artistic achievements but testaments to his lifelong struggle with the intellectual and spiritual problems that beset him; to "live" in literature was thus to record for posterity an internal drama that had never, save briefly in Hawthorne, found its adequate witness. Thoreau's writings were a still more open investment of personality, a bid for justification that came to extend even beyond persuading his contemporaries that he was the figure of his own imagining, not of theirs. It is as if, in reviewing his case against Concord and on behalf of himself, Thoreau grew aware that he was appealing to a jury whose verdict would be rendered again and again whenever his books were read. If he "drove himself fearfully in these last days,"[50] as Howarth says, it was because he was preparing his brief for the ages.

IV

In estimating these later years, it seems pointless to cite a literary "decline." What Thoreau might have accomplished had he lived to the age of Emerson or Melville, even of Hawthorne – how, particularly, he might have responded to the triumph of Darwinism – must be speculative. "The Dispersion of Seeds" would not have been another *Walden* (Thoreau was not the same man), but there are hints it might have been a remarkable performance of a different kind had Thoreau been able to finish it. The journal is itself a remarkable performance, while the four complete or semicomplete natural history essays – "Autumnal Tints," "Wild Apples," "The Succession of Forest Trees," and "Huckleberries" – are superb by any standard. Paradoxically, it was Thoreau and Melville, writers commonly supposed to have burned out by their thirty-eighth year, who enjoyed that rarity in nineteenth-century American literary careers, a second act, or what Thoreau would have called a second spring. Where Emerson had completed most of his important work by 1845 and Whitman most of his by 1860, Melville and Thoreau reinvented themselves in another genre, for another age: Melville as the poet of the vastly underappreciated *Clarel,* Thoreau as the poet-scientist just beginning to discover his subject and angle of vision when he died.

Thoreau's career, I have suggested, was preeminently a record of such "beginnings," though none was so decided as this last. His efforts to establish a workable relation to nature, society, and his own divided being gave rise to a series of adaptations which, no sooner formulated, ran up against experience, throwing him back upon himself to assess what remained and to forge yet another self-mythology. If Thoreau never quite adjusted to Concord, he at least grew wryly humorous about his maladjustment, which was almost as salutary. Measured against Emerson's or Melville's scrupulously honest charting of their spiritual journeys, Thoreau's all but willed forgetfulness of ceded positions – his incredible belief that on essential matters he had never changed his mind – seems not only self-deluded but diminishing. All that can be said is that denial was, for him, the condition for optimism, and optimism the requirement of his being. It would be more generous, and with the post-*Walden* period more accurate, to speak of Thoreau's extraordinary resilience. Examining a woodlot that had suffered "numerous fires and cuttings," Thoreau was impressed by the ability of hardwoods to regenerate themselves:

> They have commonly met with accidents and seen a good deal of the world already. They have learned to endure and bide their time. When you see an oak fully grown and of fair proportions, you little suspect what difficulties it may have encountered in its early youth, what sores it has overgrown, how for years it was a feeble layer lurking under the leaves and scarcely daring to show its head above them, burnt and cut, and browsed by rabbits. Driven back to earth again twenty times, – as often as it aspires to the heavens. (J XIV, 121)

In his endless search for analogies for his life, Thoreau may never have found a more appropriate one than in these tough old trees that never ceased to aspire. "Reimagining Thoreau" means recognizing, first of all, that he was perpetually engaged in reimagining himself in the service of this aspiration. However literary critics may plot the trajectory of his career, Thoreau himself characteristically looked ahead. The notion of his "descent" is most useful in describing how he temporarily mapped his life – not *after Walden* but even as he enlarged and revised it, and not as an extrinsic biographical matter but as a self-conception that actively shaped, or *re*shaped, the character of his book. "Reimagining Thoreau" involves tracing the course of his own reimaginings not only as they express themselves from work to work, but as they generate changing emphases *within* a work at the cost of philosophical and aesthetic unity. Finally, "reimagining Thoreau" means being a sympathetic but not uncritical observer of the procession of these self-mythologies, some of which are more honest, or productive, or capacious than others. In this respect, Thoreau was right to insist on his late ripening, for while no work of his, not even the journal, will displace *Walden* as the focus of literary attention, his final years have a deep interest not simply for the pioneering scientific and conservationist work he was doing but for the example he gives of writerly *being* – of an endless curiosity about the natural world undeformed by the psychic imperatives of the early work and expressing itself in a prose of extraordinary depth, calmness, and beauty. Recurrently in his journals Thoreau liked to symbolize himself as a hawk; it seems fitting to describe this later, freer, widely ranging Thoreauvian self as having the hawk's "poetry of motion," as ever, but also his liberties of time and space. "Enjoying each [place] as long as possible," he "most gracefully . . . surveys new scenes & revisits the old," "bravely" exploring "those parts of the wood which he had not surveyed – taking in a new segment. – annexing new territories" (*PJ* 4, 210).

Notes

Preface

1. See Michel Foucault, "What Is an Author?" in *Language, Counter-Memory, Practice,* trans. Donald F. Bouchard and Sherry Simon (Ithaca, N.Y.: Cornell Univ. Press, 1977), pp. 113–38.
2. Kenneth Burke, *The Philosophy of Literary Form,* rev. ed., abridged by the author (New York: Random House, 1957), p. 3.
3. Robert Milder, "'The American Scholar' as Cultural Event," *Prospects: An Annual Journal of American Culture Studies,* 16 (1991), pp. 119–47.
4. Michael T. Gilmore, "*Walden* and the 'Curse of Trade,'" *American Romanticism and the Marketplace* (Chicago: Univ. of Chicago Press, 1985), p. 49.
5. Gilmore, p. 49.
6. Important recent discusssions of Thoreau and literary vocation include Leonard N. Neufeldt, *The Economist: Henry Thoreau and Enterprise* (New York: Oxford Univ. Press, 1989); David Leverenz, *Manhood and the American Renaissance* (Ithaca, N.Y.: Cornell Univ. Press, 1989), pp. 22–25 and passim; and Stephen Railton, *Authorship and Audience* (Princeton: Princeton Univ. Press, 1992), pp. 50–73. Railton's work – closest to my own in its sense of literature as "performance" – appeared after my manuscript was virtually complete.
7. Frederick C. Crews, *The Critics Bear It Away* (New York: Random House, 1992), p. 77.
8. "I have not yet learned to live [in the world], that I can see, and I fear that I shall not very soon," Thoreau told Blake in December 1854 (*Corr* 354).
9. Stanley Cavell, *The Senses of "Walden"* (New York: Viking, 1974), p. 3.

Chapter 1: *"A False Position in Society"*

1. William Charvat, "American Romanticism and the Depression of 1837," in *The Profession of Authorship in America, 1800–1870: The Papers of William Charvat,* ed. Mattthew J. Bruccoli (Columbus: Ohio State Univ. Press, 1968), p. 64.
2. See Milder, "'The American Scholar' as Cultural Event," p. 123.
3. George P. Bradford, "Philosophic Thought in Boston," in *Memorial History of Boston,* ed. Justin Winsor (Boston: Osgood, 1883), vol. 4, p. 301.

4. See Robert Sattelmeyer, *Thoreau's Reading* (Princeton: Princeton Univ. Press, 1988), p. 65.

5. Leverenz, p. 73.

6. Horace Hosmer to Dr. S. A. Jones, in *Remembrances of Concord and the Thoreaus: Letters of Horace Hosmer to Dr. S. A. Jones,* ed. George Hendrick (Urbana: Univ. of Illinois Press, 1977), pp. 17, 3.

7. Richard Lebeaux, *Thoreau's Seasons* (Amherst: Univ. of Massachusetts Press, 1984), p. 35. See Robert D. Richardson, *Henry David Thoreau: A Life of the Mind* (Berkeley: Univ. of California Press, 1986), pp. 31–34.

8. "The scholar works with invisible tools to invisible ends," Emerson wrote in 1836: "So passes for an idler or worse; brain sick; defenceless to idle carpenters, masons, & merchants, that having done nothing most laboriously all day pounce on him fresh for spoil at night" (*JMN* V, 116). "The American Scholar" was Emerson's attempt to answer the sneers of "the so-called 'practical men' . . . at speculative men" (*CW* I, 59). The two Oberon stories (Oberon had been Hawthorne's college nickname) are "The Devil in Manuscript," published in 1835 and reprinted in *The Snow-Image* (1852), and "Fragments from the Journal of a Solitary Man," published in 1837 but uncollected in Hawthorne's lifetime. In "Passages from a Relinquished Work," carved out from his aborted collection "The Story-Teller," Hawthorne projects his own situation upon an aesthetically inclined youth intent "on keeping aloof from the regular business of life. This would have been a dangerous resolution, any where in the world [his narrator remarks]; it was fatal, in New-England. There is a grossness in the conceptions of my countrymen; they will not be convinced that any good thing may consist with what they call idleness. . . . The principle is excellent, in its general influence [Hawthorne's concession is typical], but most miserable in its effect on the few that violate it" (*Mosses From an Old Manse* [Columbus: Ohio State Univ. Press, 1974], p. 407).

9. Leverenz, p. 23.

10. Erik H. Erikson, *Identity: Youth and Crisis* (New York: Norton, 1968), p. 165.

11. *Collected Poems of Henry Thoreau,* enlarged edition, ed. Carl Bode (Baltimore: Johns Hopkins Univ. Press, 1964), p. 81. "What am I at present?" Thoreau asked in 1843, in the same vein: "A diseased bundle of nerves standing between time and eternity like a withered leaf that still hangs shivering on its stem" (*PJ* 1, 447). A decade later he would still be imagining himself in similar terms: "A dandelion down that never alights, – settles, – blown off by a boy to see if his mother wanted him, – some divine boy in the upper pastures" (*Corr* 303).

12. Adumbrated in the early journals, this myth appears most fully in entries of the spring and summer of 1851. See, for example, *PJ* 3, 233, 305–6.

13. H. Daniel Peck also comments on this passage in *Thoreau's Morning Work* (New Haven: Yale Univ. Press, 1990), pp. 109–11.

14. Sigmund Freud, *Civilization and Its Discontents,* trans. James Strachey (New York: Norton, 1961), p. 15.

15. Freud, *Beyond the Pleasure Principle,* trans. James Strachey (New York: Norton, 1961), pp. 30, 32.

16. Freud, *Beyond the Pleasure Principle,* pp. 36–37.

17. See Walter Harding, *The Days of Henry Thoreau* (1965; rpt. New York: Dover, 1982), pp. 94–104.

18. Wordsworth seems to have been a formative influence here. As early as January 1841,

Thoreau was quoting from the Immortality Ode ("Heaven lies about us in our infancy." – *PJ* 1, 242), a poem that became still more important for him in 1851–52 as his sense of loss deepened and he looked for mythologies to help him reconfigure his life.

19. M. H. Abrams, *Natural Supernaturalism* (New York: Norton, 1971), p. 145.

20. Erikson, *Identity: Youth and Crisis,* pp. 172–73.

21. Stephen Railton aptly uses this phrase to title his chapter on Thoreau and *Walden* in *Authorship and Audience.* See Ch. 3, pp. 53–56 especially.

22. Lawrence Buell, *Literary Transcendentalism* (Ithaca, N.Y.: Cornell Univ. Press, 1973), p. 214.

23. As Richardson observes, Thoreau seems to have used poetry to express "the emotions and the wishes he could not help feeling," and prose to set out "directions for the life he willed, the life he was setting out to create" (*Henry David Thoreau* 84).

24. On Thoreau's debt to Emerson's "Heroism," see Linck C. Johnson, *Thoreau's Complex Weave* (Charlottesville: Univ. of Virginia Press, 1986), p. 208. Robert D. Richardson traces Thoreau's interest in bravery to Aeschylus and the Roman Stoics (*Henry David Thoreau* 67–71).

25. Stephen E. Whicher, *Freedom and Fate* (Philadelphia: Univ. of Pennsylvania Press, 1953), p. 50.

26. William James, *The Varieties of Religious Experience* (1902; rpt. New York: New American Library, 1958), p. 284.

27. James, p. 282.

28. James, p. 235–36.

29. James, p. 284.

30. Robert Weimann, *Structure and Society in Literary History,* expanded edition (Baltimore: Johns Hopkins Univ. Press, 1984), pp. 7–8.

31. James Russell Lowell, "Thoreau," *My Study Windows* (Boston: Houghton Mifflin, 1895), p. 204.

32. Warner Berthoff, *Fiction and Events* (New York: Dutton, 1971), p. 165.

33. Sherman Paul, *The Shores of America* (Urbana: Univ. of Illinois Press, 1958), p. 1. Important accounts of Thoreau's early relationship to Emerson include Richard Lebeaux, *Young Man Thoreau* (Amherst: Univ. of Massachusetts Press, 1977), pp. 79–97 esp.; Harding, *The Days of Henry Thoreau* pp. 59–66 and passim; and Richardson, pp. 18–23 and passim. Although Thoreau "rarely mentioned the older man by name," his editors comment, "Emerson's presence and his influence on the early Journals are always to be inferred" (*PJ* 1, 595).

34. For a discussion of the ideological influence of "The American Scholar" on the younger generation of New England literary intellectuals, see my essay "'The American Scholar' as Cultural Event," pp. 119–47.

35. As Richardson observes, Thoreau "would have read ['The American Scholar'] even if he didn't hear it" (22).

36. Erikson, *Childhood and Society* (New York: Norton, 1950), p. 263.

37. Jerome J. McGann defines ideology, more or less representatively, as "a coherent or loosely organized set of ideas which is the expression of the special interests of some class or social group" (*The Romantic Ideology* [Chicago: Univ. of Chicago Press, 1983], p. 5). It makes an enormous difference, however, whether the class or group in question is in or out of power. For an established class, ideology serves to rationalize

and legitimate an advantageous social order. For a marginalized class, it serves to engender and validate a program of revolutionary action designed to reposition its members more favorably within society; it is "adaptational" rather than "consolidational," though it is not the less interested for that. All ideology is "false consciousness," in the Marxian sense, so far as it emerges from and speaks to the interests or values of a particular group, generalized into the progressive interests of humanity. The notion of ideology as a "map" applies best to the insurgent world-views of the disempowered, which need to be more fully articulated than the taken-for-granted assumptions of an entrenched class. The idea of a map has its American roots in Kenneth Burke, *The Philosophy of Literary Form* (1941), to which Clifford Geertz's influential essay "Ideology as a Cultural System" is much indebted (see *The Interpretation of Cultures* [New York: Basic Books, 1973], pp. 193–233). Related discussions of ideology as a mapping of experience include Erikson, *Young Man Luther* (1958) and *Life History and the Historical Moment* (1975); Lucien Goldmann, *The Hidden God* (1964) and *Essays on Method in the Sociology of Literature* (1980); and (of special clarity and value) Alvin W. Gouldner, *The Dialectic of Ideology and Technology* (1976).

38. Raymond Williams, *Marxism and Literature* (New York: Oxford Univ. Press, 1977), pp. 132, 133.

39. As F.O. Matthiessen long ago observed, Emerson liked to think of Thoreau "in the guise of his own scholar in action." *American Renaissance* (New York: Oxford Univ. Press, 1941), p. 80.

40. Steven Fink, *Prophet in the Marketplace* (Princeton: Princeton Univ. Press, 1992), p. 4.

41. Frederick Henry Hedge, "The Art of Life – The Scholar's Calling," *The Dial,* II (1840), 175. Subsequent references to Hedge's essay are included in the text.

42. Cf. Fink (14): "The expression of an inspiration [for Hedge] is a complementary activity that *completes* rather than *initiates* an action; it is essentially self-referential, and its function is therefore not to mediate between the initiated and the uninitiated."

43. Milton's sonnet opens:

> How soon hath Time, the subtle thief of youth,
> Stol'n on his wing, my three and twentieth year!
> My hasting days fly on to full career,
> But my late spring no bud or blossom show'th.

John Milton: Complete Poems and Major Prose, ed. Merritt Y. Hughes (New York: Odyssey Press, 1957), p. 76.

44. Erikson, *Identity: Youth and Crisis,* p. 156.

45. Paul, p. 97.

46. Richardson, p. 99.

47. For the causes of the initial distancing, see Robert Sattelmeyer, "'When He Became My Enemy': Emerson and Thoreau, 1848–49," *New England Quarterly,* 62 (1989), 187–204.

48. Nathaniel Hawthorne, *The American Notebooks,* ed. Claude M. Simpson (Columbus: Ohio State Univ. Press, 1972), p. 371.

49. One argument for the influence of "Man the Reformer" on *Walden* is the presence of striking echoes of language: "economy," "simplify," "extravagance," "bravery," "foundation," "awaken," and so on, down to the arcane "coenobite," the source of one of fisherman Thoreau's cleverest puns (*W* 173).

50. Paul, p. 96.
51. G. B. Shaw, quoted in Erikson, *Identity: Youth and Crisis,* p. 143.
52. John Dwyer, "'The Melancholy Savage': Text and Context in the *Poems of Ossian,"* in *Ossian Revisited,* ed. Howard Gaskill (Edinburgh: Edinburgh Univ. Press, 1991), p. 166.
53. See Dwyer, p. 169.
54. For Thoreau on Raleigh, see Paul, pp. 126–38; Fink, pp. 81–85; Sattelmeyer, *Thoreau's Reading,* p. 34; and William Howarth, *The Book of Concord* (New York: Viking Press, 1982), p. 31.
55. Paul, p. 127.
56. James, p. 288.
57. Stephen Railton treats this theme incisively in *Authorship and Audience.* The "huge disparity between [Thoreau's] ego ideal and his village reputation," Railton notes, "explains why, when he walked, he was anxious to 'make a hill or wood screen [him from every house he had to pass] – to shut every window with an apple tree' (*J* 4:118)" (Railton 54). Narrowing this disparity was one of Thoreau's lifelong projects.
58. Joel Porte, *Representative Man: Ralph Waldo Emerson in His Time* (New York: Oxford Univ. Press, 1979), pp. 136, 153. "Essaying to Be" is the title of one of Porte's chapters.
59. Frederick Garber, *Thoreau's Fable of Inscribing* (Princeton: Princeton Univ. Press, 1991), p. 18.
60. Paul uses Thoreau's "captive knight" as the title for his section on the years 1840–43 (90–139), though his reading of the Raleigh lecture is quite different from mine.
61. In Harding, *The Days of Henry Thoreau,* p. 143.
62. See Elizabeth Hall Witherell, "Thoreau's Watershed Season as a Poet: The Hidden Fruits of the Summer and Fall of 1841," in *Studies in the American Renaissance,* ed. Joel Myerson (Charlottesville: Univ. Press of Virginia, 1990), pp. 49–106.
63. See John Hildebidle, *Thoreau: A Naturalist's Liberty* (Cambridge, Mass.: Harvard Univ. Press, 1983), p. 61.
64. See Linck C. Johnson, "Historical Introduction," in *A Week on the Concord and Merrimack Rivers,* ed. Carl F. Hovde (Princeton: Princeton Univ. Press, 1980), pp. 437–41, and Johnson, *Thoreau's Complex Weave,* p. 211.
65. Hawthorne, *American Notebooks,* p. 355.
66. Lawrence Buell discusses the excursion form at length in *Literary Transcendentalism,* pp. 188–207. Also see Fink, pp. 67–78.
67. Robert Sattelmeyer, Introduction, *Henry David Thoreau: The Natural History Essays* (Salt Lake City: Gibbs Smith, 1980), p. xvi. Unlike Sattelmeyer, I do not regard Thoreau's answer to this question as a "foregone conclusion."
68. See Fink, pp. 67–74.
69. Fink, p. 69.
70. Among these "unconsummated quests" are *A Week on the Concord and Merrimack Rivers* (both in particular episodes and in its entirety), *A Yankee in Canada,* two of the three essays in *The Maine Woods* ("Ktaadn" is the exception), and *Cape Cod.* It would be hard to identify a Thoreauvian quest that *is* consummated in terms of its initial promises and expectations, *Walden* included, though in most cases Thoreau writes as if the quest had in fact realized its object.
71. Jonathan Bishop, "The Experience of the Sacred in Thoreau's *Week,"* *ELH,* 33 (1966), 72.

Chapter 2: "Under the Eyelids of Time"

1. M. H. Abrams, *Natural Supernaturalism*, p. 194. My chapter title is a variant on one of Abrams's sections on Wordsworth, "The Long Journey Home."
2. Johnson, *Complex Weave*, p. xi.
3. Richardson, *Henry David Thoreau*, p. 65.
4. See Bishop, "The Experience of the Sacred in Thoreau's *Week.*"
5. John Carlos Rowe, *Through the Custom-House* (Baltimore: Johns Hopkins Univ. Press, 1982). p. 34.
6. Peter Carafiol, *The American Ideal* (New York: Oxford Univ. Press, 1991), p. 123.
7. Hawthorne, *Mosses from an Old Manse*, p. 6.
8. Melville, *Moby-Dick*, ed. Harrison Hayford et al. (Evanston and Chicago: Northwestern Univ. Press and The Newberry Library, 1988), p. 4.
9. Melville, *Moby-Dick*, pp. 5, 7.
10. Ethel Seybold, *Thoreau: The Quest and the Classics* (New Haven: Yale Univ. Press, 1951), p. 12.
11. Joan Burbick, *Thoreau's Alternative History* (Philadelphia: Univ. of Pennsylvania Press, 1987), p. 1.
12. See Leo Marx, *The Machine in the Garden* (New York: Oxford Univ. Press, 1964). Johnson discusses Thoreau's 1848 visit to the region in *Complex Weave*, pp. 37–40.
13. Robert A. Gross, "Concord, Boston and the Wider World: Transcendentalism and Urbanism," *New Perspectives on Concord History* (Concord: Massachusetts Foundation for the Humanities and Public Policy, 1983), p. 114. See also Philip R. Yannella, "Socio-Economic Disarray and Literary Response: Concord and *Walden,*" *Mosaic,* 14 (1981), 1–24, and Lawrence Buell, *New England Literary Culture: From Revolution through Renaissance* (Cambridge: Cambridge Univ. Press, 1986), p. 330.
14. Michael T. Gilmore, *American Romanticism and the Marketplace* (Chicago: Univ. of Chicago Press, 1985), p. 35.
15. Lawrence Buell sets the matter aright when he observes, "Thoreau envisaged a model of human community that was a purified version of [the New England] social order that as a historical entity he was inclined to satirize for inertia and traditionalism" (*New England Literary Culture* 330).
16. See Harding, *Days of Henry Thoreau*, pp. 160–62. The woods-burning incident rankled Thoreau for years, as indicated by the long passages of self-justification that appear in his journal of 1850.
17. Lebeaux, *Thoreau's Seasons*, p. 132.
18. In Johnson, *Complex Weave*, p. 307. Johnson prints a reconstruction of the entire first draft. Future references to Johnson's text are included in the text and abbreviated "FD" (first draft).
19. "The Youth, who daily farther from the east / Must travel" (ll. 71–72). *The Poetical Works of Wordsworth*, ed. Thomas Hutchinson and Ernest de Selincourt (London: Oxford Univ. Press, 1936).
20. For a discussion of the history of Lowell from its paternalistic origins in the 1820s through midcentury, see John F. Kasson, *Civilizing the Machine* (New York: Penguin, 1977), pp. 55–106.
21. See Linck C. Johnson, "Reforming the Reformers: Emerson, Thoreau, and the Sunday Lectures at Amory Hall, Boston," *ESQ,* 37 (1991), 235–89.

22. Significantly, the journal source for this special kind of philanthropy appears in the immediate context of Thoreau's discussion of his 1846 arrest (*PJ* 2, 262).
23. Bishop, pp. 73–75.
24. Fink, *Prophet in the Marketplace,* p. 231. According to John Carlos Rowe, "the effort of the poet to recollect the Saddleback experience fails when he attempts to transform the divine into his own private possession" (*Custom-House* 39); in my reading, it fails when he tries to elevate his private possession into the divine.
25. As Buell remarks, the episode "conveys a strong sense of [Thoreau's] isolation from (and superiority to) other people" (*Literary Transcendentalism* 223).
26. All quotations are from Wordsworth, *Poetical Works.* Johnson discusses Thoreau's debt to Wordsworth in *Complex Weave,* pp. 29–30.
27. Fink, p. 231.
28. Peck, *Thoreau's Morning Work,* p. 28. It may be said, of course, that there is no reason why *A Week* ought to have culminated in a mountain ascent beyond the expectations one has from reading Romantic literature, Wordsworth especially. This context, however, was precisely Thoreau's own, and in "A Walk to Wachusett" he had done his best to meet its terms.
29. Peck, p. 29.
30. See Johnson, *Thoreau's Complex Weave,* p. 228.
31. William Howarth, *Thoreau in the Mountains* (New York: Farrar, Straus, Giroux, 1982), p. 85. Stephen Adams and Donald Ross, Jr., in *Revising Mythologies* (Charlottesville: Univ. of Virginia Press, 1988), also argue that "the experience on Katahdin . . . prompt[ed Thoreau] to revaluate his relationship with nature and his own earlier trip to Agiocochook" (8).
32. As Howarth observes, Mt. Washington has "some of the world's most dangerous weather. Fog – even hail or snow, in summer months – can close in swiftly and unpredictably. Hikers must use extreme caution" (*Thoreau in the Mountains* 222).
33. Carol Troyen, Catalog Note to "The White Mountains – Mt. Washington, 1851," painted by John F. Kensett, in *American Paradise,* ed. John K. Howat (New York: Metropolitan Museum of Art, 1987), p. 149. Kensett's painting of midcentury, which sets a benign pastoral landscape in the foreground against snow-topped Mt. Washington in the distance, suggests the change in the region, or in views of the region, that followed the coming of the railroad in the 1840s, after Thoreau's visit. Thoreau's Mt. Washington was probably much closer to that of Thomas Cole, who "had presented the mountains as wild, forbidding country, demonstrating on his canvases man's frailty in the face of mysterious and often violent powers of nature" (Troyen 149) – essentially Thoreau's portrait of nature in "Ktaadn."
34. See John F. Sears, *Sacred Places* (New York: Oxford Univ. Press, 1989), pp. 74–75.
35. The 1846 journal entries on the White Mountains are cast in the mode of genial travel narrative, lending force to Linck Johnson's view that Thoreau omitted the section for fear it "might have tended to domesticate Agiocochook" (*Thoreau's Complex Weave* 228; v. 25–26). But as Thoreau passed from Franconia tourist attractions like the Flume and the Old Man of the Mountains (the substance of the entries), he would have come into rougher country and confronted Mt. Washington itself, which in 1839 was not easily domesticated.
36. Fink, p. 177.
37. Edmund Burke, *A Philosophical Enquiry into the Origin of Our Ideas of the Sublime and*

Beautiful, ed. James T. Boulton (1958; rpt. Notre Dame, Ind.: Univ. of Notre Dame Press, 1968), p. 73.

38. Melville, *Moby-Dick,* p. 457.

39. Samuel H. Monk, *The Sublime* (1935; rpt. Ann Arbor: Univ. of Michigan Press, 1960), p. 228.

40. Steven Fink supplies a more ingenious rationale than Thoreau could have when he ascribes "the calculated *in*significance" of the Agiocochook section to the author's intention to write "an antitravel travelogue, in which the transcendent imagination undermines the rationale for actual travel." There is no reason why the "transcendent imagination" might not have constructed a more shapely narrative if Thoreau had had a word to deliver symbolically commensurate with the authority of New England's highest peak. The expansion of the Saddleback episode as a substitute for the anticipated account of Agiocochook is an acknowledgment he did not, and the literary consequence of the omission is a loss of whatever slight narrative line his book possessed (see *Prophet in the Marketplace* 232, 233).

41. Thoreau's attitude and tone owe much to the growing strains in his relationship with Emerson. See Sattelmeyer, "'When He Became My Enemy': Emerson and Thoreau, 1848–49."

42. As Fink remarks, "The longer *A Week* went unpublished, the more Thoreau seems to have regarded his book as a repository for all his writing that was not marketable in the magazines" (*Prophet in the Marketplace* 216).

43. Carl F. Hovde, "Nature Into Art: Thoreau's Use of His Journal in *A Week on the Concord and Merrimack Rivers*," *American Literature,* 30 (1958), 172.

44. Hawthorne, *The American Notebooks,* p. 358.

45. Hawthorne, *Mosses from an Old Manse,* p. 21.

46. Hawthorne, *Mosses from an Old Manse,* p. 25.

47. Hawthorne, *Mosses from an Old Manse,* p. 25.

48. Hawthorne, *Mosses from an Old Manse,* p. 25.

49. "For all its rivering upon the stream of time," as H. Daniel Peck remarks, "*A Week* could not open itself to the living instant of the present, the nick of time" (*Thoreau's Morning Work* 36).

50. See Thoreau's first draft of "Friday" in Johnson, *Complex Weave,* pp. 377–92.

51. In revising this passage in later drafts, Thoreau was careful to alter the possible hint of mental vacuity ("any thoughts [we might have had]") to an assertion that the rowers, indeed, "sat absorbed in thought" (*Wk* 390).

52. See Frederick Garber, *Thoreau's Redemptive Imagination* (New York: New York Univ. Press, 1977), p. 196.

53. Adams and Ross make a similar point: "[Thoreau] now [in a late stage of composition] reorganizes his various thoughts and meditations around a romance quest for heaven, which he seeks on Agiocochook but ultimately locates on earth, in a '*purely sensuous life*'" (*Revising Mythologies* 8).

Chapter 3: Deconstructing Walden

1. John Dewey, *Art as Experience* (1934; rpt. New York: Capricorn Books, 1958), p. 3.

2. *The Letters of Herman Melville,* ed. Merrell R. Davis and William H. Gilman (New Haven: Yale Univ. Press, 1960), p. 143.

3. Johnson, *Complex Weave,* p. 45. See his discussion of *A Week* as elegy (41–84).

4. See *The Letters of Herman Melville,* p. 96.

5. Warner Berthoff, *The Example of Melville* (Princeton: Princeton Univ. Press, 1962), p. 15. Also see Richard H. Brodhead's fine discussion of Melville, "The Art of the Diver," in *Hawthorne, Melville, and the Novel* (Chicago: Univ. of Chicago Press, 1976), pp. 119–33.

6. Harding, *Days of Henry Thoreau,* p. 188.

7. Because the inscribed reader in *Walden* seems manifestly male, I retain Thoreau's gender-specific word "townsmen." *Walden* was initially subtitled "Addressed to My Townsmen," and references to townsmen appear throughout the text. Justifying himself as a man in male society was always a prime motive in Thoreau's work.

8. For Carlyle's influence on Thoreau, see Sattelmeyer, *Thoreau's Reading,* pp. 39–40, and Richardson, *Henry David Thoreau,* pp. 163–65.

9. Hawthorne, *American Notebooks,* pp. 322, 334.

10. See J. Lyndon Shanley, *The Making of "Walden"* (Chicago: Univ. of Chicago Press, 1957).

11. Fink, p. 197. Fink clarifies the complicated circumstances surrounding *Walden*'s 1849 nonpublication in *Prophet in the Marketplace,* pp. 196–98.

12. See Shanley, pp. 72–73 especially, and Ronald E. Clapper, "The Development of *Walden*: A Genetic Text," diss. UCLA, 1967. See also Adams and Ross, *Revising Mythologies;* and Robert Sattelmeyer, "The Remaking of *Walden,*" in *Writing the American Classics,* ed. James Barbour and Tom Quirk (Chapel Hill: Univ. of North Carolina Press, 1990). My own understanding of the composition of *Walden,* based on an interpretation of Clapper's genetic text, is closest to Sattelmeyer's, though I tend to place much greater emphasis on the differences between the various drafts of 1852–54. My letters A–G for the successive drafts are borrowed from Clapper. Hereafter, references to Shanley and Clapper will be included in the text and abbreviated Sh and Cl.

13. See M. H. Abrams, *The Mirror and the Lamp* (1953; rpt. New York: Norton, 1958), pp. 171–75.

14. Abrams, *The Mirror and the Lamp,* p. 173.

15. Hershel Parker, *Flawed Texts and Verbal Icons* (Evanston, Ill.: Northwestern Univ. Press, 1984), p. 26.

16. Sattelmeyer, "Remaking," p. 75.

17. The "organic" reading of *Walden,* advanced by F. O. Matthiessen in *American Renaissance* (1941), was elaborated by New Critics of the 1950s and 1960s. See, for example, Lauriat Lane, Jr., "On the Organic Structure of *Walden,*" *College English,* 21 (1960), 195–202, and, most prominently, Charles R. Anderson, *The Magic Circle of "Walden"* (New York: Holt, Rinehart, 1968), still among the finest readings of Thoreau's book.

18. Sattelmeyer, "Remaking," p. 61.

19. Sattelmeyer, "Remaking," p. 58.

20. The other important recent interpretation of the composition of *Walden* is Adams and Ross's argument, which also describes two main phases of writing and turns on the notion (erroneous, to my mind) of "Thoreau's conversion to romanticism in 1851–52" (*Revising Mythologies* 63). I will return to the Adams–Ross hypothesis in Chapter 6.

21. "In reading" *Walden,* Sattelmeyer remarks, "one responds to and follows not only the

temporal structure of the Walden experience (the two years of Thoreau's life com-
pressed into a single annual cycle from one spring to the next) but also and perhaps
more subliminally the larger development of the narrator over the course of a decade
of spiritual and intellectual growth" ("Remaking" 61). Sattelmeyer's notion is a nice
rule of thumb, but it needs to be applied to any given section of *Walden* with *extreme*
caution and with the Clapper genetic text as a guide.

22. Sherman Paul, *Repossessing and Renewing* (Baton Rouge: Louisiana State Univ. Press,
    1976), p. 18. Paul's own major work on Thoreau, *The Shores of America,* written
    without the benefit of Shanley's and Clapper's manuscript findings, was unable to
    build upon this developmental sense of *Walden* and tended to read Thoreau's book as
    the product of a single fixed intention, albeit a nostalgic one.

23. Daniel B. Shea, "Emerson and the American Metamorphosis," in *Emerson: Prophecy,
    Metamorphosis, and Influence,* ed. David Levin (New York: Columbia Univ. Press,
    1975), p. 45.

24. Buell, *Literary Transcendentalism,* p. 200.

25. William K. Wimsatt and Monroe C. Beardsley, "The Intentional Fallacy," in *Critical
    Theory since Plato,* ed. Hazard Adams (New York: Harcourt Brace, 1971), p. 1015.

26. For discussions of "intention" as a shaping principle actively at work during, not
    before, the process of composition, see R. S. Crane, *The Languages of Criticism and the
    Structure of Poetry* (Toronto: Univ. of Toronto Press, 1953), pp. 140–46 especially, and
    Parker, *Flawed Texts and Verbal Icons,* pp. 21–26.

27. Burke, *The Philosophy of Literary Form,* p. 18.

28. Stanley Cavell, *The Senses of "Walden,"* p. 3.

Chapter 4: Walden *and the Rhetoric of Ascent*

1. Ovid, *Metamorphoses,* trans. Rolfe Humphries (Bloomington: Indiana Univ. Press,
   1955), Bk. XV, ll. 59–68. The lines are from "The Teachings of Pythagoras" in Book
   XV, a later section of which Thoreau quotes in "Spring" (*W* 314–16). I would like to
   thank James S. Gifford for calling my attention to the Ovid passage in relation to
   Thoreau.

2. Edmund Wilson, *The Twenties,* ed. Leon Edel (New York: Farrar, Straus & Giroux,
   1975), p. 351.

3. Joseph J. Moldenhauer, "Paradox in *Walden*" (1964); rpt. with the author's revisions, in
   Twentieth Century Interpretations of "Walden," ed. Richard Ruland (Englewood Cliffs,
   N.J.: Prentice-Hall, 1968), p. 77.

4. Buell, *Literary Transcendentalism,* p. 302.

5. Gordon V. Boudreau, *The Roots of "Walden" and the Tree of Life* (Nashville: Vanderbilt
   Univ. Press, 1990), p. 6.

6. Lebeaux, *Thoreau's Seasons,* p. 170. See Leverenz, *Manhood and the American Renaissance,*
   p. 23. Although Lebeaux and Leverenz both speak of the passage as a once-considered
   epigraph to *Walden,* Clapper identifies it as belonging to a stage F paragraph in the
   book's "Conclusion," later deleted (Cl 854); the passage first appears in a journal entry
   of February 1852 (*J* III, 293). The feelings of self-disgust it records were especially
   strong in the period 1852–53, when Thoreau recoiled at the physicality of human life,
   but the earliest drafts of *Walden* have their own suppressions – of feelings of ostracism,
   inner division, and self-doubt.

7. Stanley Fish, *Self-Consuming Artifacts* (Berkeley: Univ. of California Press, 1972), pp. 1–2.

8. Gilmore, "*Walden* and the 'Curse of Trade,'" p. 35. The ambiguity of Thoreau's purpose is intimated by the last phrase of the epigraph, "if only to wake my neighbors up," which conspicuously declines to say "*in order to* wake my neighbors up." Like chanticleer, Thoreau crows chiefly for the exhilaration of exercising his powers and asserting control over his domain; his pose of reformer is an "enabling fiction" that legitimates his brag and lays the groundwork for his relationship to the reader, but it is neither the center nor the source of *Walden*'s spiritedly satiric energies.

9. Joseph Adamson discusses the characteristic "occasion" of Thoreau's speaking in "The Trials of Thoreau," *ESQ*, 36 (1990), 139–41 especially.

10. Anderson, *The Magic Circle of "Walden,"* p. 18. See *Magic Circle*, pp. 18–38, and Moldenhauer, "Paradox in *Walden*," 73–76, for excellent discussions of Thoreau's satire in the early chapters of *Walden*.

11. Thomas Hooker, "The Preparing of the Heart for to Receive Christ," in *The Literature of America: Colonial Period*, ed. Larzer Ziff (New York: McGraw-Hill, 1970), p. 150.

12. As Thoreau's distance from Emerson widened over the years, he grew more direct in repudiating his teacher: "I have lived some thirty years on this planet [he added in stage D], and I have yet to hear the first syllable of valuable advice from my seniors. . . . If I have any experience which I think valuable, I am sure to reflect that this my Mentors said nothing about" (*W* 9).

13. *The Autobiography of Benjamin Franklin*, ed. Leonard W. Labaree et al. (New Haven: Yale Univ. Press, 1964), pp. 157–58. Though my comparison to Franklin is primarily metaphorical, Leonard N. Neufeldt explores *Walden* in relation to the guidebook tradition in *The Economist: Henry Thoreau and Enterprise*.

14. Here seems as good a place as any to address a practical difficulty inherent in reading *Walden* as a layered work. In E. D. Hirsch's words: "With a revised text, composed over a long period of time (Faust, for example), how are we to construe the unrevised portions? Should we assume that they still mean what they originally meant or that they took on a new meaning when the rest of the text was altered or expanded?" (*Validity in Interpretation* [New Haven: Yale Univ. Press, 1967], p. 233). In *Walden*'s case the problem is compounded by the fact that some late insertions draw upon journal entries from earlier years, a few of them (the sandbank passage, notably) altered in revealing ways, others left virtually intact. I confess I have no categorical answer to Hirsch's question, nor do I believe there can be one other than the pragmatic rule that the interpreter should let himself be guided by the circumstances of the particular case and by his literary and psychological instinct for what is occurring in a passage.

15. See Neufeldt, pp. 23–52.

16. Rush Welter, *The Mind of America, 1820–1860* (New York: Columbia Univ. Press, 1975), p. 135.

17. Emerson, "Address on Education," *The Early Lectures of Ralph Waldo Emerson*, ed. Stephen Whicher et al. (Cambridge, Mass.: Harvard Univ. Press, 1964), Vol. 2, p. 196.

18. Emerson, "Address on Education," p. 196.

19. Andrzej Walicki, "Marx and Freedom," *The New York Review of Books*, XXX, 18

(November 24, 1983), 52. Gilmore discusses *Walden* in terms of Georg Lukacs's idea of reification in *"Walden* and the 'Curse of Trade,'" pp. 39–40.

20. Neufeldt, p. 36.

21. See Milder, "'The American Scholar' as Cultural Event," pp. 126–29. "Beautifully sustained raids on the language of capitalism and the marketplace," Stephen Railton calls this kind of linguistic appropriation in an oxymoronic phrase suggesting at once Thoreau's ability to extend an economic trope through elaborate applications and his reluctance to establish a stationary front line (*Authorship and Audience* 63). Similarly, Frederick Garber speaks of "Economy" as "an elaborate leg-pull that plays off the terminology of the bookkeeper's ledger – the business of America as business – in order to subvert the context in which the terminology moves" (*Thoreau's Fable of Inscribing* 8).

22. Kenneth Burke, "I, Eye, Ay – Emerson's Early Essay 'Nature': Thoughts on the Machinery of Transcendence" (1966); rpt. in *Emerson's "Nature": Origin, Growth, Meaning,* 2nd ed., enlarged, ed. Merton M. Sealts, Jr., and Alfred R. Ferguson (Carbondale and Edwardsville: Southern Illinois Univ. Press, 1969), p. 151.

23. See Phillip R. Yannella, "Socio-Economic Disarray and Literary Response: Concord and *Walden,*" 9, and Richardson, *Henry David Thoreau,* pp. 166–68.

24. Railton, *Authorship and Audience,* p. 65.

25. Whatever his other interests, Thoreau never lacked time or inclination to elaborate the satire of "Economy," the only chapter he expanded in all seven manuscript drafts. One of the few instances of Thoreau's constructive social engagement in *Walden* is the villages-as-universities passage in "Reading" (*W* 108–10), drawn from journal entries of August 1852 and added to the manuscript in a late stage of composition.

26. Walter Benn Michaels, "*Walden*'s False Bottoms," *Glyph,* I (1977), 140. Thoreau's more biting remarks on trade were added to the manuscript after the failure of *A Week* in 1849 had soured him on commerce of any sort.

27. Gilmore, "*Walden* and the 'Curse of Trade,'" p. 35. Gilmore's interpretation echoes Sacvan Bercovitch's theory of the republican nostalgia behind the writing of the American Renaissance. See Bercovitch, "The Problem of Ideology in American Literary History," *Critical Inquiry,* 12 (1986), 631–53.

28. Gilmore, p. 43.

29. For example, his remark in "Baker Farm," "Enjoy the land, but own it not" (*W* 207).

30. Johnson, "Reforming the Reformers," p. 279.

31. Henry Golemba, "Unreading Thoreau," *American Literature,* 60 (1988), 393. See also Golemba, *Thoreau's Wild Rhetoric* (New York: New York Univ. Press, 1990). Let me emphasize how much I accept Golemba's argument as an account of one intention, certainly *one effect,* in *Walden.* Yet Golemba himself says he "do[es] not mean to ascribe a psychological motive to Thoreau, being more focused on his rhetorical ambitions" ("Unreading Thoreau" 397). I don't believe *Walden*'s rhetoric can be separated from its author's motives.

32. Malini Schueller, "Carnival Rhetoric and Extra-Vagance in Thoreau's *Walden,*" *American Literature,* 58 (1986), 33.

33. Richard Poirier, *A World Elsewhere* (New York: Oxford Univ. Press, 1966), p. 90.

34. Moldenhauer, p. 77.

35. Northrop Frye, *Anatomy of Criticism* (Princeton: Princeton Univ. Press, 1957), p. 52.

36. Seybold, *Thoreau: The Quest and the Classics,* p. 31.

37. Bishop, "Experience of the Sacred," p. 70.

38. Abrams, *Natural Supernaturalism,* p. 187.

39. Cavell, *The Senses of "Walden,"* p. 8.

40. William Ellery Channing, "Remarks on National Literature," *The Works of William Ellery Channing* (Boston: American Unitarian Association, 1879), p. 133. As Orestes Brownson put it in another of these pleas for a new American literature, "God in his providence has given the American people a great problem to work out. He has given it us in charge to prove what man may be, when and where he has free and full scope to act out the almightiness that slumbers within him." Brownson, "American Literature," *The Boston Quarterly Review,* III (1840); rpt. in *The Native Muse,* ed. Richard Ruland (New York: Dutton, 1972), p. 289.

41. Sacvan Bercovitch, *The Puritan Origins of the American Self* (New Haven: Yale Univ. Press, 1975), p. 174. See also Bercovitch's expanded argument in Ch. 6 of *The American Jeremiad* (Madison: Univ. of Wisconsin Press, 1978), pp. 176–210.

42. Bercovitch, *Puritan Origins,* p. 136.

43. Bercovitch, *Puritan Origins,* p. 136.

44. Buell, *Literary Transcendentalism,* p. 306. Rush Welter notes that for Americans of 1820–60 the idea of a national "experiment" contained the double meaning of *ascertaining* and *confirming* the validity of democratic principles (*The Mind of America* 23). *Walden* also plays on this ambiguity: the narrator's life at Walden was meant to "ascertain"; his book exists to "confirm."

45. See Anderson, *Magic Circle,* pp. 41–42.

46. Emerson is inconsistent on this point. While claiming the admixture of temporality in all literature and thought, he can simultaneously regard the pleasure we receive from the great English poets as "in great part caused by the abstraction of all *time* from their verses" (*CW* I, 57). At this point in his career, Emerson was unsure quite how "historical" a thinker he was, how fully he believed in the progress, or at least in the relativity, of ideas. With time, Emerson increasingly became a melioristic or protoevolutionary thinker who (as in "Circles") adopted the essentially Jamesian position that "truth" consisted in ever broader and more inclusive generalizations which put the race in a more satisfactory power-relationship to the facts of experience; in this respect, thought not only changed but progressed. Although Emerson had not reached this position by "The American Scholar," he was gradually weaning himself away from the atemporal idealism of his earlier writing, which was essentially Thoreau's in the 1849 *Walden*.

47. Hawthorne, "The Artist of the Beautiful," *Mosses from an Old Manse,* pp. 451–52.

48. See Wolfgang Iser, *The Implied Reader* (Baltimore: Johns Hopkins Univ. Press, 1974). Golemba in "Unreading Thoreau" imagines *Walden* much along the lines of Iser's reader-response theories, with the reader participating in the creation of meaning by filling in the "gaps" in the text. In Golemba's view, these gaps are intended by Thoreau as a strategy for provoking his reader.

49. As Ethel Seybold observes, Thoreau responded to what interested him in literature and sometimes took great liberties in interpreting the classics: "He wanted the heart of the matter. And to a transcendentalist the heart of the matter was what answered to a man's individual genius. . . . It was a philosophy like this which enabled him not only to select from the classics whatever he wanted, but even to read into the classics ideas which were strictly his own" (*The Quest and the Classics* 20).

50. Poirier, p. 87.
51. David Leverenz, writing from a different perspective, mounts a similar argument for Thoreau's "rivalry" with the reader: "classic male writers [of the American Renaissance] dramatize their own self-refashioning by destabilizing their narrations. . . . A self-possessed 'you' often becomes a point of departure for the flight of the self-dispossessing 'I,' whose delight in multiple perspectives and linguistic play invites readers to jump free of their slavery to a striving, anxious, manly ego based on ownership, work, competition, and social position. Ironically, the 'I-you' relationship also intimates rivalry. A lurking competitiveness reappears in the flights of the self-refashioning, reinscribing the tensions of manhood" (*Manhood and the American Renaissance* 18).
52. John Hildebidle, *Thoreau: A Naturalist's Liberty,* p. 110.
53. Cf. Whitman: "Now I see the secret of the making of the best persons, / It is to grow in the open air and to eat and sleep with the earth" ("Song of the Open Road," ll. 71–72 [*Leaves of Grass,* ed. Sculley Bradley and Harold W. Blodgett (New York: Norton, 1973)] – all Whitman citations to this text unless otherwise noted). Earlier in "Song of the Open Road" Whitman specifically repudiates hot-house culture: "Done with indoor complaints, libraries, querulous criticisms, / Strong and content I travel the open road" (ll. 6–7). And in the second section of "Song of Myself" ("Houses and rooms are full of perfumes . . .") he dramatizes the Emersonian flight from the artifice of civilization by rushing out of the house and literally or figuratively tearing off his clothes to put himself in touch with the atmosphere.
54. Sharon Cameron, *Writing Nature* (New York: Oxford Univ. Press, 1985), p. 46.
55. Peck, p. 73.
56. In Joel Porte's words, "Emerson found man and the natural world instinct with law and . . . Thoreau found them instinct with sensibility." Porte, *Emerson and Thoreau: Transcendentalists in Conflict* (Middletown, Conn.: Wesleyan Univ. Prsss, 1965), p. 192.
57. Cf. George Hochfield's brief but suggestive discussion of Thoreau's "Transcendentalist empiricism" in "New England Transcendentalism," in *Critical Essays on American Transcendentalism,* ed. Philip F. Gura and Joel Myerson (Boston: G. K. Hall, 1982), p. 478.
58. Sattelmeyer, "The Remaking of *Walden,*" p. 56.
59. See Wordsworth, "Ode: Intimations of Immortality from Recollections of Early Childhood," st. 5 especially.
60. "A Light Exists in Spring" (#812), *The Complete Poems of Emily Dickinson,* ed. Thomas H. Johnson (Boston: Little, Brown, 1960), ll. 12, 16, 17–18. All future references to Dickinson's poems will be included in the text and cited by poem number.
61. See Kenneth W. Rhoads, "Thoreau: The Ear and the Music," *American Literature,* 46 (1974), 322. In discussing Thoreau and sound I gratefully acknowledge my debt to Rhoads's fine article and to Sherman Paul's "The Wise Silence: Sound as the Agency of Correspondence in Thoreau," *New England Quarterly,* 22 (1949), 511–27.
62. Samuel Taylor Coleridge, "The Eolian Harp," *The Portable Coleridge,* ed. I. A. Richards (New York: Viking, 1950), ll. 44–48.
63. Just before the speculative passage in "The Eolian Harp," Coleridge is pictured as a kind of aeolian harp himself as he reclines tranquilly on a slope while "Full many a thought uncall'd and undetain'd, / And many idle flitting phantasies, / Traverse my

indolent and passive brain, / As wild and various as the random gales / That swell and flutter on this subject Lute!" (ll. 39–43).

64. Bishop, p. 70.

65. I am thinking here of the final pages of "Sounds" in which Thoreau turns to nature; I leave the railroad passage for later discussion.

66. "A perfect earliness [i.e., an original relation to the universe] would be free of influence," Robert Weisbuch writes of Thoreau, "and its literary statement would eschew allusion and all debate with other texts" (*Atlantic Double-Cross* [Chicago: Univ. of Chicago Press, 1986], p. 133). Weisbuch's remark gives special point to Martin Bickman's observation that "much of 'Sounds' is rendered in literary terms" (*"Walden": Volatile Truths* [New York: Twayne, 1992], p. 52).

67. Bickman eloquently makes a similar point and also contrasts Thoreau with Emerson (97).

68. William Dean Howells, *Literary Friends and Acquaintances* (New York: Harper, 1900), p. 59.

69. The portrait of Therien in the 1846–49 text is fragmentary but largely appreciative, focusing on his innocent good humor and physical health (Sh 170–73) and citing no attempts on Thoreau's part to improve him other than by reading aloud a passage of the *Iliad* – Therien being above, or below, or simply outside the townsmen-audience *Walden* proposes to reform. Post-1851 drafts darken the portrait of the woodchopper and show Thoreau trying and failing to woo him to a "spiritual view of things; the highest that he appeared to conceive of was a simple expediency, such as you might expect an animal to appreciate; and this is true of most men" (*W* 150; v. *J* VI, 36). By the time of this addition (1853–54), Thoreau had lost faith and interest in the project of converting his neighbors; moreover, as his reference to "animal" here and elsewhere in the chapter suggests, he had come to see the corporeal as irreclaimably opposed to the spiritual. A "great consumer of meat" (*W* 145), the woodchopper, like "most men," was essentially meat himself.

70. Buell, *New England Literary Culture*, p. 332.

71. Buell, *New England Literary Culture*, p. 332, and James McIntosh, *Thoreau as Romantic Naturalist* (Ithaca, N.Y.: Cornell Univ. Press, 1974), p. 248.

72. Sympathy is the mode of perception that Coleridge eulogizes, that Emerson commends in "The Poet," and that Whitman signifies by the word "became" in describing the making of the poet: "There was a child went forth every day, / And the first object he looked upon and received with wonder or pity or love or dread, that object he became." Whitman, "There Was a Child Went Forth," *Leaves of Grass: The First (1855) Edition,* ed. Malcolm Cowley (New York: Viking, 1959), ll. 1–2. Subsequent references to this edition will be included in the text and denoted "1855" to distinguish them from references to the 1892 "deathbed" edition otherwise cited.

73. Lebeaux, *Thoreau's Seasons*, p. 39.

74. McIntosh, p. 237. The passages from "Solitude" I take up are all from the first draft of *Walden* unless otherwise indicated.

75. McIntosh, p. 255. I say "nine years" because the journal origins for "The Bean-Field" date back to 1845.

76. Marx, *The Machine in the Garden*, p. 259.

77. Marx, p. 279.

78. Anderson, *Magic Circle*, p. 143.

79. Gilmore, "*Walden* and the 'Curse of Trade,'" p. 43. Gilmore sees *Walden* as moving inward after 1850, but "The Bean-Field" and "Baker Farm" both belong to the 1846–47 manuscript and in fact look back to earlier passages in the journal.

80. Burbick, *Thoreau's Alternative History,* p. 67.

81. The phrase is from "Self-Reliance": "The nonchalance of boys who are sure of a good dinner, and would disdain as much as a lord to do or say ought to conciliate one, is the healthy attitude of human nature. A boy is in the parlour what the pit is in the playhouse; independent, irresponsible, looking out from his corner on such people and facts as pass by, he tries and sentences them on their merits, in the swift summary way of boys. . . . Who can thus avoid all pledges, and having observed, observe again from the same unaffected, unbiassed, unaffrighted innocence, must always be formidable" (*CW* II, 29).

82. The passage survives in the published *Walden* but is much qualified by context (*W* 216). The first-person declaration of faith ("as I grow more resolute and faithful . . .") is also transposed to the third person to accommodate Thoreau's confessions of backsliding and indifference in "Higher Laws."

83. Michael West discusses the hawk as Thoreau's ideal image of himself as a verbal artist in "Scatology and Eschatology: The Heroic Dimension of Thoreau's Wordplay," *PMLA,* 89 (1974), 1057. I would take this specific meaning as more consistent with the themes of *Walden*'s late drafts – the significance of the passage changes with context – but I agree with West that Thoreau is portraying himself as he would like to be seen.

Chapter 5: Interregnum

1. Sattelmeyer, *Thoreau's Reading,* p. 55. I am much indebted to Sattelmeyer's account of the "quiet transformation" in Thoreau's life following the publication of *A Week* in May 1849 (*Thoreau's Reading* 54–62) and to Richard Lebeaux's chapter "Seedtime" in *Thoreau's Seasons.*

2. Fink, *Prophet in the Marketplace,* p. 258.

3. Fink, p. 258.

4. Cited in Historical Introduction to *Cape Cod,* p. 254.

5. Fink, p. 271.

6. Hawthorne, "The Hall of Fantasy," *Mosses from an Old Manse,* p. 180.

7. As Gilmore argues, "History forcibly enters *Walden* in the changes and additions made between the first draft and the published version" ("*Walden* and the 'Curse of Trade'" 49).

8. Robert A. Gross, "Concord, Boston, and the Wider World," pp. 111–12.

9. Thoreau's image is a nice example of how *Walden*'s use of wordplay invites the reader to search for meanings that may not actually have been intended by the author but *might* have been. Rightly or wrongly, one senses Thoreau on the margins of the text nodding approval at the reader's inventiveness as it confirms his own.

10. Buell, *New England Literary Culture,* p. 72.

11. For Thoreau's relation to Emerson, see Sattelmeyer, "'When He Became My Enemy': Emerson and Thoreau, 1848–49," pp. 187–204. As Sattelmeyer elsewhere observes, Thoreau's friendship with Emerson, "bound up with the fate of *A Week* almost since the book's inception, . . . began to deteriorate perceptibly during the

summer of 1849, prompting him to reexamine critically and painfully not only his notions of friendship but also his own capacity for it" (Historical Introduction, *PJ* 3, 479).

12. For example, this journal entry of April 4, 1852: "He [Emerson] finds fault with me that I walk alone, when I pine for want of a companion – that I commit my thoughts to a diary even on my walks instead of sharing them generously with a friend – curses my practice even– Awful as it is to contemplate I pray that if I am the cold intellectual skeptic whom he rebukes his curse may take effect – & wither & dry up those sources of my life – and my journal no longer yield me pleasure nor life" (*PJ* 4, 426).

13. Cameron, *Writing Nature,* p. 11.

14. Harding, *The Days of Henry Thoreau,* p. 361.

15. Sattelmeyer, "Remaking," p. 62.

16. Cf. Lebeaux, *Thoreau's Seasons,* pp. 128–29.

17. F. Scott Fitzgerald, *The Great Gatsby* (1925; rpt. New York: Macmillan, 1992), p. 189.

18. William Ellery Channing, *Thoreau: The Poet-Naturalist,* ed. F. B. Sanborn (Boston: Charles E. Goodspeed, 1902), p. 6.

19. Cf. Lebeaux, *Thoreau's Seasons,* pp. 138–41.

20. As Lebeaux remarks, Thoreau "oscillated between the polarities of age and youth, between thinking of himself as young, still capable of renewal, and old, dried up, his best days behind him" (*Thoreau's Seasons* 126).

21. "The Pulley," *The Poems of George Herbert* (London: Oxford Univ. Press, 1961).

22. See Sattelmeyer, *Thoreau's Reading,* p. 58, and "Remaking," pp. 56–57.

23. Abrams, *Natural Supernaturalism,* p. 188.

24. Leary, " 'Now I Adventure': 1851 as a Watershed Year in Thoreau's Career," *ESQ* 19 (1973), 143.

25. "Natural piety" occurs in Wordsworth's three-line epigraph to the Immortality Ode ("The Child is father of the Man; / And I could wish my days to be / Bound each to each by natural piety"), which is drawn in turn from the short lyric "My heart leaps up." That Thoreau had Wordsworth close in mind is evidenced by a phrase from the entry on natural piety: "My heart leaps into my mouth at the sound of the wind in the woods" (*PJ* 3, 368).

26. Cf. Lebeaux, *Thoreau's Seasons,* pp. 138–39.

27. Walter Pater, *The Renaissance* (New York: New American Library, 1959), pp. 157, 158.

28. Lebeaux also discusses Wilkinson's influence on Thoreau (*Thoreau's Seasons* 136–37).

29. Adams and Ross, *Revising Mythologies,* p. 63.

30. Hochfield, "New England Transcendentalism," p. 478.

31. Peck, *Thoreau's Morning Work,* p. 43.

32. As Sharon Cameron observes, "analogies [in the journal] do not inaugurate connections between nature and the mind" (*Writing Nature* 46). John Burroughs is even more emphatic: "Thoreau was in no sense an interpreter of nature; he did not draw out its meanings or seize upon and develop its more significant phases. Seldom does he relate what he sees or thinks to the universal human heart and mind. He has rare power of description, but is very limited in his power to translate the facts and movements of nature into human emotion." Burroughs, *The Last Harvest* (Boston: Houghton Mifflin, 1922), p. 140.

33. While less interested in the chronology of Thoreau's development, Martin Bickman

sees Thoreau transforming a sense of childhood loss into "a more general mythography of culture," with *Walden* itself "an attempt to create structures that will make possible a reintegration of ourselves with the world, and of the mind with itself" (*"Walden": Volatile Truths* 95).

Chapter 6: Defying Gravity

1. Richard Wilbur, "Juggler," *New and Collected Poems* (New York: Harcourt Brace, 1988), ll. 1–7.
2. Fitzgerald, *The Great Gatsby*, pp. 111–12.
3. Sattelmeyer, "Remaking," p. 61.
4. Here I borrow Raymond Williams's terms for historical processes. See *Marxism and Literature*, pp. 121–27.
5. Except in degree (a important qualification), there is nothing extraordinary about this kind of temporally layered composition, even in academic prose. As I reworked this manuscript during the summers of 1993 and 1994 I introduced ideas and emphases not present in earlier drafts (this end note, for example), but I also elaborated arguments that dated back two years or more and that I could not have begun to conceive in later years. I liked to think that I was revising everything according to my current understanding of Thoreau, but any reader so inclined could compare my chapters on the early writings and *A Week* with an essay on the same materials published in 1991 and discover not only the changes in my thinking over the years but the survivals in my present manuscript of older ideas I am not even conscious of having outgrown. Comparing essay and book, my hypothetical reader-critic might conclude, "Milder's framework is more or less the same in his book [dominant], but he is moving away from idea X about Thoreau even as he expresses it more cogently [residual], and he is beginning to think in terms of idea Y, which barely occurred to him earlier [emergent]. Doesn't he see his inconsistency?" If my reader were truly astute, he or she might ignore the published essay entirely and find these disjunctions in the book itself, though in the absence of datable external evidence (notes, superseded drafts, class transcripts, library slips) it would be hard to determine which ideas were residual and which emergent. See my essay "An 'Errand to Mankind': Thoreau's Problem of Vocation," *ESQ*, 37 (1991), 91–139.
6. Wilbur, "Year's End," *New and Collected Poems*, ll. 26–27.
7. See Frye, *Anatomy of Criticism*, pp. 131–239.
8. Cf. Whitman: "The greatest poet has less a marked style and is more the channel of thoughts and things without increase or diminution. . . . He swears to his art, I will not be meddlesome, I will not have in my writing any elegance or effect or originality to hang in the way between me and the rest like curtains. . . . What I experience or portray shall go from my composition without a shred of my composition." Preface 1855, in *Leaves of Grass 1855*, ed. Cowley, p. 13.
9. I am not suggesting that Thoreau is not an "artist" in his writings; my point, rather, is that in many of them (the travel books, especially) he prefers to think of himself as a finder of meaning in experience rather than as a creator of it in words.
10. Hawthorne, *American Notebooks*, p. 395. Even the rude shanties of the Irish, Hawthorne continues, seemed not to profane "the repose and sanctity of the old wood," which "overshadows these poor people, and assimilates them, somehow or other, to

the character of her natural inhabitants" – Walden as "'God's Drop'" (*American Notebooks* 396).

11. Hochfield, "New England Transcendentalism," p. 481.

12. Lionel Trilling, "Huckleberry Finn," *The Liberal Imagination* (1951; rpt. London: Mercury, 1961), p. 108.

13. William James, *"The Will to Believe" and Other Essays in Popular Philosophy* (Cambridge, Mass,: Harvard Univ. Press, 1979), p. 29.

14. "For Once, Then, Something," *The Complete Poems of Robert Frost* (New York: Holt, Rinehart, 1958), p. 276.

15. See Chapter 5, section I.

16. Frye, *Anatomy of Criticism,* p. 328.

17. Mary Gordon, "The Deadly Sins/Anger: The Fascination Begins in the Mouth," *New York Times Book Review,* 13 June 1993, 3.

18. See Michael West, "Scatology and Eschatology," pp. 1049–50.

19. See Stephen Railton's fine article, "Thoreau's 'Resurrection of Virtue!,'" *American Quarterly,* 24 (1972), 210–27.

20. Milan Kundera, *The Unbearable Lightness of Being,* trans. Michael Henry Heim (New York: Harper & Row, 1984), p. 246.

21. Railton, "Thoreau's 'Resurrection of Virtue!,'" 213, 214.

22. West, p. 1047.

23. Cf. Sattelmeyer, "'The True Industry for Poets': Fishing with Thoreau," *ESQ,* 33 (1987), 198.

24. Richard Bridgman, *Dark Thoreau* (Lincoln: Univ. of Nebraska Press, 1982), p. 118.

25. Philip Young, *Hawthorne's Secret: An Un-told Tale* (Boston: Godine, 1984), p. 66. See Frederick Crews, *The Sins of the Fathers* (New York: Oxford Univ. Press, 1965), p. 85. Even Hyatt H. Waggoner, no friend of psychosexual readings, concedes that "it is certainly possible to speculate that masturbation may lie *behind* the story" (Waggoner, *The Presence of Hawthorne* [Baton Rouge: Louisiana State Univ. Press, 1979], p. 108).

26. Cf. Emerson in the Divinity School Address: "Thus; in the soul of man there is a justice whose retributions are instant and entire. He who does a good deed, is instantly ennobled himself. He who does a mean deed, is by the action itself contracted. He who puts off impurity, puts on purity" (*CW* I, 77–78). See also "Compensation" (*CW* II, 55–60 esp.).

27. Sattelmeyer, "Fishing with Thoreau," p. 199.

28. In the published text, for example, Thoreau concludes the paragraphs on sensuality with an oblique admission: "I hesitate to say these things, but it is not because of my subject, – I care not how obscene my *words* are, – but because I cannot speak of them without betraying my impurity" (*W* 221). Draft E is more explicit: "I am not afraid that my words will be obscene – nobody is – I am only afraid that you will think me obscene – because I *am*" (Cl 594).

29. Peck, *Thoreau's Morning Work,* p. x.

30. I gratefully acknowledge my debt to Lanya Lamouria for suggesting the lines of my reading of the owl passage. An interesting analogue to the passage is Thoreau's 1852 journal description of an encounter with a woodchuck (*PJ* 4, 453–55).

31. William Howarth, *The Book of Concord,* pp. 80, 81.

32. Whicher, *Freedom and Fate,* p. 111.

33. Shanley notes that three leaves from what is now "The Pond in Winter" are missing

from draft A and "probably contained some of the material of [the present] paragraphs 9 through 15, and certainly the beginning of 16" (Sh 199). It is impossible to say with certainty that the material I discuss from paragraphs 6–12 dates originally from drafts E, F, and G. Some of it draws upon journal entries of 1852 and could not have belonged to the initial *Walden;* still other passages make use of earlier journals but thematically revise them in a way consistent with datable changes in drafts E through G. Equally convincing, to my mind, are the attitudes taken in the paragraphs, which reflect Thoreau's positions of 1853–54, not of 1845–49.

34. Thoreau was by no means alone in this belief; following Kant, Leon Chai observes, "Romantic authors [were] able to discern in poetry and science two aspects of a common endeavor, the attempt of the mind to assimilate all realms of experience, whether as aesthetic sensation or as cognitive apprehension." Chai, *The Romantic Foundations of the American Renaissance* (Ithaca, N.Y.: Cornell Univ. Press, 1987), p. 146. M. H. Abrams also refers to the belief of Romantics like Schelling who saw "the redemptive goal of human life . . . as that ultimate stage of the collective consciousness of mankind when, by the fullness and perfection of its power of organized knowing, it will utterly repossess everything which it has, in its earlier stages of imperfect and partial knowledge, separated and alienated as object to itself as subject" (*Natural Supernaturalism* 189). In his efforts to wring optimism from the defeat of the individual's hopes, Emerson develops a similar position in the essay "Fate," first delivered in lecture form in 1851.

35. Paul, *The Shores of America,* p. 59.

36. Jonathan Edwards, *Images or Shadows of Divine Things,* ed. Perry Miller (New Haven: Yale Univ. Press, 1948), p. 44.

37. Edwards, pp. 50–51.

38. Perry Miller, Introduction to *Images or Shadows,* pp. 6–7. See also Charles Feidelson's discussion of types and tropes in *Symbolism and American Literature* (Chicago: Univ. of Chicago Press, 1953), pp. 77–118.

39. Hildebidle, *Thoreau: A Naturalist's Liberty,* p. 98.

40. Possibly I exaggerate somewhat here. There are moments in the journal when Thoreau, feeling himself fallow, opens his senses to nature and is rewarded by a perception that stimulates a train of thought and lifts him beyond his dullness (v. *PJ* 4, 3–4). But this is not the same as "blessedness." Between these two levels of experience is a difference in degree amounting almost to a difference in kind. By 1853, moreover, even nature, though a continuous source of interest, was losing its power to stimulate reflection – or so the journals seem to testify.

41. Coleridge, "Dejection: An Ode," *The Portable Coleridge,* ll. 45–46.

42. Garber, *Thoreau's Redemptive Imagination,* p. 170.

43. Whitman, "As I Ebb'd with the Ocean of Life," *Leaves of Grass,* ll. 43, 11–12.

44. Stevens, "The Snow Man," *Collected Poems* (New York: Knopf, 1967), ll. 1, 48. Strictly speaking, Thoreau's problem was different from the snow man's. Thoreau saw a great deal that was "not there" (the visions of the imagination) as well as "the nothing that is" (the impenetrable world of nature); his frustration was that he could neither join the two (distilling poetry from fact), nor live in the imagination alone.

45. Martin Bickman, *The Unsounded Centre* (Chapel Hill: Univ. of North Carolina Press, 1980), p. 39.

46. Bickman, *The Unsounded Centre,* p. 39.

47. Coleridge, "Dejection: An Ode," l. 39. See also st. 4.

48. Whitman, "As I Ebb'd With the Ocean of Life," *Leaves of Grass,* ll. 78–79.

49. Quoted in James R. Mellow, *Nathaniel Hawthorne in His Times* (Boston: Houghton Mifflin, 1980), p. 216.

50. Robert Frost, "The Oven Bird," *Complete Poems,* l. 14.

51. Stephen Whicher, "Emerson's Tragic Sense," in *Interpretations of American Literature,* ed. Charles Feidelson, Jr., and Paul Brodtkorb, Jr. (New York: Oxford Univ. Press, 1959), p. 155.

52. Bickman, *"Walden": Volatile Truths,* p. 65.

53. For a potential consumptive like Thoreau, Michael West points out, regretful brooding may also have been tantamount to death, since contemporary medical opinion and folklore urged "deliberate cheerfulness" as essential in forestalling tubercular attacks. West, "Scatology and Eschatology," p. 1055.

54. Sattelmeyer, *Thoreau's Reading,* p. 80.

55. Loren Eiseley discusses progressionism in *Darwin's Century* (Garden City, N.Y.: Doubleday, 1958), pp. 91–97. For an account of Thoreau's relation to Agassiz's views on "special creation," see Sattelmeyer, *Thoreau's Reading,* pp. 87–89, and Richardson, *Henry David Thoreau,* pp. 362–68.

56. See Eiseley, pp. 108–15, and Gertrude Himmelfarb, *Darwin and the Darwinian Revolution* (New York: Norton, 1962), Chs. 8–9 especially.

57. Robert Chambers, *Vestiges of the Natural History of Creation,* quoted in Himmelfarb, p. 218.

58. See Robert Sattelmeyer and Richard A. Hocks, "Thoreau and Coleridge's *Theory of Life,*" in *Studies in the American Renaissance: 1985,* ed. Joel Myerson (Charlottesville: Univ. Press of Virginia, 1985), pp. 269–84. Sattelmeyer and Hocks note that Thoreau "read and copied extracts from [Coleridge's *Theory*] shortly after its posthumous publication in 1848" (270) and imply that he was deeply influenced by it almost immediately: "His reading of the *Theory of Life* . . . came just at the beginning of a subtle but profound shift in Thoreau's stance toward nature, a shift that amounted to adopting the study of natural history, along with writing, as the principal occupation of his life. In this context, Coleridge's treatise offered him a philosophical underpinning for his work, and more importantly provided him with a bridge between the transcendental idealism of his youth and the detailed and scientific study of nature that occupied his maturity" (279). Coleridge's theory was certainly fitted to serve Thoreau well, yet judging from the absence of resonances in the journals (Thoreau seldom mentioned books or authors directly), he seems not to have digested it fully or given it prominence in his thought for some time, probably not before 1853. The reason for this, I think, is that his concern, through 1852 at least, was primarily with his own spiritual development and only (very) subordinately with the vast, impersonal reaches of time and purpose suggested by cosmology. Thus an analogist like Wilkinson who seemed to promise a moral knowledge of the immediate was more pertinent to Thoreau's interests of 1851–52 than was Coleridge. It was only when Thoreau, frustrated in his hopes for personal metamorphosis, began to look beyond the life of the individual for consolation and meaning that Coleridge assumed the kind of significance Sattelmeyer and Hocks ascribe to him.

59. West, "Scatology and Eschatology," p. 1047.

60. Kundera, p. 245.

61. Marx, *The Machine in the Garden,* pp. 261, 264. In Marx's view, Thoreau transfers paradise from history to consciousness, where it belongs, in response to the technological progress that renders his pastoral world an anachronism. By drafts F and G, however, Thoreau has long since finished with the themes of pastoralism, technology, and history that Marx traces so ably through earlier sections of *Walden.* What the imagination is driven to resist and compensate for in "Spring" is not "progress" but the withholdings of life itself: the impassable gulf between fact and truth, matter and spirit, earth and heaven.

62. Michael West, "Charles Kraitsir's Influence upon Thoreau's Theory of Language," *ESQ,* 19 (1973), 266. See also Philip F. Gura, *The Wisdom of Words* (Middletown, Conn.: Wesleyan Univ. Press, 1981), pp. 124–41.

63. For Trench's influence on Thoreau, see Gura, pp. 115–18.

64. Kraitsir, *Glossology* (1852), quoted in West, "Kraitsir's Influence," 267.

65. West, "Kraitsir's Influence," 267, 269.

66. Gura, p. 135. See also West, "Kraitsir's Influence," 269.

67. Quoted in West, "Kraitsir's Influence," 270.

68. West, "Kraitsir's Influence," 270.

69. Hawthorne, *Mosses from an Old Manse,* pp. 469–70.

70. Poirier, *A World Elsewhere,* p. 20.

71. West, among others, also finds the hawk an image of the Thoreauvian artist. "Not obsessive but fundamentally liberating," West writes, Thoreau's "wordplay is just that, *play,* the stylistic expression cultivated by a spirit that learned to cope with its isolation by imitating (albeit in the medium of language) the flight of that supremely contented hawk" ("Scatology and Eschatology" 1057).

72. Wilbur, "Juggler," *New and Collected Poems,* l. 12.

73. Frost, "Birches," *Complete Poems,* l. 56.

74. Wilbur, "Juggler," *New and Collected Poems,* l. 30.

75. Albert Gelpi, *Emily Dickinson: The Mind of the Poet* (Cambridge, Mass.: Harvard Univ. Press, 1966), p. 96.

76. Gelpi, p. 161.

77. Wallace Stevens, "Adagia," *Opus Posthumous* (New York: Knopf, 1957), p. 163.

78. Stevens, "Adagia," p. 164.

79. Anderson, *Magic Circle,* p. 260.

80. Lebeaux, *Thoreau's Seasons,* p. 212.

81. "The great works of American literature," Poirier writes, "are alive with the effort to stabilize certain feelings and attitudes that have, as it were, no place in the world, no place at all except where a writer's style can give them one" (*A World Elsewhere* ix). Richard Lebeaux echoes the idea when he observes that "rather than 'Life in the Woods,' a more apt and accurate subtitle for *Walden,* by the time it was completed, would have been 'Life in the Words'" (*Thoreau's Seasons* 209).

82. Cavell, *The Senses of "Walden,"* pp. 108, 109.

83. Paul, *The Shores of America,* p. 281.

Chapter 7: "A Point of Interest Somewhere Between*"*

1. F. Scott Fitzgerald, "My Lost City," *The Crack-Up and Other Essays,* ed. Edmund Wilson (New York: New Directions, 1945), p. 31.

2. Richardson speaks of Thoreau's "nearly limitless capacity for being interested" in things (Richardson 376).

3. Lebeaux, *Thoreau's Seasons*, p. 204.

4. Richardson, *Henry David Thoreau*, p. 323.

5. See Harding, *Days of Henry Thoreau*, pp. 341–42.

6. "Life without Principle," published posthumously in 1863, is a revised version of the lecture alternatively titled "Getting a Living" and "What Shall It Profit?" that Thoreau reworked on and off for several years. In the absence of an extant draft of the 1854 lecture, I make reference to the published text on the assumption that it preserves the argument and spirit of the original, if not demonstrably and in all cases the exact wording. See "Textual Introduction" to "Life without Principle," *Reform Papers*, pp. 369–73.

7. Neufeldt, *The Economist*, p. 80.

8. See Fink, *Prophet in the Marketplace*, p. 271.

9. Leonard N. Neufeldt says Thoreau speaks in a voice "presumed to be both superior and normative," and "disparages, insults, harangues, cajoles, humors, proscribes, prescribes, and, like the prophet Isaiah, is willing to reason on the basis of his assumptions; but he is not hopeful of meeting many of his terms." Neufeldft, pp. 80, 81.

10. Harding, *Days of Henry Thoreau*, p. 342.

11. See Fink, pp. 271–72.

12. Howarth, *The Book of Concord*, p. 109.

13. See Howarth, *The Book of Concord*, p. 128.

14. See Sattelmeyer, *Thoreau's Reading*, pp. 78–110.

15. Walter Harding, "A Bibliography of Thoreau in Music," in *Studies in the American Renaissance: 1992*, ed. Joel Myerson (Charlottesville: Univ. Press of Virginia, 1992), p. 291. "His choice of music," Harding adds, "was astonishingly conventional and sentimental for such an iconoclastic individual" (p. 291).

16. The "cranberrying" journal entry of August 1856 (discussed later in this section) draws a memorable line from the episode: "I get my new experiences still, not at the opera listening to the Swedish Nightingale [Jenny Lind], but at Beck Stow's swamp listening to the native wood thrush" (*J* IX, 3).

17. Seybold, *The Quest and the Classics*, pp. 75, 77. As Thoreau wrote in January 1854, "If the writers of the brazen age are most suggestive to thee, confine thyself to them, and leave those of the Augustan age to dust and the bookworms" (*J* VI, 68; cited in Seybold, 75).

18. As Leo Stoller observes, "It seems impossible to avoid the conclusion that in relation to slavery in 1854 Thoreau was still chiefly concerned with the internal cleansing of a man who held that reform was first of the soul and only secondarily of the world" (*After "Walden"* [Stanford: Stanford Univ. Press, 1957], p. 141).

19. Harding, *Days of Henry Thoreau*, p. 416

20. See Harding, *Days of Henry Thoreau*, p. 417.

21. Henry Adams, *The Education of Henry Adams* (Boston: Houghton Mifflin, 1961), p. 7.

22. Channing, *Thoreau the Poet-Naturalist*, p. 16.

23. See Howarth, *The Book of Concord*, p. 155. My reading of "Chesuncook" has much in common with Howarth's, which helps demythologize some of the clichés about Thoreau's attitude toward wild nature and toward the actual (as opposed to the ideal) Indian.

24. Lebeaux, *Thoreau's Seasons,* p. 182.
25. Thoreau can be drily ironic about Indian etymologies. Curious about the origin of "Quebec," Thoreau and his companion are told that "'when the English ships came up the river, they could not go any further, it was no narrow there; go back, – go-back, – that's Que-bec.' I mention this to show the value of [Tamnunt's] authority in other cases" (*MW* 142).
26. Although Thoreau was always fascinated by woodsmen and Indians, as by primitives of any sort, his admiration for them has been vastly overemphasized by his readers. Ambivalence was his characteristic emotion. The noble Joe Polis of "The Allegash and East Branch" is the creation of Emerson in his funeral oration and of Thoreau's critics, not of Thoreau himself, whose Indian guide, though almost preternatural in his woodcraft, displays virtually no moral or intellectual being and alternates between sullen silence and pointless garrulity – an Alek Therien without the good nature and originality, and not above capitalistic self-interest, a concern for the regularity of his meals, and minor religious hypocrisy. Philip F. Gura's description of Polis is a sample of the reigning mythology that all but obscures Thoreau's warts-and-all portrait: "Here was no rancorous Christian but a truly religious man: Joe's natural piety, his heightened sense that the world was animated and that his words were so expressive that they became one with the things named, marked him a man to be treated with utmost respect" ("Thoreau's Maine Woods Indians: More Representative Men," *American Literature,* 49 [1977], 378). This is the Indian Thoreau hoped to meet in the woods but hardly the one he portrayed. Among other things, Polis is a Christian convert who voices surprise that Thoreau and his companion should think to travel on Sunday, who squares this with his conscience by deciding not to accept Sunday wages, and who then forgets his vow and accepts them anyway, as Thoreau notes with dry bemusement. Polis fascinated Thoreau by his instincts for the forest, which were seldom translatable into cognitive thought, let alone communicable in words, and which rarely, if ever, struck Thoreau as partaking of the spiritual. Gura's portrait is a response more to the preexperiential theorizing about Indians Thoreau sometimes engaged in than to his un-(but not necessarily dis-)illusioned presentation of the actual man. For a more balanced view of Thoreau on Polis, see Howarth, *The Book of Concord,* pp. 151–53. At his death Thoreau left more than three thousand pages of notes on Canada and (especially) North American Indians, so his presentation of Polis and Aitteon can hardly be said to show fully his attitude toward the Indian.
27. Howarth, *The Book of Concord,* pp. 156–57.
28. Hildebidle, *Thoreau: A Naturalist's Liberty,* p. 83.
29. Howarth, p. 156.

Chapter 8: "Annexing New Territories"

1. *Keats: Poetical Works,* ed. H. W. Garrod (London: Oxford Univ. Press, 1966), ll. 23–24.
2. As Sattelmeyer and Hocks argue, one's evaluation of "the character and quality of [Thoreau's] scientific work" largely shapes one's "estimation of the overall trajectory of his career: did the years after *Walden* manifest a decline in imaginative power related to his increasing absorption in the collection and classification of natural history data, or did these studies form the basis of important and large-scale projects that his early death prevented him from completing?" ("Thoreau and Coleridge's *Theory of Life*" 269). I

would modify these words only to emphasize that it is as *writing*, not as anticipations of modern scientific theory and method, that Thoreau's late essays need to justify themselves.

3. William L. Howarth, *The Literary Manuscripts of Henry David Thoreau* (Columbus: Ohio State Univ. Press, 1974), p. 294.

4. Sattelmeyer, Introduction to *The Natural History Essays*, p. xxxi.

5. Sherwood Anderson, *Winesburg, Ohio* (1919; rpt. New York: Viking, 1964), p. 35.

6. Fink, *Prophet in the Marketplace*, p. 279.

7. Fink, p. 280.

8. Fink, p. 281.

9. McIntosh, *Thoreau as Romantic Naturalist*, p. 280.

10. As Fink observes, Thoreau seems to have "learned how to appeal to two audiences," a middlebrow popular audience and a more discerning literary one (285); in this he was like Melville in his magazine pieces of 1853–55. I am less sure than Fink that Thoreau is writing for the discerning audience at all; for once in his career it seems enough for him to write for himself, though a part of this gratification would come from a sense that his calm self-sufficiency has registered upon *someone*.

11. Richardson, *Henry David Thoreau*, pp. 357–62.

12. Richardson, p. 359.

13. According to Richardson, Thoreau read Ruskin's *Elements of Drawing* "by late November 1857" (*Henry David Thoreau* 360), which leaves it unclear how far Ruskin might have been responsible for the October 1857 entries. Even so, Richardson's argument for a Ruskinian influence on "Autumnal Tints" is generally persuasive.

14. Sattelmeyer aptly calls the essay "a kind of literary precursor to the fall foliage tour." Introduction, *The Natural History Essays*, p. xxvii.

15. Hildebidle, p. 84.

16. Hawthorne, *Mosses from an Old Manse*, p. 7; see *American Notebooks*, pp. 318–19. Curiously, Thoreau made the same observation on the pond lily six years later: "How sweet, innocent, wholesome its fragrance! How pure its white petals, though its root is in the mud!" (*J* IV, 147). Hawthorne's journal observation dates from August 1842, when he was living at the Old Manse and occasionally seeing Thoreau, so it is possible Thoreau originally suggested the analogy to him. On the other hand, Thoreau, while no reader of fiction, knew *Mosses from an Old Manse* well enough to cite it in *A Week*, so it is equally possible that Thoreau's analogy was kindled, consciously or not, by Hawthorne's.

17. A sign of this extroversion is the paucity of the pronoun "I," which, as Hildebidle points out, "occurs . . . only three times in the first six paragraphs of 'Autumnal Tints' and then is swept aside by a flood of 'we' and 'our'" (*A Naturalist's Liberty* 88).

18. Wilbur, "Year's End," *New and Collected Poems*, p. 302.

19. Howarth, *The Book of Concord*, p. 216.

20. Cole quoted in Oswaldo Rodriguez Roque, "The Exaltation of American Landscape Painting," in *American Paradise*, p. 26.

21. Roque, p. 44. Richardson calls Church's "oil sketches of Katahdin and of fall foliage in New England . . . exact visual counterparts of 'Ktaadn' and 'Autumnal Tints'" (*Henry David Thoreau* 339).

22. See Barbara Novak, *American Painting of the Nineteenth Century* (New York: Harper & Row, 1979), p. 94.

23. Harding, "*Walden*'s Man of Science," *Virginia Quarterly Review,* 57 (1981), 48.

24. See Sattelmeyer, *Thoreau's Reading,* pp. 90–91, and Richardson, pp. 373–76.

25. Harding, *Days of Henry Thoreau,* p. 437.

26. Kathryn Whitford, "Thoreau and the Woodlots of Concord," *New England Quarterly,* 23 (1950), 294. See also Donald Worster's informed and helpful discussion of Thoreau in *Nature's Economy* (San Francisco: Sierra Club, 1977), Ch. 3 especially.

27. Stoller, p. 81.

28. Howarth, *The Book of Concord,* p. 195.

29. See Charles Darwin, *The Origin of Species* (New York: New American Library, 1958), pp. 81, 83. Sattelmeyer also notes the relevance of Darwin's observations to Thoreau's current projects (*Thoreau's Reading* 89).

30. *The Autobiography of Charles Darwin,* ed. Nora Barlow (1958; rpt. New York, Norton: 1969), pp. 119, 161.

31. Betty Flanders Thomson, *The Changing Face of New England* (Boston: Houghton Mifflin, 1977), p. 121 (see also pp. 28–30).

32. Thomson, p. 30.

33. Thomson, p. 121.

34. See Worster, pp. 71–72.

35. Thomson, p. 122.

36. Peter J. Bowler, *Evolution: The History of an Idea,* rev. ed. (Berkeley: Univ. of California Press, 1989), p. 214. An example of this method in "The Dispersion of Seeds" is Thoreau's movement toward an explanation of why white pine seedlings spring up in a pitch pine forest though pitch pine seeds vastly outnumber white pine seeds ("Dispersion of Seeds" 152–53).

37. Darwin, *The Origin of Species,* p. 74.

38. Gertrude Himmelfarb, *Darwin and the Darwinian Revolution* (New York: Norton, 1959), p. 165. Darwin speaks directly of the universal struggle for life as "the doctrine of Malthus applied with manifold force to the whole animal and vegetable kingdom" (*Origin* 75). In fact, Malthusianism was more than an analogy to the theory of natural selection; it was, as Darwin acknowledged, the fundamental catalyst for his formulation of the theory in 1838. See Darwin, *Autobiography,* p. 120.

39. See Darwin, p. 436.

40. Sattelmeyer, Introduction to *The Natural History Essays,* p. xxvi.

41. Hildebidle, p. 94.

42. Darwin, p. 438. In the *Origin* Darwin prudently equivocated on the theological implications of nature's appalling "waste," but in his private correspondence he sometimes shows himself troubled to the point of blasphemy. He addressed the matter directly in a passage from the *Autobiography* that caused much dissension among his family after his death and that was not printed until granddaughter Nora Barlow's edition of the *Autobiography* in 1958. The passage reads in part: "[The] very old argument from the existence of suffering against the existence of an intelligent first cause seems to me a strong one; whereas . . . the presence of much suffering agrees well with the view that all organic beings have been developed through variation and natural selection" (*Autobiography* 90).

43. In his groundbreaking discussion of the late writings Leo Stoller argues for Thoreau's "acceptance of industrial capitalism as impersonally dictated necessity." "Each of Thoreau's investigations of silvics," he observes – for example, "his study of the

growth rate of various trees, especially pitch pines, to determine the most profitable age for cutting – was adding to the foundation for a modern forest management and thus increasing the possibility of a union between satisfactory profits and the preservation of nature" (*After "Walden"* 71). Thoreau's labors did have this effect and, to a degree, this intention, but not, his comments make clear, because he relented in his antagonism toward market values.

44. Howarth, *The Book of Concord,* p. 191.
45. Herman Melville, *The Confidence-Man: His Masquerade,* ed. Harrison Hayford et al. (Evanston and Chicago: Northwestern Univ. Press and Newberry Library, 1984), p. 124.
46. Cited in Harding, *The Days of Henry Thoreau,* p. 465.
47. See Harding, *The Days of Henry Thoreau,* pp. 457–59, and Howarth, *The Book of Concord,* pp. 215–18.
48. In Jay Leyda, *The Melville Log* (New York: Harcourt Brace, 1951), p. 832.
49. Hawthorne, quoted in Leyda, p. 529.
50. Howarth, *The Book of Concord,* p. 218.

Index